THROUGH A GLASS DARKLY

Through a Glass Darkly

ESSAYS IN THE RELIGIOUS IMAGINATION

edited by
JOHN C. HAWLEY

FORDHAM UNIVERSITY PRESS
New York • 1996

© Copyright 1996 by FORDHAM UNIVERSITY PRESS
All rights reserved.
LC 96-5318
ISBN 0-8232-1636-5 *(hardcover)*
ISBN 0-8232-1637-3 *(paperback)*

Library of Congress Cataloguing-in-Publication Data

Through a glass darkly : essays in the religious imagination / edited by John C. Hawley.
   p. cm.
   Includes bibliographical references.
   ISBN 0-8232-1636-5. — ISBN 0-8232-1637-3 (pbk.)
   1. Religion and literature. 2. Religion in literature.
3. Christianity and literature. 4. Christianity in literature.
5. Literature—History and criticism. I. Hawley, John C. (John Charles), 1947– .
PN49.T46 1996
809'.93382—dc20   96-5318
                                                                                CIP

for my parents, Charles and Lilian

CONTENTS

Acknowledgments ix

Introduction xi

I
CHRISTIAN EUROPE

1. The Gospel of Mark as Myth
   Brenda Deen Schildgen — 3

2. An Early Renaissance Guide for the Perplexed: Bernardino of Siena's *De inspirationibus*
   Franco Mormando, S.J. — 24

3. Between Earth and Heaven: Ignation Imagination and the Aesthetics of Liberation
   Paul G. Crowley, S.J. — 50

4. Erasmus, Education, and Folly
   Christiaan Theodoor Lievestro — 70

5. Blind Prophecy: Milton's Figurative Mode in *Paradise Lost* and in Some Minor Poems
   William Franke — 87

6. A Lesson in Reading: George Eliot and the Typological Imagination
   Jo Ellen Parker — 104

7. Rouault and the Catholic Revival in France
   Jane Kristof — 119

8. A Life of Allegory: Type and Pattern in Historical Narratives
   Edward T. Oakes, S.J. — 134

II

INTO THE TWENTY-FIRST CENTURY

9. A View from the Far Side
   Andrew Greeley 153

10. The Tyranny of the Secular Imagination
    Gavin D'Costa 177

11. Religious Polyphony in the Novels of Nuruddin Farah
    Norman R. Cary 194

12. The Social and Political Vision of Sri Aurobindo
    K. D. Verma 206

13. Feminist Providence: Esther, Vashti, and the Duty of Disobedience in Nineteenth-Century Hermeneutics
    Joyce Zonana 228

14. The Buddhist Imagination in Chinese Fiction
    Sheng-Tai Chang 250

15. "Behind the Curtain": Derrida and the Religious Imagination
    Terrence R. Wright 276

Contributors 297

ACKNOWLEDGMENTS

I wish gratefully to acknowledge *The Toronto South Asian Review* (now known as *The Toronto Review of Contemporary Writing Abroad*), which first published K. D. Verma's article, and *Streven*, which first published Christiaan Lievestro's article.

INTRODUCTION

> Tom's God was bright, and gave light to the world. My God was different: was the darkness around the world.
>
> ——DAVID PLANTE, *The Accident*

I

> I fled Him, down the labyrinthine ways
> Of my own mind
>
> ——FRANCIS THOMPSON

THE QUESTION THAT SO DISTURBED Christ's contemporaries resonates even now: "Who do you say that I am?" (Matt. 16:15). Paradoxically, the answers his disciples boldly or clumsily offer seem to define *them* far more clearly than describe their teacher. The New Testament stands as a record of their subsequent obsession with the question, with what they remember their answers to have been, and with how this radically creative interrogation ordered their remaining years. Throughout the centuries their own disciples, variously aided and obstructed by these confessions, used the question as a litmus test not only in their prayer and in their personal relations, but, eventually, in their global politics, as well.

Whatever else may be said about the writers of the New Testament, it is interesting that they would wish to portray their Messiah as someone concerned with the response to such a question—as if the call to imagine and give "shape" to this other person was crucial, for both the respondent and the questioner. Their conception of God apparently entailed imaginative "recognition," either on the spot ("You are the Christ, the Son of the living God" [Matt. 16:17]) or in retrospect ("Did not our hearts burn within us as he talked to us on the road and explained the scriptures to us?" [Luke 24:32]) as a moment of conversion and Wordsworthian recovery—a powerful emotion recollected in tranquillity. What they had in mind reverberates with echoes of Eden, where Adam and Eve recognized the true identity of all around them and called everything by its appropriate name. The answer to this one question shaped their answer to all others.

At any rate, New Testament epiphanies proceed as an entrance into truth: there is room only for "yes, yes" and "no, no" in their newly imagined world. But in their subsequent ministry disciples soon enough saw that posing God as a question does not guarantee a response, let alone a "recognition." The question in some cases is spoken too soon, too loudly, or in a foreign tongue. "Each of us," as William Mathews notes, "has a question history that unfolds spontaneously within our lives" (35), and that spontaneity is a precious gift. Charles Darwin, for example, while fascinated by the world of nature, observed with some dismay that he was completely unmoved by questions of beauty in the arts: "I am a withered leaf for every subject except Science," he told a friend in 1868 (qtd. in Fleming 219). Shakespeare he found nauseating, and music and paintings oppressive. There are, it seems, some "questions" that a particular imagination cannot, for one reason or another, hear—as though a sense had been dulled or damaged, or has yet to develop.

But if the question should not be forced, neither should it be ignored. Imagination, after all, in both the larger social setting and the private world of the individual, requires a nourishing environment or it will atrophy—and imagination is at the heart of the question asked by any religious leader. Regarding the "moral" imagination, for example, Jonathan Jacobs notes that "an understanding of what it is to be a person or a rational animal is an appreciation of what it is to have a certain characteristic kind of life, and the special sort of subjectivity that that involves" (28). Walking an imagined mile in another's shoes, so the folk wisdom has it, pre-empts an objectifying alterity that frees us from moral kinship. But, if this is difficult enough when it demands empathy for those outside our family circle, what sort of subjectivity can a human being project for a *transcendent* other? Even in a theology that centers on Incarnation, how can a moral imagination cope with the immanence and imagined familiarity of one like us in all things but sin?

Yet, the mention of "coping" suggests the expenditure of energy, veering possibly toward entropy—and this exhaustion, of course, is exactly what imagination counteracts. Martin Marty speaks of a "pastoral" imagination which, "when it catches on to the fact that it *gets* to be used [rather than *has* to be used] has less in common with the wings of an ostrich and more with the wings of a dove" (8). Imagination is a gift, given to some and not to all, and is not a burden. In this context, the question Jesus asks is not an inscrutable problem, incapable of solution; it is not even a koan, though that may come a bit closer to the truth. It is an opportunity for invention, for relaxation. The religious imagination has always been a *source* of energy, for better or worse.

If, in other words, the question remains hanging in the air, this is not for lack of answers. In fact, it is met throughout the ages with an uproar of competing responses. Joseph Feeney notes that American Catholics, for example, when asked to describe their religious experiences, resort to a matrix of images that may be classified as secular (e.g., sex, finance, music, nature) or sacred (e.g., saints, Scripture, parish events). In both cases what is remarkable, if sometimes controversial, is the volatility and ever-renewed versatility of the imagining. "In colonial America," he writes, "the Puritans once tried to discipline the religious imagination by restricting its sources to the Bible and to common, everyday life. In modern America, by contrast, the Catholic imagination can—does—roam widely and, in Joseph-like fashion, puts on myriad colors" (219).

As the essays collected here hope to demonstrate, this variegation in religious imagination (the "pied beauty" of Hopkins's poem, in one sense) has a history, like the ripples in a pond that expand out from a remembered splash. In Part I the examples to which our chapters resort are principally Christian, but their implications touch upon any form of imagination that deals with the transcendent—with, in Justin Kelly's words, "the question of how the absence of God becomes the presence of God" (1). Like a great sculptor approaching a marble block, we use our religious sensitivities as "the means by which the still hidden truth declares itself to us" (4).

The reference to David Plante's novel *The Accident*, which begins this introductory essay, recalls Kelly's reading of Yeats's poem "The Song of Wandering Aengus." Yeats speaks of plucking "The silver apples of the moon, / The golden apples of the sun," and Kelly concludes that they are, of course, the very same apples, seen first by moonlight and then by sunlight. "And the metamorphosis of one into the other symbolizes the very movement from ideal to real, from one nocturnal glow of imagination to the full daylight of vision" (5). Though the two characters in Plante's novel live side by side, they inhabit two quite different worlds.

The full daylight that Kelly describes, and the various procedures of metamorphosis that lead individuals to this "clearer" vision, are addressed in the essays that follow. Some are directly historical studies, some tangentially so, and others explicitly ahistorical. Brenda Deen Schildgen's, for example, follows Paul Ricoeur's lead and considers the Gospel of Mark not so much as a document of its age as a symbol system that follows the rules of mythmaking from many cultures and times. Such a study, interested in structures and patterns, attempts to examine a sort of knowledge beyond that familiar to Darwin: in fact, a "poetic" knowledge.

Christiaan Lievestro's, on the other hand, is an examination of context as much as content, and offers an interesting working-through of the relationship between the Ignatian and Erasmian notions of humanism, especially as played out in Jesuit schools of the Renaissance. Where might their imaginations have taken them if their respondent had not been there to narrow the focus, or to light unlikely alleys? Edward Oakes's study directly addresses the "in-between" area embodied in historical narratives. His focus is on narratological questions regarding the gaps between fact and fiction, and the search for transcendent meaning through immanent story-telling. Truth—what is that?—remains another biblical question that reverberates through time.

Like Lievestro's, Paul Crowley's essay draws its inspiration from recent celebrations of the 450th anniversary of the founding of the Society of Jesus. But Crowley's essay, beginning with Pozzo's ceiling in the Gesù church in Rome and moving to the meditation techniques employed in Ignatius Loyola's *Spiritual Exercises*, examines the baroque imagination prompted by the attempted visualization of a space somewhere between heaven and earth. Such an attempt typifies the baroque confidence and verve that celebrates the invasion of one space by another. Where cannot the religious imagination focus in its search: on the foreground, on the backdrop, on the shifting interstices?

Jane Kristof's discussion of Georges Rouault is both a contextualization and a literal visualization, a reminder that this most important Roman Catholic painter of his day was a member of a revival of religious imagination that stressed both individual expression and pious tradition. What is the role of the larger community in the shaping of one's notion of God? A tradition of piety like that of Rouault is given a detailed treatment by Franco Mormando in his humorous examination of Bernardino of Siena, the most popular preacher of his day. Bernardino's highly imaginative and startlingly graphic sermons made this Franciscan the most important student of the discernment of spirits until Ignatius. His interplay between pious interiorization and sensuous description has been, and remains, a controversial source of religious energy. And to what ends is such energy to be directed?

William Franke and Jo Ellen Parker also focus their studies on precursors, and on the anxiety of the influence they wielded. As Franke shows, Milton's task was to "protestantize" Dante by separating image from truth. The image, so important in Roman Catholic imagination, no longer functions for Milton as an outward manifestation of how things "really" are, but rather feeds the reader's personal experience of his poem, in which truth can be encountered, it is hoped, with greater spiritual immediacy. Where, then, for Milton does this reality reside? Is God, in fact, the process of encounter that the poet hopes his work will promote? And is this not imagination itself? In Parker's essay, George Eliot must contend both with a massive tradition of typological reading of the Bible and with Ludwig Feuerbach! The layers of responses to earlier imaginations are put on like multiple sweaters, and can disguise the shape within. As Parker demonstrates, Eliot seeks to expose the inadequacy of Feuerbach's representation of the Protestant iconography of celibacy and marriage. In whose interest would Feuerbach so imagine the topic?

II

"Lovely in limbs, and lovely in eyes not his"

—Gerard Manley Hopkins

The essays, taken together, seek not only an answer to the questions asked by Jesus of his disciples, but also to anticipate an equally contentious query: *How* do you say who I am? Thus, in the book's second section we turn our attention to the contemporary scene, a world in which divisions between religious cultures are less fixed and the avenues for imagination intersect in interesting ways. If Part I demonstrates the effects of time on the "Christian" imagination, Part II suggests even more clearly the variety of imaginative paradigms that one can bring to question transcendence. One might say that we are now living in an age of imaginative permeability, an age, some would argue, of postdenominationalism. At the same time as the close of our millennium engenders apocalyptic fears in some, defensive fundamentalisms dully erect a Maginot line against the beauty and wit of other belief systems. And to what purpose? What god worth his or her salt would willingly lie in Procrustes's bed?

In a study similar to our own, Stanley Hopper notes that the deeper themes of current literary works focus on "modern man's search for a soul, for comradeship, for inner peace, for a 'place' in the cosmos, for hope, for creative satisfactions," and he goes on to suggest that "it is an odd paradox that just as religious dogmas were being relaxed through the liberalizing movements of the nineteenth and early decades of the twentieth centuries, the literary world should have been renewing these and making them a point of appeal" (xi). This estimate is at least optimistic, if not outright wrong; many in the Western world would point to contemporary literatures as evidence of *despair* over the hope for transcendence rather than of renewal.

We therefore turn our attention to religious imaginations that some will find unfamiliar or questionable, and we begin with one very close to home: Andrew Greeley's. It is simplistic to describe his approach to God as sexual, but it will do as a place to start. He is by no means the first priest to write controversial novels for religious purposes (think, for example, of Queen Victoria's chaplain, Charles Kingsley), but he is the first to be so prominently displayed at the checkout line in local supermarkets. His essay confronts head-on the criticism of his celebration of the "happy fault" that leads his characters to a very attractive God.

Gavin D'Costa then introduces us to a methodology for approaching unfamiliar religious imaginations as a pre-catechesis for an approach to God. As he notes, "Imaginative empathy in this new mode is the key to understanding the Other." His intriguing argument attacks the false objectivity of the secular imagination, and opts for the greater honesty of engaging the other from within one's own committed belief system. The Bakhtinian overtones of the "conversation" D'Costa envisions become the structural framework for Norman Cary's examination of the Islamic imagination of Somali novelist Nuruddin Farah. K. D. Verma shows the Hindu imagination that led to Sri Aurobindo's political philosophy, and how this had such important ramifications in the life of Gandhi and his followers. Joyce Zonana, in turn, demonstrates the interesting ramifications of "orientalism" in the nineteenth-century's assimilation of Jewish stories for political purposes much closer to home. With passing reference to Confucianism and Taoism, Sheng-Tai Chang provides an overview of Buddhism's influence in the literary imagination of China, focusing on the dialectic of "simultaneously detaching oneself from the world and engaging it."

Finally, T. R. Wright takes a surprising look at deconstruction. "Right from the beginning," he writes, "there was a deeply religious vein in Derrida's thought." In a sense, what Wright says about Derrida might be said of our own collection, as a whole: "for Derrida, all representation will always be incomplete, always in need of interpretation, . . . enmeshed in codes. . . ." We hope that our collection will be a helpful examination of some of those codes.

We feel there are many persuasive reasons for continuing such an examination, and one of the most compelling is offered by Emmanuel Levinas. As he notes in his controversial 1948 essay on reality and its "shadow," "the phenomenology of images insists on their transparency," but he sees them as opaque.

> The intention of one who contemplates an image is said to go directly through the image, as through a window, into the world

it represents, and aims at an *object*. Yet nothing is more mysterious than the term "world it represents"—since representation expresses just that function of an image that still remains to be determined. (134)

Levinas offers a challenge to the esthete who would celebrate the atemporality of such images—the beautiful stained-glass windows that fix, forever, a never-to-be-repeated time of innocent belief, a little gem of human history. He condemns the evasion of responsibility that any such fixed reality might falsely allow, and calls instead for the imposition of criticism to chart the distance between the myth proposed by any art and *reality*, from which questions of transcendence may emerge:

> In the vision of the represented object a painting has a density of its own: it is itself an object of the gaze. The consciousness of the representation lies in knowing that the object is not there. The perceived elements are not the object but are like its "old garments," spots of colour, chunks of marble or bronze. These elements do not serve as symbols, and in the absence of the object they do not force its presence, but by their presence insist on its absence. They occupy its place fully to mark its removal, as though the represented object died, were degraded, were disincarnated in its own reflection. The painting then does not lead us beyond the given reality, but somehow to the hither side of it. It is a symbol in reverse. (136)

Such astringent philosophy scours from any superficial picture of God the sense of completion; it erases from any narrative theology the sense of an ending. In effect, it asks once again: Who do you say that I am? With this sharp reminder of the limitations of the human imagination, this introductory essay concludes by returning to David Plante, the author with whom it began. His recent novel, stereotypical of the contemporary quest described by Stanley Hopper, centers in a rape and the search for a Russian painting of the Annunciation—reminiscent, somehow of Yeats's "Leda and the Swan." Plante's book concludes with ambiguity, and with a stark faith in the imagination as the language of transcendence, arising anew in each culture, age, and individual:

> Falling asleep that night, Claude thought: No, I don't believe in God, but I can imagine him. I imagine him as the darkness in

which images occur, the darkness that, when I shift my attention from an image to what is around the image, I see spreading in all directions beyond my sight. That vast dark space behind the image of a sunlit glass of water is the only way I can imagine God. (*Annunciation* 346)

University of Santa Clara JOHN C. HAWLEY

WORKS CITED

Feeney, Joseph, S.J. "The Varieties of the American Catholic Religious Imagination: A Contemporary Taxonomy." *Thought* 56.2 (June 1991): 206–20.
Fleming, Donald. "Charles Darwin, the Anaesthetic Man." *Victorian Studies* 4 (1961): 219–36.
Jacobs, Jonathan. "Moral Imagination, Objectivity, and Practical Wisdom." *International Philosophical Quarterly* 31.1 (March 1991): 23–27.
Hopper, Stanley Romaine, ed. *Spiritual Problems in Contemporary Literature*. New York: Harper, 1957.
Kelly, Justin, S.J. "Absence into Presence: A Theology of Imagination." Warren Lectures Series in Catholic Studies 16. U of Tulsa. 8 Sept. 1991.
Levinas, Emmanuel. "Reality and Its Shadow." *Les Temps Modernes* 38 (1948): 771–89. Trans. Alphonso Lingis. In *The Levinas Reader*. Ed. Seán Hand. Oxford: Blackwell, 1989. 129–43.
Marty, Martin. "Pastoral Imagination." *Church* 7.3 (Fall 1991): 5–8.
Mathews, William, S.J. "The Questioning Imagination." *Milltown Studies* 27.1 (Spring 1991): 14–27.
Plante, David. *The Accident*. New York: Ticknor, 1991.
———. *Annunciation*. New York: Ticknor, 1994.

I · CHRISTIAN EUROPE

1 • The Gospel of Mark as Myth

Brenda Deen Schildgen

TO EXAMINE THE GOSPEL OF Mark as myth is to take it temporarily outside of time and history and to consider its communication as poetic knowledge. Viewing the Gospel in this way opens us to psychological and ontological dimensions which may be less apparent in time-specific historical or sociological studies. In myths certain fundamental human concerns and situations are expressed through ancient, inherently biological and culturally primal, symbolism. This symbolism adheres as Paul Ricoeur has suggested "to the most immutable human manner of being in the world, whether it be a question of above and below, the cardinal directions, the spectacle of the heavens, terrestrial localization, houses, paths, fire, wind, stones, or water" (*Interpretation* 65).

Through looking at the Gospel outside of history, and examining how it employs mythic themes, we can approach some understanding of how the Gospel attempts to say something about "reality," and about how to live in the world *sub specie eternitatis*. However, myths are usually projected back into a time before time, what Paul Ricoeur calls "mythic time," but in the case of Mark the narrative is set in the present time. Narratives set in this "mythic time" represent an imagined time before "fragmentation" overtook the human condition, when all the differences, whether sky and earth, male and female, God and humankind, etc., were in harmony. Consciousness of differences did not exist, because human transgression had not created them. Obviously, the Gospel of Mark does not describe such a time, but it does present the possibility of overcoming this bifurcated human condition by modeling a "way of being in the world" by which these differences can be harmonized. Thus, "mythic time" in the Gospel of Mark is an "allegory of possible time" when human "communitas" can be restored (Turner, *Ritual*). The mythological dimensions of the Gospel show a way and point to a future opportunity to overcome the human fragmented condition, thus bringing the imagined tranquillity and loss of the mythic past into play as a dynamic utopian future.

Because the Western intellectual traditions combine the Judeo-Christian tendency to historicize myth with the Greek tendency to philosophize and rationalize it and the Roman tendency to politicize it, we have overlooked how the central Christian myth or sacred story makes use of synchronic narrative patterns. These symbolic narrative patterns may involve subject matters, such as the human quest for knowledge, understanding, adventure, or personal transformation, the relationships between the sexes, family organization, and related issues, the role of kings and priests, for example, as well as narrative patterns using devices such as trebling, the journey, descents, ascents, and crossings over. Narratives articulate "human action" through words and symbols, and patterns, and norms, while culture determines symbols and makes their meaning public (Ricoeur, *Time* 57).

An exploration of the mythic characteristics of the Gospel of Mark will suggest how Mark's Jesus is a mythological figure and conversely how Mark's Jesus subverts mythology. An essential mythic model for the religious reformer in the West finds its imaginative source in the character and life of Jesus as narrated in the Gospels. Because it is a major force in forming the religious imagination of Christians, this story has imprinted a model of religious heroic expectation on those who listen to or read the story. In the Gospel of Mark, Jesus accepts his mission, rejects the comfort of the "home" environment, selects a few chosen followers, presents a program for reform, encounters challenge and conflict, courageously stands up for the program's convictions, experiences failure even with the chosen disciples, and accepts whatever tragic or triumphant acts conclude the reforming journey—these actions and events seem to characterize the path of the reformer.

Though this pattern may not differ markedly from many other myths, the ontology which accompanies it transforms mythic expectation. Rather than re-enforcing the fears which maintain cultural and social codes, the main character preaches the subversion of fear, and shows how to successfully overcome its power. But his actions and teachings are shown to be liminal in terms of space and time, and although his actions undermine social structures enforced by fear, the ultimate success of his mission is shown to depend on the conquest of fear by trust, even though the possibility of this victory is left paradoxically open. In the story, history and myth intersect, for both myth and history present characters and events according to shared rhetorical patterns. While the narrative makes absolute "truth" claims, they are made within the context of myth and story. Hans-Georg Gadamer discusses this characteristic of myth in *Truth and Method* (72–73, 118–19). Likewise Hayden White in *The Content of the Form* remarks that because history writing in the West emerged out of literary discourse, which shaped itself against the background of myth, history differentiates itself from literature by virtue of its subject matter rather than its form. History, he suggests, claims "truth" for its own, whereas literature is relegated to the imaginary (44–45). As a "true" sacred history, the Gospel story has functioned partly to form the mythic model of exemplary action for the Christian religious imagination.

If we consider one conventional function of myth as showing us how to be at home in the world, as not answering questions, but as suspending and deflecting questionability (Blumenberg 126), then we can see that in the setting of the Gospel of Mark, "the unquestionable known" of traditional culture, society, and ritual is in a state of flux and conflict. Conventional mores as preserved in these traditions are no longer assumed. The certainties protected by Hebraic traditions are no longer unquestioned, and a world of possibilities has filled the chasm created by their demise. Mark, through his recounting of the mythic journey of Jesus, is constructing a new myth to subvert the old decaying one, which shows that man can live and die in a world of contingency as long as he does not fear, and this knowledge is the central uncontingent reality of being. He is showing that man and the divine can reconcile through the transformation of fear to trust. Mark presents this new myth as the story of the challenging reformer willing to take on suffering and death as essential to his mission of conversion. Mark shows fear as the force which can undermine this new way of being in the world and which will direct the conventional anxieties about suffering, ethical paradox, and intellectual bafflement. In other words, Mark creates a myth in which the struggle to exist in the world requires the conquest of fear. The essence of this revelation is timeless, for its message transcends the particular historical moment of the Gospel.

Fear creates the semiotic, emotional, and ethical confusions in the Gospel. The failure of trust and understanding leads many characters to surrender to cowardice in an attempt to control and own their world. In contrast, Jesus, experiencing what we can assume is the most excruciating fear and facing the absolute reality of his impending death in grief-stricken horror and dismay, hoping that "this cup could pass" from him (14:34–36)[1] does not yield to fear. Rather, he shows that he cannot possess the world, that the way to live and die in the world is to trust in what God wills, not seek what man wills. In a vulnerable social and political setting, controlled by religious and political forces, whether taboos or armies, people are susceptible to fear and terror, but Mark presents an uncontingent reality of being in the world which he pits against the fragmenting certainties of a disordered "communitas" and a compromised way of being. Jesus's actions show that "being at home in the world" and trusting in its own fragile realities can overcome the power that disease, hunger, diabolical forces at work in people, nature, the unknown, and even death have over humans. Such fearlessness can break the alienation between God and man, and reconcile man to God. On the other hand, surrendering to fear will lead to ethical, semiotic, and political chaos, where desire for immediate and tangible power over the world conceals the always-present reality of certain death.

II

Mark, of all the Gospels, has an extraordinarily "magical" setting: the large number of curing wonders (1:23–27, 29–34, 40–44; 2:3–5; 3:10–12; 5:21–43, passim); the commissioning of the disciples as "proclaimers of the gospel" and "drivers out of devils" (3:13–16); the identification of perverse human behavior with the devil and diabolic spirits (5:1–17; 8:33; 9:14–27, 38–40); the two multiplication-of-food stories (6:35–44; 8:1–9); the transfiguration (9:2–13); the taming of the sea (4:35–41; 6:45–52) (Thompson, *Motif-Index*, "Magic Control of the Seas," Motif # D 2151.1, Vol. 2: 386); the three predictions of forthcoming suffering, death, and resurrection; and the empty tomb and announcement that he had risen just as predicted (16:1–8). Many of these are standard folklore motifs as "culture hero banishes demon" (Motif A 531.1.1, Vol. 1: 122), "dying culture hero teaches people how to die" (Motif A 565, Vol. 1: 124), "culture hero establishes customs" (Motif A545, Vol. 1: 124), and "culture hero tames winds and regulates rivers" (Motifs A532; A533, and A533.1, Vol. 1: 123). Mark's attention to the miraculous and the extraordinary in which demonic powers oppose salvific ones specifically locates his historical narrative against the backdrop of cosmic time, the setting for myth, thus emphasizing the eternal and cosmic significance of the activities and the human potential for reconciliation and conquest of the demonic, whether spiritual or physical, or in the form of devils, disease, physical handicap, hunger, moral depravity, or death.

Myth assumes such an extra-real literary environment, but not to avoid reality. On the contrary, the extra-real is an allegory of possibilities, a temporary environment where the conditions of biological and existential living outside of time and outside of conventional spaces can be fully explored. Yet, it is the fundamental condition of living in real space and real time which forms the central concern of myth. As such, myth is a literary environment, the world of the imagination, whether unrestricted by convention or consciously transgressing the conventions (social, political, religious, or cultural) which regulate human behavior. Myth is the extra-ordinary space-time where the extra-ordinary human possibility can be worked out. The conventions of ordinary space-time and ordinary life are abrogated during the extra-ordinary circumstances. In the Gospel of Mark, the extra-ordinary events, their prime actor, and the "way of being" he adopts create a new community which temporarily replaces conventional structures and expectations and these changes direct the Gospel's readers or listeners to the possibility of a new community formed out of this utopian human opportunity. These are the circumstances or situations in which the imagined model of the reformer operates. His reforming activities are liminal as is the time in which the activities take place. Normal expectations, structures, and understanding are momentarily overturned, questioned, or at least spotlighted in the narrative.

In the Gospel of Mark, Jesus is a mythic presence, a way of "being in the world," whose actions and journey show that all the biological, environmental, and existential dangers which oppress humans—even death itself—can be overcome. Mark's exaggeration of perverted, disordered, dangerous, or painful physical and mental conditions, whether hundreds of devils in a single person, excessive femaleness in a twelve-year menstrual flow, or the double provision of "bread" to the starving thousands, or death itself, serve to emphasize the power of Jesus's "way of being" to transform the human experience of the natural world. As he confronts the distress of "living as humans," Jesus consistently identifies and challenges fear (*phobos*) as the source of the human environmental, biological, or ontological crisis. If myth promotes a fearful view of the universe and re-enforces terror by showing what happens to transgressive humans who step outside the boundaries of human place in the cosmos and society, the Gospel of Mark's myth works against this hereditary fear, showing that the conquest of fear leads to the erasure of the "different" or "other" status of man.

Instead of explaining away fear or re-enforcing fear-driven taboos, as is more common in myth, the Gospel identifies fear as the emotion that threatens to return chaos, and therefore prompts humans to seize control of the world. Fear-laden taboos rule human relationships, whether between social and ethnic groups, families, political power structures, or ritual practices. Fear creates and controls the distance between human and human or human and the divinity. As a projection of mankind's deepest anxieties, "fear" reminds man of his fugitive status and makes him conscious of his own "otherness" in relationship to the cosmos, to the society in which he sojourns, to his family, and most of all to his own consciousness. But, in revealing and preserving man's alienated status, "fear" also makes possible the potential for reconciliation. If humans create and preserve their own alienation, they must also have the potential for reconciliation. Jesus's "liminal" mission is a brief interlude in human affairs when this potential becomes present.

The antidote for these fears and their attendant desires is simply not to yield to fear, but to trust. Such an act of trust makes the numinous present in human experience and closes the gap between the "self" and the "other." What I mean by the "numinous" here follows Rudolf Otto's extended discussion, in *The Idea of the Holy*, of the awesomeness experienced in the face of the *mysterium tremendum*. When Jesus crosses over from the ontological territory of the habitual "self" (structured by rigid custom and taboo, and sustained by fear of the natural world or fear of social, political, biological, religious, or other personal differences) to the utopian world where such rigid structures collapse, his act restores the divine to the human experience. Jesus's radical actions subvert fear and the taboos enforcing it as he accepts humanity's powerless and fragile place in the world. This vulnerability unsettles the boundary between the divine and the human, making possible the return of the divine to the human experience. The exposure of human weakness and fragility hints that to abandon the ego, with all its desires and fears, is simultaneously to abandon all the social and human structures supporting it. It is, as it were, to retrieve the prelapsarian state before fallen humankind realized its own separation from the divine and constructed social mores and familial alliances in an effort to control the world in which its vulnerable "self" might subsist.

The Gospel therefore presents Jesus as a mythic figure confronting his own ontological crisis, his "aloneness" and "isolation," as cosmic powers, social and political structures, family alliances, and friends all flee from him, persecute him, or fail him. His mission and death show that fear drives people to delude themselves into thinking they can control the world. Jesus's experience proclaims that fear promotes the desire for power over other people, both politically and socially-culturally (as in the case of the High Priests, Pontius Pilate, and Herod), over tradition (as with the Scribes and Pharisees), over life and death (as with the disciples and Jairus), over God (as shown by all the miscreant acts in the Gospel), and even over one's own will (as with Judas, Peter, and the women at the tomb). Fearlessness, on the other hand, as a declaration of the human's powerless place on earth, shatters the boundaries between humans (whether social, ethnic, familial, or individual), between society and nature, and between the divine and the human, and reconciles them.

Fear characterizes the emotions of the unknowing as well as the evil characters and propels their actions in the Gospel. Fear defines the insiders and outsiders, aligning followers with betrayers and opponents with intimates. Almost every major character and many minor ones express fear, whether it be Herod, the disciples, the woman bleeding for twelve years, the disciples, the chief priests, Pontius Pilate, the elders and scribes, or the women who attend Jesus at the tomb.

Mark identifies the motive for some of the most perverse actions in the Gospel as fear. The murders of the two holy men, John the Baptist and Jesus, are prompted by fear. In the John the Baptist story, "Herod feared John" (6:20)—and this fear actually kept John alive though incarcerated (6:20)—but Herodias nursed a grudge against him (6:19), prompted by her fear for her place as rightful wife of Herod. The ultimate consequence of this fear was the death of John.

It is fear, too, that inspires the political and religious powers to conspire against Jesus. When Jesus assaults the established cultic practice and its practitioners (11:17), the chief priests and the doctors of law respond with a plan to kill him, because "they were afraid of him" (11:18). Not only are they afraid of him, but their cowardice has also spread to their fear of his power over people, their own religious constituency (11:32; 12:12). Although Mark does not use the word fear to describe Pontius Pilate's mood as he decides to capitulate to the crowd's demand to "crucify him," he does make clear that Pilate's action is motivated by a desire to "satisfy the crowd," suggesting that Pilate was afraid of the power this mob might exercise if not satisfied.

The other group of fearful is the "unknowing," and it includes Jesus's closest followers and those for whom he performs miracles. "Trust" opposes fear as the ontological condition that can conquer the power of fear over human's lives, but this message seems to elude all the inhabitants of the Gospel. The first time the disciples express their fear, during the first crossing of the water (4:41), this opposition is introduced. When observers cannot understand how the Gerasene demoniac could be freed from a legion of devils (5:16), this opposition appears once more. The hemorrhaging woman is afraid when she realizes that Jesus's magic has cured her, as is Jairus when he discovers that his daughter is already dead (5:35–36). But in both these cases, Jesus informs these distressed people that "trust" can overcome the most oppressive dangers if one only abandon fear (5:36).

Again when Jesus predicts his forthcoming suffering, death,

and resurrection, his disciples do not understand this riddle, and are afraid: "they did not understand what he said, and were afraid to ask" (9:32). On the way to Jerusalem, his disciples are astounded, while those who follow are afraid (10:32). Peter's failure to admit that he knew Jesus when challenged by one of the High Priest's serving maids (14:68–70), even though his motive is not provided by Mark, is another case where cowardice overcomes trust. The Gospel also paradoxically concludes with "fear": "They said nothing to anybody, for they were afraid" (16:8). Even the women who did not flee the crucifixion but watched from a distance (15:40) capitulate to fear when their normal human expectations are disrupted by the empty tomb.

Though the highlighting of fear points to the normal condition of humans, and at the same time shows Jesus's opposition to its power, his action is presented as a liminal experience. This "limen," or margin, a common motif of myths, is a brief interval or interruption of the normal, a boundary experience when the past is momentarily suspended, and the future has not yet begun; it is a time of possibility when everything known and assumed is suddenly tentative and contingent (Turner, "Liminal" 44). In this liminal space-time, the history of the final time of Jesus's life, the time of his public ministry unfolds. There are a number of ways in which such liminal conditions set the atmosphere of the Gospel. The larger scope of the entire Gospel, the narrative of the last, or only, events in Jesus's life which the Gospel records, can itself be considered a "limen." It is a narrative of his public life, the space between his life as it was in Galilee, about which we learn very little, and his death. In contrast to most myths where the hero crosses the boundary into exile, whether the forest, desert, or jungle, Jesus's crossing is into the public arena, the streets of local and distant villages and eventually Jerusalem itself. Rather than a withdrawal from the security of home into the unknown natural terrain, Jesus's exile from the security of home takes him into the hostile and unknown territory of contemporary Palestine and environs, essentially into history.

In this period of his public life, he challenges the conventional structures that regulate social, political, and religious life, and we are shown how the fear and anxiety that sustain these structures can be overturned. After divine sanction has been conferred on Jesus by the heavenly voice, "You are my beloved son. In you I am well pleased" (1:11), Jesus announces the beginning of the marginal time which becomes the central apocalyptic time when his public ministry begins (1:15). His proclamation that "the time has arrived," a cue to a turning point in the narrative, dismisses ordinary time, ordinary kingdoms, and ordinary messages in favor of *metanoia* and trust. This proclamation reverses worldly conventions, whether of time, space, or being. Many contemporary worldly conventions are suspended (such as family allegiances and cultic practices), and the marginal and liminal in the form of charismatic wandering, wonderworking, and teaching take their place. The "liminal" experience is a self-imposed exile from human business as usual, when a totally new community or "way of being" can emerge in contrast to the normal condition of human alienation. This alienation or separation is of two kinds: one is for humans to act only in terms of social or political structures; the other is to yield to fundamental selfish urges no matter how much one harms fellow human beings (Turner, *Ritual* 105). While Jesus, his disciples, and followers participate in the temporary abrogation of social, cultic, and familial convention and avoid self-centered actions, the Gospel draws up sides, in the pattern of myths, which radically divide the world into those who conform to codes, taboos, or other social expectations and conspire in selfish acts *vs.* those who follow Jesus and his reform movement. In the liminal interlude, Jesus creates a community in which he abandons these structures and base urges and in which altruistic action takes their place. The possibility of the restored prelapsarian utopia and the reality of man's obduracy create the narrative tension in this liminal space-time. "Faith," "trust," and "openness" make this reconciliation possible, but the Gospel also shows that fear subverts it, and cements the power that conventional forces have over people.

In his conflict with the doctors of the law (2:15-3:6; 7:1-3), Jesus addresses the opposition between culture and nature; the Herod-*vs.*-John the Baptist intercalation (6:14-29) exposes the struggle for power between kings and priests; Jesus identifies himself with a mission in the towns in contrast to John's mission in the wilderness (1:35-38); he is the purifier who cleanses those with unclean spirits (1:23, 33, 34, 39; 5:1-20, passim); Jesus promises a future life which will conquer the powers of death (8:34-38, 9:31,

10:29–31, etc.); God *vs.* Satan (8:33) is yet another opposition, as is land *vs.* water (4:36–41, 6:45–52).²

Mark's narrative explores situations where the conventions determining insiders and outsiders, that is, those who follow the authoritative teachings on the family, patriarchalism, sex and gender roles, eating and cleanliness rituals, and clan solidarity condoned in the Hebrew bible, are often modified. Although he reaffirms the Law repeatedly (7:8–10; 10:17–22; 12:29–34), Mark's Jesus, nevertheless, redefines familial and clan alliances, choosing a group of followers who represent different social statuses and political affiliations (1:16–20; 3:13–19), specifically seeking those outside his own ethnic clan (7:24–30; 5:1–20), and rejecting his family on the grounds that "Whoever does the will of God is my brother, my sister, my mother" (3:35).

Nor are Mark's negations of social and cultural convention restricted to issues of status and familial alliances. His version of the Jesus story shows his hero confronting and undermining cultic practice, redefining insiders and outsiders by confronting the "doctors of the law" and the priesthood, those who hold the religious, intellectual and cultural power in the setting of the story (2:13–3:6, 12:13–27, 14:1–2, passim).

In the Gospel of Mark, Jesus's actions take place within traditional mythic political structures in which power is equally divided between king and priest (Dumézil). It could be argued, however, that, in contrast to the conventional pattern, history has ruptured myth and challenged Hebraic sociopolitical practice. It has restructured the balance between king and priest, because the Roman presence has made Israel a client state under the management of the Roman procurator Pontius Pilate, with the puppet king Herod in Galilee and the temple priesthood continuing cultic practice as usual in Jerusalem. Instead of the king and priest acting as mediating forces, the Gospel presents a perverse figure, Pontius Pilate, as the ironic or subversive mediator between these historically and mythologically balancing powers. Likewise, it could be argued that the mythic structures have adapted themselves to "real" historical circumstances. In the balance of power between king and priest, Mark's Jesus is hardly a mediator. Rather, his mission and activity seem to be directed against the structural mythic political conventions that have continued these powers in their hereditary positions, even though he does not take a political position against the Romans, insisting perhaps ironically that Caesar, like God, should receive his due (12:17). The Gospel, nevertheless, shows that king and priest have abandoned their traditional mythic roles as protectors of the certainties that rule the clan's life and sustain its identity while ensuring its survival. On the contrary, it is they who are undermining "Israel's" laws, traditions, and customs by murdering its prophets and charismatic religious leaders (6:14–29; 14:1–2, 55–64). Neither Jesus nor Mark spends much attention on the tyranny of the Roman presence, which is supported by self-evident military power, but Mark shows Jesus in direct confrontation with those holding cultural and social power as he attempts to expose their presumed righteousness which is sustained by tradition, taboo, habit, and prejudice.

III

The narrative surface does not present Jesus as a mediator between oppositions, but because he is in active opposition to them, he is consciously exposing them and showing a way of being which would eliminate their dichotomous power over humans. Paul Ricoeur, like Louis Marin in his structural study *Semiotics of the Passion Narrative*, argues that underlying narrative structures do not merely re-present themselves figurally, but "initiatives get taken" on the surface of the narrative which introduce contingencies into the story and govern the transformations taking place on the deeper levels ("Interpretive" 244). Jesus's public ministry, the only part of his life that Mark has chosen as his subject, is essentially liminal activity, a brief period in real time when conventions are momentarily challenged. This liminality is both creative and destructive. It calls into action a new human being by questioning conventional structures and foregrounding their limitations. As Turner points out, liminality invites critical thinking and even opposition to "social structural man," but liminality also presents, whether directly or by implication, a possibility for human society which is an unstructured but homogeneous "communitas" composed of the human species ("Liminal" 47). Such a situation cannot be sustained for long, for it is an interval, a period in which all structural conventions are momentarily denied or abrogated

(*Ritual* 94–130). Jesus's public ministry, therefore, is such a momentary period when the possibility of a new community outside these structural conventions takes hold of the people's imaginations and behavior. Jesus's charismatic activities and fearless presence direct this momentary hiatus.

In addition to the Gospel's narrating the "liminal" final period in Jesus's life, a number of threshold events also characterize Jesus' mission. The first of these occurs in Chapter 2. Jesus is "at home," which represents his home in Galilee, his tradition, and his social and religious training. He proclaims his message from the security of this home environment, while the crowd listens in the "space in front of the door" (2:2). At this point in the Gospel, despite the fact that the "time has come" (1:15), and Jesus's public ministry has begun, he has not crossed the threshold into the public arena, but remains within the domain of his home in Galilee, with all the security that offers. But there are so many people occupying the threshold that the crowd "opens the roof," thus annulling the normal conventions of "inside" and "outside" and "up" and "down." It is through this action, and his response to it, "Your sins are forgiven" (2:5), that Jesus crosses the "limen" which initiates the conflict with his opponents (2:6–8) and establishes the opposition between "good" and "evil," between the fearful and the fearless. This "limen" is between "things as they are," held together by fear and taboo—the security of home, family, clan, society, ritual, custom, and culture—and a new, unknown territory where social, cultural, and political predictability, with the exception of prophetic foreknowledge, dissipates. Thus, Mark deploys the mythic theme in which a culture hero crosses the threshold, but in contrast to myth, the journey the hero undertakes will re-assess how to live in the world rather than confirm the cultural norms and conditions preserved by custom or law. This is why, for example, it is such an important detail that Jesus teaches his first recorded parable from the "sea" (4:1–20) while the crowds listen from the land. The "sea" also denotes a "limen" as a metaphor for the mythic "natural" environment, outside civilization, culture, and tradition as we know it, where he can preach a totally new social and moral message, a new way of being, constructing a new "communitas," which he describes in the Parable of the Sower (4:3–34).

Immediately following this first parable, Jesus tells his disciples,

"Let us cross over to the other side of the lake" (4:35), traversing the mythical "boundary" between the known and the unknown, the world as it is and the world he will show his disciples can exist. This is not an easy crossing for the disciples (Starobinski), although for Jesus it is very tranquil: "he was in the stern asleep on a cushion" (4:38). In the crossing, the new ontology of being human is specifically presented: because the disciples in their usual frayed state are terribly frightened, "Master, we are sinking! Do you not care?" (4:38), and Jesus, having calmed the waters (Thompson, Motif # D. 2151, Vol. 2: 385), confronts them with their cowardice, "Why are you such cowards? Have you no faith even now?" (4:40). Again, Jesus takes his disciples onto the dangerous and unknown mythic environment of the water, both a physical and a social threat to humans, and reminiscent of Jonah's ill-fated sea journey. It is a symbolic environment which is menacing precisely because it is nature uncontrolled by man; it is outside social rules and habits, that is, the taboo-ridden world created out of human fears. At any moment, it threatens to destroy man's sense of predictability, in his normal fear-bound condition, the static world he counts on to continue his existence. But Jesus's actions show the disciples that unknown, threatening natural forces and the unknown territories of human ontology or sociology they symbolically represent, are not menacing if we do not allow "fear" to rule us. He is taking them across the boundary between the known and the unknown, but he is showing them the ontological condition that must characterize this crossing. As the disciples recognize Jesus's power over the water, a moment of spontaneous "communitas" occurs; although the disciples are awestruck and confused by the event, it is, nonetheless, a moment of mutual understanding when all the anxieties separating humans from one another, from God, and from nature, are suddenly exposed.

In the second sea journey, again a mythic crossing over the unknown, Jesus walks on the water (Motif # D. 2125.1, Vol. 2: 376), while the wind exercises its will (the disciples were "laboring at the oars against a head wind") (6:48), showing the disciples it is possible to cooperate with the unknown, despite its dangers. The disciples are once more terrified (6:50), and Jesus tells them, "Don't be afraid," giving the revelation formula for divine presence, "It is I," and advising them once more to avoid fear (6:50).

The primal fear of water, which threatens to conquer and destroy man's tranquillity in his known and stabilized environment, can be diverted by the abandonment of fear, a transformation which makes the divine present in human experience. The danger of unknown and untamed nature, which might break in on humankind and its known conventions at any moment, creates fear, but the human conquest of fear makes the numinous present to them.

The final threshold Jesus crosses is the entrance into Jerusalem, which happens three times (11:11, 15, 27). The confrontation with Jerusalem is between "his way" and the practices of the times. In his first entrance, he is greeted as a leader, the traditional "liberating" king (11:9–10), the savior who enters the temple in a traditional "king"-*vs.*-"priest" pattern. He traverses the boundary between his established ministry in the towns and villages of the countryside into the ultimate confrontation with the "city," historical site of Israel's regal and religious past and its present form. Mark merely notes that "he entered Jerusalem and went into the temple, where he looked at the whole scene" (11:11). He makes no comments on what Jesus might have observed there, and Jesus himself is silent. Mark constructs a dramatic scene which pits the "cult hero" against the locale of traditional sacred rite and priestly purview, leaving narrative gaps which will be filled in by the second and third entrances into Jerusalem. Whether Jesus's reaction was fear, revulsion, anger, or acceptance, we do not know, although all these emotions will characterize his actions once the Jerusalem drama actually begins.

Prior to the second entrance, Jesus curses the "fig tree," symbolic representation of Israel, a precursor to his angry cleansing of the temple (11:15–18), and a link to the first entrance into Jerusalem. His cursing acts as a narrative clue to his emotional response to what he had seen in Jerusalem on his first visit. Righteous anger prompts both actions as he transgresses the boundaries of cult and prejudice overseen by the official powers who will determine his inevitable death (11:18–19). The fig tree's "unreadiness" parallels the unreadiness of the temple practitioners for the reforms Jesus demands. His violation of the fig tree confronts the complacency of Israel and its rigid stasis that refuses change. In the final entrance, he is challenged on the authority for his actions (11:28), to which he responds by dismissing the conventions of temporal authority, telling the parable of the vineyard with its veiled allegory of Israel's historic rejection of its prophets or divine missionaries (12:1–9). He is asked by what right he violates the sanctified boundary separating the priestly cultus from others, and his fearless response in the form of the parable of the vineyard, answers that the right comes from the divinity, the right of prophets who are outside the priestly-aristocratic domain. He is not a mediator, but a reformer, the liminal purveyor of the divine mission.

The temple practice, or religious business as usual, Jesus deems a profligate violation of "communitas." His confrontation with the temple is his final act of opposing the established power and exposing its corruption. His actions frame the apocalyptic choice between contemporary social and religious custom in the temple and God's house. Excoriating the temple practitioners (11:17), he quotes Jeremiah, "My house shall be called a house of prayer for all nations," and dismisses all human structures, whether of cult, clan, or nation, and reminds his listeners of the utopian "communitas" where all humans are joined in common prayer in God's house.

The Gospel ending, nevertheless, implies the paradoxical potentiality of a continued or renewed "communitas" only if its listeners accept the "road" Jesus's mission reveals. When Jesus's followers (Judas, Peter, and even the women) succumb to fear and desert him, they figuratively join his opponents as betrayers of the kerygmatic mission and its potential to restore the prelapsarian ontological condition. Their acquiescence to fear on the narrative surface also reworks the underlying structures defining insiders and outsiders, God's world and the human world, and convention and unconvention. If the arrest is the final turning-point in the narrative when the liminal period concludes and the restructuring which had overtaken Jesus's inner society and the narrative comes to an end, it is also at this point that the old structure returns, but it is God and Jesus on one side and all those who have forfeited their wills to fear on the other.

From this point on, Jesus's magical power disappears, just as it had when he visited his own hometown earlier in the Gospel (6:4–6), which Mark explains on the grounds of lack of faith. It is also from the arrest forward that Jesus withdraws as actor and subject, to whom everyone reacts, becoming instead the acted upon and object in the drama, although still the prime agent, as he assumes the role of scapegoat and passively inspires action in his opponents. Though superficially the narrative appears to reclaim the conventional structures which the priests and leaders reappropriate to themselves, with all the people falling into their respective places, in fact a totally new structure has taken over, and it is no longer liminal. Jesus as a fearless, intensely suffering sacrificial offering offsets all the fear-driven agents who participated in or looked at the spectacle of the liminal events. Just as power and prophecy desert him, so does speech, for he remains mostly silent, although his three utterances during this span of the narrative (from the arrest to his death) are central to the mythic communication. The first is to answer the question, "Are you the Messiah, the Son of the Blessed One?" (14:61), to which he responds by recalling the divine revelation formula, "I am" (14:62), while also quoting Daniel's prophecy of the coming of the Son of Man (14:62). In the second, a response to Pilate's question, "Are you the king of the Jews?" (15:2), he passively turns back to the speaker, "The words are yours." His third and final statement is the lament from the cross in Aramaic, recalling Psalm 22, "My God, my God, why hast thou forsaken me?" These three quotes reflect the overall ambiguity of the Gospel, as they move from a statement of divine presence through a refusal to acknowledge human structures to a divine absence. Nevertheless, all three emphasize Jesus's outsider status from worldly structures and his denial of their ultimate power, and at the same time show his acceptance of his vulnerable status in the cosmic drama. His death demonstrates that he, unlike all the other characters in the Gospel, who gave in to fear in their desire to control the world, has accepted his vulnerability because he cannot control the world. The Roman centurion's statement, "Truly this man was a Son of God" (15:39), conferring divine affiliation on Jesus, points to his death as an act of reconciliation. Such an act of reconciliation closes the gap between God and man and the separation which accompanies it. Now the opposition is between the deserted man on the cross, whose only appeal is his own forsaken condition, and all the other compromised ways of being, whether of betrayal, power-seeking, cowardice, or other malicious behavior.

In the liminal space-time all the conventional dichotomies in human experience, whether between male and female, life and death, old and young, culture and nature, or village and city, priests and kings, polluted and clean—what Lévi-Strauss called binary opposition—are present, and the narrative of Jesus's life shows how to set aside these dichotomies, but whether anybody in the Gospel rises to the invitation and demonstrated possibility is left paradoxically open. Jesus's command of *metanoia*, in fact, is a demand not for action but for ontological change, which may show itself in action. It is a reversal, an apocalyptic invitation to turn from the normal and toward the liminal. In contrast to the structured dichotomies, the narrative or mythic revelation shows there is only one dichotomy: God's way and man's way, and this too can be reconciled. As the surface *peripeteia* of the Jesus narrative unfolds, two parallel reversals take place. The conventional social and political structures are first exposed and undermined by Jesus's street actions, and during this time a contingent model for recovering the divine in the human emerges. The narrative exposes the difference between the space and time of the divine world and the human world and presents the model for overcoming the separation between these worlds (Ricoeur, "Interpretive" 244–47).

The Gospel of Mark seems uniquely prepared to overturn the conventional dichotomies, in fact, to present a story which probes and even opposes social adherence to custom. In this respect, in contrast to Bronislaw Malinowski's theory (72–124) about myth's functional role, the Gospel does not re-enforce social and moral responses or sustain the norms of social structure. For example, Jesus (5:25–43) confronts the taboos which separate the sexes, and dismisses the opposition between Jew and gentile (5:1–20, 7:24–30, passim). His choice of followers reflects his distrust of social conventions of status and political affiliation, for he includes rich, poor, political zealots, Roman collaborators, fishermen, and bureaucrats (1:16–20; 2:13–14; 3:13–19). He also dispels the opposition between city and country because his mission takes him to both places. The structural conventions or dichotomies, thus, undergird the space where the liminal action of Jesus's public career takes place; they rule the world he enters, and we might assume that they hold sway at his death, but whether or not they triumph after his death is left paradoxically open for those who read the narrative as adherents or deniers of "the way."

Therefore, though Jesus's mission points to the possibility of an uncontingent abrogation of the structural opposition, whether the Gospel shows how this will happen is questionable. The Gospel cannot absolutely resolve the tension of opposition. In fact, the tension of the Markan ending (16:8) reflects that the conflict between the chaos and order of life is overcome not in arriving but in being on the way. While the liminal time may have temporarily overturned the ordinary human manner and expectation, the crucifixion and empty tomb, and all the human action of betrayal, abandonment, desire for power, and cowardice which made these events possible, emphasize the contingency of human behavior and "being in the world," in contrast to God's absoluteness as embedded in the kerygmatic communication of the narrative. The opposition is the setting for Jesus's mythic journey; the narrative breaks through these underlying patterns because Jesus's action violates their power. The apparent restoration of the opposition at the end of the Gospel punctuates the contingency of the impact of his journey. But the failure of his most intimate followers to live up to the challenge does not attack them or the message; just the contrary, the narrative presents the model for the liminal experience, and leaves open the possibility for any listener to follow it, difficult as it may be.

Though Jesus's way is uncontingent, the capacity for humans to travel it is contingent. Mark presents Jesus, not as a "divine figure," despite the fact that he is called "the son of God" on three important occasions (1:11; 9:7; 15:39), but as an heroic cult figure, a human being who is the primary actor in the mythic and cultural context. The mythic context is the occasion for working out the potential of a new uncontingent ontology. If traditional myth expresses "man's awareness that he is not lord of his own being" (Bultmann 10–11), the Gospel of Mark shows man how he can become lord of his own being, by showing him how the divine can be present in his life. In the Gospel of Mark, a myth, in the sense of an uncontingent narrative truth, is in the process of being constructed. The cultural and social norms in the historical setting of the Gospel are collapsing, and the political environment is unsettled and violent. They are shown to be constructions of human anxiety and trepidation, the motives that propel humans to appropriate the world. Jesus exposes these social and political realities as corrupt and diseased, so the usual certainties of the mythic context dissipate, and suffering, intellectual bafflement, and ethical paradox take their place. Jesus's dichotomy between "fearing" (*phobein*) and "trusting" (*pistein*) confronts this crisis and shows the way to overcome it. Thus, Mark's Gospel shows a new ontology of being, ready to replace the old, which is in a state of collapse; in the process of creating a myth, Mark's Gospel is setting a pattern of religious expectation and presenting an imaginative narrative model of the reformer who accepts both the promise and the vulnerability of his mission and his own role in it.

Notes

1. All scriptural quotations are from *The New English Bible*.
2. See Malbon for an elaborate structural analysis of this topographical, architectural, and geopolitical opposition in the Gospel.

Works Cited

Blumenberg, Hans. *Work on Myth*. Trans. Robert M. Wallace. Cambridge, MA, and London: MIT P, 1985.
Bultmann, Rudolf. "New Testament and Mythology." In *Kerygma and Myth: A Theological Debate*. Vol. 1. Ed. Hans Werner Barsch. Trans. Reginald H. Fuller. London: SPCK, 1957. 1–44. 2 vols.
Dumézil, Georges. *Mitra-Varuna: An Essay on Two Indo-European Presentations of Sovereignty*. Trans. Derek Coltman. New York: Zone, 1988. Trans. of *Mitra-Varuna: Essai sur deux représentations indo-européenes de la souveraineté*. Paris: Gallimard, 1948.
Gadamer, Hans-Georg. *Truth and Method*. New York: Crossroad, 1986.
Lévi-Strauss, Claude. *Anthropologie structurale*. Paris: Plon, 1958.
———. *The Raw and the Cooked: Introduction to a Science of Mythology*. Vol. 1. Trans. John and Doreen Weightman. New York: Harper, 1969.
———. *Structural Anthropology*. Trans. Claire Jacobson and Brooke Grundfest Schoepf. New York: Basic Books, 1963.
Malbon, Elizabeth Struthers. *Narrative Space and Mythic Meaning in Mark*. San Francisco: Harper, 1986.
Malinowski, Bronislaw. "Myth in Primitive Psychology." *Magic, Science and Religion, and Other Essays*. Selected and intro. Robert Redfield. Boston: Beacon, 1948.
Marin, Louis. *Semiotics of the Passion Narrative: Topics and Figures*. Trans. Alfred Johnson, Jr. Pittsburgh: Pickwick, 1980.
The New English Bible. New York: Oxford UP, 1972.

Otto, Rudolf. *The Idea of the Holy*. Trans. John W. Harvey. London and New York: Oxford: Oxford UP, 1931.

Ricoeur, Paul. "Interpretative Narrative." *The Book and the Text: The Bible and Literary Theory*. Ed. Regina Schwartz. Oxford: Blackwell, 1990. 237–57.

———. *Interpretation Theory: Discourse and the Surplus of Meaning*. Fort Worth: Texas Christian UP, 1976.

———. *Time and Narrative*. Vol. 1. Trans. Kathleen McLaughlin and David Pellauer. Chicago and London: U of Chicago P, 1984.

Starobinski, Jean. "Le Démoniaque de Gérasa." *Analyse structurale et exégèse biblique: Essais d'interprétation*. Ed. R. Barthes, F. Bovon, F. J. Leehardt, R. Martin-Achard, J. Starobinski. Neuchâtel, Switzerland: Delachaux et Niestlé, 1972.

Thompson, Stith. *Motif-Index*. 2nd ed. 2 vols. Bloomington: Indiana UP, 1966.

Turner, Victor W. "Liminal to Liminoid." *Ritual to Theatre: The Human Seriousness of Play*. New York: Performing Arts Journal Publications, 1982.

———. *The Ritual Process: Structure and Anti-Structure*. Chicago: Aldine, 1969.

White, Hayden. *The Content of the Form: Narrative Discourse and Historical Representation*. Baltimore and London: Johns Hopkins UP, 1987.

2 • An Early Renaissance Guide for the Perplexed: Bernardino of Siena's *De inspirationibus*

Franco Mormando, S.J.

> Another one of these [self-proclaimed prophets from the woods] was going around begging with one of his sisters and painting angels. They were saying that she was pregnant with the Holy Spirit and were distributing her milk—he used to squeeze the milk from her, putting his hands all over her breasts! What outrageous depravity! Do you think that's a rational thing to do, going around squeezing the milk from a woman? I don't care who's doing it, I say these things are not pleasing to God. And, oh, oh, by the way, the milk of the Virgin Mary! Ladies, are you listening? And you, fine sirs, have you seen any of it? You know, they're passing it off as a relic. It's all over the place. Don't you believe in it for a moment. It's not real. Don't you believe in it! Do you think that the Virgin Mary was a cow, that she would give away her milk in this way—just like an animal that lets itself be milked?
>
> —Bernardino of Siena, "Similmente" 209

THE PICTURE OF EARLY FIFTEENTH-CENTURY Europe which the historical facts and contemporary eyewitness accounts convey is one of upheaval, confusion, and apprehension on a massive scale affecting all realms of society. It is a landscape of catastrophic warfare between nations, towns, political factions, and rival families, repeated traumatizing outbreaks of the unconquerable "Black Death," widespread economic depression, and chronic famine. In addition to this, the Church had to endure the continuance of what was to be nearly forty years of the "Great Western Schism," with two, at times three, popes simultaneously competing for the allegiance of and authority over the faithful. The schism, as we well know, represented a major disruption of temporal and spiritual governance at all levels throughout the continent and had itself followed an even longer and likewise disruptive exile of the papacy in Avignon. Moreover, impeding as it did the sorely needed, long-called-for reform of the Church "in head and members," this sad episode in papal history was ultimately one of the causes of that even sadder sequence of events of the next century commencing in October 1517 when one Augustinian monk disseminated from Wittenburg his theses against indulgences.

The faith and religious practices of the ordinary laywoman and -man did not fail to reflect the disorientation of the times: searching for truth, security, and guidance amid the general chaos and apocalyptic expectation, large numbers fell prey to the deceits of false prophets and of their own misguided perceptions and distraught imaginations. "Small wonder, then," observes Oakley, "that it was an era during which . . . religious feelings [were] frequently expressed in extreme and violent form" and "that religious phenomena that smack to us of the pathological periodically surfaced" (115).[1]

To be sure, the deceptions of the "spirit of darkness" have always been a real and present danger for humanity in every period, but this particular moment in history—which fed its collective religious imagination with every literal detail of the Book of the Apocalypse—certainly stands out as an epoch of exceptional turmoil. The perennial questions of the spiritual life—"Whom are we to believe?" "In what are we to put our trust?" "How do we know when and where God is leading us?"—acquired an urgency that the more confident Christendom of the preceding centuries had not known.

One of the spiritual leaders to whom people turned in their distress was the popular preacher Bernardino of Siena. Though there are scattered around the world many churches and towns bearing his name, Franciscan friar Bernardino of Siena is nowadays not a well-known figure in history. Yet, grand preacher-reformer-saint, he was the "voice most eagerly listened to" in early Quattrocento Italy, "the golden age of Franciscan preaching" (Wilkins 133; Iriarte 127).

By the time of his death "perhaps the most influential religious force" on the peninsula (*Oxford* 163), the friar spent his entire adult life—nearly forty years—traveling from town to town in northern and central Italy, instructing, admonishing, exhorting, and, yes, entertaining the crowds who gathered in ever-growing numbers to listen to his word. In that age before movable type, preaching was indeed the most important means of mass communication, and successful popular preachers like Bernardino were thus the influential information-disseminators and opinion-makers of the day. Once his fame was established at the age of 37 and until his death at the age of 64, Bernardino was obliged to preach in the open town squares, for the basilicas and cathedrals could no longer contain the audiences who came to hear his Lenten, Advent, and other sermon cycles. Bernardino's success was due not only to his captivating colloquial eloquence, his intimate knowledge of the facts, issues, and psychology of contemporary everyday life, and his reputation for wonderworking sanctity, but also to his well-rounded secular learning and his thorough—albeit decidedly medieval—command of Scripture, theology, philosophy, and canon law. In an age of crisis in ecclesiastical authority, Bernardino was one of the few representatives of the Church who found trust among the people. We are fortunate in possessing nearly twenty volumes of his works, an opulent mine of detailed information and rare insight into the *mentalité* and everyday world of early Renaissance Italy.

Responding to the demands of his flock for guidance as to how one knows the will of God in the midst of discordant voices within and without oneself, Bernardino addressed that specific topic repeatedly in his vernacular sermons. But his most important response was the exhaustive Latin treatise *De inspirationibus*, "Concerning Inspirations."[2] (We shall see in due time what the friar means by the word "inspirations.") Brought to completion late in his career, most likely in 1443, the year before his death, it is Bernardino's contribution to that ancient genre of spiritual literature called "the discernment of spirits."[3]

One of the fundamental premises of the Christian faith is that the "Spirit of truth" resides in each woman and man (John 14:16–18). This means, in effect, that if we wish to know the will of God, we often do not have to go far; we need only listen to our own heart. We have direct access to God through the "voices" we hear inside our very selves. But, discerning the voice of the Spirit of truth from the many other voices within us is, in reality, no easy task, especially since "even the devil can quote Scripture," that is, uses the appearance of good to lead one into evil. The New Testament itself warns: "Beloved, do not believe every spirit but test the spirits to see whether they are from God" (1 John 4:1). Hence, throughout the ages since the time of Jesus, many a master and mistress of the spiritual life has attempted to assist the faithful in this difficult but vital responsibility by composing treatises on the topic of "the discernment of spirits." In these works they offer advice, caveats, and, beginning with Bernardino, precise rules to help their spiritual children steer their way through the at times confusing and conflicting promptings of their interior lives. (Thus, those tracing the historical development of the Western understanding of the psyche and its dynamics will find these works a valuable resource.) Written in the isolated calm of Bernardino's cloister cell overlooking the towers, steeples, and terracotta roofs of Florence and Siena, the *De inspirationibus* represents the definitive, autumn-of-life synthesis of a much-experienced, much-traveled teacher who was also a principal player in the drama of early Renaissance Italian society and politics.

THE SOURCES OF THE *DE INSPIRATIONIBUS*

As research into the sources of Bernardino's manual has shown, much of its contents is drawn directly from earlier works that treat the same or allied subjects. Indeed, in acceptable premodern fashion, Bernardino frequently lifts verbatim entire passages from previous "authorities," sometimes revealing their origin, oftentimes not. This should not surprise us: as itinerant preacher to the minimally lettered masses, Bernardino saw his role, above all, as a catechist, as a summarizer and popularizer of official Church doctrine, not as a speculative theologian engaging in original, groundbreaking scholarship. Yet, however extensive his borrowings, Bernardino's own psychological insight, personal experience, and literary genius are also present here in large doses and ultimately meld to create a work distinctive in both its personality and its contribution to the subject matter it addresses.

The most important source for the present treatise is the work of a nowadays obscure Franciscan poet and mystical writer Ugo Panziera (d. ca. 1330, not to be confused with the Dominican preacher Ugo da Prato, who died in 1322). The author of widely diffused poetical hymns, *laudi*, in the style of his more famous Franciscan predecessor Jacopone da Todi (d. 1306), Ugo also produced fourteen treatises, notes, and letters on diverse questions of the spiritual life known collectively as the *Trattati spirituali*. Among these works is one entitled *A che si possono conoscere le spirationi se sono da mettere in operatione per acquistare salute. Et perchè le virtù sono in salute meritorie* ("How one may know which inspirations are to be put into operation in order to gain salvation. And why the virtues are meritorious for our salvation"). Bernardino, who owned a personal copy of Panziera's *Trattati*, studied the latter portion (number 8 of the collection) with particular attention, as the extant manuscript (Cod. I.II.15, Biblioteca Comunale di Siena), with annotations in the friar's own hand, reveals. There is hardly a page of the *De inspirationibus* which is not beholden in some way to Panziera's treatise, the most important debt of all being the rules for discernment themselves: the first ten of these twelve rules come verbatim from *A che si possono conoscere*.

A second author on whom Bernardino depends heavily is the English scholastic master Alexander of Hales, *Doctor irrefragilis* (ca. 1186–1245), one of the intellectual luminaries of the early Franciscan order at the University of Paris. For information and guidance on the most diverse of questions, Bernardino will consult and cite by preference Alexander's *Summa theologica*, as he does extensively in the present treatise. Completed under papal mandate by William of Middleton (Melitona) and brethren, this encyclopedia of the faith was one of Bernardino's—and the Franciscan order's—prime textbooks, having been imposed on the Franciscan schools by the order's ministers general. Loyal to his own order's traditions and *auctoritates*, Bernardino quotes Thomas Aquinas only on scant occasion. In the *De inspirationibus*, the Dominican is utilized only in the section (277–82) dealing with the question of scandal.

The remainder of the list of Bernardino's sources is too lengthy to describe in detail, representing works and authors cited with far less frequency by the friar. Not surprisingly, another great Franciscan luminary, Bonaventure, figures among these remaining names. It must be noted, however, that the one book, the *Centiloquium*, which Bernardino cites several times, believing it (as did everyone until late into our own century) the work of Bonaventure, is actually by a certain Marchesinus de Regio. Yet, about this Marchesinus I have been unable to find any information beyond his bare name supplied without comment by the Quaracchi editors. Other sources for the *De inspirationibus* are, by and large, the standard authorities of the period: Cassian, Augustine, Jerome, Isidore, Bernard of Clairvaux, Nicholas of Lyra, and Hugh of St. Cher, among others. Like most of the other religious handbooks of that age, Bernardino's treatise is both a mirror of its specific generation and a *summa* of many centuries of Church history and teaching. Bernardino wrote in an age in which "tradition" still ruled supreme and "novelty" was met with suspicion and hostility. This he well knew, for the friar was himself the victim of an ample dose of the latter as a result of his preaching of devotion to the Holy Name of Jesus centered on the IHS-sunburst monogram tablet which he designed for public worship.[4]

Further names which may be less familiar to us today but represent important sources for Bernardino are the thirteenth-century Franciscan David of Augsburg (*De exterioris et interioris hominis compositione secundum triplicem statum incipientium, proficientium, et perfectorum*); Matthew of Sweden (Matthia de Svetia), author of one of Bernardino's *livres de chevet*, the *Expositio in Apocalypsim*; and Hugh Ripelin Argentinensis, thirteenth-century Dominican author of the *Compendium theologiae veritatis*, until recently attributed to Albertus Magnus. Bernardino does not fail to quote, as well, one of the "pillars" of the Observant branch of the Franciscan family (successor to the earlier, controversial "Spiritual" faction), his much-beloved Pietro di Giovanni Olivi. Olivi, along with Ubertino da Casale (author of yet another of Bernardino's *vademecum*s, the *Arbor vitae crucifixae Iesu*), was part of the much-persecuted leadership of the Spiritual Franciscan movement in the century before Bernardino's entrance into the order. The specific work of Olivi's used by Bernardino in the present treatise is his *Remedia contra spirituales tentationes*, quoted several times but never identified as a source, perhaps out of prudence in this case, for Olivi's name (like Ubertino's) was still shrouded in the suspicion of heresy and schism.

INSPIRATIONES: A DEFINITION

Bernardino divides the *De inspirationibus* into three "sermons" (together representing 88 pages of printed text in the Quaracchi edition), to be used as the basis for preaching to the general public on three separate days in the octave of Pentecost. The first "sermon" treats "the various kinds of *inspirationes*," classified, as we shall see, according to their origin—from God, from angels, from the devil, etc. The second "sermon" is entitled "The discernment of *inspirationes*" and gives us the friar's twelve rules. The final sermon, "The many illuminations by which to know what *inspirationes* are to be acted upon; and why they bring us merit and what merit they bring us," clarifies the distinction—already taught, in effect, in the preceding sermon—between *inspirationes* to be carried out "in will but not in deed," "in deed but not in will," "both in deed and in will." Sermon Three also explains in detail the how, the why, and the how much of the merits gained by us through good *inspirationes*.

Before proceeding any further in our examination of the treatise, we need to ask the question we have thus far postponed. What exactly is Bernardino's understanding of that spiritual-psychological phenomenon he calls *inspirationes*? The friar gives us a precise definition, taking it verbatim from his principal source, Ugo Panziera: "An *inspiratio* is a certain arousal of the mind which impels us toward a worthy, unworthy, or indifferent action" ("Inspiratio est quaedam excitatio mentis ad aliquod meritorium aut demeritorium seu indifferens operandum," 224). Bernardino's definition requires some explanation.

To begin with, the issue of translation of terms. When used in the present genre of literature, the term *inspiratio* is more properly rendered into English as "spirit" rather than "inspiration." *Spiritus* is the traditional Latin term for the phenomenon in question here, and that is conventionally translated as "spirit."[5] Bernardino's use of *inspiratio* rather than *spiritus* in this context appears to be unique: at least among the long inventory of works on the subject reviewed by the authoritative *Dictionnaire de spiritualité* it is the only one to use such vocabulary. Though unusual, *inspiratio* does have the advantage in that *spiritus* (like the English "spirit") can refer to several entities—the third person of the Trinity (the Holy Spirit), angels or devils (good or evil spirits), the human soul or life-force ("Father, into your hands I commend my spirit," Luke 23:46). Bernardino uses the word *spiritus* to refer to all three entities. But except for the already cited verse from 1 John 4:1 which Bernardino's Vulgate renders as "Nolite omni spiritui credere, sed probate si ex Deo sunt" (223) and in which the word is clearly a synonym for *inspiratio*, the friar consistently adheres to the latter term, *inspiratio*, in referring to that potentially good, bad, or indifferent "arousal of the mind" he is investigating here for his audience of perplexed souls.

In sum, despite the difference in vocabulary between Bernardino and the mainstream of "discernment" literature, given the definition we have just read and the exposition that follows, we can be sure that involuntary movement of the psyche originating beyond consciousness which the friar calls an *inspiratio* is indeed what other spiritual masters intend by the term *spiritus* and what all modern works in the genre call in English a "spirit." Nonetheless, to avoid confusion in the discussion and translations that follow and to keep us alert to the fact that we are dealing with a technical term, I will keep Bernardino's *inspiratio* or its plural, *inspirationes*, in their untranslated state.

A further word about Bernardino's devils and angels (two of the sources, as we shall see, of *inspirationes*) and their commerce with humankind is appropriate here. Put simply: as far as the cosmology and the anthropology informing all the friar's teaching is concerned, Bernardino is completely a person of his times. The *forma mentis* of the orthodox Christian believer as so vividly depicted, for example, in Dante's *Divine Comedy* is, with hardly a modification, that of Bernardino of Siena as well. Accordingly, in that realm of the supernatural pertinent to our topic, angels and devils are all real, acting, intelligent incorporeal agents external to our consciousness, continually engaged, with or against the Almighty, in the cosmic struggle over possession of our souls. Bernardino's sermons are filled with tales (which the friar will at times even introduce with historical "verifications" such as "just a few years ago in the nearby town of . . .") "documenting" in graphic detail the work of these creatures of good and evil in the lives of everyday women and men. *De inspirationibus* itself contains no such tales, but there is enough explicit reference to angels and devils to convince us that Bernardino is not simply making use of symbolic language, as far as he is concerned.

What interests Bernardino more is not the depiction of the physiognomy of the good and the bad spirits but rather the classification and analysis of *inspirationes*, that is to say, the means by which angels and devils—on behalf of or in opposition to God—do their work within our hearts and minds. In other words, mirroring the continuing tendency in the historical development of the doctrine of discernment (Sweeney 151), he focuses his attention primarily on the psychological phenomena (in terms of both thought and affect) by which we are drawn to or repelled from union with God.

As the definition states, *inspirationes* are of three moral types (good, bad, indifferent) and, as is stated in the same paragraph, can be traced (again in the exact words of Panziera) to seven distinct sources: God, the angels, one's own virtue (*a propria virtute*), the devil, one's own vice (*a propria malitia*), some temporal necessity, some temporal convenience (224). The first three represent good *inspirationes*; the next two, evil *inspirationes*; the final two, indifferent *inspirationes*. Yet, as we shall see when we turn to his list of specific rules of discernment, the distinction on which Bernardino, above all, bases his practical advice is of an eminently empirical nature: spirits are divided according to whether they counsel an act that will bring pain ("quae ad laborem inducunt," 244), pleasure ("quae ad delectationem inducunt," 258) or a simultaneous mixture of both ("quae inducunt ad laborem et delectationem," 274). As his subsequent exposition and examples reveal, by *labor* and *delectatio*, Bernardino means both physical and mental pain and pleasure. Thus, the two categories include but exceed Ignatius of Loyola's categories of "desolation" and "consolation."

As we have seen, Bernardino does make a categorical judgment as to the ontological status of these *inspirationes*. But, in the discussion that follows, he admits that when in the throes of an *inspiratio*, we, in reality, have little certainty (at least initially and perhaps even beyond that) as to its ultimate nature ("De impossibilitate seu difficultate discretionis quae in his septem generibus inspirationum cadit," 236ff.). The friar supplies us with many specific details regarding the *modus operandi* of each of the above-mentioned agents, details that represent entirely the orthodox teaching of his day. For example, as Alexander of Hales states, angels do not create or send good thoughts (*bonas cogitationes*) to our mind; they only remove obstacles therein to such thoughts; God alone is their author and dispenser (224–25, 228). In addition to the above-named seven agents or sources, Bernardino also recognizes the influence of the "humours" of our body (as explained by medieval medicine) and the planets and stars on our state of mind (see "De merito inspirationum quae naturaliter fiunt, et de variis inclinationibus quae fiunt ex constellationibus vel natura," 309–11) but gives little attention to such influence beyond noting that the *inspirationes* deriving therefrom are subject to the same criteria and rules mandated for all other classes of *inspirationes*. The same applies to his stance on demonic possessions and various forms of what we would today call psychopathology (265–71): again, one need not know their origin in order to know which *inspirationes* to ignore, which to fulfill; the rules will guide you.

The Friar's Twelve Rules of Discernment

As befits its times, the *De inspirationibus* opens with a tone of apprehension: following the enunciation of the already-quoted *thema*, "Do not believe every spirit, but test the spirits to see whether they are of God" (1 John 4:1), Bernardino sounds the warning:

> Navigating through this world as though on the open sea, we must employ great caution lest we endanger our lives. For often we are deceived under the appearance of the good; and unless we seek to be directed in our actions by the divine lights, we will necessarily fall into the snares of many dangers. (223)

The friar then tells us that he writes with great hesitation on so difficult a topic, yet, as we have already said, does so to satisfy the demand of so many of the faithful (224).

Never one for abstract discourse, Bernardino gives many examples of "this deception under the appearance of good" and the aberrant behavior he has seen likewise passing under the name of piety. One example he cites is the much-condemned but largely fictitious "heretical movement" of the "Free Spirit," supposedly exemplified by Marguerite Porete's *Mirror of Simple Souls* (248).[6]

Another example given is the strange but historically documented case (Rusconi 233–35) of that gullible band of souls who were convinced by some "prophet" to make a pilgrimage from Italy to Jerusalem "naked as when they came from their mother's womb." These pious souls got no further than the Adriatic coast where, to their great chagrin, the waters did not part for them as their leader had promised and they were seized by the local lord (256). The friar was not speaking from mere detached observation of the lives of those around him, however: in one of his vernacular sermons on discernment referred to above, "Come si de' domandare a Dio che c'insegni a fare la sua volontà" ("How we must ask God to teach us to do His will," Siena 1427), we are granted a more intimate insight into Bernardino's personal confrontation with self-illusion and the maturation of his understanding of the dynamic of discernment of spirits. This autobiographical episode, which Bernardino describes in a cheerful tone of self-mockery, represents a turning point in his spiritual life:

> Oh ladies, since this crazy zeal once touched even me, I can say something about it from experience; I want to tell you about the first miracle I ever performed—it was before I became a friar, after the "Bianchi" [Flagellant Movement]. There once came to me the desire to live like an angel, not like a human . . . the thought came to me that I could live just on water and weeds, and I decided to go and live in the woods . . . and I said to myself: Good, now, I will do just as the holy fathers [of the desert]; I will eat weeds when I'm hungry and when I'm thirsty, I will drink water. And so I made up my mind to do just that. . . . And in my head I tried to figure out a place where I could go and roost. . . . [Finally after much indecision over the locale:] And so I went over there beyond the Follonica Gate [in Siena] and I began to gather a salad of sow-thistle and other weeds, and I had no bread or salt or oil, and I said to myself: Okay, for this first time, we'll wash and scrape it, but the next time, we'll just scrape it and not wash it, and when we get more used to it, we won't even clean it and after that we won't even go and gather it. And so in the name of blessed Jesus, I began with a fistful of sow-thistle, and put it in my mouth and began to chew on it. I chewed and I chewed but it wouldn't go

down. Not being able to swallow, I said to myself: Okay, let's start by drinking a little bit of water. No use! The water went down, but the sow-thistle stayed in my mouth. To make a long story short, I had drunk I don't know how many sips of water with that one mouthful of sow-thistle, and I still couldn't get it down. Do you get my point?

That one mouthful of sow-thistle was enough to chase away this temptation [to go off and be a hermit], because that is what I know it certainly was, a temptation . . . sometimes [our desires] seem so good but turn out to be very bad! (2: 788–90)

The episode taught Bernardino a lesson for life. Subsequent study and experience led him eventually to the conclusion that though humanity is, yes, handicapped by a great deal of "excusable ignorance" as to the precise nature and "secret workings" of these *inspirationes* (236), we can still avail ourselves of reasonably certain, precise guidelines telling us which spirits to act upon and which to ignore.[7] Thus, he gives us his twelve rules for discernment which we now examine, one by one.

Rule 1. You must always listen to the *inspiratio* which in itself represents a cross to bear, or which leads you to pain independent of any utility or temporal pleasure for oneself or for another whom you love whether naturally or sensually or sinfully. (244)

The title of the *capitulum* which introduces Rule 1 tells us that it is especially directed *contra deliciosos*, that is to say, at those "delicate" pleasure-loving, pain-fleeing individuals. In reality, to some degree, all humanity falls into this category "since, because of original sin, we are always drawn to carnal pleasures and to the delights of this world . . . [and] since our infected flesh is a bilge of concupiscence and of every sort of evil" (244–45).

As the friar explains (244), there are three components to this rule: first, the presence of pain, "the cross"; second, the absence of temporal utility and nonspiritual pleasure for oneself; and, third, the absence of the same kind of utility and pleasure for a loved one. Bernardino explains his use of the key term, "cross," and its synonyms: "It is to be noted, first of all, that by the words 'pain' or 'cross' or 'labor' and so on in the present treatise we mean always something painful borne for the love of virtue; just as the long vertical bar of the cross supports the horizontal one, so, too, does love support pain through virtue" (244).

The second component is straightforward and calls for no comment, and likewise the third—except for that string of adverbs distinguishing the types of love: "naturally or sensually or even sinfully." In place of an abstract explanation of the three categories, Bernardino simply gives concrete examples: "natural love," e.g., that between parent and child; "sensual love," e.g., that between husband and wife, and "sinful love," e.g., that between two fornicators. By "sinful" love, the friar specifically intends *mortally* sinful love, as the subsequent discussion makes clear.

We shall see that Bernardino later (under Rule 5) makes a similar but not identical threefold distinction between types of *delectatio*, pleasure: "sensual," "natural," and "spiritual." There we are told that *all* "sensual" pleasure is mortally sinful while, at the same time, that "natural" pleasure in this postlapsarian world is "rarely" unstained by at least some shade of venial sin (259). Because he uses the same adjectives in both sets of distinctions and because love is a form of *delectatio*, the startling conclusion would seem, therefore, that the love between parent and child is in most cases stained by venial sin while that between husband and wife always by mortal sin. It could well be that Bernardino did not intend the two sets of categories to overlap and is simply guilty of a lapse in his distinction-making. But such a severe, pessimistic judgment is by no means uncharacteristic of the moral judgments the friar makes in other parts of his teaching.[8]

> **Rule 2.** The *inspiratio* must be listened to when the inspired painful and arduous action is compatible with the natural endurance of one's body, that is to say, when it does not surpass the bounds of prudence. (248)

Rule 2, as the chapter heading announces, is especially directed to "those who chastise the body with immoderate rigidity" (248). Certainly, there was much in the way of pathology in many of the contemporary penitential practices, and Bernardino, pastor of souls, had seen his share of them and their disastrous consequences in the lives of such penitents: "There are those, who, even in sickness, take on [penances] which leave one speechless: they afflict their body with severe fasts, with interminable vigils, with ferocious flagellations, going about shoeless, not protecting themselves against inclement weather, and doing all of this against the advice of the experts and sometimes in disobedience to the clergy" (250). Young people, in their impressionability and recklessness, he adds, are especially prone to such excess (249). The friar reminds his reader: "the human body is created by God and although, through labor and penances, it, like a slave, must be keep under the yoke of reason, we, however, must not skin it alive or kill it, since God loves it, having in mind the future beatitude of the soul . . ." (248). Furthermore, when the body is weakened, the soul, too, is weakened and has all the greater difficulty in carrying out the good (248). To illustrate his point, Bernardino gives the example of a wildly drunken man on a horse haplessly attempting to arrive at his destination. Bernardino spends considerable time and energy extolling the virtue of prudence, "mother of all virtues," and proportion: nothing in excess, neither too little nor too much; everything in due degree and amount, like the parts of a handsome human face, the perfectly tightened strings of a musical instrument (250).

Rule 3. The *inspiratio* is good if the painful effort can be endured by the strength of the soul. (252)

Just as the body has its limits so, too, does the soul. It is not, says Bernardino, that the soul can die, for it is immortal (248); but the weight of an excessive spiritual, emotional, or mental burden can "lead to a great perturbation and to a true disorientation of the spiritual energies" (252). An elaboration of the caveat just given under Rule 2, what the friar is now warning against are dangers that run from psychological illness (temporary or permanent) to the very loss of one's soul to the devil. Especially susceptible to such perils are those who attempt spiritual feats of one kind or another which are simply beyond their capability. In fact, this is one frequent way—under the guise of a spiritual good (253)—in which the "ancient serpent" deceives the unsuspecting Christian. Furthermore, however well-intentioned they may claim to be, the individuals in this category are usually also motivated, we are told, by presumption, curiosity, foolhardiness, or just plain stupidity (252).

Examples given from contemporary experience include retired mercenary soldiers who attempt the penitential life of a desert hermit, those who think they can save their souls by remaining in the world instead of entering the protective cloister of religious life, those who think they can perform miracles, those "complete ignoramuses and idiots" who, "under the guise of zeal and love of souls, presumptuously meddle in confessions, preaching, and pastoral care" (254). Not surprisingly, the whole realm of sexuality, as well, is fraught with danger: just when we think we have become impervious to the promptings of the flesh, just when we think "Satan appears to be sleeping" and unmindful of us, that is when we are most susceptible to temptation. Bernardino mentions in this regard the heretical, wife-swapping sect of the "reformer" Fra Dolcino (d1307) and then cites the case of one overconfident woman, who, in order to prove her victory over the flesh, climbs into bed with a young man. The friar's terse conclusion: "I pass over in silence whether she lost or won the battle" (255).

> **Rule 4.** The *inspiratio* must be listened to if the toil and the pain, be they corporal or spiritual, are reasonable. (255)

"Reason," Bernardino explains, is "a certain movement of the soul which renders the sight of the mind acute and distinguishes true from false" (255). The friar has already told us much about the need for prudence and reason in previous sections and here in slightly different terms only repeats his exhortation. What is added under Rule 4 is (in keeping with his scholastic love of distinctions) a list of the seven generic varieties of unreasonable behavior. The list need not detain us here. It is, by the way, in this section of the treatise that we encounter the already cited example of that band of ingenuous souls who, stark naked, attempted their march to the Holy Land only to be halted by the uncooperative waters of the Adriatic (256).

> **Rule 5.** The *inspiratio* must be accepted, if, in its execution, without mortal sin, the natural pleasure is less than the spiritual pleasure. (258)

With this rule we pass into the realm of those *inspirationes* which lead, not to pain, but to pleasure. Now, no pleasure, it is explained, is good or bad in itself; what makes it good or bad is its object, place, time, manner, or degree. Furthermore, as we have already seen, there are three types of pleasure, classified "according to the different pleasurable objects": sensual, natural, and spiritual. In sensual pleasure, "reason, spiting God, is made slave of the flesh." This is mortal sin and is excluded right away as a legitimate form of pleasure for Christians. In natural pleasure, instead, "reason is united with sensuality; however, neither reason nor sensuality predominate completely" (258–59). In other words, the two maintain each other in balance, at least in theory. In fact, such a balance is rarely achieved or maintained: "the corporal senses derive a little more pleasure than is reasonable and thus most of the time venial sin is committed" (259).

In the third type of pleasure, "spiritual," "both our natural and spiritual natures are supernaturally gratified." The vehicles of such pleasure may be those of the created, that is, material, world, but the object is completely spiritual: God, Jesus, Mary, etc. Now, Bernardino warns us, sometimes what may initially appear to be spiritual pleasure is in fact or may become in fact sensual, therefore, mortally sinful, pleasure. The friar gives us an example: "I know of a person who, while contemplating the humanity of Christ on the cross (it is shameful to say and horrendous just to imagine), sensually and foully polluted and defiled himself (herself?). I don't consider this a matter to be preached openly about" (259). The only other specific case Bernardino discusses is one that meets the conditions of the Rule perfectly: it is the case of a man who is fasting "with great fervor" on just leeks or onions. Although deriving "more natural pleasure" in this food than normally would be the case, he should not give up his fast for the greater spiritual merit and pleasure he is in fact experiencing at the same time (260).

Rule 6. The *inspiratio* must be accepted if in the inspired action, through virtue or grace, there is only spiritual pleasure. (260)

Rule 6 opens with a scholastic excursus on virtue and grace—what each is, how the one differs from the other. The former is defined (in the words of Augustine) as "a good quality of the soul through which we live rightly, which no one uses for evil and which God produces in us and without us" (261). The latter, instead (according to Bonaventure and, "to a certain extent," Paul as well), is a "manifestation of the Spirit for the [spiritual] utility [of another person]" (261).[9]

Bernardino's laconic, textbook definitions, in truth, would call for explanation and illustration, but these go unsupplied by the friar whose interests lie elsewhere. Instead, he devotes the remaining space in this section (263–64) to the more practical question of how one might know whether a pleasure is purely spiritual or not. There are, he says, five signs: "trepidation" (i.e., awe and reverence), "a humble sense of self," "avidity for the cross," "elation" (such as that of "the Apostle" in Galatians 2.20) and, finally, a "variety of gifts" such as "an ineffable peace of soul," "a certain aptitude and disposition toward loving God," "a certain dominion overall of the corporal senses and delights of the flesh," the acquisition of a new virtue or the removal of an old vice and, finally, the cure of some incurable infirmity.

> **Rule 7.** The *inspiratio* is holy if, because of the spiritual pleasure, the soul comes to feel more humble. (264)

In effect, what was just given as one of the signs of purely spiritual pleasure, "a humble sense of self," becomes the subject matter of a rule of discernment of its own. Not only does it become a rule of its own, it also represents one of the most extensively commented upon rules in the treatise. Of all the ways the "ancient enemy" uses to deceive and manipulate humanity, pride, in all its forms, is his favorite and most potent, Bernardino suggests here. Was it not pride that brought Lucifer himself to his fall from the "divine sweetness" of heaven (264)?

The type of pride the friar concentrates on in this section is especially that of presuming oneself the divinely chosen instrument of special, personal messages, revelations, visions, or prophecies. The devil easily capitalizes on the vanity of such self-proclaimed visionaries, mystics, and prophets, and this is particularly the case in the present day (266). It is in this section of the treatise that the spiritual turmoil and apocalyptic hysteria of the early fifteenth-century Church comes unmistakably to the forefront. The friar—who himself had to do battle with such apocalyptic rabble-rousers (Origo 211–12)—makes no attempt to mask his disgust with such instruments of the devil: "we are filled with these prophecies to the point of nausea: for example, those predicting the coming of the Antichrist, the signs of the coming judgment, the persecution and the reform of the Church, and the like." Even if these prophecies were true, adds Bernardino: "nonetheless, the servants of God could easily find other things with which to occupy themselves more fruitfully, since our Lord Jesus Christ has scolded on many occasions such curious investigators of the future" (267).

There are those whose presumption and fantastications reach such a point as to cause them to believe they are worthy of the papacy itself. "I've known more than one person" in this category, states Bernardino, who goes on to decry, with a pun on words, the renewed outbreak of schism with the 1440 election of the antipope, Felix V, by the Council of Basel: "And what great a danger lies in this, unhappy [*infelix*] Christendom itself is experiencing in our own days right now: how unhappy [*infelix*] she is under the pseudo-Felix since, precisely because of such an illusion, . . . the deluded Anti-pope has given rise to such a horrible and monstrous scandal in the heart of the Church. This is the greatest crime and negation of the Most High Lord" (268). Ironically, a few years before, Bernardino had occasion to meet and, in subsequent preaching, to praise the man in question, who, as Amadeus VIII, duke of Savoy, had been so zealous in his punishment of usurers (268, note 1).

After further deprecation against these "messengers of the Antichrist," Bernardino then singles out another "horrible" and scandalous example of presumption and hallucination, that of those individuals who supposedly experience "spiritually consoling" sexual encounters with Christ or the Virgin: "Nor must it be passed over in silence, I believe, that many are so horribly seduced and deceived that they claim Christ or the blessed Virgin herself to have appeared to them and to have been caressed by them not only with kisses and embraces but even with indecent gestures . . ." (269). The entire paragraph has actually been lifted verbatim from one of Bernardino's sources, David of Augsburg, a fact duly noted by the Quaracchi editors (269, note 2), but we can well imagine that the well-informed friar in the course of his long and active apostolate had heard enough stories himself of this type to warrant such a warning in his own treatise. The section closes thereafter with a reminder (in the form of another neat, scholastic list of distinctions) that such deception, when not diabolic, can also have its origin in what we have come to term psychopathology and sheer mental deficiency (269–71).

> **Rule 8.** The *inspiratio* must be accepted if, because of the spiritual pleasure, the soul is illuminated and strengthened in the truths of faith and mores. (271)

The message communicated under the rubric of Rule 8 is simple and straightforward: all our beliefs and our actions must conform to the official teaching of the Church. Therefore, any *inspiratio* that suggests otherwise is to be discarded as evil. This official teaching, says the friar, is succinctly summarized by the Apostles' Creed, which embraces the "threefold Scripture" of the Church, that is to say, the New Testament, the Old Testament, and, the body of doctrine and legislation contained in canon law and in the "approved" portions of the writings of the Fathers of the Church.

Oblivious to the fact of the historical evolution, and the internal ambiguities and contradictions of this mass of "scripture," Bernardino does not even raise the possibility of dissent with the teaching of the magisterium or question its contents or judgments in any way. Nor does he seem at all aware that, throughout the history of the Church, there have, in fact, been many subsequently canonized women and men whose personal *inspirationes* represented at times radical departures from the teaching, canon law and/or tradition of the Church, a prime example being Francis of Assisi himself. Bernardino simply repeats his categorical condemnation of these bearers of new, private revelations (274). Moreover, lest he not have been sufficiently clear in the previous section in his feelings about the bothersome preachers of the Apocalypse, he returns to the subject in his conclusion to this section:

> Is it not true that in the time of the blessed Bernard, and before and after him—not only then, but even in our own times, when I myself was a child fifty years ago—is it not true that there was spread around the deception of many revelations and visions which claimed that the Antichrist had already been born? These revelations—because of the apparently holy life and reputation of those who were preaching and writing about it—were believed to be true; yet, as I have never tired of preaching, with my own experi-

ence to back me, they have all proven to be truly diabolical deceptions. . . . (274)

"The shrewdness of the ancient serpent," he adds yet again, has obtained great results for itself through such teaching.

Rule 9. The *inspiratio* must be accepted if the pleasure or pain is not an occasion of scandal for one's neighbor illuminated by God.

Rule 9 brings us to the final category of *inspirationes*, those which lead to both pain and pleasure. Bernardino announces four rules in this group (274) but in reality there are only three: the final, twelfth, one represents a general rule, above and beyond the pleasure/pain distinction, to be applied in cases of particular challenge.

Bernardino takes from the *Glossa ordinaria*'s entry on Matthew 18:7 his definition of scandal ("an unseemly word or deed which is the cause of ruin for another," 275) and proceeds in his usual, scholastically methodical, distinction-making way to give us a thorough instruction on the topic. (For instance, we learn that of the first type of scandal, "necessary" scandal, there are, in turn, three subtypes, the first of which, "necessity or inevitability," has, in turn, three qualities: *inculpabile, ineligibile,* and *immutabile*.) In fact, this instruction on scandal is so thorough that the friar must excuse himself for its unintended length (283). But, aware of the "scandalous" times in which the treatise came to be, one can well understand the friar's insistence on the topic. Unfortunately, Bernardino does little to relieve the tedium of this scholastic disquisition in the way of vivid examples taken from his own experience which we so appreciate in his own preaching. Finally, as far as the qualification "illuminated by God" is concerned, Bernardino gives only a brief explanation: he equates this "neighbor" with the "just person" and suggests as his or her opposite the "carnal," "natural," or "unspiritual" person of 1 Corinthians 2:14.

Rule 10. The *inspiratio* must be accepted if, barring mortal sin, even a resultant vitiated natural pleasure is less than the pain of a virtuous suffering. (284)

The tenth rule returns us to the distinction between "natural," "sensual," and "spiritual" pleasure made familiar to us by the friar's exposition of Rule 5. The exposition of the present rule is, in fact, largely repetitive with respect to the earlier, closely allied one and thus is necessarily brief. The friar even makes use of the same example as before: the case of those persons who, in the midst of the "virtuous suffering" of a fast, find that they are taking a greater than normal pleasure in what little food they are permitting themselves. Again, given the greater good of the "virtuous suffering," this perhaps venially sinful gastronomic, leek-and-onion pleasure is indeed permitted. But one must be on one's guard against its becoming the occasion for mortal sin (285)!

> **Rule 11.** All conditions being equal, a lesser good must be relinquished for a greater good, and, consequently, a greater good must be placed before a lesser good. (285)

The dictate of common sense, Rule 11 is largely self-explanatory, and Bernardino's task here is simply to make explicit the hierarchy of "greater" and "lesser" goods. "In the present life," he tells us, the good can be of three types: "the first is great, the second is greater, the third is the greatest. The first is the temporal, the second is the corporal, the third is the spiritual" (285–86). Obviously, spiritual goods must always be pursued before either corporal or temporal goods, but, in the realm of spiritual goods (as in each realm), there is, in turn, a further hierarchy of good, better, best. In confirmation of this teaching, Bernardino quotes the imperative of Jesus, "If your right eye causes you to sin, pluck it out and throw it away" (Matt. 5:29), and immediately offers a concrete (if unconsciously and implicitly misogynistic) example: "This 'right eye' is conversation with a woman done with a spiritual intention: but if it is scandal to you—that is to say, if it is an occasion of ruin, or of disgrace—pluck it out and throw it away" (286). Another example (287) is supplied by St. Paul who, according to the friar-preacher, asserts the superiority of the office of preacher over that of baptizer: "For Christ did not send me to baptize but to preach the Gospel . . ." (1 Cor. 1:17).

Finally, Bernardino proceeds to explain, it is better, by the same token, to commit a venial sin to avoid a mortal sin, a smaller venial sin to avoid a greater venial sin and a lesser mortal sin to avoid a greater mortal sin. He takes from the Old Testament a somewhat startling example of the latter instance and says that

Mosaic Law permitted divorce (Deut. 24:1) in order to prevent the greater evil of uxoricide (288).

Rule 12. In doubtful and arduous actions, before proceeding, one must investigate as to the certainty of the will of God. (288)

As we have already pointed out, this twelfth and final rule is, in reality, a general one which departs from the pain/pleasure schema of the preceding three with which the friar illogically classifies it. Here it is a question, not of pain or pleasure, but of doubt and difficulty. With the inclusion of this final instruction, Bernardino seems to be saying: "if, after applying the pertinent advice of the above eleven rules, you still cannot decide a course of action, then here's what to do next." "What to do next," the further investigation, entails three elements: seeking the advice of worthy, "illuminated" spiritual superiors, praying assiduously, and, finally, simply letting a certain amount of time pass. The first two elements require no explanation for us here; as for the third, simply waiting is what the friar suggests when all else fails:

> Time indeed achieves many things that cannot be achieved through the will or the industry or the power of men. Time calms the agitated sea, brings fruit to ripeness; through it the animals, the fish, the birds receive their growth. At times, God wishes to illuminate us in a choice of action, not through an angel or in another way, but through the means of time, most especially if we persevere in prayer; since time changes and along with it change many things, and in all things it is God who sheds light on judgment and doubts. . . . (290)

It is on this note that Bernardino's exposition of the twelve rules of discernment—his safe and reliable guide for the perplexed souls of his age—ends. The work was to remain a "guide for the perplexed" for many generations. At the friar's death and especially after his canonization (1450), the treatise was given wide circulation through the vast Franciscan network, all parts of which—"even . . . barbarian nations"—requested copies of the friar's collected works, as we are told by John of Capistran (Barnabo da Siena 114, note h). The product of a world that had come to an end, it was eventually forgotten by the Church, superseded and overshadowed (together with nearly all other previous such works) by the appearance of Ignatius of Loyola's *Spiritual Exercises*.[10] Yet, neglected as it has been and obsolete as it is as a handbook of spiritual or psychological guidance, the treatise can make claim to a place of distinction in the long history of the development of the Western doctrine of discernment.[11] It was not simply one more work added to an already long list: "To Bernardino must be accorded the honor of having been the first . . . to have drawn up a treatise on spirits and their discernment representing a compendium of all that the Catholic tradition had taught in preceding centuries" (Guidetti 140). "[T]he undeniable fact [is] that Bernardino is the first . . . who succeeded in finally producing a complete treatise on so difficult a subject" (Pacetti, *Trattato* 1: xxiv). Though, certainly, credit must be given to the sources (especially Ugo Panziera) from which Bernardino draws heavily in his treatise, my own research thus far into the matter has been unable to contradict the substance of these judgments on Bernardino's place in the "discernment tradition." In any case, even if subsequent findings were to change the above evaluation, this carefully wrought product of so engaged, so long, so insightful a participant in and shaper of the life and psyche of the early Renaissance Church remains a document worthy of the attention of posterity. It is a valuable point of entry into the religious imagination of Western Christendom in its eleventh hour before the rude awakening of the Protestant Reformation.

Notes

1. While confirming the admittedly dreary (at least to our modern sensitivities) conditions of popular religion in the "waning of the Middle Ages," Oakley interprets these data in their fuller historical-social context and, as a result, is inclined to see therein "signs of a deepening piety" (120) rather than of the degeneration of the faith traditionally pictured by historians.

2. Though an annotated Italian translation exists (Bernardino, *Trattato* 1929), the *De inspirationibus* has not been translated into English. All translations in the present study from the Italian and Latin are my own. Among the secondhand *reportationes* of the friar's public preaching, we find as well three pairs of sermons devoted to the same topic and delivered as part of three separate sermon cycles (Florence 1425 and Siena 1427). However, it is on the scrupulously prepared Quaracchi critical

edition of the *tractatus* that I will base my exposition of Bernardino's doctrine of the discernment of spirits, since this version comes directly from the friar's own pen. Time and space unfortunately do not here allow us to compare and contrast these earlier transcribed sermons with the Latin treatise, as interesting and as valuable as such a study would be. When all is said and done, however, we would find that the main differences between the Latin and the vernacular works are principally stylistic: Bernardino bases himself in both cases on the same scriptural and ecclesiastical authorities, using the same arguments and outlines. In preaching to the largely unlettered crowds in the town squares, the friar adopts a lively, highly colloquial speech filled with colorful domestic imagery, artfully crafted *exempla*, intimate, conversational asides, and the host of emotion-rousing theatrical techniques counseled by the medieval *artes praedicandi* which made his preaching so effective a means of communication. In contrast, the prose of the Latin treatise appears more subdued and succinct, the contents largely (though by no means always) reduced to the bare bones of the friar's argument.

3. The term comes from St. Paul who, in 1 Corinthians 12:10, lists it as one of the gifts given to some by the Spirit. But what the Apostle means by this and the other gifts mentioned is not clear: "precise definitions are impossible" (Murphy-O'Connor 810). For a survey of the "discernment of spirits" tradition, see Guillet et al., and Sweeney. The first half of Sweeney's study is a comparative analysis of the teachings of the major authorities on the subject, from the New Testament to Ignatius of Loyola, but Sweeney does not treat or even mention Bernardino's work.

4. The most complete treatment of this episode of Bernardino's life is still Longpré's.

5. *Discretio spirituum* is the Latin for "discernment of spirits."

6. "Misunderstanding, prejudice born of tensions in towns between secular and regular clergy, unpopularity of the unprotected women of the beguinages, and certain potentially perilous teaching about the mystical way stimulated authority to define a heresy and sect which, as a coherent and organized whole, never existed" (Lambert 393).

7. The *Dictionnaire de spiritualité*, we may here note in passing, errs when it states (Guillet et al. 65) that it is only with Ignatius of Loyola and J. B. Scaramelli that we reach "precision" in the formulation of the rules of discernment. Whatever else one may fault Bernardino's rules for, lack of precision is certainly not one of them. (The *Dictionnaire* does, however, devote a short paragraph to *De inspirationibus* [Guillet et al. 73–74]).

8. On both the contradictions and the severity of Bernardino's moral judgments, see Mormando.

9. Bernardino's Italian translator, Pacetti, clarifies the definition with the addition of the bracketed words (1: 108).

10. Did Ignatius know of and/or study the Bernardinian treatise? As Guidetti reports (28–29), the specific sources of the *Spiritual Exercises* have never been securely identified. He wonders, however, could, for example, Teodosio da Lodi, Ignatius's Franciscan confessor in Rome both before and after 1541 (the year of the publication of the *Exercises*), have brought *De inspirationibus* to the attention of his spiritual directee?

11. The present study is the first one to appear in English on Bernardino's treatise. The bibliography on the *De inspirationibus* is scant. Pacetti's translation is preceded by a long introductory essay, while Heerinckx gives a brief summary of the work in his article on Bernardino in the *Dictionnaire de spiritualité*. I have already had occasion to cite the even briefer notice elsewhere in the *Dictionnaire* (Guillet et al.) and Guidetti's work. The only other published study of Bernardino's treatise I have thus far uncovered is Vassallo's. Both Guidetti and Vassallo are interested in the treatise primarily as a theological-spiritual manual.

Works Cited

Barnabo da Siena. *Vita Sancti Bernardini Senensis*. Acta sanctorum, Maii, V: 107–17.

Bernardino da Siena. "Come si de' domandare a Dio che c'insegni a fare la sua volontà." *Prediche volgari sul Campo di Siena 1427*. Ed. Carlo Delcorno. Vol. 2. Milan: Rusconi, 1989. 761–96. 2 vols.

———. *De inspirationibus*. Opera omnia. Vol. 6. Quaracchi, Florence: Collegio S. Bonaventura, 1950–65. 223–311. 9 vols.

———. "Similmente, che Idio c'insegni a fare la sua santa volontà." *Prediche volgari sul Campo di Siena 1427*. Ed. Carlo Delcorno. Vol. 2. Milan: Rusconi, 1989. 797–820. 2 vols.

———. *Trattato delle ispirazioni*. Trans. Dionigio Pacetti. 2 vols. Siena: Cantagalli, 1929.

Guidetti, Armando. *Il discernimento degli spiriti in S. Bernardino da Siena e in S. Ignazio di Loyola: Introduzione a uno studio di confronto*. Rome: Centrum Ignatianum Spiritualitatis, 1982.

Guillet, Jacques, et al. *Discernment of Spirits*. Trans. Sr. Innocentia Richards. Collegeville, MN: Liturgical P, 1970. Trans. of "Discernement des esprits." *Dictionnaire de spiritualité: Ascetique et mystique, doctrine et histoire*. Paris: Beauchesne, 1932.

Heerinckx, J. "Bernardin de Sienne." *Dictionaire de spiritualité: Ascetique et mystique, doctrine et histoire*. Paris: Beauchesne, 1932.

Iriarte, Lazaro. *Franciscan History: The Three Orders of St. Francis of Assisi.* Trans. Patricia Ross. Chicago: Franciscan Herald Press, 1983.

Lambert, Malcolm D. *Medieval Heresy: Popular Movements From the Gregorian Reform to the Reformation.* 2nd. ed. Oxford: Blackwell, 1992.

Longpré, E. "S. Bernardin de Sienne et le nom de Jésus." *Archivum Franciscanum Historicum* 28 (1935): 443–76; 29 (1936): 142–68, 443–77; 30 (1937): 170–92.

Mormando, Franco. "To Persuade Is a Victory: Rhetoric and Moral Reasoning in the Sermons of Bernardino of Siena." *The Context of Casuistry.* Ed. J. Keenan and T. Shannon. Washington, DC: Georgetown UP, 1995.

Murphy-O'Connor, Jerome. "The First Letter to the Corinthians." *The New Jerome Biblical Commentary.* Ed. Raymond E. Brown, s.s., Joseph A. Fitzmyer, s.j. and Roland E. Murphy, O.Carm. Englewood Cliffs, NJ: Prentice, 1990.

Oakley, Francis. *The Western Church in the Later Middle Ages.* Ithaca: Cornell UP, 1979.

Origo, Iris. *The World of San Bernardino.* New York: Harcourt, 1962.

The Oxford Dictionary of the Christian Church. Ed. F. L. Cross and E. A. Livingstone. 2nd ed. rev. New York: Oxford UP, 1984.

Rusconi, Roberto. *L'attesa della fine: Crisi della società profezia ed Apocalisse in Italia al tempo del grande scisma d'Occidente (1378–1417).* Rome: Istituto Storico Italiano per il Medio Evo, 1979.

Sweeney, Richard J. "Christian Discernment and Jungian Psychology: Toward a Jungian Revision of the Doctrine of Discernment of Spirits." Diss. Graduate Theological Union, 1983.

Vassalo, Francesco S. *Risposta dell'uomo a Dio: Studio per una teologia delle ispirazioni secondo S. Bernardino da Siena.* Naples: Dehoniane, 1980.

Wilkins, E. H. *A History of Italian Literature.* 2nd ed. rev. Cambridge, MA: Harvard UP, 1984.

3 • Between Earth and Heaven: Ignatian Imagination and the Aesthetics of Liberation

Paul G. Crowley, S.J.

"ACHIEVING LIBERATION OF THE OPPRESSED is now seen to be incumbent upon believers. Liberation," Jon Sobrino concludes, "is now seen to be the central reality, the merger of the historical and the personal, the blending of present exigency and scriptural norm" (2). No statement of the program of the theology of liberation could be more imbued with the Ignatian imagination. And perhaps few spiritual visions could so aptly capture the liberation esthetic as the Ignatian, which springs from an ardent desire to see salvation accomplished.

The theology of liberation has by now entered the common lexicon not only of theologians, but of many people who have until recently expressed little interest in theology.[1] It is a theological genre or, better, a "movement" issuing out of and responsive to the experience of the poor and suffering of history, based upon a conviction that the Gospel has direct pertinence to the concrete human condition. It calls for a liberating practice as the way salvation is to be realized in history. A theology of liberation understands the Gospel as a divine challenge to any exercise of political and economic power that would threaten the very survival of human beings. The Gospel itself calls for a transfiguration of the earthly city and human history into an image of the kingdom of

God. Thus, a theology of liberation moves in two directions: toward the fulfillment of human history in the absolute freedom of eternal life, and the working out of salvation within history itself. As Roger Haight has put it:

> [H]ere faith involves a form of praxis, a mode of being and acting in the world. This response says in the name of Jesus Christ that God is essentially Savior and that this salvation is operative as a process of humanization or liberation within history. This salvation gives meaning to history because it leads toward eternal life and because it gives meaning to history here and now as something that is meant to increase the capacity of human freedom itself. This humanization process will lead to absolute or final human fulfillment or freedom. But the condition for affirming this experientially, meaningfully and with conviction is praxis, that is, participation in the historical movement itself. (42)

The absolute cannot be reached except through the concrete, historical, and, especially, the human. Liberation theology limns through praxis the circuit of salvation "between earth and heaven."[2]

A certain mystique, even romantic aura has been associated with the theology of liberation, especially its Latin American manifestations, as it has been so closely identified with heroic and near-heroic people who have taken the Gospel to heart as a summons to praxis. The multitude of martyrs in recent years, most of them tied in some way to the inspiration engendered by the patterns of liberation thinking and practice, have firmly established the theology of liberation, not only as a theological methodology, but as a source of spirituality and religious esthetic. One cannot visit the graves of the Salvadoran martyrs who had totally identified with the poor without the feeling that one has come near a still-quickening holiness, a place where the desires of heaven have met the intransigence of the earth.

Many of the leaders of the first generation of Latin American theologians have been Jesuits. The martyrs of El Salvador in particular have been a great inspiration to Jesuits all over the world, evoking a sense of holiness and mission which inspiring words alone cannot accomplish. Is there a connection between this esthetic experience of the holy, arising out of the experience of the suffering and death of the poor and their witnesses, and the religious imagination of Ignatius? In order to begin to answer the question, we might go back 350 years to the city of Rome, where stories of heroic witness to the faith, once inspired by the letters of Xavier, gave way to an entirely new religious esthetic.

Pozzo's Ceiling

On the ancient site of the Temple of Isis in the city of Rome stands the Church of San Ignazio, a church originally intended for completion in 1640 for the centenary anniversary of the founding of the Society of Jesus. The church was to serve as the chapel of the already fabled Roman College, an institutional embodiment of Jesuit ideals in both humanistic education in the post-Reform era and missionary activity for the Catholic faith in the newly discovered worlds of America and Asia. As such, it was to be a glorious monument to the genius of the founder of the Jesuits and an illustration of his expansive religious vision. The imposing façade of this new temple, a somewhat cleaner version of the Gesù Church nearby, comes suddenly into view as one meanders through the narrow streets in back of the Roman College and, passing through a thin opening, comes upon the salon-like baroque Piazza of San Ignazio, which has all the appearance of having been constructed for the staging of opera.[3] One wall of this intimate outdoor opera house is the façade of San Ignazio.

As one enters the church, one's gaze is almost immediately adverted to the central ceiling panel, a *trompe-l'oeil* masterpiece, completed in 1694 by the famed Jesuit artist Brother Andrea Pozzo, entitled *The Glory* [or *Apotheosis*] *of St. Ignatius*. Pozzo, a master of perspective and foreshortening, succeeded not only in rendering three dimensions on a virtually flat surface, but also in opening up the ceiling of the church to the virtual infinity of celestial height. As the viewer stands firmly planted on the marble floor of the church, the temple seems to explode upward toward the central figures of Christ and St. Ignatius, who appear to be ascending into the heavens. Surrounding St. Ignatius are angels, and some of the newly named saints of the Society, among them "Italians, Spaniards, Poles, French and Flemish . . . [who] symbolise St. Ignatius' international and supernatural idea" (Calvo 7).[4]

Surrounding these international figures are clusters of groups representing human beings in all their variegation and multiplicity, misery, confusion and need, as they struggle with idolatry, heresy, and other forms of darkness. And these are not only European or Roman people; they comprise the palette of humanity from Europe to Asia, from Africa to the Americas—the entire expanding world toward which the young Society of Jesus was turning, especially through the ministry of the Roman College. In Pozzo's ceiling, God's saving light moves downward from the heavens, through the ministry of Ignatius, to all the peoples of the earth; the entire earth is suffused with illumination of the heavens.[5] At the same time, the viewer, along with the entire sweep of humanity, is drawn back up to that very focal point of heavenly glory toward which the ceiling is perpetually open. Pozzo has managed to depict a kind of back-and-forth movement of the religious imagination of the viewer between earth and heaven.

A yet closer look at the ceiling will demonstrate more clearly how this back-and-forth movement of the imagination functions. The geometrical focal point of light in the canvas is clearly St. Ignatius, but Ignatius is not placed dead center in the composition. That place is held by the glorified Christ, who bears upon his shoulder the cross of salvation. He is gesturing toward Ignatius, electing him to the glory which is now recognized by the Church as belonging to Ignatius, a grace realized only through heroic ministry to the entire suffering world, a world to which Ignatius belongs as Christ's companion. Those familiar with the life of St. Ignatius will recognize here a reference to the vision of Ignatius at La Storta, where Ignatius, upon entering Rome, had a vision of Christ bearing his cross—a vision that resulted in a confirmation of his calling to Rome and in special devotion to the name of Jesus (Ignatius 66–67). The movement between earth and heaven therefore finds its central mediation not in the glory of Ignatius, but in the contemplation of the glory of God in Jesus Christ, who himself became human, even unto death, "so that at the name of Jesus, every knee should bend, in heaven and under the heavens" (Phil. 2).

This closer examination reveals something even more telling about the religious imagination at work here. The figure of Christ is not seated alone in the heavens. He is part of the triune Godhead that includes the Father and, in the form of a dove, the Holy

Spirit. The Father and the Holy Spirit are together sending Christ down toward the world of Ignatius, and, through him, to the world of the viewer. Jesus Christ is depicted here as the second person of the Trinity who becomes incarnate, a reality which is metaphorically represented by the monogram of the name of Jesus—IHS—borne by a floating angelic figure at the bottom of the composition. This figure and the emblem appear directly above, and quite close to, the viewer, so that the Holy Name descends vertically from the heavens directly upon the viewer standing below it. The viewer, in turn, gazes upon the name of Jesus, and with the entire earth, bows in glory before the Lord who, through his crucifixion and vanquishing of sin and death, draws all the earth back to himself.

A circular movement between earth and heaven begins with God "above" in the sending of the Word, involves the human world "below" where that Word becomes incarnate, and through the Word incarnate draws this human world back to God, where the human world achieves its plenitude in the heavenly vision. This movement is not abstract: it involves real flesh and blood, actual people in specific places, in the unyielding though passing corporeality of human life, bound as it is by all the texture of space and time, open as it is to the infinite.

The Movement of the Ignatian Imagination

Pozzo was a magnificently gifted artist; he was also a Jesuit artist. One can see in this ceiling the lines of the Ignatian religious imagination found in the *Spiritual Exercises* of St. Ignatius, the fundamental inspiration of the Jesuit approach to the Gospel (see de Guibert 534–39).[6] Even the La Storta vision, which is clearly a source for this canvas, must be read within the broader context of the *Exercises*, where the main dynamics of Ignatian imagination are clearly indicated.

The *Spiritual Exercises* of Ignatius of Loyola are often considered archetypal of what was later called Counter-Reformation spirituality. The *Exercises* profoundly influenced other spiritualities that emerged from the post-Reformation period, almost all of which "reproduced in one form or another the fundamental elements dear to St. Ignatius: systematic use of the imaginative powers and the interior senses, deliberate incitement of the affections, ascetic and moral application" (Cognet 13). Unlike some earlier medieval forms of mysticism, the *Exercises* as Ignatius composed them did not focus upon a purgation of the senses with a view toward suprasensual union with the divine through a bypassing of earthly existence—the purely contemplative pole represented by some spiritual paths strongly influenced by Neoplatonism (Cognet 14–16).[7] And unlike some forms of spiritual life emanating from Renaissance humanism, the *Exercises* did not entertain a facile optimism about human nature, or take their focus from the efficacy of earthly works alone (Cognet 78). While Ignatius certainly recognized that the path to God is through the human, and through the natural world in general, he was also deeply aware of a fundamental fissure in this world and saw the plain marks of sin and darkness within it. While human nature is essentially good, the Ignatian view envisages a battle of the spirits within the drama of human history, a battle depicted in the *Exercises* in the meditation on the Two Standards and the Kingdom Meditation (see below).

The *Exercises*, then, chart a path that moves through the imagination, between contemplative and active poles, between an eschatologically ordered love of God, and life amid the terrestrial pageant of good overcoming evil. A fundamental relation between heaven and earth lies at the heart of Ignatian mysticism, which is an active apostolic mysticism intended to cultivate a person *simul in actione contemplativus* (a person at once both contemplative and active).[8] Although the conclusion of the *Exercises* is the contemplative pole of the "Contemplation to Attain Divine Love" [the *Contemplatio*], this end is attained only within the theater of the world of human actions, for it is only through this graced and struggling movement of the human that one can adore the great works, the *magnalia*, of the triune God. Love for God in God's great works of salvation is "precisely the object of Ignatian contemplation, of apostolic contemplation" (Daniélou 358). Ignatian contemplation calls for a full exercise of the religious imagination, finding in the real human world the absolutely transcendent struggle of God's working out the liberation of the world itself and pointing to an end beyond history.

This movement between earth and heaven finds its resolution for Ignatius in the centrality of the Incarnation, where both poles find their relation to each other in the singularity of human personhood, a personhood celebrated by Pozzo in the descending love of God in Jesus, the incarnate Son sent by the eternal Godhead for the salvation of all people, and in the drawing of Ignatius and all of humanity with him upward toward God. The finality of the *Contemplatio* cannot be attained apart from the pivotal contemplation on the Incarnation. The movement between earth and heaven is set up in the meditation on the Incarnation, finds its plenitude in the *Contemplatio*, and is resolved in the centrality of Jesus.

Hugo Rahner described this movement "between earth and heaven" in his classic *Ignatius the Theologian*. In the lead essay of this book, he notes the importance of the notion of *de arriba*, from above, in the Ignatian religious world-view. For Ignatius, the source and goal of all created reality is "from above." Although human beings are clearly creaturely beings, and while one comes to a love for God through created things, one does not find the fullness of being by embracing only the creaturely state. While one finds God in all created things, one arrives at a love for God by, somewhat paradoxically, stripping oneself of all love for created things. And this is possible only for that person

> who has been graced with this consolation and consequently, through his own union with this "above", moves downwards with a cosmic, universal love towards created things, towards everything the world encloses. [One] embraces everything because it has come from God and belongs only to God. (H. Rahner 7)

In Rahner's interpretation, a motion of the soul is therefore established which begins at the creaturely level and in one's love for creation, moves upward toward the source and goal of creation in God, and then, having received and been transformed by God's love, returns to the creaturely level, but now detached from it, because one is in possession of a sense that everything belongs first to God and is constituted lovable because it is first loved by God.[9] In all these movements, the initiative comes from God, not as from a prime mover, but as heavenly source of grace and life in human history.[10] As Rahner puts it, "the essential note of Ignatian theology is the way of descent" (H. Rahner 9).

Both motions, the downward and the upward, find their union

in the "middle": the Church and, in the Church, the "Mediator" (H. Rahner 10). That Mediator is, of course, Christ, who embodies the union of downward and upward movements. Ignatian spirituality is focused upon this middle in Christ,[11] perhaps nowhere more than in the contemplation on the Incarnation. In the context of liberation theology, it is fitting that we focus here upon the contemplation on the Incarnation, which is for Ignatius the imaginative construction of the movement between earth and heaven whereby God's saving work is accomplished.

The Contemplation on the Incarnation

The contemplation on the Incarnation is situated within the Second Week of the *Exercises*, a phase during which the retreatant, having already savored the consolation of knowing that one is a sinner loved by God, is now freed to focus on his or her desire for and generosity in serving God in one's life. The exercitant has already undertaken the "Kingdom" contemplation, in which one is asked to consider Jesus's invitation: "Whoever would like to come with me is to labor with me that following me in the pain, that person may also follow me in the glory" (*Sp Exx* [95]).[12] The exercitant was further invited to consider the following type of prayer of oblation, where, with the help of God's infinite goodness [*infinita bondad*], one expresses the "want and desire and deliberate determination . . . to imitate you in bearing all injuries and abuse and all poverty of spirit, and actual poverty, too, if your most Holy Majesty wants to choose and receive me to such life and state" (*Sp Exx* [98]). It is with this spirit of open generosity and gratitude that the exercitant now turns to the Incarnation.[13]

The contemplation on the Incarnation is actually part of a five-part exercise. First, we have the contemplation on the Incarnation itself, which approaches the subject matter "from above," i.e., from the starting point and viewpoint of the triune Godhead, but in descent. This is followed by a contemplation on the Nativity, which views the same subject matter seen "from below," from the human standpoint of the poverty of the stable, the experience of Mary and Joseph, and all the human and sensual factors attendant thereto. Then follow two "repetitions" in which the relation between these two contemplations is considered, especially as they lead to responses in the exercitant, either toward consolation or toward desolation. Finally, there is the application of the senses, in which the imagination works to allow the mystery of God-become-human to be savored in the humanness of the retreatant, through a consideration of that very humanness which, as in Pozzo's ceiling, yearns for the salvation that comes to it in the humanity of the Second-Person-of-the-Trinity-become-incarnate.

The contemplation on the Incarnation itself consists of a brief preparatory prayer, three preludes, three points, and one so-called colloquy. The downward-upward pattern of this contemplation is evident in the construction of the preludes and points, and in the harmony that relates the preludes and points to each other.

The first prelude begins with a colloquy among the three divine persons in the heavens, perhaps like the divine cluster at the center of Pozzo's ceiling. As Ignatius frames it:

> Here, it is how the three divine persons looked at all the plain or circuit [*redondez*] of all the world, full of people, and how, seeing that all were going down to hell, it is determined in their eternity, that the second person should become human to save the human race. . . . (*Sp Exx* [102])

The initiative of a movement between earth and heaven begins entirely with God, *de arriba*, in the interest of saving lost humankind.

The second prelude shifts the focus from the Trinity to that singular, unique human person, Mary of Nazareth, to whom the Trinity has chosen to communicate itself. Mary is seen "within the great capacity and circuit of the world, in which are so many and such different people" (*Sp Exx* [103]). Here, the gaze of the imagination is drawn toward the richly variegated human world, depicted in Pozzo's canvas by so many different types of people, and ultimately, to a consideration of the particularity of each person, especially that most particular person, Mary. Here, it might be noted, the visual lines of the Pozzo canvas move to the divine action upon the singular viewer who stands directly beneath the Holy Name held by the angelic figure, much as God's Word, through Gabriel, was communicated to Mary. The viewer, in his or her particularity, thus becomes a participant, like Mary, in the divine drama. Such a participation is indeed one of the aims of this Ignatian contemplation on the Incarnation.

The third prelude is an exercise in drawing the first two together through an "interior knowledge [*conoscimiento interno*]" of Jesus, "Who for me has been made human, that I may more love and follow him" (*Sp Exx* [104]). The economy of heaven and earth, the divine action made on behalf of all humanity, is also made "for me" with the end in mind that, like Mary, I might live for God's ends in my own human particularity.[14] The Mediator, Jesus, is therefore "at once in heaven and here below." The exercitant's focus upon Jesus draws one's imagination up into the mystery of God and, united in love with God, back down in love, through Jesus's self-emptying, to help accomplish the work of salvation on earth.

Now Ignatius invites the retreatant to experience this movement of the imagination through the mediation of the bodily senses. (This part of the contemplation on the Incarnation is not to be confused with the application of the senses, which occurs after a consideration of the Nativity and two repetitions, later in the day). At this point, the mediation of the bodily senses becomes an integral part of the function of the religious imagination—an imagination exercised not in abstraction from, but precisely through, human corporeality, because it is in the radically concrete that God works.

In the first point, the movement we have already sketched is repeated, this time through the sense of vision. Here, instead of beginning with the heavens, we begin from the standpoint of the earth, "first those [persons] on the surface of the earth, in such diversity [*diversidad*], in dress as in actions: some white and others black; some in peace and others in war; some weeping and others laughing; some well, others ill; some being born and others dying, etc." (*Sp Exx* [106]). The imagination is invited to roam those places in human reality represented by the lower reaches of the Pozzo canvas, below and, in a sense, within which we ourselves stand.

Then, having surveyed the scene in all its multifarious detail, our sight is directed upward, to the center. There we are "to see and consider the three divine persons, as on their royal throne or seat of their Divine Majesty, how they look on all the surface and circuit of the earth, and all the people in such blindness, and how they are dying and going down to hell" (*Sp Exx* [106]). The exercitant, of course, as a human being, has some experience of this blindness, and of this backsliding toward eternal loss, an experience depicted spatially by Pozzo in that the viewer stands literally below even those who are being cast down to the netherworld by the forces of truth.

Finally, we are "to see Our Lady, and the angel [Gabriel] who is saluting her, and to reflect in order to gain profit [*sacar prouecho*] from such a sight." As we suggested above, the viewer of the canvas is in the place of Mary, and a floating heavenly figure salutes us with the name of Jesus itself. The exercitant, in his or her humanity, becomes the place of continuing Incarnation here on earth.

This sense exercise is repeated, first by focusing on *hearing* what the people of the earth are saying, what the divine persons are saying among themselves, and what the angel and Mary say to each another, so that the exercitant may draw profit from such words (*Sp Exx* [107]). In the third point, the spotlight is on actions—what the people of the earth are *doing*, what the divine persons are doing, "namely, working out the most holy Incarnation," and what occurs between the Angel and Mary of Nazareth (*Sp Exx* [108]). All this is done with a view toward the conclusion of the contemplation on the Incarnation, entreating [*pidiendo*] the Trinity, the eternal Word incarnate, or Mary "according to what I feel in me, to follow and imitate Our Lord more, who has, in a time so very recent, become incarnate [*ansí nuevamente encarnado*]" (*Sp Exx* [109]).[15] And one should bear in mind, again, that this contemplation is itself placed in relation to that which follows, the contemplation on the Nativity. The entire five-part movement, which stresses the fact that God became human, and that salvation is worked out by God through his human intermediaries, points to the conclusion of the *Exercises*, the *Contemplatio* where the ultimate focus is upon God as both giver and gift, from whom "all the good things and gifts descend from above [*de arriba*] . . . as from the sun descend its rays . . ." (*Sp Exx* [237]).

Hugo Rahner has elegantly described what is happening in this kind of movement of the religious imagination. We might keep in mind here the Pozzo canvas as we consider this description:

> Thus this Ignatian theology of Christ effects a sort of "reduction" of "above" to "below", by way of the divine Majesty put to death on the cross. . . . The royal throne of the Father is confronted by

"the face and circumference of the earth" [*Sp Exx* (102, 103)], and below this again is the utmost abyss beyond which no further descent is possible: the hell into which [people] must "descend" [*Sp Exx* (102)], though they are able to rise again from it in the Mediator to the glory of the Father, because the Word—as the radiant source—had himself "come down from above" [*Sp Exx* (237)] and is thus "at the feet of the most Holy Trinity," where he "implores the Trinity for forgiveness." In Christ, then, the "above" of the Father has become permanently fused into the elements and atoms of the world "below." The dialogue on the royal throne ends in the room at Nazareth. (17; translation slightly emended)

The "room at Nazareth" is, of course, the space and time on earth occupied by the exercitant, or by the pilgrim who gazes, either literally or figuratively, through the Ignatian imagination, upward toward the Trinity.

Ignatian Imagination and the Aesthetics of Liberation

The Ignatian imagination is certainly something other than flight of fancy; it is more than the ability to picture scenes or compose places, although this may be partly suggested by Ignatius; it is even more than the application of the senses, although it includes some exercise of the senses, as the three points of the *Contemplatio* suggest, and as the fifth movement of this five-part exercise will prescribe.[16] The application of the senses is an imaginative exercise, but it does not in itself exhaust the substance of Ignatian imagination. The Ignatian imagination is a "faculty" of interpreting reality in its totality, spiritual and corporeal. While it is other than sensory fantasy, it is dependent upon the very corporeality that the senses imply. At the same time, it extends beyond the bodily senses to include the entire range of spiritual senses which the human person possesses as a spiritual being.[17] It is thus a form of remembering the manifold ways in which God has descended into the physical and spiritual matter of our own lives. It implicates all the coordinates of space and time as these define, condition, modify, or mediate earthly existence; these become the point of departure for the human response to God's initiative. Once implicated, they find their natural fulfillment in their cooperation with the saving work of God in Jesus Christ.

That which distinguishes the Ignatian imagination from various other understandings of imagination is, therefore, (1) its utterly concrete referentiality to the time and space within which human existence takes place, and within which God becomes incarnate, and (2) its simultaneous transcendence of ordinary sensory experience such that the meaning of such experience is found in God and the fulfillment of human existence in cooperation with God's desires. The imagination for Ignatius is firmly planted in the human reality of space and time; it is within that reality—its temporality, spatiality, architecture, perspective, and motion—that God is experienced.[18]

For Ignatius, therefore, the imagination is an indispensable medium for the experience of God; intrinsic to human nature, it is a natural instrument of religion. The imagination leads from earth to heaven in the human desire for God; at the same time, it leads from heaven to earth in God's desire, working through the willing cooperation of human beings, for the salvation of the world. The religious imagination depicted at San Ignazio, and more subtly limned in the *Spiritual Exercises* of St. Ignatius, provides an aesthetic within which the theology of liberation might be understood today. Jesuit theologian Jon Sobrino, one of the chief architects of the theology of liberation, has noted the historic gap between spirituality and the practice of Christian faith, a gap that the theology of liberation has endeavored to bridge through a dialectic of contemplation and action (Endean 2). The spiritual life, he reminds us, is never purely spiritual; it must include real "incarnated" life, the edges of history as people experience and construct history. It is in this historical theater of human experience that the Incarnation has taken place, not outside it. As the assassination of his brother Jesuits in 1989 attested, such a conviction is bound to bring with it a certain definite rejection and persecution, responses that would not exist if real life were not the basis for a spiritual vision (Endean 3–4). Spiritual life, therefore, is planted "from below," from the standpoint of the one "looking up" to the God who liberates human beings from the structures of sin which pull them down.

At the same time, it must be said that historical life is never purely historical, i.e., never purely concrete. It is also a matter of spirit (Endean 4). This is a fundamental insight of the Hegelian dialectic of history, which sees history as the unfurling of the

Spirit through human contingencies. In Jesus himself, it is not merely his own initiative, but the initiative of the Spirit which draws him, through his freedom, toward undertaking a ministry of salvation, indeed of liberating the lowliest from their oppression. The ultimate impetus for the saving work of Christ comes "from above" as the triune God elects to become one with humanity in the form of a lowly person—one "who emptied himself and took the form of a slave" (Phil. 2:7).

Sobrino specifies four prerequisites for a liberation spirituality, which we might call here a liberation esthetic, one deeply imbued with the Ignatian imagination. The first is "honesty to the real," which means beginning with the human condition as it is. The theology of liberation begins with a firm stance in the world of the poor, those who have been systematically excised from pictures of what is "real." The Ignatian imagination, however, insists on including the poor, and on identification with the poor, even to the point of becoming poor. This is a major and repeated theme in Ignatian spirituality. It is certainly remarkably represented in the Pozzo canvas, with teeming masses of poor humanity of all colors reaching up to heaven for salvation. The viewer of the canvas stands spatially within the world of this teeming poor humanity, not above them, nor to the side, merely looking on. The esthetic effect is one of total identification with "those on the lowest rung of the ladder of history" (Gutiérrez, "Expanding" 12).

The second prerequisite of a liberation spirituality is "fidelity to the real," which Sobrino describes as

> perseverance in our original honesty, however we may be burdened with, yes, engulfed in, the negative element in history. Our first knowing is shrouded in obscurity by a certain non-knowing, and the power of negativity will challenge that first hope of ours. We shall know only that we must stay faithful, keep moving ahead in history, striving ever to transform that history from negative to positive. (18)

Again, we find ourselves planted so firmly in the "below" of history that the vision of an integral liberation can be clouded. Looking "up" we can, perhaps, fail to see that a central mediation of the liberating work of the Gospel is the suffering of the Cross borne by the one who descends to become incarnate within human history. Fidelity to the real reveals that liberation is a matter not of theoretical dialectic, but of a certain historical dialectic between flesh and spirit, and therefore, of suffering and even martyrdom. Fidelity to the real, furthermore, has a praxic dimension, which means actively participating in the work of liberation. In Pozzo's ceiling, the triune God establishes the pattern for active participation: full incarnation in human reality in its poorest forms, a participation reflected by Pozzo in the sending of Jesuits with hearts on fire to the four corners of the world.

This leads to the third prerequisite of a liberation spirituality: the willingness to be swept along by the "more" of reality (Sobrino 19). Here Sobrino strikes a familiar Ignatian theme, the idea of the "more" or the *magis*. But here it does not denote some superhuman striving, but, rather, an active openness to the totality of human reality, and the willingness to be caught up in it. The Ignatian imagination, therefore, de-centers the world of the familiar, the world that is given, and turns one's attention to the world as God sees it, in its comprehensive totality and fundamental unity. The focus here is not on "diversity," but on the universality of God's liberating love.

And this raises the fact that the liberating work of the Gospel will take on different shapes and forms in different cultural settings. "An authentic universality does not consist in speaking precisely the same language but rather in achieving a full understanding within the setting of each language. . . . The goal, then, is not uniformity but a profound unity, a communion or *koinonia*" (Gutiérrez, "Expanding" 23). An esthetic of liberation will revel in the particularity which finds its value in the unity of a final integrating vision. In Pozzo's ceiling, Europe, the only world familiar to most seventeenth-century viewers, is relativized and even reduced in status to of the four corners of the earth, on a par with the Americas, Asia, and Africa. At the same time, it finds a new sense of itself as a culture among cultures, where human misery and poverty are shared transculturally, as much in need of the liberating work of the Incarnation as Africa, Asia, or the Americas are. While in each of these mythic places the Gospel becomes allegorized according to native custom and costume, a new center now holds, not in the culture of Europe, but in the liberating work of Christ.

Finally, Sobrino points to the essential prerequisite of the experience of God (Gutiérrez 20–21). And here we return to our starting point, the movement of the imagination between earth and heaven. There can be no pure, unmediated experience of God in the Christian sense. There is no spiritual experience that is not historicized, and, in the movement of Ignatian imagination, that experience is the experience of salvation, of an integral human liberation involving both historical and transcendental coordinates. The experience of God, finally, is an ongoing experience which takes place within the theater of human suffering, especially the suffering of the poor, whose particular world the Incarnate One entered. In the last analysis, we are speaking here of an esthetic which is most accessible not in the texts of various editions of the *Exercises*, or in the visual texts of great frescos and canvases, but in the texts of human lives, which Ignatius in his genius saw as yearning for salvation. This spiritual path through the motion of the religious imagination is of particular pertinence in our own day, when the earthly and transcendent poles are often enough proposed as mutually exclusive opposites, and where God is reserved to the realm of private judgment, or worse, to pure flights of fancy. A religious imagination thoroughly grounded in concrete human experience, as this one surely is, can only conclude to a God who is correlatively real and liberating.

Notes

1. See, for example, Gustavo Gutiérrez' discussion of liberation theology, where he notes that it "has stimulated an interest in reflection on the Christian faith—an interest previously unknown in Latin American intellectual circles, which have traditionally been cool toward Christianity or even hostile to it" ("Expanding" 4). For an account of one of the more spectacular openings to some dimensions of Christian faith, partly in response to the initiatives of the theology of liberation, see Gutiérrez' *Fidel*.

2. The phrase is taken from Hugo Rahner (12). Rahner's description of the theological dialectic to be found in Ignatius is discussed below.

3. Indeed, in 1727, Pope Benedict XIII ruled that funds earmarked for the completion of the dome of San Ignazio be spent instead on the piazza outside, giving Rome "one of her most 'theatrical' urban spaces." See Levy 216.

4. With Ignatius, early Jesuits like Jerónimo Nadal "affirmed straightforwardly that for the members of the order 'the world' was their 'house' [and] . . . that the Society was essentially a group 'on mission,' ready at any moment to travel to any point where there was need for its ministry." The *doing* of the saving work of the Gospel anywhere in the world is firmly planted in the Jesuit imagination. See O'Malley 18.

5. Admittedly, this approach to the fresco does not take into account the standard reading of it as "a dialectic between the name of Jesus, chosen for the Society by the saint, and 'ignis,' fire, a pun on the name of Ignatius." "Depicted at the center of the field, high above the four parts of the earth, the saint is struck by rays of light emanating from Christ's wounded side. . . . From the heart of Ignatius, as from a mirror, light issues to the four corners of the earth. The converting power of this light or flame is mediated by the Jesuit saints who travelled to the four continents as missionaries. The sending of the missionaries and the spreading of fire on earth are taken from the gospel and communion antiphons, respectively, for Ignatius' mass proper" (Levy 216). Calvo writes that Pozzo confirms the connection between the name of Ignatius and the motto *Ignem veni mettere in terram*. "Pozzo himself supplies a precise explanation of the significance of his fresco: 'Jesus illumines the heart of St. Ignatius with a ray of light, which is then transmitted by the Saint to the furthermost corners of the four quarters of the earth, which I have represented with their symbols in the four sections of the vault.' Referring to the missionaries of the Society of Jesus he writes: 'The first of these indefatigable workers is St. Francis Xavier, the Apostle of the Indies, who is seen leading a vast crowd of Eastern converts towards Heaven. The same kind of scene i[s] depicted with other members of the Society of Jesus in Europe, Africa and America'" (29).

6. The rich biblical foundations of the *Exercises*, and their rendering as a kind of pedagogy of Scripture, can be found in much current literature, notably in Cusson.

7. Cognet associates this tendency especially with the Northern or Rheno-Flemish school of spirituality. It must be said, however, that early *Directories* to the *Exercises* saw a relation between the "weeks" of the *Exercises* and "the three traditional 'ways' of Christian spirituality—purgative, illuminative, and unitive." See O'Malley 22.

8. Philip Endean, s.j., invokes Emerich Coreth, who "argued powerfully that [Gerónimo] Nadal's description of Ignatius as 'simul in actione contemplativus' implicitly involved a radical correction of philosophical habits going right back to antiquity: the preference for knowing over loving, the interior over the exterior, the individual over the collective" (413). The Coreth article he cites is "Contemplation in Action," in Gleason 184–211

9. Daniélou cautions against reading the Ignatian path to God through creatures in too facile a manner. "It would be imprudent to believe that one could go very quickly to God through creatures. This is the error of a certain modern humanism. St. Francis of Assisi chanted the 'canticle of the Sun,' but only after having been the stigmatist of Alverno" (366).

10. Michael Buckley stresses this initiative from God, this *privilegium* of grace, as foundational to an understanding of an Ignatian sense of devotion. "It was important that if Ignatius and any particular Jesuit was able to find God in anything whatsoever, it was because God has first found them" (27). I am deeply indebted to Father Buckley himself for the stimulus to begin thinking about the dialectical structure of the contemplation on the Incarnation, a subject which he has discussed many times with fellow Jesuits.

11. "The [one] who looks from below up to the above understands in the descent from above, in the outpouring of the divine source upon the world below, that he is bound up with the above and, precisely because he recognizes his own position, with the below. He realizes, too, that if consolation is 'poured' into him, it is only because God, the very source, himself descended and became Mediator. Above and below are bound up together through the mediating activity of the one Mediator. Indeed, it is possible to conceive of the below only in terms of the above, and this by fixing one's gaze upon the middle, which evokes the interior attitude of *acatamiento*, awe" (H. Rahner 11;. translation slightly emended).

12. Quotations from the *Spiritual Exercises* are abbreviated as *Sp Exx*, followed in brackets by the standard paragraph number. All quotations are from the Mullan translation, which appears in Fleming. In some places, where Spanish appears in brackets, I have compared the Mullan translation with the Spanish "Autograph" text in *Monumenta*.

13. This generosity, or magnanimity, is an essential note of Ignatian spirituality. It is the human correlate to the *magnalia* of God, and is the precondition for an apostolic engagement in God's saving work. Ignatius specifies generosity toward God and willingness to be used as God's instrument as a precondition for making the *Spiritual Exercises*. See "Fifth Annotation" [5]. Daniélou writes: "The Apostle indeed ought to be engaged in the great works of God. He must have then, through the spirit, a soul corresponding to these great works, which are difficult because they are great. . . . It is only by the power of God that one can accomplish the works of God" (362–63).

14. Hugo Rahner elaborates: "Ignatius first makes the exercitant as a sinner run swiftly through the whole of this space between the 'royal throne' of the Trinity and the 'circumference of the earth' [*Sp Exx*. 58],

and then fills it out with the middle of the incarnation [*Sp Exx* 102–106]. But this also means that he is teaching the exercitant to contemplate even this below and middle from above; in other words, he is measuring all created things, good and defective alike, against the goodness and wisdom of God above [*Sp Exx* 59, 237]" (13).

15. We find here an indication of the importance of a sense of time and history in Ignatius's spirituality, and in the exercise of Ignatian imagination. The distance of the event of the Incarnation from the present moment is considerably reduced by considering it to have occurred but lately, *nuevamente*. Here the imagination does more than reconstruct a past event; it is the vehicle by which the palpable present reality of that event is brought home to the exercitant through the collapsing of human time into the salvation time of God.

16. Philip Endean notes that this application of the senses comes at the end of the Ignatian day of prayer (as the fifth part), in a movement "from reflection *on* the scene to reflection *of* the scene, one of deepening imaginative involvement. Instead of simply thinking about past events, retreatants are challenged to react to the events of Christ's life, and to imagine how their own lives might become responses to those events" (404).

17. Karl Rahner so argues in "'The 'Spiritual Senses'" and in "The Doctrine." In the latter article, he holds that a relationship can be discerned between Bonaventure's doctrine on the spiritual senses, and Ignatius's doctrine of the senses in the *Exercises*.

18. Philip Endean notes: "In Ignatian imaginative prayer, we are invited to experiment with new ways of understanding the world. . . . We seek to let the Gospel symbols be reflected in our own selves, generating new patterns of interpretation and action. . . . An awareness of dependence on God enables and expands us to be who we are. Our ultimate categories are relational" (410).

Works Cited

Buckley, Michael. "'Always Growing in Devotion . . .': Jesuit Spirituality as Stimulus to Ecumenical Involvement." Regis College 1988 Chancellor's Address. Toronto: Regis College, 1989.

Calvo, Francesco. *Church of St. Ignatius, Rome*. Bologna: Officine grafiche Poligrafici il Resto del Carlino, 1968.

Cognet, Louis. *Post-Reformation Spirituality*. Trans. P. Hepburne Scott. New York: Hawthorn, 1959.

Coreth, Emerich. "Contemplation in Action." Gleason 184–211.

Cusson, Giles. *Pédagogie de l'expérience personnelle: Bible et exercices.* Paris: Desclée de Brouwer, 1968.
Daniélou, Jean. "The Ignatian Vision of the Universe and of Man." *Cross Currents* 4 (1954): 358.
Dupré, Louis and Don E. Saliers, eds. *Christian Spirituality: Post-Reformation and Modern.* New York: Crossroad, 1989.
Endean, Philip, s.j. "The Ignatian Prayer of the Senses." *Heythrop Journal* 31 (1990): 413.
Fleming, David. *The Spiritual Exercises of St. Ignatius: A Literal Translation and a Contemporary Reading.* St. Louis: Institute of Jesuit Sources, 1978.
Gleason, R. W. *Contemporary Spirituality: Current Problems in Religious Life.* New York: Macmillan, 1968.
Guibert, Joseph de. *The Jesuits: Their Spiritual Doctrine and Practice—A Historical Study.* Trans. William J. Young. Chicago: Institute of Jesuit Sources, 1964.
Gutiérrez, Gustavo. "Expanding the View." In *Expanding the View: Gustavo Gutiérrez and the Future of Liberation Theology.* Ed. Marc H. Ellis and Otto Maduro. New York: Orbis, 1988. 3–39.
———. *Fidel Castro y Religión: Conversaciones con Frei Betto.* Mexico City: Siglo Veintiuno, 1986.
Haight, Roger. *An Alternate Vision: An Interpretation of Liberation Theology.* New York: Paulist, 1985.
Ignatius of Loyola. "Autobiography." *St. Ignatius' Own Story: As Told to Louis Gonzalez de Camara, with a Sampling of His Letters.* Trans. William J. Young. Chicago: Loyola UP, 1980.
Levy, Yvonne. *Saint, Site, and Sacred Strategy. Ignatius, Rome and Jesuit Urbanism.* Ed Thomas M. Lucas. Rome: Biblioteca Apostolica Vaticana, 1990.
Monumenta Historica Societatis Iesu, Vol. 100, *Monumenta Ignatiana,* ser. 2a, vol. 1. *Exercitia Spiritualis,* ed. J. Calveras and C. Dalmases. Rome: Institutum Historicum Societatis Iesu, 1969.
O'Malley, John, s.j. "Early Jesuit Spirituality." Dupré 3–28.
Rahner, Hugo, s.j.. *Ignatius the Theologian.* Trans. Michael Barry. New York: Herder, 1968.
Rahner, Karl, s.j. "The 'Spiritual Senses' According to Origen." *Theological Investigations* 16: 81–103.
———. "The Doctrine of the 'Spiritual Senses' in the Middle Ages." *Theological Investigations* 16: 104–34.
Sobrino, Jon. "The Importance of Spiritual Life Today." *Spirituality of Liberation: Toward Political Holiness.* Trans. Robert R. Barr. New York: Orbis, 1989.

4 • Erasmus, Education, and Folly

Christiaan Theodoor Lievestro

As a longtime student of Erasmus, I looked forward to testing an intriguing statement by William Harrison Woodward when I first came to teach at a Jesuit university twenty-five years ago. In his now-classic study *Desiderius Erasmus Concerning the Aim and Method of Education*, Woodward wrote: "Perhaps it was in the Jesuit schools that the curriculum of Erasmus was most adequately represented" (84).

When I studied the tradition and practice of one of those schools, I was both pleased and startled by my new perceptions. I saw that the great Christian humanist Erasmus, a Catholic priest, would indeed be satisfied that many of his ideals and aims in curriculum were realized in Jesuit schools. More of that in a moment.

But, another startling fact quickly became apparent, confirmed more and more as I gained a circle of wonderful Jesuit colleagues and carefully studied the history of the Jesuits. Both in name and in his works, Erasmus was distinctly not in favor. Moreover, according to tradition, the works of Erasmus had been condemned early on for study by the Jesuits themselves and in their schools—since, in fact, the last days of Ignatius in 1556.

That anti-Erasmus tradition still prevailed in my encounters with Jesuit colleagues, especially the older generation. In Ganss's notes to his translation of the 1970 official edition of Ignatius's *Constitutions of the Society of Jesus* is the persistent argument—and error—that Ignatius read the beautiful and inspiring *Enchiridion* (*Handbook of a Christian Soldier*) of Erasmus at Barcelona about 1525 and "ever after held Erasmus in suspicion" (Ignatius 219).

We know now that Ignatius could not have read the *Enchiridion* at Barcelona. Rather, it was at Alcalá that this controversial encounter took place. Georg Schurhammer, S.J., described the circumstances effectively:

> When Iñigo was a student at Alcalá in 1526, many individuals, including his own confessor Miona, had advised him to read the *Enchiridion militis christiani* of Erasmus, which his benefactor, the publisher Miguel de Eguia, had a short time before printed in Latin and Spanish. But when Iñigo learned that certain preachers and persons in authority had already found fault with this author, he refused to have anything to do with him, saying that there were books about which no evil was spoken, and that these were the books that he wanted to read. The condemnation of Erasmus' work by the Theological Faculty of Paris strengthened Iñigo in his rejection of the humanist in Basel. (168–69)

As a colleague, James W. Reites, S.J., an Ignatian scholar, recently pointed out to me,, "The attitude of Ignatius [toward Erasmus] is not entirely clear. I suspect that he changed over time: early on he was a bit of a puritan, and offended by Erasmus; later he might have been less severe on him."

A major study by John Olin of Fordham University, first written in 1967 and later amended, identified the source for that tradition of antipathy. Pedro Ribadeneira, Ignatius's first biographer and, in later years, his close Jesuit confidant, wrote in 1567–69, that "the reading of that book [*Enchiridion*] chilled the spirit of God in him and gradually extinguished the ardor of devotion." Olin tells us that the biographer maintained thereafter that Ignatius "conceived such an aversion for the author . . . that he would not permit Erasmus' books to be read in the Society" (77, 80). The anti-Erasmus tradition that Olin identifies was strongly reinforced by another important source, Juan Alonso de Polanco, personal secretary to and intimate of Ignatius; in his 1574 biography he repeated the story about the *Enchiridion* directly from Ribadeneira's account (80). Although Olin's study is helpful in revealing these important sources, the fact of some antipathy on the part of Ignatius toward certain works of Erasmus cannot be discounted.

It is clear that the anti-Erasmus tradition maintained a nearly official character until fairly recently. The well-known theologian Hugo Rahner wrote that "[Ignatius] felt an almost instinctive aversion for the literary trivialities of Erasmus, whose *Handbook of a Christian Soldier* had the effect of leaving him strangely cool in his religious dealings with God" (86). The source he cites in 1953 for this assertion is Ribadeneira! Here, apparently, was the explanation for the contradiction I initially encountered between Woodward's impressive statement and the facts I confronted in my first acquaintance with a Jesuit university.

I have wrestled for years with that contradiction, and this essay is an attempt to summarize my thoughts as I continue to ponder that paradox. I should stress at once that I have found this wrestling both instructive and inspiring. In the spirit of Erasmus and in the tradition of the French *moraliste*, I find that ongoing confrontations with a dilemma of this kind make me truly *engagé*, as the *moraliste* would have it, deeply engaged with a profound literary and spiritual problem. Important scholarly revision in recent years has addressed this difficulty. More, I trust, will continue.

The focus here is primarily on the greatest, most famous, and one of the most controversial works by Erasmus, *The Praise of Folly*. To place this discussion in historical context, attention is also directed to a fuller review of Jesuit attitudes toward him and his major educational writings.

Nothing demonstrates more dramatically the fate of Erasmus and his reputation as the greatest humanist scholar than the fact that he was offered a cardinal's hat by Pope Paul III in 1535. Two decades later, Erasmus was denounced by Pope Paul IV as "the leader of all the heretics" and his works condemned to be burned and placed on the Index of Forbidden Books.

As Erika Rummel has shown, Erasmus came under suspicion by the Spanish Inquisition as early as 1527 and by the Paris faculty of theology in 1531. After his death in 1536, "Erasmus was placed in the first category of heretics whose works were to be shunned in their entirety" when the Council of Trent first created the Index in 1559 (11).

Although a priest of the Church, Erasmus came to be judged anticlerical as the hierarchy felt its authority increasingly threatened by the reformers. The nature of his scholarship also alarmed Church leaders. Because Martin Luther's German translation of the New Testament was based on Erasmus's revised Greek text, the very important Greek scholarship of Erasmus became a particular anathema. In Paris, the war cry of Catholic students left no doubt: "Anyone who learns Greek is a secret Lutheran!" (Barthel 31). Moreover, in his popular student texts for the study of Latin, the *Colloquies* and the *Adages*—and even more in the soon-notorious *Praise of Folly*—Erasmus disparaged abuses by the Church and her clerics in a humorous, at times mocking, tone. However appropriate some of this criticism, it appeared to reinforce that of the militant reformers. In addition, the irrepressible wit and ironic humor of his brilliant writing offended the rigid and uncompromising sensibilities of beleaguered Church authorities.

Since Ribadeneira's biography, too much has been made of the contrast between the humanist spirit of Erasmus and the supposed antihumanism of Ignatius. What began as an error or overstatement has become merely a colorful convention, at times repeated to glorify one man at the expense of the other. The antithesis is often illustrated by the coincidence that Erasmus, Rabelais, Calvin, and Ignatius all attended the medieval monastic Collège de Montaigu. In Paris it was called "the cleft in the buttocks of the Mother of Theology" for its disgusting, miserable conditions (Mitchell 32; Barthel 32). Erasmus loathed the place as a brutal, ignorant horror, and Rabelais would have had it burned to the ground. Calvin, on the other hand, and supposedly Ignatius, approved of its grim austerity, which moved one writer to conclude that "here we have one of the great cleavages of the sixteenth century, between the Humanists and the Puritans" (Johnson 270).

Thus, Olin rightly noted that "the Ribadeneira text has given posterity the general picture of an Ignatius hostile to Erasmus and his spirit from the start, . . . but . . . Ribadeneira is describing essentially a very personal experience at second hand more than forty years after the event itself and . . . his description would seem to be a faulty and inaccurate ex-post-facto reconstruction" (77).

The polarity between Erasmus and Ignatius was evident to most writers and was maintained well into the present century. Yet, the standard account does not do justice to the religious imagination or the complex moral and educational positions of either man. Impressive scholarship of the past several decades has led to a more sophisticated appreciation of both Erasmus and Ignatius.

We know from Aldo Scaglione and several previous commentators that in his last years Ignatius became uncomfortable with the continued use of Erasmus's excellent texts for the teaching of Latin in Jesuit schools. Nevertheless, either openly or by some transparent rationalization, many of his works were frequently used. Because his books were easily pirated, it was convenient (with a bit of awkward sophistry) for the Jesuit college in Rome to advise the rector in Bologna in 1561: "This book is not by Erasmus . . . though he may have revised or amended it. In this case it can be read. But even if he composed it, the Company has the privilege of using it, also for the students of our schools. Furthermore, in Rome it is sold publicly and anyone can obtain it" (qtd. in Scaglione 79). Woodward demonstrated that the *Colloquies*, for example, were pirated in every country in Europe (24). And from the comprehensive record of the curriculum at the first Jesuit college at Messina, we have clear evidence of precisely which of Erasmus's texts were used in each Latin class (Farrell 49; Ganss 107).

John O'Malley, s.j., has made emphatically clear in two important studies ("Counter-Reformation"; "Fourth Vow") that "the familiar story of St. Ignatius' antipathy to Erasmus" is highly dubious. He defers to Olin and others who had shown "conclusively that there is no record that Ignatius issued to the Society a general prohibition on the reading of Erasmus' works"("Counter-Reformation" 17). In fact, as Olin had pointed out, "Erasmus was read in the Jesuit colleges and presumably by the members of the Society" (80).

O'Malley's perceptions of the "compatibility between Ignatian and Erasmian piety" stem from his appreciation of the "more accurate and authentic portrait of Erasmus" in major recent scholarship. O'Malley has put this revision in perspective.

> The antipathy of Jesuit authors like Broderick, Tacchi–Venturi, and most others to Erasmus sometimes surpasses that of the early Jesuits themselves, and they scold Erasmus almost as severely as they do the Protestant heretics. In the light of researches of the past twenty years, Erasmus has emerged vindicated on many issues. . . . Scholars now recognize in Erasmus one of the great theologians of his age, who so towered above his contemporaries in erudition and methodological presuppositions that they could not appreciate him. ("Fourth Vow" 7)

In his recent major study *The First Jesuits*, Fr. O'Malley persuasively confirms not only Professor Olin's earlier perceptions but also his own prescient insights regarding Jesuit attitudes toward Erasmus. He casts considerable doubt on the hoary tradition that Ignatius "was turned against Erasmus during his studies in Spain . . . by reading of the *Enchiridion*," noting that "the style and content of this work, especially in the Castilian translation, contained so much that was compatible with Ignatian *pietas* and little or nothing that ran counter to it." O'Malley stresses, however, the increasing virulence of Erasmus's enemies, which caused Jesuits "to avoid running the risk of such labeling [heresy] for their own new and fragile institutions." Clearly, prudence and caution, not strong antipathy, governed Ignatius's views about the works of Erasmus.

The second traditional "fact," O'Malley adds, that Ignatius "as general forbade all Jesuits read anything Erasmus wrote . . . is false. Ignatius never issued to the Society a universal binding prohibition of Erasmus's works." O'Malley concludes that:

> None of the early Jesuits, however, understood what Erasmus fully intended in those many works. Had they done so, they would have found much in them that was congenial to their own *pietas* and much that was helpful in dealing more effectively with the "mystical theology" they espoused. But their own training and the hatred for Erasmus that filled the atmosphere around them prevented them from appreciating his religious and theological message. (*First Jesuits* 260–64)

My own experience confirmed this recent revision (or "renaissance," as O'Malley called it) in Jesuit attitudes in education regarding Erasmus when four seminarians were assigned to my course in the Comparative Literature of Christian Humanism several years ago. The central reading in that course was the work of Erasmus. To my surprise, all four of those young Jesuits were enthusiastic about Erasmus and strongly recommended that, in the future, more time and emphasis be given to his work.

Woodward's statement (84) about the Jesuit curriculum would have prepared me for the reaction of these seminarians if the readings had been limited to Erasmus's inspiring *Enchiridion*. In that spiritual guide with its metaphor of the "soldier" of Christ was the familiar tone Ignatius so often employed. However, the seminarians also read with special enthusiasm and appreciation *The Praise of Folly*, particularly condemned by Jesuits. But then, these young men had a delightful sense of humor, and they could appreciate the sophistication of the playfulness in the "wisdom of the fool." That was certainly not the case with the grim and severe educators of the Counter-Reformation, particularly when Ignatius himself had been on the defensive against the Spanish Inquisition which had twice challenged his statements and then imprisoned him, first in Alcalá, and later in Salamanca (Bangert 13). To be associated in any way with the subtleties of Erasmian humor, let alone his criticism of false piety or corruption of true Christian ideals, was intolerable, even dangerous, for first-generation Jesuits.

Add to this that theological extremists found humor and consequent ambiguity in their violent strife to be worse than frivolous. As O'Malley notes, by the 1570s, when one of the first Jesuits, Alfonso Salmerón, was writing his commentaries on Erasmus's New Testament, "he deeply resented Erasmus' supposed failure to take a stand in the subsequent controversies and his committing the terrible 'crime of neutrality'—*crimen neutralitatis*" (*First Jesuits* 264). Nevertheless, Woodward correctly identified the Jesuits' cautious use of classic texts in their study of Latin directed toward moral instruction as the Erasmian curriculum in the *Ratio Studiorum* of 1599.

The *Ratio*, which remained in force until the suppression of the Society in 1773, was original neither in its program of study nor in the methods of instruction. It was a careful collection of rules regarding school practices; pedagogical principles were only inferred, not stated. In introducing the first English translation, Edward Fitzpatrick described it as "a practical handbook in educational method and school and class management. The system is greater than its expression. What made the Jesuits the schoolmasters of Europe was organization" (32).

This comprehensive system and purposeful organization, so well presented in the classic study by Francis Donnelly, s.j.., was truly original and highly effective for centuries. As John Donohue, s.j., noted more recently: "Erasmus may have recommended the same sort of methodology as the Jesuits, but Erasmus founded no network of schools" (30). The *Ratio* did indeed reflect the very best of the new humanist values and standards in education. It retained the merits of the medieval tradition while committing fully to the most progressive humanistic pedagogy put forward by the such Renaissance theorists as Erasmus, Vives, Piccolomini, and others.

Still, as Donohue observes, "It was not the love of learning for its own sake that inspired Ignatius" in the *Constitutions* to urge the preparation of the *Ratio*, but rather a practical moral purpose. This is what "sharply distinguished Ignatius from Erasmus whose . . . Christian humanism called for a simple amalgam of classical culture with Christian faith. One cannot imagine St. Ignatius talking about love of letters at all" (13). In fact, according to McGucken, Ignatius "was certainly not a scholar and had little of the humanist about him" (5).

Here, then, is the complexity in the achievements of Ignatius and Erasmus pointed to by O'Malley which makes their relationship so subtle to appreciate. Erasmus was as committed to the moral values of humanistic education as Ignatius was. But the great Dutch scholar had in mind a somewhat elite concept for the education of select young students in settings akin to tutorials, the only teaching he had ever practiced. Not so with the founders of the Jesuit schools or the authors of the *Ratio*.

O'Malley recently reviewed the gradual Jesuit commitment to the teaching mission, one that Ignatius most certainly had not originally intended or anticipated ("How Jesuits Changed" 28). The result was profound both in the schools' full engagement in classical learning using pagan texts, and in such modern studies as astronomy, physics, and, to great effect, theater, music, and dance.

Yet, certainly in the early years when the greatest tension between the Erasmian spirit and the counter reformers became most acute, a vast distinction was evident. With the authors of the *Ratio*, Erasmus was generally a reformer of morals, of society, and of the Church. But the Jesuit aims, according to McGucken, were far more deliberate and focused. He judged that Loyola and his Company could be called "utilitarian" in their employment of education to prevent heresy. "Once get control of the youth, train them in right principles, impart to them at the same time an education the equal or superior of any in Europe, and the whole world is saved for the church. Here was the concrete realization of Loyola's dream of conquering the land of the infidel" (McGucken 9; Ganss 173). Erasmus had no such plan.

In an important essay on Ignatius and humanism, François de Dainville, S.J., gives clear evidence of the delicate, rather precarious balance between Jesuit humanist classical scholarship and Jesuit dedication to a fervent moral purpose. Ignatius accepted the study of the classics as indispensable to the defense of Scripture and the Church. This was a lesson learned from his teachers at Alcalá University, where its founder, Cardinal Cisneros, had introduced a strong Erasmian influence. As Ignatius wrote in the definitive edition of the *Constitutions*, it was "proper to despoil Egypt of its ornaments to use them for the service and honor of God." Professor George Hardin Brown of Stanford University recently pointed out to me that Ignatius's use of "the venerable patristic allusion 'despoiling the Egyptians' shows that [he was] following some strong and safe precedents." Despite a certain uneasiness and concern about using the pagans, Ignatius maintained in a letter of 1555 to a young teacher that, as St. Paul said, "I have become all things to all men that I might save all" (qtd. in de Dainville 205).

It is in this context that we must understand the very complex relationship between Jesuit education and its use of Erasmus's theory and texts. True, Erasmus's works were banned by the Council of Trent. Yet, it is also true that "the early Jesuits, at least, came very near to venerating his memory and the Jesuit St. Peter Canisius spoke very highly of him" (Levi 28). The *Ratio Studiorum* took up many of his educational theories, and his *De copia*, an elaborate aid to the teaching of Latin composition, remained widely used in most Jesuit schools. The *Adages*, Latin composition examples from classical sources, and, most surprising, some of the highly ironic or satirical *Colloquies* were also used. Preserved Smith, in his splendid study of Erasmus, notes that these were often attacked as "depraved, obscene, impious, seditious." The *Adages* in Margaret Phillips's translation and the *Colloquies*, translated by Craig Thompson, reveal the full range of risks and hazards in using them, however selectively, to teach Latin in Jesuit schools.

The one Erasmian composition definitely not permitted in Jesuit education was the infamous *Praise of Folly*. Here, in its enigmatic, paradoxical, and sometimes caustic wit, was the dramatic antithesis to the straightforward moral rigor of the *Ratio Studiorum*. When we confront carefully all the necessary qualifications concerning the hoary convention of hostility by Ignatius toward Erasmus (who, after all, was decades older and never knew Ignatius or his work), we are left with a distinct contrast of religious imaginations in their methods of moral instruction, particularly in the enormously challenging *Praise of Folly*.

The story of the composition of Erasmus's *Folly*, this masterpiece of irony, is a familiar one. When Erasmus arrived in England in 1509 at the home of his beloved friend Thomas More, he was ill from the long journey. To amuse himself while he was recovering, he composed his *Moria Encomium* in several days simply from the vast store of learning in his memory. His title and dedication to More, whose wit was as delightful as that of his guest, played upon his host's name and the Greek *moria*, or folly. Together Erasmus and More had, on a previous visit, translated Lucian, the second-century Greek wit and satirist. The *Encomium* itself is a classic example of the Greek and Latin virtuoso mock-praise of, for example, the flea or of baldness. More was delighted with the result and urged Erasmus to publish this seemingly private bit of fun between guest and host. The *Folly* was soon greatly popular when it was widely circulated in many translations, a result of the new printing presses.

The absurdity of this artful composition should have been transparent to informed critics. The brilliant tribute to folly is delivered by Folly herself! How could anything be taken seriously in the sixteenth century when spoken by Folly and by a woman? Still, because both Erasmus and More were known to be strong advocates of equal education for women (as Woodward, and also Smith, demonstrated emphatically), one might have suspected a hidden irony.

As a matter of fact, as Folly's charming nonsense and drollery about our human foibles begin to take on a serious tone about church and political abuses, the reader is confronted with the famous paradox of the Cretan who declared that all Cretans are liars. Near the end of Folly's dazzling display of wit, she brings us to that magnificent and final paradox of the "wisdom of the fool," the famous "folly of the cross" and the "Christian fool" from Paul's First Letter to the Corinthians. And, finally, to leave us with the ultimate dilemma of the paradox, Folly concludes her oration with foolish comedy.

The ingenuity and subtlety of *Folly* make it one of the greatest works of world literature. To understand it, we must return to Greek comedy. Erasmus himself anticipated the comparison and attempted to deflect criticism. In his preface and dedication to More, he wrote: "I don't doubt that there will be busybodies to condemn the book. They will thunder out comparisons with the Old Comedy and the satires of Lucian" (Adams 4). Erasmus and More had translated a number of Lucian's satires into Latin, most of them by Erasmus, as we know from Thompson's English translation of their combined work. There is another significant clue in Erasmus's *De ratione studii* (1511), his method of instruction to learn Greek and Latin grammar. As "sound models of style . . . instructive by reason of their subject matter," he recommends the reading of Lucian as his first choice among Greek prose writers. Of the poets, in order of preference, he selects Aristophanes, Homer, and Euripides. "Menander, if we possessed his works, would take precedence of all three" (Woodward 164).

Erasmus was justified in denying identity with Greek Old Comedy, best exemplified by Aristophanes, because its harsh buffoonery lampooned individuals by name. This the Dutch humanist never did, certainly not in *Folly*. His preference for Menander, whose comedies we have only in imitation by the Romans Plautus and Terence, clearly connects Erasmus with Greek New Comedy. This was akin to the English comedy of manners of the Restoration and later, which satirized types and social groups rather than specific individuals. On the other hand, Erasmus could not so easily deny identity with Lucian's brilliant, rather caustic wit or his vigorous satire.

At the heart of the profound challenge in *The Praise of Folly* are its irony and paradox. The ability to recognize irony is often identified as one of the greatest tests of sophistication and intelligence. And paradox, as Rosalie Colie demonstrates in her splendid study, "necessarily attends upon those men brave enough to travel to the limits of discourse" (23).

All Christian mystery derives ultimately from the well-known paradox *credo quia absurdum est*, that is, belief in the "absurd" fact of the Incarnation. Erasmus's own greatest aim in his biblical exegesis and translations was to restore the vision and ideals of original Christianity, for which he has sometimes been labeled "primitivist." So he did indeed address emphatically the absurd in the Christian paradox. Olin notes the parallel with "St. Paul's famous transposition of wisdom and folly in the first letter to the Corinthians [I Cor. 1:18–28, 3:18–20, 4:10]." He observes that *Folly* "mirror[s] the ambiguity and puzzle of life itself," and that "Folly in her own person illustrates [St. Paul's] theme. Indeed her whole encomium may be called a sermon on this text and an exercise for her listener or reader in judging wisely what she has to say" (54, 55).

It is also important to understand the character of the "absurd" in Erasmus's Greek comedy model, and in the *Folly* itself. Werner Jaeger, in his brilliant *Paideia*, points out that the human person was defined in later Greek philosophy as more than a talking, thinking animal, as, rather, the only animal capable of laughter. "Thereby they placed laughter on the same plane with thought and speech, as an expression of intellectual freedom" (359). For Erasmus, freedom of the will and the intellect was a hallmark of the man in all his life and his work. That is why he moved from one European city to another whenever he foresaw restrictions imposed on his freedom to write as he felt he must. Also, his debate with Luther on free will, his *De libero arbitrio* (1524), was almost a manifesto of his commitment to intellectual freedom.

Plato, particularly in his *Symposium* and *Phaedo*, revealed that life is both a comedy and a tragedy, that the poet should be both a tragedian and a comedian. Jaeger adds: "The Olympians themselves became a laughing audience at a comedy. If even the mighty gods could laugh and be laughed at in this frankly comic way, the Greeks obviously felt that every human being . . . had not only the power of feeling heroic emotion and serious dignity, but the ability and the need to laugh." Thus, Attic theater coupled a tragedy with a comedy to show our complete humanity in the eternal spectacle of human nature and its weaknesses, as well as the ideal of classical perfection (Jaeger 360).

In *Homo Ludens,* his classic study on the play-element in culture, Johan Huizinga derives much of his concept of play and the ludic from Erasmus. The ludic, he asserts, is not ludicrous or ridiculous but playful, full of joy. "Play does not exclude seriousness." He saw the genius of Renaissance comedy in its essential ludic character. "Nothing could be more playful than Rabelais . . . while Cervantes remains the supreme magician of laughter and tears" (181). But the extremists of the Reformation and the Counter-Reformation could not tolerate the ludic manner in which Erasmus approached holy issues, the jocosity of his irony, and the "blithe wit he can never completely do without" (181). As Erasmus protested in a letter to one stiff-necked opponent: "In my opinion, it is quite unnecessary to act in the Schools as you act when playing cards or dice, where any infringement of the rules spoils the game. In a learned discussion, there should be nothing outrageous or risky in putting forth a novel idea" (qtd. in Huizinga 156).

Olin described *Folly* as "a kind of seriocomic joke," but not with the straightforward moral instruction of the *Enchiridion*. By employing the "wit, the irony, and the guile of the mischievous jester," Erasmus has caused readers much confusion and misunderstanding when they are shocked by the mockery of sacred things. Although Olin, quoting Louis Bouyer, found that Erasmus was "simply laughing at humbug," religious fanatics, so usual in his day, were outraged by *The Praise of Folly* as well as by many of his *Adages* and *Colloquies* for their ironic humor (8).

A new study by Walter Gordon on the seriocomic art of Erasmus also identifies the Lucianic wit in *Folly* and the *Colloquies*. Gordon is especially helpful in recognizing the "merry seriousness . . . the *aner spoudogeloios*, the festively grave men" in the Greek models of Lucian, Aristophanes, and Plato (63). His last chapters "Toward a Ludic Theology" present an important reconciliation of the serious and the ludic in Christian thought. He notes that Lucianic seriocomedy did "advance its own modest morality," but that the far more purposeful moral teaching of Erasmian seriocomedy was not easily recognized. The paradoxical irony of *Folly*, its "mingling the joke with more urgent material, [caused readers to become] confused as to where one leaves off and the other begins" (43).

What we have, then, in *The Praise of Folly* is a classic display of Socratic irony (Erasmus called him "St. Socrates") and a superb example of Montaigne's "Platonic paradox." In fact, it was Montaigne, who wrote often of his admiration for Erasmus, who best exemplified the French tradition of the *moraliste*, with irony and paradox as a challenging moral teaching method in the Socratic tradition.

Contrary to the English term "moralist"—one who admonishes in direct prescription and didactic instruction ("Thou shalt . . . thou shalt not . . .")—the *moraliste* confronts us with moral dilemmas in problem exposure. If we are sensitive to the moral problems, we must agonize or be fully *engagé* with our morality. The existentialist continues that tradition. The familiar term *Angst* comes, of course, quickly to mind. Or we can turn back to Job, the most profound of all the books in the Hebrew testament and the first great existentialist work, to appreciate the brilliant and troubling paradox displayed in *The Praise of Folly*.

Thus, it is entirely reasonable to me that the authors of the *Ratio Studiorum* would find it foolish to employ the indirect, confusing, and disturbing paradoxical method displayed in *The Praise of Folly*. Our experience with the ongoing debates about the meaning of the Book of Job and the effect of Socratic irony makes clear that such an approach to teaching is too complex and sophisticated for the straightforward moral purpose of the *Ratio*—which was directed toward youthful, not mature, students.

But, for mature readers, the moral teaching method of Erasmus in *Folly* is enormously effective in its own way. We should keep in mind the distinction made by William James between the "tough-minded" like Machiavelli and the "tender-minded" thinkers of the Renaissance like Erasmus, Ficino, Pico, Montaigne, and the Cambridge Platonists. With Erasmus, the true spirit of *caritas*, as in the teachings of Paul, enlightens his dazzling ludic moral paradox. Erasmus, the "Prince of Humanists," as Schurhammer calls him, is a teacher with compassion, fully aware of our foibles and ignorance, and amused (and bemused) at our contradictions, inconsistencies, and self-delusion. That same awareness is splendidly realized later in the *Essays* of Montaigne. With him as with Erasmus, humor is not frivolous or trivial. Rather, it is seriocomic, charitable, sympathetic, and *true*.

Erasmus would have agreed with Horace Walpole's familiar comment in 1776, that life is a comedy to those who think and a tragedy to those who feel. It is again the comedy and tragedy of life in Plato's *Philebus*. And, it is the ultimate paradoxical confrontation, the "folly" of our existence, with which the *moraliste* would leave us forever morally *engagé*. But, again, I accept that such sophisticated and disturbing ambiguity could never be appropriate moral instruction according to the intentions of the *Ratio Studiorum*.

Think of the effect in the classroom of posing such dilemmas as Erasmus does! We so often hear Thomas Gray's familiar words "Ignorance is bliss." But the apparent source of that popular irony is not Erasmus's meaning in *Folly*, although simplistic reading may suggest it. The spirit of the work is far more profound and disturbing: If ignorance is bliss, 'tis folly to be wise. We are left to ponder the meaning of wisdom in contrast to learned and pompous nonsense, as well as the desirability or even possibility of ignorance. Such *moraliste* teaching seems a great folly to many educators. Think of Socrates's "Know thyself," to which I add, "if you dare." Would we risk Leoncavallo's *Pagliacci* in the classroom when Canio, at the end of the comedy, actually stabs his own wife, Nedda, to death, then steps to the front of the stage and informs the audience, "*La commedia è finita*"?

Mikhail Bakhtin observes the duality in the seriocomic in an essay on Rabelais and the complex nature of medieval carnival laughter that perceives the world in its laughing aspect: "[I]ts final and complete expression at the highest level of the Renaissance [is] Erasmus's *The Praise of Folly*, one of the greatest creations of carnival laughter in world literature" (qtd. in Adams 317).ä And Carlos Fuentes in his essay on Don Quixote noted "the influence of Erasmus on Cervantes in three themes common to the philosopher and the novelist: the duality of truth, the illusion of appearances, and the praise of folly" (193).

Such problems in ambivalence and paradox are hardly the kind that the traditional and conventional moralist would expose to students who are to be formed with a prescribed morality. Fr. O'Malley's perception about a new, more sophisticated, appreciation of the complex teachings of Erasmus is important to us. We have now both a clearer sense of "the compatibility of Erasmian and Ignatian piety" *and* a helpful recognition of the enormous difference in the religious imagination and the methods of two great moral teachers.

Works Cited

Adams, Robert M., ed. and trans. *Desiderius Erasmus: The Praise of Folly and Other Writings*. New York: Norton, 1989.

Bangert, William V., s.j. *A History of the Society of Jesus.* St. Louis: Institute of Jesuit Sources, 1972.
Barthel, Manfred. *The Jesuits.* Trans. Mark Howson. New York: Morrow, 1984.
Colie, Rosalie L. *Paradoxia Epidemica: The Renaissance Tradition of Paradox.* 1966. Hamden, CT: Shoe String P, 1976.
Dainville, François de, s.j. "Saint Ignatius and Humanism." Trans. J. Robert Barth, s.j., and John M. Culkin, s.j. *Jesuit Educational Quarterly* 21 (1959): 189–208.
Donnelly, Francis P., s.j. *Principles of Jesuit Education in Practice.* New York: Kenedy, 1934.
Donohue, John W., s.j. *Jesuit Education.* New York: Fordham UP, 1963.
Erasmus, Desiderius. *The Colloquies of Erasmus.* Trans. Craig R. Thompson. Chicago and London: U of Chicago P, 1965.
———. *The Translations of Lucian by Erasmus and St. Thomas More.* Trans. Craig R. Thompson. Ithaca: Vail-Ballou, 1940.
Farrell, Allan P., s.j. *The Jesuit Code of Liberal Education.* Milwaukee: Bruce, 1938.
Fitzpatrick, Edward A., ed. *St. Ignatius and the Ratio Studiorum.* New York: McGraw-Hill, 1933.
Fuentes, Carlos. "Don Quixote or the Critique of Reading." *Wilson Quarterly* Autumn 1977: 186–202.
Ganss, George E., s.j. *Saint Ignatius' Idea of a Jesuit University.* Milwaukee: Marquette UP, 1954.
Gordon, Walter H. *Humanist Play and Belief: The Seriocomic Art of Desiderius Erasmus.* Toronto: U of Toronto P, 1990.
Huizinga, Johan. *Homo Ludens: A Study of the Play-Element in Culture.* 1950. Trans. R. F. C. Hull. Boston: Beacon, 1955.
Ignatius of Loyola. *The Constitutions of the Society of Jesus.* Trans. and intro. George E. Ganss, s.j. St. Louis: Institute of Jesuit Sources, 1970.
Jaeger, Werner. *Paideia.* Vol. 1. 1939. Trans. Gilbert Highet. Oxford: Oxford UP, 1969. 3 vols.
Johnson, Paul. *A History of Christianity.* New York: Atheneum, 1976.
Levi, A. H. T. Introduction. *Praise of Folly.* By Desiderius Erasmus. Trans. Betty Radice. Middlesex: Penguin, 1971.
McGucken, William J., s.j. *The Jesuits and Education.* New York: Bruce, 1932.
Mitchell, David. *The Jesuits.* New York: Watts, 1981.
Olin, John C. *Six Essays on Erasmus.* New York: Fordham UP, 1979.
O'Malley, John W., s.j. *The First Jesuits.* Cambridge, Massachusetts: Harvard UP, 1993.
———. "The Fourth Vow in Its Ignatian Context." *Studies in the Spirituality of Jesuits* 15 (1983): 1–45.

———. "How the Jesuits Changed: 1540–56." *America* 27 July 1991: 28–32.

———. "The Jesuits, St. Ignatius, and the Counter-Reformation." *Studies in the Spirituality of +Jesuits* 15 (1982): 1–28.

Phillips, Margaret Mann. *The "Adages" of Erasmus: A Study with Translations*. Cambridge: Cambridge UP, 1964.

Rahner, Hugo, s.j.. *The Spirituality of St. Ignatius of Loyola*. Trans. Francis J. Smith, s.j. Chicago: Loyola UP, 1953.

Rummel, Erika, ed. *The Erasmus Reader*. Toronto: U of Toronto P, 1990.

Scaglione, Aldo. *The Liberal Arts and the Jesuit College System*. Amsterdam: Benjamins, 1986.

Schurhammer, Georg, s.j. *Francis Xavier: His Life and Times*. Trans. M. Joseph Costelloe, s.j. Rome: The Jesuit Historical Institute, 1973.

Smith, Preserved. *Erasmus*. New York: Harper, 1923.

Woodward, William Harrison. *Desiderius Erasmus Concerning the Aim and Method of Education*. New York: Teachers College, Columbia U, 1964.

5 • Blind Prophecy: Milton's Figurative Mode in *Paradise Lost*

William Franke

PARADISE LOST PRESENTS ITSELF as Christian prophetic poetry. By invoking the "Heav'nly Muse" that inspired Moses, and by endeavoring to soar above all the classical founts of poetic inspiration, Milton places his poem in the tradition of sacred poetry originating in the Bible and claiming to deliver not merely human wisdom but divine truth.[1] Yet Milton's theological outlook made it by and large impossible for him to adopt the characteristic poetics of this tradition as it was handed down to him through such works as the *Divina Commedia*, the *Gerusalemme Liberata*, and the *Fairie Queene*. All these works share the problem of representing a human story, or we might even say *the* human story, as having a wider and deeper significance, a higher truth, in the light of Christian revelation. If human affairs by the aid of Christian revelation can be seen in their ultimate meaning, then it is the prophetic poet's task precisely to find the means of figuring that meaning in the story he relates.

The methods of accomplishing this developed by *Paradise Lost*'s Christian prophetic forebears can generally be subsumed under various forms of allegory. Whether allegory is conceived Neoplatonically, as it generally was by Christian poets, as relating the visible world to "the invisible things which are above" in "heavenly places in Christ," or after the fashion of biblical typology as establishing an analogy between what we *now* see as in a glass darkly with what we will *then* see face to face, Christian allegory constitutes a mode of externalizing spiritual truth, giving it some intuitable shape that human intellect can grasp.² Milton, however, for reasons of his own, or rather of his Reformed religion, was not able to accept, if not in strictly limited ways, such methods. For the status of the image as vehicle of truth had been undermined by the Reformation's ardent iconoclasm. He needed to redefine radically the status of imagery from that of being a gross embodiment or shadowy type of invisible truth to that of a heuristic device used and consumed in provoking an immediate, subjective, nonobjectifiable relation to a truth that could not be iconographically realized at all.³

In other words, Milton as a prophetic poet could surrender neither the image nor the truth. Using a third option, he retained both but disconnected them, so that the image no longer functioned as an outward manifestation and representation of how things really are, but rather fed the reader's personal experience of the poem, where truth could be encountered in spiritual immediacy. In this way, the direct address of the Word to each individual conscience, which became paramount in the Reformation, might find a channel in prophetic poetry. This peculiar (and proto-Symbolist) figurative mode had far-reaching consequences for Milton's style and for the structural dynamics of his poem.

A close reading of a not atypical passage will serve to isolate characteristic stylistic effects of Milton's image-suspicious poetics. The concluding lines of Book II, relating Satan's emergence from Chaos into sight of the created world, illustrate the aptitude of Milton's style for shedding an emotional aura rather than achieving sharp imagistic definition:

> But now at last the sacred influence
> Of light appears, and from the walls of Heav'n
> Shoots far into the bosom of dim Night
> A glimmering dawn; here Nature first begins
> Her fardest verge, and Chaos to retire
> As from her outmost works a brok'n foe
> With tumult less and with less hostile din,
> That Satan with less toil, and now with ease
> Wafts on the calmer wave by dubious light
> And like a weather-beaten Vessel holds
> Gladly the Port, though Shrouds and Tackle torn;
> Or on the emptier waste, resembling Air,
> Weighs his spread wings, at leisure to behold

> Far off th' Empyreal Heav'n, extended wide
> In circuit, undetermin'd square or round,
> With Opal Tow'rs and Battlements adorned
> Of living Sapphire, once his native Seat;
> And fast by hanging in a golden Chain
> This pendent world, in bigness as a Star
> Of smallest Magnitude close by the Moon.
> Thither full fraught with mischievous revenge,
> Accurst, and in a cursed hour he hies.
>
> (II.1034–55)

Beginning with the phrase "the sacred influence / Of light appears," Milton prefers a generally felt, rather than specifically seen, "influence" as grammatical subject, even though what actually "appears" must be the light itself, which in a more exact statement would assume the nominative (rather than a genitive) function. This slight displacement of predication toward the impalpable gives priority to emotional radiance over image, as does a phrase like "living Saffire," where whatever may be living about the sapphire cannot be directly seen but only sensed. Both "sacred" and "living" are highly radiant adjectives, charged with the wonder and warmth of the divine, within the poem's Christian-symbolic idiom.

This iridescence at the linguistic level overlays a represented world (laminal Chaos) which is left "dim" and "glimmering." Heaven itself is not clearly seen but is conceptualized instead in explicitly indeterminate terms as "undetermin'd square or round," thereby thematizing the unfocused, in fact unrealizable, quality of what is described. The enriching of verbal resonances but blurring of the object represented is further promoted by recurring redundancies which multiply opaque folds in the verbal veil of the verses. Expressions such as "first begins" and "fardest verge" give a stirring ring of ultimacy to the words as signifiers but do not help to delineate referential content any more than does "hanging . . . pendent."[4]

On closer examination, however, these redundancies, while contributing nothing to the narrative, turn out to be among the devices by which Milton suggests thematic issues for the reader's consideration. The word "first" in this poem, as previously heard in "first disobedience" and "first seduc'd," invests what is being described with archetypal significance, inscribing it within Milton's story of all things, the alpha and the omega. The word "fardest" bears the same weight of totality implicit in the archetype, transposing it into a spatial dimension. All nature and history are thus encompassed, and this desired universality motivates the lack of distinctness in particulars that we have observed. In like manner, the other narratively superfluous repetition, the double allusion to the fact of the earth's being suspended from heaven, upgrades this structural element to a moral and theological theme: such dependency, by being doubly stated, is confirmed as the all-important characteristic of the sublunary world. As the chain from heaven to earth tautens into a tautology, this dependency becomes the necessary general character of the terrestrial.

To similar effect, when we are told that the earth is "in bigness as a Star," but then are immediately checked in our imagining this bigness by the sequel "Of smallest Magnitude," this thwarting of our smooth reception of the image actually facilitates our grasp of the meaning standing behind, or perhaps getting in front and in the way of, the image: it impresses on us the utter relativity of all earthly greatness, the bigness we have conceived being undercut one line lower.

The other similes in the passage similarly work not to specify and resolve descriptions, but rather to set up patterns of thematic coherence at one remove from the story line. These similes, like those in Book I, suffer from syntactic dislocations that impede their smooth integration into the narrative: for instance, the uncertain connection of the "That Satan" clause with what precedes it and the conflation of tenor and vehicle in "like a weather-beaten Vessel holds / Gladly the Port, though Shrouds and Tackle torn." These descriptive imprecisions work like the simile clusters in Book I which digress from the actual situation of the fallen angels on the abyss of fire, defeating its accurate depiction, but indirectly suggesting its thematic significance for a reader. The Leviathan figure for Satan, for example, leads to a story about a navigator by night mistakenly anchoring in the "scaly rind," which is irrelevant to picturing Satan supine on the fiery lake, although it is proleptically ominous considering the poem's overall theme.

Something else which undermines or at least ironizes the similes in our passage as aids to the realization of the narrative is that they are for the most part disanalogies to the situation and action represented. Chaos's retiring is compared to an army's retreating, but "With tumult less and with less hostile din." Likewise, the qualification of "the emptier waste" in which Satan spreads his wings as "resembling Air" serves more to stress that there is only a semblance of air than to provide any concrete vehicle for visualization; a resemblance to air is too vague to be imagined anyway, and we are left rather with a concept of what the empty waste is not.

The information-bearing value of Milton's images is often nil, for they do not articulate an objective state of affairs, which would be to represent truly. Instead they communicate tone and other such musical values, stirring emotion which may lead the reader to inward apprehension of an unarticulated and inarticulable truth. Exactly homologous to the reader's immediate relation to truth, in this account, is the prophetic poet's relation to his Heav'nly Muse, from whom he claims to receive the words of his poem as by a kind of mental automatic writing. She is invoked as

> . . . my Celestial Patroness, who deigns
> Her nightly visitation unimplored,
> And dictates to me slumb'ring, or inspires
> Easy my unpremeditated Verse. . . .
>
> (IX.21–24)

In this description of his inspiration Milton is being dictated to; he does not see anything. He is not, like Dante—a foil to which he will recur frequently in examining Milton's representations of transcendence—a traveler through fully objectified worlds beyond the grave. His poem is the record of his being visited rather than his visiting, and so it is not all his but also "Hers who brings it nightly to my *Ear*" (IX.46–47; emphasis added). For Milton, to "see and tell" of things invisible to mortal sight seems to be all one thing, bypassing the mediation of the visual object; and in this sense his prophecy is blind.

Milton would undoubtedly have taken satisfaction in thinking that this came close to what the Hebrew prophets meant by such phrases as "The word of the Lord came upon me" and "Then I was in the spirit. . . ." Whatever truth is communicated does not inhere in the images as some sort of "real presences." It is in the nonobjectifiable connection with the divine. Of course Milton does not avoid images. His poetry is as rich in them as any. But they do not embody truth, not even the truth which his poem would communicate about the ways of God to men. The imagery is in this relative sense irrelevant.[5]

Nevertheless, and perhaps all the more for this reason, Milton's images work upon the reader's feelings, instilling a sense of grandeur, arousing emotion, bringing about the heightened state of sensitivity in which one is susceptible to immediately confronting the truth about things, by the light of Christian revelation, and understanding with sudden moral insight the reality of one's own life-story in its identity with the universal human story. Thus, the images have a sacred function; they are used paraenetically, as if in preaching, to exhort and edify. But they are emphatically not sacramental, in the way of images in the *Inferno*, which are manifest embodiments that enable us to see God's judgment, the absolute and final truth about each individual, in each visible detail of form and gesture. For Dante, the ways of God, the divine punishments and rewards in which human lives attain their absolute significance, are fully manifest in symbolic representation.[6] For Milton, representation is radically alien from God, though like everything in creation, including evil, potentially an instrument for achieving God's purposes.

This theologically motivated dissociation of truths from its representation stands behind many of the quite unorthodox and perplexing features of Milton's style. In numerous cases elaborate descriptions are undercut and whisked away, detailed development notwithstanding, as mere fictions: Orpheus's mother, for instance, invoked in the proem of Book VII to save her son, turns out in the very last words of the verse paragraph to be an "empty dream," and simultaneously in her train vanish not only the Thracian bard himself but the whole "wild rout" of Bacchus and revelers, until then seen rioting in the woods of Rhodope. Or again, Mulciber's picturesque fall like a shooting star from the "Crystal Battlements" of Heaven is drawn out "from Morn / To Noon . . . from Noon to dewy Eve, / A Summer's day; and with the setting Sun . . ." (I.742–44), only to be cast off as a flight of fancy in the ensuing line with the jolt of an enjambment: "Thus they relate, / Erring." Such illusory displays, as they thus turn out to be, are in this way demoted from the status of primary figurations of the poem's central myth or truth.[7] They are not accorded this highest degree of poetic reality.

The fully elaborated objectifications of the poem swing loose from its divine meaning and message. They are not allowed to incarnate the poem's true significance. The relation to truth in *Paradise Lost* remains that of sheer immediacy, of the blind poet to his directly dictating Muse, or of the reader to apprehensions stimulated by the poem in its powerful music and emotion, but not symbolically crystallized in the abundant materializations of the poem, which drift off as not belonging to its essence, as having merely facilitated the experience without permanently embodying the poem's intrinsic meanings.

The problem with Milton's style (and with the figurative mode it embodies) is not that it fails to achieve concreteness or externality. There is much more abstract theology in the *Divina Commedia* than in *Paradise Lost*. The problem is that the really quite impressive realization at the visual surface is not anchored to truth; the poem's materializations do not (nor are they meant to) adequately represent its deeper meanings. The relation of sacramentality, whereby the divine manifests itself materially in the world, has been broken. Whereas Dante's imagery as a rule asserts its veracity as unequivocal representation of truth, Milton's imagery tends to call attention to itself *qua* imagery, i.e., to its status as untruth, as mere poetic invention. As soon as he departs from the express word of Scripture and its postulated truth, Milton's representations of the Garden of Eden are merely hypothetical and are even tagged as such:

> . . . Hesperian fables true,
> If true, *here only*. . . .
>
> (IV.250–51; emphasis added)

Milton's lack of a figurative code for representing the true world in images results in the structures of doubling and parodic imitation which pervade *Paradise Lost*. It is no longer possible to assign univocal meanings to imagery as in Dante's World. Thus, "heaven resembles hell" (II.268), and the Father's relationship with his "Only begotten Son" (II.80) is mirrored by Satan and his "own begotten" (II.782) perfect image, Sin, as well as by the calamitous couple, equally parthenogenetic, Adam and Eve. The poet himself whose song "with no middle flight intends to soar" (I.15) cannot escape comparison to Satan who "soars" (II.634), as well as association with Jove usurping and his Olympians in the "middle air" (I.514–16). Similarly, uncontrollable proliferation of parodies riddles the imagery of prospect as it travels from God to Adam and Satan and to the poet's own implicit prospect over all the scenes narrated in the poem, taking on a series of contradictory connotations with no clear criteria of distinction between good gazing and evil. And the same must be said for the language of dominion and monarchy which invests by turns Adam, Satan, and the Almighty. In all these instances, figuration in a world which lacks objectivity and in which the truth of things is dissociated from their visual image has become equivocation.

Often lexical links, such as the "link of nature" language used to describe both Adam's attachment to Eve after her fall and Sin's desire for her father, whom she pursues by building a bridge across Chaos, point up parody and ambiguity at the linguistic surface. But even at the poem's foundations, the pervasive ironies which riddle the structure of *Paradise Lost*, and which have been interpreted as undermining Milton's orthodoxy, can be understood as consequences of the ineradicable equivocity of Milton's figurative mode. The fact that God seems to be represented as a self-serving tyrant made gratuitously ogre-like and a power-mongre in Book III, just as if the Devil spoke truth about him in Books I and II,[8] may be understood as deriving from this intrinsic equivocity. Like the absolutely good person, God himself, so also the absolutely good place *a priori*, the Garden, assumes an ambiguous valence with the suggestion that perhaps only expelled from Paradise can Adam and Eve be "happier far" in the "Paradise within."

The fact that representation is incurably equivocal is effectively pointed up by the exact equivalence of the celestial and the infernal courts in the scenes representing, respectively, Satan's and the Son's volunteering for tasks that daunt all the others. Just as in hell "all sat mute, / Pondering the danger with deep thoughts" (II.420–21), so "all he Heav'nly Quire stood mute . . . [none] durst upon his own head draw the deadly forfeiture . . . (III.217–21). The implication of such coinciding imagery seems inescapably to be that both courts are full of self-servers and that God like Satan exploits the situation for self-glorification.

Parallels and parodies which seem to vitiate the poem's ostensible program crop up incessantly where they could be easily avoided. It seems perverse that, just after Eve's satanically inspired dream enticing her to covet the forbidden fruit in order to become Godlike, Raphael should turn up talking about food and suggesting it may constitute a way of participating with angels and transcending corporeality:

> . . . time may come when men
> With Angels may participate, and find
> No inconvenient Diet, nor too light Fare:
> And from these corporal nutriments perhaps
> Your bodies may at last turn all to spirit,
> Improv'd by tract of time, and wing'd ascend
> Ethereal, as we, or may at choice
> Here or in Heav'nly Paradises dwell. . . .
>
> (V.493–500)

The voice in the dream, extolling the "Fruit Divine . . . able to make Gods of Men," had coaxed:

> Taste this, and be henceforth among the Gods
> Thyself a Goddess, not to Earth confined,
> But sometimes in the Air, as we, sometimes
> Ascend to Heav'n, by merit thine, and see
> What life the Gods live there, and such live thou.
>
> (V.77–81)

Satan's false promise of being able to fly to heaven is unmistakably reprised in Raphael's divinely commissioned words, with verbatim echoes such as "ascend" in metrically emphatic positions, and the very same pattern of inference and persuasion.

A related consequence of the dissociation of meaning and image is uncontrolled fertility in both images and meanings, none of which, however, is definitive. The visible heavens seem to manifest an excess of creativity—beyond the measure of the useful—which bothers Eve. When she asks Adam the reason, he produces an excess of explanations, which nonetheless do not adequately explain why there should be so many stars shining at night, as is proved by his later posing to Raphael the same question of

> How Nature wise and frugal could commit
> Such disproportions, with superfluous hand. . . .
>
> (VIII.26–27)

The unchecked fecundity of creation is similarly a problem arousing anxiety when Eve worries that the garden is getting out of control—that is why she suggests to Adam that they separate, since they are losing time from work because of amorous dalliance made inevitable by close proximity. And again after the Fall the fear of her own fertility prompts Eve to propose a suicide pact with Adam. All these anxieties are erroneous but inevitable in a world whose true meaning cannot be made manifest. Such anxieties are not allayed by rational demonstrations—such as Dante receives in such abundance from his guides Vergil and Beatrice, whose discourses on love and the generation of the soul, free will, predestination, and the influence of heavenly bodies on human character, moon spots, angelic hierarchy, faith, and everything else that raises doubts in Dante's mind end by satisfying his intellect within its inherent limitations. The solution for Milton's creatures can lie only in practical virtue and trust; that is, in

> . . . What thou canst attain, which best may serve
> To glorify thy Maker, and infer
> Thee also happier. . . .
>
> (VII.115–17)

In the injunctions to know only what is useful (cf., e.g., VII.112–20; VIII.191–97), Adam and Eve are denied all knowledge of what is true *per se*. What it is right for them to believe depends on a morality of obedience rather than on how things actually are and can be seen to be. Small wonder, then, that Milton should be unable to represent truly the things that are above (or are to come), since

> God to remove his ways from human sense,
> Plac'd Heav'n from Earth so far, that earthly sight,
> If it presume, might err in things too high,
> And no advantage gain.
>
> VIII.119–22)

From a Catholic and Dantean perspective, the basic problem is loss of the interpretative key which enables human beings to know by means of their senses the true meanings of things. For Dante this key was provided by the Incarnation. All the perceptible world pointed to a true Being revealed through God's entering the world, taking on body, and becoming man. Theologically, Milton hedges on the doctrine of the Incarnation; this is entailed by his Arianism, all but explicitly avowed in *The Christian Doctrine*, and evinced by the disparities, even clashes, between the Father and the Son in Book III of *Paradise Lost*. In Milton's poetry the incarnation of the Word transmogrifies it from revelation to equivocation. Everything divine, when reflected in the created universe, is susceptible to Satanic perversion.

These and an entire interweave of other ambiguities and equivocations can be understood as deriving from lack of a symbolic mode for expressing truth objectively. Because there is no objective origin in extra-verbal vision, a transcendental signified that can stand as the unifying sense of the variety of poetic signifiers, Milton's figuration tends to disaggregation and to inadvertent, or in any case subversive, parody. The figurative becomes equivocal. Milton does claim continuity with the Christian prophetic tradition, but in his re-enactment of the office of prophetic poet prophecy has become blind. What the poet sees and makes seen is a powerfully moving stimulus to that moral fervor in which alone the truth may be apprehended. But that truth is never made visibly objective. It is to be encountered—even by the reader of *Paradise Lost*—only in the blinding immediacy of inspiration in the Spirit. This "Protestant principle," which effectively governs the poetics of Milton's prophetic work, by extension from his Reformed way of reading Scripture,[9] is clinched near the conclusion of the poem by the archangel Michael's reference to

> . . . the truth
> With superstitions and traditions taint
> Left only in those written Records pure,
> Though not but by the Spirit understood.
>
> (XII.512–14)

Milton's Early Poems and Reformed Religion

In retrospect, the theologically motivated figurative mode that was to come to maturity in *Paradise Lost* can be discerned as emergent in Milton's early poems. We have seen that Milton's conception of poetic inspiration as direct action on the poet's faculties of the Heav'nly Muse, his "Celestial Patroness," who dictates to him unpremeditated verses while he sleeps, with no mediation through visual objects, shows up lucidly against the backdrop of certain orientations of Protestant religion, specifically its stress on the immediate relation between the individual and the divine, bypassing church hierarchy and the sacramental system. Milton's early poems in the prophetic mode record his development toward a style of prophecy consonant with these accents of Reformed theology. Indeed, certain of his early efforts register the impulse toward immediacy in the relation with divinity to such a degree as sometimes to threaten to cancel out altogether expression in poetry, with its projection of a verisimilar world of manifest forms. The palpable embodiment in images and in an externalized field of figures that is so essential to prophetic poetry as we find it in Dante—to revert one more time to this touchstone—runs a risk in the early poems of losing its ability to mediate the divine, like Catholic ceremony and sacramental rite, no longer needed or tolerated in Reformed religion.

Signally revealing of Milton's impatience with embodiment of religious truth in poetic imagery is his conflicted approach to (and withdrawal from) the theme of the Incarnation. Milton would come to reject the fully Catholic doctrine of the Incarnation and embrace Arianism only later,[10] but at this point the theological tendency and its correlative poetics are already clearly detectable.

The inaugural poem of Milton's career as prophetic poet,[11] "On the Morning of Christ's Nativity," thrusts straight to this theological crux, and yet betrays an aversion to its own central theme, the incarnation of a divine being, God the Son, as a human being, what the Fourth Gospel declares in the phrase: "the Word became flesh and dwelt among us." This is seen first in the way Nature, in the poem, recoils from a material incarnation of divinity, shrinking in shame at the approach of her Maker, taking advantage of the wintry season to "hide her guilty front with innocent Snow" (ll.39). Like Nature hiding her outward, sensuous form, Milton writes shy of any material representation adequate to his divine theme, invoking rather a musical modality of pure immediacy, which induces a state of rapture that knows no external visual representation. Indeed, the heavenly music that accompanies the birth threatens to short-circuit the whole history of redemption in which Christ is embodied in his Church and its work: "For if such holy song / Enwrap our fancy long, / Time will run back and fetch the Age of Fold . . ." (XIV.133–35). Time may run back or forward—it hardly matters—to the unfallen state of concord with God or "perfect diapason," as in "At a Solemn Music," where again music represents the modality of the immediate apprehension of the divine.

More than celebrating the Incarnation, the Nativity Hymn grasps after Apocalypse. This is evident, for example, in the marshal imagery of "helmed Cherubim / And sworded Seraphim" (XI.112–13), which upstages Luke's pastoral scene of angels appearing to the shepherds, and in the persistence of allusions such as those to the trumpets clanging on Mount Sinai "while the red fire and smouldering clouds out brake" (XVII.159). This apocalyptic impetus forces the narrator to try to apply brakes—"But wisest Fate says No, / This must not yet be so, / The Babe lies yet in smiling Infancy" (XVI.149–51)—so as to give time to the baby Jesus to grow up, as well as time to the Church for its one and two-thirds' millenia, and however much longer, of history. As much as it may be deferred, however, still the clamor of apocalypse encroaches by the end even of this very stanza: "Yet first to those ychained in sleep / The wakeful trump of doom must thunder through the deep" (XVI.155–56).

Divinity is essentially to be heard and not seen, because it belongs to another world which sounds can announce, rather than to anything that can actually be seen and represented in the flesh. "At a Solemn Music" presences the vision of God enthroned in heaven, saluted by "divine sounds of Saintly shout and solemn Jubilee," as an essentially musical experience, invoking Voice and Verse, "pledges of Heaven's joy," in order that they "to our Highrais'd fantasy present / That undisturbed Song of pure concent" (5–6). Similarly "Il Penseroso" dissolves its richly symbolic and almost sacerdotal religious imagination, figuring a cathedral service, into music as the mode in which transcendence is "seen" through the ear:

> There let the pealing Organ blow
> To the full voic'd Choir below
> In Service high and Anthems clear,

> As may with sweetness, through mine ear,
> Dissolve me into ecstasies,
> And bring all Heav'n before mine eyes.
>
> (162–67)

The resort to music in these poems, as in the Hymn on the Nativity itself, gestures toward an ultimate revelation and unveiling beyond images.

Only by a deflection from the Incarnation (i.e., the union and organic integration of the divine with the human) to the rout of the pagan idols, drawn out over seven full stanzas, is the Nativity Ode able to create the imaginative space necessary for poetry as opposed to apocalypse, and so allow for elegiac and pastoral modes, as in

> The lonely mountains o'er
> And the resounding shore,
>   A voice of weeping heard, and loud lament;
> From haunted spring and dale
> Edged with poplar pale,
>   The parting Genius is with sighing sent;
> With flower-in woven tresses torn
> The Nymphs in twilight shade of tangled thickets mourn.
>
> (XX.181–89)

This lament of the departing local spirits, not part of the Gospel tradition at all (though suggested by Jeremiah's voice of lamentation and the weeping of Rachel for her children cited by Matthew as a prophecy of the slaughter of the innocents), opens an elegiac vein which runs luxuriously throughout a leisurely and picturesque poetic dilation: "Nor is Osiris seen / In Mempian grove or green, / Trampling the enshowered grass with lowings loud . . ." (XXIV.213–15) Only thus is the poem saved from foreclosing, by a premature apocalyptic event, the salvation history that begins a new phase with the Incarnation.

A similar pressure of immediacy, which in the Nativity Ode tends to press poetry into apocalypse, altogether impatient of the veils, deferrals, and endless mediations that characterize a tradition of poetry as prophetic revelation by means of allegory, can be felt especially strongly even in the diptych made up of "L'Allegro" and "Il Penseroso," where Milton conceives the ambition to "attain / To something like Prophetic strain" (173–74). There is a scheme of specular correspondences between the two poems whereby each successive motif—from shepherds to Shakespeare—in one is loosely matched in the other by some comparable theme given a different twist and emphasis. The "beauty" in "L'Allegro"—potentially Milton's Beatriceä—who in the tower "lies / The cynosure of neighboring eyes" (79–80) turns out in the correlative tower image of "Il Penseroso" to be none other than Milton himself, alone—"Or let my lamp at midnight hour / Be seen in some high lonely tower"—contemplating the constellations by "immortal mind" (85ff.). Here again there is no external object for Milton's prophetic faculty, but only immediate inspiration. Prophetic/poetic power is connected with the absence of the image, and that perhaps explains why Orpheus loses his "half-regained Eurydice" (105) in the outward-oriented activity and poetry of "L'Allegro" but recovers her ("made Hell grant what love did seek" [108]) in the inward contemplation of "Il Penseroso." In *Paradise Lost* Milton would fully realize what already seems to be anticipated here: prophetic sight accrues with loss of the view of Nature's book (III, proem).

By the time he wrote *Paradise Lost* Milton had learned how to manage the compulsion toward immediacy in the apprehension of the divine, so as to allow room for poetry and its mediation, its unfolding in rhetoric and images, of ecstatic experience. He had learned methods of indirection, whereby the divine, although not symbolically concretizable, can be suggested to the individual reader's experience through music and imagery.

The loosening up of symbolic as well as of syntactic structure that we observed in *Paradise Lost* affords Milton the opportunity to employ the persuasive and affecting resources of poetry, rather than apodictic statement and sacramental image of truth as in Dante, to the end of provoking in the reader an apprehension of the divine. This experience of immediacy, of transcendence, of accession of imaginative power in the Spirit, is Milton's substitute for an objective language of truth. Thus, debate as to whether the symbolism in the Garden (e.g., of the "four main streams" that flow from Paradise's fountain and ramify into "mazy error") is Neoplatonic or typological (Madsen 2) misses the fundamental point that either type of symbolism, if there, is there primarily for "effect." For these are for Milton not modes of figuring the true and the real but at most techniques of creating resonances or a sense of foreboding—with the proviso that the calculated effect may be as momentous as religious conversion.

Notes

1. Quotations of Milton's works are from Hughes, ed. I wish to acknowledge that my participation in the seminar on Milton under the direction of Stephen Knapp at the University of California, Berkeley in spring 1988 was the seed-bed of a number of points developed in this essay.

2. More detailed consideration of Milton's stance vis-à-vis antecedent traditions of poetic allegory and prophecy can be found in Kates and in Samuel.

3. The view that sees Milton's poetry as a kind of "self-consuming artifact" is associated especially with the approach of Fish.

4. Observations on the characteristic "indistinctness and inconsistency" of Milton's descriptions, to borrow a phrase from T. B. Macaulay's famous *Essay on Milton* (1825), are commonplace throughout the critical tradition. Cf. especially T. S. Eliot's classic remarks on Milton's style and imagery, including the statement that "Milton never saw anything."

5. Eliot's reading of Milton's imagery as symptomatic of a "dissociation of sensibility" is given an interesting postmodern twist by Herman Rapaport. Rapaport argues that "Milton's desire was to defetishize the image, to empty words of their corporeality, their parousia, which to Milton was but an illusion to begin with" (243). Rather than the incarnate poetic word in which signified and signifier become one, Milton proffers "a word divested of the divine, differed and deferred from the signified" (16).

6. A classic discussion of Dante's figurative technique for representing the eternal world in images of temporal phenomena can be found in Auerbach.

7. Isabel MacCaffrey treats Milton's poem as "true myth," explaining that myth "doesn't stand for anything else; it is what everything else stands for . . . " (55). See also Frank Kermode on the poem's "basic myth" as symbolizing contemporary and universal human experience.

8. These are favorite themes of Empson.

9. See MacCallam for Milton's adherence to Protestant models of exegesis.

10. The issue of Milton's Arianism is thoroughly explored by Patrides.

11. Milton writes about the genesis of this poem in his verse letter in Latin to Charles Diodati known as the "Sixth Elegy." Cf. Northrop Frye's observations on Milton's discovery of himself as a "priest of poetry": "The poet's images are derived from human life, but the major poet must also use those human symbols to convey to man some inkling of the eternal worlds beyond human knowledge, 'singing now the holy counsels of the gods above, and now the deep regions where the fierce dog (Cerberus) barks,' to quote again from the *Sixth Elegy*" (v).

Works Cited

Auerbach, Erich. "Figura." *Scenes from the Drama of European Literature: Six Essays*. Gloucester, MA: Meridian, 1969. 12–67.
Eliot, T. S. "Milton I." *On Poetry and Poets*. New York: Farrar, 1957. 156–65.
———. "Milton II." On Poetry and Poets. New York: Farrar, 1957. 165–84.
Empson, William. *Milton's God*. London: Chattro, 1965.
Fish, Stanley. "Discovery as Form in *Paradise Lost*." In *New Essays on "Paradise Lost."* Ed. Thomas Kranidas. Berkeley: U of California P, 1971. 1–15.
———. *Self-Consuming Artifacts: The Experience of Seventeenth-Century Literature*. Berkeley: U of California P, 1972.
———. *Surprised by Sin*. New York: Macmillan, 1967.
Frye, Northrop, ed. *"Paradise Lost" and Selected Poetry and Prose*. New York: Holt, 1951.
Hughes, Merritt Y., ed. *John Milton: Complete Poems and Major Prose*. New York: Odyssey, 1957.
Kates, Judith. *Tasso and Milton: The Problem of Christian Epic*. Cranbury, NJ: Associated UP, 1983.
Kermode, Frank, ed. *The Living Milton: Essays by Various Hands*. London: Routledge, 1960.
MacCaffrey, Isabel. *Paradise Lost as "Myth."* Cambridge, MA: Harvard UP, 1959.
MacCullum, H. R. "Milton and Figurative Interpretation of the Bible." *University of Toronto Quarterly* 31.4 (1962): 396–415.
Madsen, John. *From Shadowy Types to Truth: Studies in Milton's Symbolism*. New Haven: Yale UP, 1968.
Patrides, C. A., W. B. Hunter, and J. H. Adanson. *"Bright Essence": Studies in Milton's Theology*. Salt Lake City: U of Utah P, 1973.
Rapaport, Herman. *Milton and the Post-Modern*. Lincoln: U of Nebraska P, 1983.
Samuel, Irene. *Milton and Dante: The "Commedia" and "Paradise Lost."* Ithaca: Cornell UP, 1966.

6 • A Lesson in Reading: George Eliot and the Typological Imagination

Jo Ellen Parker

I

GEORGE ELIOT'S EARLIEST FICTIONS are thoroughly informed by typological discourse and imagery; in fact, her effort to bring readers into a renewed relationship with what I will call the "typological imagination" is central to her imaginative and moral purposes. She begins her fictional project with the conventions of biblical typology for two reasons: in the first place, because they rest upon a specific and fundamental set of moral and metaphysical assumptions which have meanings independent of her fictional uses of them and, in the second, because they connect her work to a tradition and a discourse which define an already existing historical community to which she can safely assume her readers belong.

George Landow cites the returns of an English religious census taken on Sunday, March 30, 1853, to conclude that at a conservative estimate "three-quarters of the congregations assembled on a Sunday in the 1850's or 1860's would have heard some form of Evangelical doctrine" (*Types* 16). Victorian Evangelicalism relied heavily on typological discourse in its sermons, literature, theology, and hymns, and thereby spread not only specifically typological ideas but also a more broadly defined set of typological interpretive and rhetorical strategies. Typology is a method of biblical hermeneutics, originating in the commentaries of the early Fathers of the Church, which assumes a complex and indissoluble relationship between the Old Testament and the New, a relationship best understood as a web of correspondences. Old Testament persons or events, viewed as "types," are interpreted as figures or images of New Testament persons or events, their "antitypes," which in turn figure or image some person or event in the kingdom of heaven. In this kind of reading, for example, the chosen people of Israel in the Old Testament will be seen as the type of those choosing and chosen by Christ in the New, and these in turn as the type of the Elect or the saved in heaven. In addition to these historical levels of figuration, a typological reading can include an allegorical interpretation which is general or abstract. For instance, the type of Israel/Disciple/Believer can lead to some abstraction like "the righteous minority must endure persecution but will be rewarded."

More generally, typological interpretation subverts the common-sense perception of the linear nature of time, for it perceives two or more widely separate historical moments as bound into one timeless instant of prophecy and fulfillment in the mind of God. It delights in "paradox and enigma," assuming that "everything can be an emblem if we learn to see properly" (Landow, "Moses" 344). It perceives all things as existing simultaneously in two realms, the material and the spiritual, and, as a system of ideas about how words mean typology, has wide-ranging implications for the understanding of metaphor.

Eliot's youthful exposure to Evangelicalism assures us that she was familiar with both the specific images and the interpretive method of typology. Her early fictions, centered as they are on typological images and on typological discourse as a topic, clearly demonstrate that her adult rejection of Evangelical convictions may have caused a re-evaluation of these images but did not diminish their centrality in her imagination.

As a case in point, we have the Reverend Amos Barton, title character of the first of the three short stories which constitute *Scenes of Clerical Life*. Mr. Barton is an Evangelical clergyman whose sermons and meditations are deeply but incompetently imbedded in typological imagery. In his language Amos invokes the typological vocabulary which Eliot and her readers share and which therefore creates an interpretive community for his story, but because he does not comprehend this vocabulary—because he cannot properly read his own words—we who do comprehend are made to look on him with condescension and pity.

The first time we see into Amos's thoughts he is walking home from a dinner party and contemplating his plans for the parish lending library. He is excited about an anti-Dissent tract which he plans to add to the library.

> Dissent, he considered, would have its head bruised in Shepperton, for did he not attack it in two ways? He preached Low-Church doctrine—as evangelical as anything to be heard in the Independent Chapel; and he made a High-Church assertion of ecclesiastical powers and functions. Clearly, the Dissenters would feel that "the parson" was too many for them. Nothing like a man who combines shrewdness with energy. The wisdom of the serpent, Mr. Barton considered, was one of his strong points. (53)

In his thinking Amos employs an image from the typological tradition to describe the anticipated effect of his anti-Dissent activities: that is, the type of Christ bruising the head of the serpent. This type is founded on the passage in Genesis in which Eve is told that as a result of her sin her descendants will bruise the head of the serpent and the serpent will bruise their heels. This prophecy is fulfilled, according to the standard interpretation, by Christ, who crushes Satan and incurs the suffering of the Crucifixion in so doing.

Amos's application of this type expands our understanding of his character in several ways, chiefly by poking fun at him. The figure he uses compares Amos himself to Christ and Dissent in his village to Satan. The ludicrous self-aggrandizement of the equation tells us either that Amos does not understand what he is saying or that he has no sense of perspective, showing us stupidity coupled with arrogance and a combative view of the world. Further, Amos applies the type incompletely. The essential significance of the type is its prediction of the Passion of Christ. Even when considered on the abstract or ethical level alone, the type is generally taken to mean that evil can be conquered only at a price. Consequently, if Amos understood his own figure of speech correctly, he would foresee that some suffering will be called for on his part. But he does not, and goes on his way cheered by his visions of triumph and honor.

In fact, in his last phrase Amos considers that "the wisdom of the serpent . . . was one of his strong points" (53). This reference, to Matthew 10:16, is to the instruction Jesus gives the apostles to use the "wisdom of the serpent" as they begin the work of evangelism among the Gentiles. Although it seems that the reference may have occurred to Amos associatively because it too uses the image of the serpent, the allusion clearly conveys his distorted perception of himself and the situation in Shepperton as he allusively places himself among the apostles and compares his mission to theirs, facing a hostile people. In several earlier scenes, however, we have long since seen that his parishioners' attitude toward Amos is more like benevolent amusement than hostile resistance and that they seem very little in need of converting. His is the only point of view from which this allusion makes sense, and its evident senselessness serves to impeach his point of view.

By stressing the disparity between Amos's understanding of his language and our own, Eliot both increases our understanding of his character and reduces our sympathy for him by revealing his arrogance, stupidity, and self-dramatization. But there is a final and ironic twist to Eliot's, as opposed to Amos's, use of these images. For what Amos does not see and we do—the painful but necessary cost of bruising the serpent's head—does in fact come to pass, as Amos finds himself widowed, scorned, and desolate by the narrative's end. Our correct reading of the image Amos uses incorrectly gives us an accurate prediction of the imminence of Amos's personal Calvary. In this way the conventional meaning of the type remains intact and constitutes a code shared by Eliot and her readers but unavailable to Amos. Readers who can interpret this code have the advantage of a clear guide to the story, while Amos cannot bring its metaphors into any coherent relation with his experience.

Eliot insists that the ability to manipulate language effectively is at the heart of religious and moral community. She introduces Amos's fellow clergymen by identifying them with their characteristic figures of speech. "Mr. Furness preached his own sermons, as any one of tolerable critical acumen might have certified by comparing them with his poems; in both, there was an exuberance of metaphor and simile entirely original, and not in the least borrowed from any resemblance in the things compared" (93). Mr. Pugh may not write poems, but he does create metaphors with his wardrobe: "He . . . might be seen any day sallying forth on his parochial duties in a white tie, a well-brushed hat, a perfect suit of black, and well-polished boots—an equipment which he probably supposed hieroglyphically to represent the spirit of Christianity" (93). But we are told that any hieroglyphic representation of Christianity in Mr. Pugh's clothing is only "supposed"; he too has no adequate medium for the expression of his vocation. A third member of the group, Mr. Cleves, lacking the poetic figures of the one and the sartorial figures of the other, is "the true parish priest . . . the surest helper under a difficulty . . . Mr. Cleves has the wonderful art of preaching sermons which the wheelwright and the blacksmith can understand . . . because he can call a spade a spade, and knows how to disencumber ideas of their wordy frippery" (93). Lest we think that his simplicity and clarity signify that Cleves lacks intelligence or sophistication, Eliot emphasizes that "for all this, he is perhaps the best Grecian of the party" (94). Thus, he is both the best interpreter and the most easily interpreted of the clergymen present, and he is, not incidentally, also the most effective pastor. Because he can express ideas without "frippery" he stands in a clear relationship to his parishioners, and because he is the best Grecian he stands in a clear relationship to the sacred texts. Both relationships are essential to an effective ministry, to allow his parishioners an effective reading of him and of Christianity through him.

Amos is in direct contrast. "Mr. Barton had not the gift of perfect accuracy in English orthography and syntax, which was unfortunate, as he was known not to be a Hebrew scholar, and not in the least suspected of being an accomplished Grecian" (59). Amos's ignorance of Hebrew and Greek cuts him off from the sources of Scripture, and his inability in English cuts him off from his parishioners as well. His parishioners seem to sense Amos's exclusion, choosing an animal, rather than a human, image to describe him as a preacher: "But when he tries to preach wi'out book, he rambles about, and doesn't stick to his text; and every now and then he flounders about like a sheep as has cast itself and can't get on its legs again" (48). Here, again, Eliot uses traditional Christian imagery that communicates directly with her readers in a way that is over the heads of her characters, so to speak. Mr. Hackit, speaker of these lines, shows no sign that he takes his image as anything more than a vivid representation of Amos's verbal and intellectual floundering. We see, however, that it neatly expresses Amos's special problem. He who should be the pastor, the shepherd, of this particular flock, is by virtue of his verbal ineptitude actually one of its needier sheep.

In "Amos Barton," reading and interpreting are bound up with integration and community. Communication and community are mutually necessary: when they come together they create the kind of communion that makes Mr. Cleves "the surest helper under a difficulty." This communion of human understanding and sympathy is the essence of Eliot's much-discussed "religion of humanity." What has been underrecognized is the role of traditional religious discourse in articulating that religion.

The potential for community in "Barton" expands outside the story itself because of the presence of traditional religious discourse in the story. Typological imagery invokes a community extending back to the past and out to the reader, establishing a history which includes Eliot and the reader but excludes Amos. These types are used by Eliot with their conventional meanings intact, and these conventional meanings are both validated and used to create ironies in the structure of the plot. The predictions of Amos's types—that the serpent will bruise his heel, that he will be as a stranger in a strange land—come true in his experience, so the reader who recognizes them has a reliable guide through the story. Such a reader sees a clear foreshadowing where Amos cannot, just as Mr. Hackit's sheep metaphor relies on the image of the pastor as shepherd to convey its fullest meaning from Eliot to her readers while bypassing its own vehicle, Mr. Hackit, who probably would not understand it if it were pointed out to him. Typology retains its value as a gloss on experience for those who understand it, but those who do not are shut out from the meaning it imparts to everyday events and finally misunderstand not only their language but also their lives.

Writing her first fiction under the influences of Strauss and Feuerbach, Eliot explores in "Amos Barton" some of the most fundamental questions raised by the theology of the Higher Criticism. What meaning, if any, can scriptural images have? How can that meaning be determined? What is the relation of Scripture to common, in both senses, life? The sad fortunes of Amos Barton force Eliot's reader to confront those questions. Through him Eliot illustrates her conviction that how we understand Scripture both reflects and influences our experience. She refuses to treat the typological conventions as esoteric, allowing them still to define a moral and imaginative community which is not the community she depicts but the community she creates with and among her readers. Conventional, typological imagery, then, appeals to Eliot because of its traditional and communal nature. It defines a community, facilitates communication within that community, and refers precisely to its central metaphysical ideas. But to say that these aspects of the convention appealed to her is not to say she entirely endorses the traditional content of the images she uses. Other aspects of "Amos Barton" illustrate some of the difficulties that Eliot found inherent in the typological images, especially as they define the status of women in the Christian mythos.

II

Although we can see clearly enough the ways in which Amos's linguistic and imaginative limitations define his failure as a clergyman, the text insists that we consider him as a husband as well. It is more the story of a marriage than of a ministry, and our final assessment of Amos has to take into consideration his relations with his wife, Milly, and the Countess Czerlaski. Clearly Eliot, in her *Scenes of Clerical Life*, is not attempting to depict the Victorian clergy as the male institution it actually was; but if she wanted to tell love stories, why choose clergymen to tell them about, as she does in each of the three stories that make up *Scenes*?

The choice is perfectly consistent with the influence of typology and Feuerbach on her thinking, as both agree in perceiving marriage as essentially religious. Typology expresses this connection by identifying the marriage relationship with the clerical relationship in the type of the Bride of Christ. Feuerbach believed that the sexual relationship was the highest expression of his humanist religion. In both cases human marriage comes to represent the redemptive possibilities of relationship. Eliot, for her part, subjects both theories of marriage to the test of human experience— and pointedly of female experience—and finds both wanting.

In order to explore the traditional Christian iconography of sexuality and marriage in its relationship to physical and religious experience, Eliot structures *Scenes* around the type of the Bride of Christ, one of the most complex and most central in the tradition. Through this type marriage is seen, in the words of the Book of

Common Prayer, as "signifying unto us the mystical union that is between Christ and his Church." The basis for the Bride of Christ type is the interpretation of Adam as a type of Christ. Adam alone among men, except for Christ, was created without sin. Both were created directly by God and not through the usual processes of human sexuality, and so both represent a beginning for humanity. Thus, it becomes conventional to speak of the Old Adam and of Jesus as the New or Second Adam as a way of emphasizing that with Adam man was created and with Jesus he was re-created. This typology is present in the Scriptures, especially in the Gospels of Luke and Mark. Samuel Mather sees Adam's similarity to Christ chiefly in this role as representative and founder of a people: "*Adam* and *Christ* both stood in stead of all that belonged to them. *Adam* was the Head of the *first* covenant, *Jesus Christ* is the Head of the second covenant" (64). Adam and Christ are involved in a reverse-type as well. Adam fell and Christ redeems: "Adam conveys and communicates Sin and Death; But Christ Righteousness and Life" (65). This view, also, is present in Scripture, especially in the Pauline material: "For as in Adam all die, even so in Christ shall all be made alive" (1 Cor. 15:45).

The typological interpretation of Eve, bride of the Old Adam, is rather more complex. The conventional reading is that as Eve is the bride of the Old Adam the Church is the bride of the New.

> And as *Adam* was a Type of Christ; so we may carry the parallel a little further, and so *Eve* may be considered as a Type of the *Church*. . . . She was taken of his side, while *Adam* was asleep, and afterwards married to him. So the Church was taken out of Christ's Side, while he was in the Sleep of Death, and joined to him as his Spouse by the covenant of Grace. (Mather 65–66)

The relationship between Adam and Eve, Christ and the Church, serves as a model for all marriages. Thus, in the Anglican wedding ceremony the bride is exhorted to make her groom the head of their household as Christ is the head of the Church, thereby conforming to the order instituted in Eden. "For the husband is the head of the wife, even as Christ is the head of the Church. . . . Therefore as the Church is subject unto Christ, so let the wives be to their own husbands in everything." The typological analogy extends thus: wife is to husband as Eve is to Adam as Church is to Christ. And, since the relationship between each human pastor and his particular congregation is to be modeled on that between Christ and his Church, we can add as congregation is to minister.

The Church's identification with Eve proves especially difficult because of a deep dichotomy in traditional perceptions of Eve. She is both the mother of us all and the cause of our fallen state. Eve involves both Mary the Virgin and Mary the Magdalen in the type, and through her both the Madonna and the Magdalen are associated with the Church. Eve, like the Virgin, is created sinless; Eve and Mary in this way are female parallels to the male figures of Adam and Christ. Further, the prophetic type of the bruising of the serpent's head, which we have already seen Amos misconstrue, connects them, for the seed of Eve which it prophesies is the Son of Mary. Eve and the Virgin Mary are thus also involved in a reverse-type, as are Adam and Christ. Adam sinned; Christ comes to atone for sin. Eve brought death into the world; Mary, the life which will abolish death. Mary, like the Church, is the earthly vessel of God's Grace.

Even so, this identification of Eve, the Virgin, and the Church does not purge the taint of Eve the temptress, the cause of our fallen state, allied with the fallen Magdalen. And so this identification taints the Church, the bride, and the congregation, at least implicitly, and the "female" elements of the type are associated with transcendent purity as well as with carnality and susceptibility to temptation. "The Lord from Heaven stands distinctly revealed in the character of the second Adam. As such, He must also have His spouse, and has it in part now; but shall have it in completeness hereafter, in the company of faithful souls who have been washed from their sins in His Blood" (Fairbairn 257). The temporal manifestation of the Church, in Fairbairn's view, is always susceptible and therefore only a partial fulfillment of its typological role. Only in Heaven will the Church be purified of its "female" taint. This too is a thoroughly scriptural, or at least Pauline, notion: "I have espoused you [the church at Corinth] to one husband, that I may present you as a chaste virgin to Christ. But I fear, lest by any means, as the serpent beguiled Eve through his subtilty, so your minds should be corrupted from the simplicity that is in Christ" (2 Cor. 11:2-3). The proper role of the "male" elements is to preserve the purity and prevent the temptation. This husbandly duty is expressly urged in the marriage ceremony; "Husbands, love your wives, even as Christ also loved the Church, and gave himself for it, that he might sanctify and cleanse it."

This type is central and much applied. It is this series of typological analogies that defines both ecclesiastical and social order. The type of Christ as the New Adam and the Church as his Bride is at the heart of the Christian world-view, expanding as it does into an image of divine, social, and sexual order and imaging this order as one in which authority is rightfully vested in the male and the priest, justifying patriarchal social and ecclesiastical structure and symbolically assigning women to antithetical moral extremes. Women represent man's fall and man's salvation. It is perhaps unnecessary to point out that they are consequently imaged in relational terms: the Helpmeet of Adam and the Bride of Christ; Mother Eve, Mother Mary, and Mother Church. Feuerbach perceived that this imagery distorted and oppressed human sexuality and human relationships. He attempted to purge sexuality of its association with weakness and downfall in his own account of the traditional images, but like them he too exalted marriage and idealized it as a redemptive relationship.

For Feuerbach, all human relationships, "of child and parent, of husband and wife, of brother and friend," are "*per se* religious," but the sexual relationship, he implies, is the most religious of all human relationships (271). Throughout *The Essence of Christianity* Feuerbach stresses the centrality of the sexual relationship to his view of humanity. "He who lives in the consciousness of the species, and consequently of its reality, lives also in the consciousness of the reality of sex" (170). Feuerbach's materialism requires that all human relationships, all "I-Thou" relationships, be regarded as strictly non-Platonic. I and Thou are not related as more or less perfect reflections of some essence of humanity or some Idea of Man. They are related as eating, breathing, physical creatures, through sensuous and sensory experience, and thus the "consciousness of the reality of sex" is no abstraction but is born of experience. Therefore for Feuerbach it is the marriage relationship which is the highest expression of religion, for it offers the most complete relationship of person to person. Human sexual awareness and involvement removes the "spiritual center" of human life "from heaven to earth" and suggests to human beings their own spiritual sufficiency (Feuerbach 170).

However, the Christian tradition, Feuerbach says, in its effort to keep heaven the "spiritual center" of human life, has radically alienated the sexual impulse. "The more the sensual tendencies are renounced, the more sensual is the God to whom they are sacrificed" (26). The institution of the celibate clergy and the upholding of celibacy as an ideal for layfolk on earth has made necessary a compensatory image of the complete human family in heaven. So, Feuerbach says, with the medieval rise of Mariology Mary is "inserted" into the relationship between Father and Son as "the representative of the maternal principle to create a perfect image of the human family," as the "truly religious consecration of the sexual impulse" (70). Protestantism, in instituting marriage for its clergy and thus diffusing the impulse behind this alienation, has in Feuerbach's view diminished its conception of the Divine by removing the female principle; "respect for Mary" is crucial to conceiving of the fullness of God, and "Protestantism has weakened itself by rejecting Mary" (72).

If Protestant theology has diminished, however, Protestant morality has flourished, or so Feuerbach implies when he says that "Catholic morality was the *Mater Dolorosa*: Protestant morality a comely, fruitful matron" (139). (This "comely, fruitful matron" reminds us immediately of such Eliot characters as Milly Barton and later Gritty Moss.) Protestantism is less alienating to human sexual nature, the essence-of-human-species nature, and therefore morally richer, if theologically and iconographically poorer.

Thus, Feuerbach argues, essentially, that because it has returned the family relationship from heaven to earth Protestantism is less alienated, more moral, and thus in his terms more truly religious than Catholicism. Where typology sees the symbolic Bride of Christ as the path to human salvation, Feuerbach sees the human brides of Protestant ministers as the source of moral elevation. He has replaced the old paradigm of sexuality fallen and redeemed with his own polarity of sexuality alienated and fulfilled.

On this point Feuerbach's arguments are ultimately unsatisfactory. His materialistic emphasis on the actual celibacy or marriage of the clergy leads him to disregard the iconography of celibacy and marriage shared by Protestantism and Catholicism. Since he does not speak of the alienated imagination, but only of the alienated sex drive—or, more precisely, since he does not address symbolic, non-institutional influences on behavior—he never comes to grips with the effects and implications of these images. At the same time, despite his emphasis on the significance of concrete experience, he fails to recognize the abstraction of his own system. In this particular case he does not ask the obvious question whether Protestantism is actually, and not theoretically, morally superior. He does not subject his assumption that it is to a test.

In constructing her tales of clerical life Eliot is addressing precisely these questions, constructing such a test, in such a way as to suggest her critique, from a woman's position, of Feuerbach's ideas about sexuality and marriage. In them she examines the relationship between the typological iconography of sex and marriage and the everyday experience of three Protestant wives. But the experiences of these women bear out neither the typological nor the Feuerbachian view of marriage.

In "Amos Barton," to take the case at hand, we have Amos bracketed by two women. One is a Madonna, an angel; the other, a worldly husband-hunter. Milly could have been drawn directly from Feuerbach's representation of Protestant morality. She is a mother, five times over: "a large, fair, gentle Madonna" (54). "Milly's memory hallowed her husband, as of old the place was hallowed on which an angel from God had alighted" (111). She has a special relationship with Divine love and an infinite faith in its mercies. "Her heart so overflowed with love, she felt sure she was near a fountain of love that would care for her husband and babes better than she could foresee" (58). Milly is an icon of feminine Christian virtue; in fact, she is so much an icon that "you would even perhaps have been rather scandalized if she had descended from the serene dignity of being to the assiduous unrest of *doing*" (54).

"You" would have been continually scandalized, however, for Milly is constantly doing—darning socks, recovering books for the parish library, minding the children, salting bacon, and rising at five to get it all done. In the character of Milly, Eliot has combined the Madonna as a traditional icon with the reality of a poverty-stricken housewife's life in a large family. As a Madonna Milly is just what any minister's wife should be; as a darner of socks she is just what Amos Barton's wife needs to be.

The "you" of the above passage posits a general public or social tendency to adopt a view of Milly in which the reader is implicated, a view defined by traditional Christian iconography. Amos and the Countess, unlike the servants and children who see Milly at all her daily tasks, take this iconographic view of Milly as well, and their one-dimensional perception prevents them from recognizing the reality of her other life, her active life, and the threat that it poses to her health and very existence. In other words, those in the story who see Milly too much as a saint overlook her true saintliness, which is in doing, not in being. Those who see her as a Madonna cannot properly value her motherhood.

Eliot's comment on the typological thinking here is subtle. True, she is showing that typological conceptions can block the accurate perception of reality. But she says so by applying a perfectly accurate type. Those in the story who read Milly as a Madonna are not mistaken in revering her selfless motherhood. In its content the image is perfectly accurate. The error is in seeing Milly as an iconic, rather than an active, Madonna; as an image of a mother and not as the woman who enacts the image. As we have noted before, in "Amos Barton" Eliot preserves the integrity of the types while insisting on complete and proper application. The type in this case tells the truth so long as it is not abstracted from concrete and immediate reality; the image of the Madonna needs the reality of motherhood to give it meaning. This is the innovation Eliot brings to her use of typological imagery. Alert and intelligent readers who share the typological traditions are in a privileged position for understanding her intentions. However, readers ingrained in ignorant or morally lazy habits of typological misreading are kept from understanding precisely and ironically because of their familiarity with the vocabulary she invokes.

Caroline Czerlaski is equally, although less fatally, misinterpreted. Amos, in his gullibility, accepts her at face value, but the parish generally persists in reading her as a whore and an adventuress. This conception of the Countess, while supported by circumstantial evidence, seems also to be encouraged by its contrast to the public perception of Milly. The Madonna must be set off against the Magdalen, the Mother against the fallen woman. And so, their perceptions influenced by the iconography of their faith, the townspeople find it quite natural to identify the Countess as a sexual adventuress out to steal Milly's husband and their pastor. In doing so they overlook the true nature of the threat she poses to Milly, which is the economic drain she creates upon the family.

It is literally labor that kills Milly, in both senses of the word. She has been weakened and worn by ceaseless housework and dies in the struggle to give birth to her sixth child. In this fact is the essence of Eliot's critique of Feuerbach. She knows that the sexual life he celebrates is sometimes the death of "fruitful matrons" and that for women the sacredness of the marital state is perhaps less apparent than the immediacy of its demands. In Eliot's imagination women's labor is the insistent reality which finds no expression in the images of women she inherits from the biblical tradition and from Feuerbach. In fact, by the end of this story we are likely to see Milly not in any conventionally female role but in the iconographically masculine role of Christ. Her death operates as a redemptive sacrifice, giving Amos a moment of moral insight and redeeming his reputation and his memory in the parish. Thus, if we remember the typological alignment of Christ, husband, pastor and Eve, wife, and Church, this story ultimately suggests a realignment of the conventional values which could be considered a feminist one. Redemption and purity are found in the bride and parishioner; weakness and gullibility, in the husband and pastor. It is Amos whose vanity leads him astray, as Eve's led her. Christ is sacrificed for the redemption of His Bride, but Milly is sacrificed to and redeems her husband and pastor. So that, although the idealization of Milly may at first glance seem a conventional enough instance of the Angel in the House, coupled with Eliot's refusal to idealize Amos, it suggests a challenging of typology's conventional ethical implications and of Feuerbach's revisionist reinterpretation of marriage. Moral authority, "Amos Barton" suggests, cannot be presumed in husbands or in pastors, just as marriage can be as much Calvary as heaven on earth.

Works Cited

Eliot, George. *Scenes of Clerical Life.* Ed. David Lodge. New York: Penguin, 1973.

Fairbairn, Patrick. *The Typology of Scripture.* 1856. Grand Rapids, MI: Zondervan, 1952.

Feuerbach, Ludwig. *The Essence of Christianity*. 1854. Trans. Marian Evans. New York: Harper, 1957.

Landow, George. "Moses Striking the Rock." *The Literary Uses of Typology*. Ed. Earl Miner. Princeton: Princeton UP, 1977.

———. *Victorian Types, Victorian Shadows: Biblical Typology in Victorian Literature, Art, and Thought*. Boston: Routledge, 1980.

Mather, Samuel. *The Figures or Types of the Old Testament*. 1705. New York: Johnson, 1969.

7 • Rouault and the Catholic Revival in France

Jane Kristof

GEORGES ROUAULT has often been seen as a somewhat anachronistic figure in twentieth-century art, a painter isolated by his deep religious commitment from the cultural milieu in which he worked. The opening lines of James Thrall Soby's monograph on the artist sum up this generally accepted image:

> Georges Rouault: a solitary figure in an era of group-manifestos and shared directions; a devout Catholic and devotional painter in a period when artists more often have run the gamut of anti-religious feeling, from indifference to irreverence; a painter of sin and redemption in the face of prevailing estheticism and counter-estheticism.... (5)

This view is, of course, accurate up to a point, but only up to a point. Rouault was certainly by far the most important Catholic painter of his day, but he was not unique. The beginnings of his career, around the turn of the century, coincided with a remarkable literary, intellectual, and, to a lesser degree, artistic renewal in the French Church, the so-called Catholic revival. Moreover, his confirmation in the Catholic faith, which occurred in the 1890s when he was in his twenties, was one of a series of conversions among a disillusioned cultural elite. The writers J.-K. Huysmans, Paul Claudel, Charles Péguy, Jacques and Raïssa Maritain, and Jacques Rivière, and the painter Émile Bernard all turned or returned to Catholicism at the end of the nineteenth and the beginning of the twentieth centuries. (In many cases they had, like Rouault himself, been baptized Catholic and subsequently become disaffected.)

How does Rouault's artistic development reflect the spiritual climate of his formative years? In answering this question it will be convenient to distinguish between two groups, the Catholic painters and the Catholic writers, and examine the influence that either of these might have had upon Rouault.

His relation to the first group, the Catholic painters, can be discussed rather briefly since it seems to have consisted of mutual indifference. The most prominent figure in an effort to resuscitate liturgical art that paralleled the Catholic literary revival was the symbolist painter Maurice Denis. Denis was an almost exact contemporary of Rouault's and the two were acquainted, yet they seem almost to belong to different eras. The precocious Denis is generally remembered as an artist of the nineteenth century while Rouault stands unquestionably in the twentieth. Rouault was evidently quite conscious of this distinction. In remarking on the changes that had occurred in the course of his long career he is reported to have said: "I knew Maurice Denis when he was considered an *avant gardiste* . . ." (qtd. in Courthion 248).

The very personal style that Rouault evolved had, in fact, almost nothing in common with the flat, decorative manner, pallid coloring, and narrative or symbolic content characteristic of the Denis group, which sought to perpetuate into the twentieth century the style of Puvis de Chavannes. In a rare reference to Denis, contained in a letter of 1924, Rouault describes a retrospective exhibition of his work as "très retrospective" (Rouault and Suarès 193), while Denis, in a long and profusely illustrated survey of twentieth-century religious art, published in 1939, devotes only one half-sentence to Rouault: "And let us not forget . . . Rouault, a strange and powerful artist, the most audacious of the deformers" (303). He includes no illustration of Rouault's work.

Rouault was also a friend of Georges Desvallières's, cofounder with Denis of the Atelier de l'Art Sacré and perhaps the most forceful member of the latter's circle. Desvallières had been, like Rouault himself, a student of Gustave Moreau's and an admirer of Léon Bloy. Another somewhat older artist of the same orientation was Albert Besnard, whose subjects, however, tended to allegory rather than religion. Besnard, in 1890, asked Rouault to execute stained glass windows for the École de Pharmacie from his cartoons. The then nineteen-year-old Rouault had already served a five-year apprenticeship in a stained-glass workshop and had developed a lasting love for the medium, so that the offer must have been particularly tempting to him. His rejection of it would seem to indicate a determination, even at this early age, to find his own idiom in painting.

By contrast, Rouault's relations with several Catholic writers and thinkers were extremely close and fruitful. First, in order both of time and of importance, were J.-K. Huysmans and Léon Bloy. Rouault's *Souvenirs intimes* of 1926, consisting of impressions of a small number of artists and writers who had played a crucial role in his development, contains recollections and lithograph portraits of both of them (figs. 1 and 2).

Huysmans was a critic and novelist of the naturalist school whose dramatic conversion to Catholicism is recorded in his trilogy of novels, *En Route, La Cathédrale,* and *L'Oblat.* The last of these books describes Huysmans's efforts to establish a colony of religious artists in conjunction with the Benedictine monastery of Ligugé, an experiment that, after a couple of years of precarious existence, was terminated by a 1901 law against unauthorized religious communities. Rouault made a pilgrimage to Ligugé in the spring of 1901 and remained there for six months until the dissolution of the monastery. Many years later he recalled:

> We were a few friends who formed a little group around Huysmans and tried to lay the foundation for artistic and intellectual work that would be dedicated and selfless. Huysmans wanted to bring together men who, having abandoned the farce of Paris, would count neither money nor influence; no Bachelor's or Doctor's degrees and no specialists; just men who had put behind them all that was nonessential in life: degrees, medals, prerogatives. He wanted to organize this with me . . . and a few others. . . . (qtd. in Courthion 78)

In 1904, having been deeply affected by Léon Bloy's novel *La Femme pauvre,* Rouault arranged to be introduced to its author, who, until his death in 1917, was to be a close friend and spiritual mentor. Bloy dedicated the first chapter of his *Belluaires et porchers* to Rouault, and one of the artist's rare works based on a literary theme is his *Monsieur et Madame Poulot* of 1905 (private collection), derived from a couple of Bloy characters. This painting outraged the author, however, as did all of Rouault's mature art. "For nothing on earth would I accept such an 'illustration' as this," complained Bloy to his diary (qtd. in Courthion 103–104).

Bloy expressed his opinion of his friend's art frequently and with characteristic vehemence, as, for instance, in a letter of 1907: "Today I have two things to say to you, and only two . . . : First, you are attracted solely to what is ugly; you appear to have a sort of vertigo of hideousness. Second: if you were a man who prayed, a religious man, a communicant, you could not paint those horrible pictures" (qtd. in Courthion 104).

This line of attack is puzzling coming from Bloy, who was himself a considerable specialist in sordidness and degradation. The Poulot couple, for instance, are at least as unsavory in the writer's presentation as in the artist's. A partial explanation is that Bloy's tastes were arrested in the art of his beloved Middle Ages—characteristically, the painter-hero of *La Femme pauvre* illuminates manuscripts in a medieval manner—or, as Rouault himself contended, that his friend lacked artistic taste altogether (199; qtd. in Soby 36).

The problem may have gone deeper than a verbal-visual dichotomy, however. Bloy was a man of extremes whose writings veered between an insistent brutality on the one hand and an equally assertive and occasionally sentimental piety on the other. During Bloy's lifetime (he died in 1917), Rouault echoed only the writer's somber side, largely avoiding explicitly religious motifs. His painting afforded little comfort, either human or formal. Presumably it was the unrelieved darkness of his vision that so offended Bloy, who might perhaps have been more appreciative of Rouault's later art as he had once been of his student efforts.

On more than one occasion Rouault depreciated attempts to represent him as "the Léon Bloy of painting," citing the intrinsically visual character of his works as well as Bloy's extreme aversion to them (103; qtd. in Courthion 152). Nevertheless, affinities between the writer and the painter are, as will be seen, so striking that critics have persisted in pointing them out.

Bloy's writings were instrumental in the conversion to Catholicism of Jacques and Raïssa Maritain, and it was at his house that Rouault met this couple who were to be among his most intimate friends—indeed for a period of several years he dined almost weekly at their home. They were also early and ardent champions

Fig. 1. Portrait of Huysmans. Lithograph from *Souvenirs intimes*, 1926. Photographie Giraudon.

Fig. 2. Portrait of Bloy. Lithograph from *Souvenirs intimes*, 1926. Photographie Giraudon.

Fig. 3. *Monsieur X*, 1911. Albright-Knox Art Gallery, Buffalo.

Fig. 4. *Miserere*, Plate 16. "The society lady fancies she has a reserved seat for Heaven." Collection, The Museum of Modern Art, New York.

Fig. 5. *Prostitute at Her Mirror*, 1906. Musée d'Art Moderne, Paris.

Fig. 6. *Men of Justice*, c.1913. Musée d'Art Moderne, Paris.

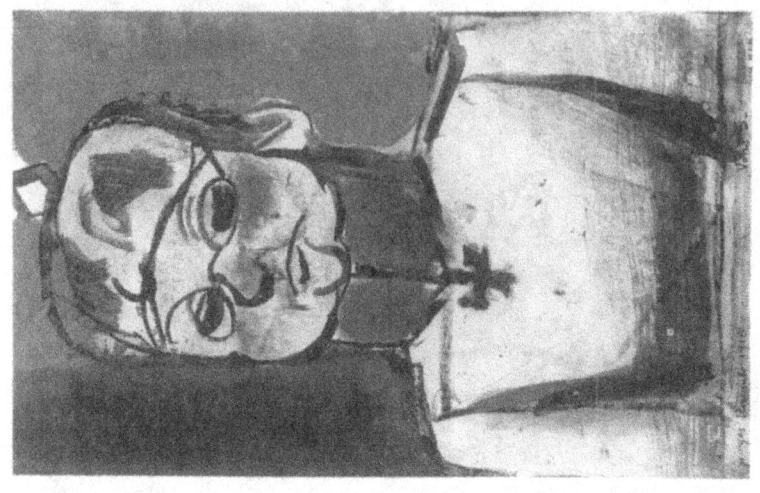

Fig. 7. *The Reformer*, 1915. Musée d'Art Moderne, Paris.

Fig. 8. *Von F.*, 1915. Musée d'Art Moderne, Paris.

Fig. 9. *Miserere*, Plate 49. "The nobler the heart, the stiffer the collar." Collection, The Museum of Modern Art, New York.

Fig. 10. *Crucifixion*, 1918. Philadelphia Museum of Art, Collection of Henry P. McIlhenny.

of his art, and it was his example that inspired Maritain to write *Art and Scholasticism*, which first appeared in 1919.

Rouault's relations with other leading spirits of the Catholic revival were less important and less direct. Jacques Rivière, a younger writer much under the influence of Claudel, wrote, on the occasion of Rouault's first one-man exhibition in 1910, one of the most sensitive and sympathetic reviews of his work to have appeared to that date (San Lazzaro 17–18). François Mauriac was a warm admirer of Rouault whom he described as " painter after my own heart" (qtd. in San Lazzaro 73–80). Rouault's longtime friend, collaborator, and correspondent, André Suarès, was also a close friend of Claudel's and biographer of Péguy. The former was considerably influenced by Huysmans and had visited the monastery at Ligugé a few months before Rouault's stay there; the latter had a close relationship with the Maritains, so that both were very much a part of the artist's ambient.

Having noted Rouault's close personal associations with many of the leaders of the religious renaissance of the early twentieth century, it remains to trace some of the relationships of his art to their thought. A warning, though, is perhaps in order. These relationships should not be expected to take the form of direct transcriptions of philosophical or theological ideas into painting. Rouault himself insisted that "with me nothing was *calculated, worked out, oriented* by theories . . . , literary or even spiritual theses . . ." (199). Rather, his art was a product of intuition and paint. "Images and colors for the painter are his way of being, living, thinking, feeling" (29). Nevertheless, his essentially visual expression in many ways parallels the literary approaches of his colleagues.

Turning first to specifically artistic matters: there was virtual unanimity among the Catholic intelligentsia as to the deplorable state of contemporary sacred art. Huysmans wrote several diatribes on this subject, of which perhaps the most brilliant is his description of what he calls the "hemorrhage of bad taste" at Lourdes, which he attributes to the direct intervention of the devil (101–14). Bloy maintained that art and religion had become more and more estranged with each century since the Middle Ages until, in his own day " . . . the contempt or horror of modern Christians for all . . . superior art . . . appears to be another and more devilish kind of iconoclasm. Instead of slashing paintings

... we stifle souls of light in the sentimental slime of an idiotic piety ..." (110). Maritain likewise regarded conventional religious art, the so-called "art of St. Sulpice," as a "devilish ugliness, an offense to God and much more harmful than is generally believed to the spread of religion ..." (140).

These sentiments were fully shared by Rouault. When asked about the "art of St. Sulpice," he replied simply that it "does not exist" (140). His contempt for popular sacred art seems to explain why, during the first decade of the century, when his religious fervor was perhaps most intense, he avoided traditional Christian subjects almost completely, fearing, as he later explained, to create works "into which a sullen convention might have slipped" (qtd. in Rubin 96). In place of the biblical themes that had dominated his student days, Rouault now devised a new iconography, and, perhaps taking his cue from Huysmans and Bloy, turned to the presentation of contemporary life and contemporary types seen in a pervasively religious or moral context.

Moreover, the social viewpoint implied in these early works of Rouault's is clearly in keeping with the prevailing mood of the Catholic intelligentsia. A common denominator of such traditionalist movements as Action Française, which attracted the Maritains, and the Christian socialism of Péguy was pity for the poor and outcast and, often still more conspicuously, bitter condemnation of the bourgeoisie.[1] In particular, Bloy's loathing for the rich frequently exceeded the bounds of Christian charity, as when the thought of several millionaires drowning in the wreck of the *Titanic* filled him with "sweetest consolation," or when he reflected with unconcealed satisfaction on the deaths of about four hundred "unclean bourgeois" in a disastrous fire at the Opéra Comique (Heppenstall 11).

It is against this background that the often biting caricatures of Rouault's early career must be understood, his *Monsieur X*, of 1911, in Buffalo, for instance (fig. 3), and several studies of judges. Raïssa Maritain recalls him "fainting with indignation" at overhearing a society woman, who was later to appear in Plate 16 of *Miserere* (fig. 4), remark: "I'll go straight to heaven" (25). The other side of this outrage was, however, the compassion of his many studies of poor families and depressed suburbs, of weary, aging clowns and dancers, often reminiscent of Daumier.

The very mention of Daumier, however, suggests Rouault's

distance from the artistic tradition of social criticism in France. His focus is neither political nor economic. The situation of the poor, their deprivation, their discouragement in an inhospitable environment, is not, for Rouault, simply a societal aberration. It is rather, as William Dyrness emphasizes, the archetype of the human condition (130–33). It will be ameliorated not by radical action or progressive legislation but by family solidarity, as in *Faubourg of Toil and Suffering* (1912, Philippe Leclerq Collection) and its many variations, or by the presence of Christ, as in *Christ in the Suburbs* (1920, Fukushima Collection) or *Christ and the Poor Man* (1937, formerly Vollard Collection).

In the first decade of the century Rouault was particularly concerned with a category of social outcast that also figured importantly in the writings of both Huysmans and Bloy (and of another of his favorite authors, Dostoevsky), namely, the prostitute.[2] An impressive example of this genre is *Prostitute Before a Mirror* of 1906 in the Musée d'Art Moderne, Paris (fig. 5). His depiction of these women of the streets, with their pimply faces, sagging bodies, and dingy rooms, seems to owe something to the relentless naturalism of Huysmans, while the note of pity and righteous indignation may well have been inspired by Bloy. There is also, of course, ample painterly precedent for Rouault's prostitutes, particularly in the Degas-Lautrec tradition, but a number of commentators, starting with the artist himself, have discounted his indebtedness to this source (qtd. in Charensol 23). Degas's and Lautrec's brothel scenes are human, casual, and often comic. Rouault's prostitutes by contrast have an iconic quality, with their heavily outlined, monumental forms and their often intense gaze. They seem to personify corruption and, at the same time, vulnerability. There are often allusions to traditional embodiments of sensual beauty, explicitly in a title like *The Fallen Eve* or implicitly in compositions that recall Venus at her mirror or the Odalisque. In characterizing Rouault's treatment of this subject Kenneth Clark uses the terms "idol" and "ideal" (346–47). Again, Rouault's approach is ultimately neither sociological nor psychological but religious.

The process of the law was another favorite subject of Rouault's early career and one that likewise afforded him a means of expressing his social sympathies directly and his religious values more obliquely. Presumably borrowing the theme again from Daumier, who occasionally made ironic use of the symbol of a crucifix in the courtroom,[3] Rouault wrote a poem that helps to clarify the significance this series had for him:

> The condemned man went away
> indifferent and weary
> his lawyer in phrases hollow
> and imposing
> had proclaimed his innocence
> a red-robed prosecutor thundering
> rose up
> held society blameless
> and charged the accused man
> under a crucified Jesus
> now forgotten there.
>
> (153–54)

A visual translation of these lines is found in a 1913 watercolor entitled *Men of Justice* (Musée d'Art Moderne de la Ville de Paris), in which two callous but complaisant judges confer, oblivious of a crucifix that dominates the upper part of the painting (fig. 6). Some lines from this poem reappear as inscriptions for the *Miserere* plates, and here the figure of the condemned, Plate 18, is identical to that of Jesus in Plate 21, except for the halo and crown of thorns. In other courtroom scenes there is a variation of this theme with the face of one of the judges or warders mirroring that of the prisoner.

In view of their generally humanitarian and anti-establishment bias, it is surprising to find that the French Catholic writers of the early twentieth century tended to be nationalistic often to the point of chauvinism, and that their adherence to a supranational, "catholic" faith did not mitigate, but actually intensified this nationalism. Church and country, even God and country, seem frequently to have overlapped in their minds, as when Péguy attributes to the Deity a special preference for the French (234–37) or when Bloy contends that they have succeeded the Jews as His chosen people (324–25). A perfect embodiment of the convergence of patriotic and religious ideals was found in Jeanne d'Arc, who was the heroine of works by Bloy, Claudel, and Péguy.[4] Rouault also painted two splendid images of Jeanne, completed in 1949 and 1951, and alluded to her frequently and reverently in his writings (104, 122, 162).

With the outbreak of the First World War, Martin Luther emerged as Jeanne's negative counterpart, personifying the heretical perversity of Germany just as she epitomized the faithful Catholicism of France. Bloy, in a rather tortuous metaphor, contrasts the wooden cross that consoled Jeanne at the stake with the iron cross, symbol of German militarism, which he calls "Luther's masterpiece" (327–29). In Claudel's blatantly propagandistic play *La Nuit de Noel 1914*, the German soldiers are described as "the hordes of Luther," while the French army is said to be inspired by Ste Jeanne, as well as Ste Geneviève and the Virgin Mary (572). Raïssa Maritain writes of a course her husband offered in 1914–15, "in which he endeavored to bring out the principal characteristics of German philosophy from Luther to our times. This was combat duty, a sort of intellectual contribution to the war against an aggressor who had begun by cutting himself off spiritually from the community of Western nations . . ." (213). After the war this rather jaundiced view of Luther was incorporated into Maritain's *Trois Réformateurs: Luther, Descartes, Rousseau*, published in 1925.

In the same spirit is Rouault's caricature of 1915, *Le Réformateur*, in the Musée d'Art Moderne de la Ville de Paris (fig. 7), in the corner of which is inscribed "on Luther," and which a catalogue describes, perhaps with a touch of embarrassment, as "plus anti-allemande qu'anti-protestante" (Musée National 62). A somewhat less partisan satire from the same year and in the same Museum is *Von F* (fig. 8), in which the artist simply transfers to a Prussian officer the same pudgy pomposity that he had already noted in his own compatriots such as *Madame X* (Musée d'Art Moderne de la Ville de Paris) and *Monsieur X*. Even a work so deeply and universally human in tone as *Miserere* (originally entitled *Miserere et guerre*) contains some nationalistic elements: two of its more repugnant images, Plates 49 and 51, are identifiably German, the former even bearing a striking resemblance to Kaiser Wilhelm (fig. 9).

Turning from public to more personal issues: many Catholic intellectuals, including Huysmans and more especially Bloy, cultivated a sort of mystique of suffering which evidently appealed strongly to Rouault's naturally melancholic temperament. Huysmans in his last, agonizing illness refused morphine, protesting:

"Ah! You want to prevent me from suffering! You want to change the sufferings of the good God for the evil pleasures of earth!" (Laver 258). In *L'Oblat* he personifies suffering as the bride of Christ and mother of the Church. Bloy wrote several panegyrics to suffering, of which the following is typical: "Suffering! here is then the key word! Here the solution for every human life on earth! the springboard for every superiority, the sieve for every merit, the infallible criterion for every moral beauty. . . . It is the backbone, the very essence of moral life" (275).

The exaltation of suffering among the Catholic intellectuals perhaps explains why Rouault in his early period transformed symbols of pleasure, the "fille de joie" and the circus clown, into tragic figures, and why when, around 1912, he gradually returned to more explicitly Christian themes, he concentrated almost exclusively on the passion and death of Jesus, at least until the 1930s when he started to paint the more serene biblical landscapes. "Being a Christian in these hazardous times," he wrote, "I can believe only in Jesus on the Cross" (103). Like Bloy, he loved Pascal's phrase, "Jesus will be in agony, even to the end of the world . . ." and used it as an inscription for Plate 35 of *Miserere*.

This almost exclusive preoccupation with Christ's suffering could strain the limits of orthodoxy, as when Bloy reacted to Easter Sunday by declaring: "I do not succeed in feeling the joy of Resurrection, because—so far as I am concerned—the Resurrection never comes. I always see Christ in His agony, Christ on the Cross, nor can I see Him in any other way" (42). Rouault's piety is certainly more balanced. Although his friend André Suarès omitted any reference to the Resurrection from the text of their joint publication *Passion*, Rouault included a wood engraving of the risen Christ among the plates, explaining: "I did not know whether or not Suarès believed in the resurrection of Jesus which I have never doubted" ("A la Galerie" 25). However this engraving seems to be one of only two depictions of this theme among literally dozens of Passion scenes. (The other is a painting, *Christ with Raised Arms*, in the S. S. White Collection, Ardmore, Pennsylvania.) It might also be noted that the only event of Jesus's infancy that attracted him was the Flight into Egypt with its overtones of menace and alienation.

In fairness it should be noted that in his later years Rouault, having overcome the hypersensitivity of his youth and found fulfillment both in his art and in his family life, occasionally took exception to the critics' emphasis on his somber side. "Now a certain critic calls me melancholy, morbid, and Lord knows what else," he protested in 1931. "I am as gay a dog as ever trod this earth" (108).

A final point of convergence between Rouault and the Catholic literati was their common suspicion of the modern world and nostalgia particularly for the Middle Ages. Claudel observed that the men of his generation and circle bore "a fundamental grievance against the present" (Chaigne 260). Huysmans, Bloy, Maritain, Péguy, and Claudel were all ardent admirers of medieval art and life, as was, of course, Rouault himself. He once remarked, "I do not feel as if I belonged to this modern life . . . ; my real life is back in the age of the Cathedrals" (qtd. in Speaight 63).

It may be surmised, however, that the Middle Ages represented to this group as much a romantic ideal as an historical era. Huysmans's writings on medieval art and symbolism rested as much on intuition as on research, while Maritain's Thomism was notable less for its dogmatic fidelity to the thought of St. Thomas than for its adaptability and venturesome approaches to such twentieth-century phenomena as political democracy and abstract art.

Similarly, Rouault, for all his deep feeling for "the age of the Cathedrals," did not actually visit Chartres until 1939, his sixty-ninth year, when the windows were being removed for wartime safekeeping, and this despite the fact that he had lived in and around Paris all his life.[5] A preference for the subjective image over the historical reality must, however, be regarded as a healthy thing for his art. Especially in his later career, it often imparted to his paintings a romantic and exotic glow without their ever becoming archeological. His luminous reds and blues, heavy dark contours, and often iconic compositions sometimes evoke, but never imitate, Gothic stained glass. "There is far too much imitation of the past, a superficial approach to the beautiful and the sublime," he warned. "Just as we do not wear the same clothes as our ancestors, it would be artificial to imitate at all costs the faith of the Middle Ages" (qtd. in Courthion 348).

Rouault's sense of the futility of resurrecting a bygone past may well have been rooted in his early experience with the colony of religious artists organized by Huysmans at Ligugé, described above. He continued to cherish the goals of the Ligugé colony, as is seen by his frequent nostalgic references to the anonymous, communal art of the Middle Ages. But, the very limited success and ignominious end of the project probably convinced him of the impossibility of attaining these ideals in the twentieth century.

> The anonymous builder of a great work, how far superior he was to many pseudo-personalities of our epoch, when the ideal collaboration between architect, painter, and sculptor has been abolished. The art of the cathedrals is at once collective and personal, but we cannot revive artificially such a mode of living, of feeling, of understanding, of loving. We can do other things, but we cannot re-create what the spontaneous collective effort of generations built with the faith that was theirs. (127–28)

After the experiment at Ligugé, Rouault never took part in any further group religious enterprises, and, what is more surprising, he showed little interest in programs of church decoration. This was not entirely a matter of choice, of course, since ecclesiastical authorities largely ignored his art, at least until the last two decades of his career. However, although he was always generous in permitting the adaptation of his finished works to church decoration, he refused a request in 1937, by the architect Henri Videl, to design a stained-glass window for a church in the Cité Ouvrière of Tavaux (on grounds of lack of time), and four of his five windows for the Church at Assy, commissioned in 1945, as well as the tapestry for the Chapel at Hem of 1957, are simply translations of oil paintings not originally intended for church settings (Rubin 84–99). Apparently he was not eager to participate personally in that "ideal collaboration between architect, painter and sculptor" that he so much admired in medieval art. Rouault was, by all accounts, a shy and private person, but his ambivalence toward such liturgical commissions probably reflects also his acknowledged horror of pretentiousness in religious art (108). For him, faith was evidently less a communal than a personal or even a mystical experience.

It is a measure of his success as a twentieth-century religious painter, however, that he was able to convey both the complexity and the power of that personal experience. He imparts a spiritual dimension to everyday life so that there are no sharp boundaries between his secular and his sacred themes. (Interestingly two of his five windows for the Church at Assy are floral still-lifes which would normally fall into the former category.) As Suarès once assured him: "Everything you do is religious, even your clowns . . ." (qtd. in San Lazzaro 7).

The figure of Jesus appears with increasing frequency in Rouault's later paintings, beginning in the second decade of the century. A fine early example is the *Crucifixion*, of about 1918, in the Philadelphia Museum of Art (fig. 10). These images have the impact of a direct encounter: Christ is usually shown in close up, or, if placed in a landscape or interior, in quiet communion with two or three other figures. Yet the abstraction of forms and the intensity of colors imbue these scenes with a sense of mystery, of transcendence. Paradoxically, too, for all their intimacy, these visions are seen through the filter of centuries of devotional tradition. The recollection of Gothic stained glass has already been mentioned; sometimes a painted frame within the frame suggests the presence of a hallowed icon, or a crucifixion takes on almost the character of a crucifix; often the rich surface of pigment and the luminous effect of chiaroscuro recalls Rouault's early idol, Rembrandt, or his beloved teacher, Gustave Moreau. The synthesis of individual expression and allegiance to pious tradition, characteristic of the Catholic revival as a whole, is nowhere better seen than in these works.

In conclusion, then, it may be seen that if Rouault felt himself a lonely figure in the twentieth century, it was at least a loneliness shared with some of the most select and creative spirits of his generation.

Notes

1. An enlightening discussion of the social and political views associated with the Catholic revival is to be found in Griffiths, esp. chaps. 10 and 12. Rouault's social views may also have been shaped in part by his father, Alexandre Rouault, a cabinetmaker and admirer of the originally Catholic radical Felix de Lamennais. The senior Rouault became estranged from Catholicism and sent his son to a Protestant school because of the Church's condemnation of Lamennais.

2. Prostitutes are among the protagonists of Huysmans's *Marthe, Histoire d'une fille,* and *Les Soeurs Vatard,* and of Bloy's *Le Desespéré.* As

Courthion suggests (99), Rouault's prostitute studies bring to mind "Dostoevsky, and particularly the Dostoevsky revealed in *Crime and Punishment.*" However, Rouault's correspondence with Suarès indicates that it was not until 1911, by which time he had largely abandoned the subject of prostitution, that Rouault first read *Crime and Punishment* with "la joie de Christophe Colomb apercevant le Nouveau Monde . . ." (3).

3. As in a courtroom scene in the Boymans Museum, Rotterdam, and in a watercolor entitled *Articles Produced in Evidence* in Melbourne, Australia. James Ensor also juxtaposes the bleeding feet of Christ on a crucifix to the malicious faces of a panel of judges in *Les Bons Juges* (1891, private collection) and in an etching based on this painting.

4. Péguy's first book was *Jeanne d'Arc*, published in 1897. Claudel supplied the text for Arthur Honegger's *Jeanne au bûcher*. Bloy wrote *Jeanne d'Arc et l'Allemagne* in 1915. The cult of Jeanne and its ideological ramifications is outlined in Warner.

5. Courthion (341) quotes Rouault as having told him: "I never rush things. It was not until 1940, the beginning of the last war, that I saw Chartres for the first time." However, Rouault's recollection of the date seems to be mistaken since a poem entitled "L'Oasis," commemorating this visit is dated August-September 1939, which also corresponds more closely to the beginning of the war (166). The thought of the rose window at Chartres inspires Rouault to an outburst of lyricism in a letter to Suarès in 1925, but he adds that he has never seen it to his "shame and regret" (Rouault and Suarès 199).

Works Cited

"A la Galerie Charpentier Rouault peintures inconnues ou célèbres," *L'Art Sacré*, 7–8 (March-April, 1965).

Bloy, Léon. *Pilgrim of the Absolute*. Trans. John Coleman and Harry Lorin Binsse. Ed. Raïssa Maritain. New York: Pantheon, 1947.

Chaigne, Louis. *Paul Claudel: The Man and the Mystic*. Trans. Pierre de Fontnouvelle. New York: Appleton, 1961.

Charensol, Georges. *Georges Rouault: L'homme et l'oeuvre*. Paris: Éditions des Quatre Chemins, 1926.

Clark, Kenneth. *The Nude: A Study in Ideal Form*. Bollingen Series 35. New York: Pantheon, 1956.

Claudel, Paul. *Théâtre*. Vol. 2. Paris: Bibliothèque de la Pléiade, 1956. 2 vols.

Courthion, Pierre. *Rouault*. New York: Abrams, 1961.

Denis, Maurice. *Histoire de l'art religieux*. Paris: Flammarion, 1939.

Dyrness, William A. *Rouault: A Vision of Suffering and Salvation.* Grand Rapids, MI: Eerdmans, 1971.
Griffiths, Richard. *The Reactionary Revolution: The Catholic Revival in French Literature, 1870–1914.* New York: Ungar, 1965.
Heppenstall, R. *Leon Bloy.* New Haven: Yale UP, 1954.
Huysmans, J.-K. *Les Foules de Lourdes.* Paris: Plon, 1915.
Laver, James. *The First Decadent: Being the Strange Life of J.-K. Huysmans.* London: Faber, 1954.
Maritain, Jacques. *Art and Scholasticism with Other Essays.* Trans. J. F. Scanlan. New York: Scribner's, 1937.
Maritain, Raïssa. *Adventures in Grace.* Trans. Julie Kernan. New York: Longmans, 1945.
Musée National d'Art Moderne. *Georges Rouault: Exposition du Centenaire.* Paris: Ministère des Affaires Culturelles, 1971.
Charles Péguy. "Dieu et la France." *Basic Verities, Prose and Poetry.* Trans. Ann and Julian Green. New York: Pantheon, 1945. 234–38.
Rouault, Georges. *Sur l'art et sur la vie.* Paris: Denoel/Gonthier, 1971.
Rouault, Georges, and André Suarès. *Correspondance.* Paris: Gallimard, 1960.
Rubin, William. *Modern Sacred Art and the Church of Assy.* New York and London: Columbia UP, 1961.
San Lazzaro, G. di, ed. *Homage to Georges Rouault.* Trans. Joan Sanchez. New York: Tudor, 1971.
Soby, James Thrall. *Georges Rouault: Paintings and Prints.* New York: Museum of Modern Art, 1947.
Speaight, Robert. "Homage to Rouault." *Dublin Review* 209 (July 1941).

8 • A Life of Allegory: Type and Pattern in Historical Narratives

Edward T. Oakes, S.J.

> A man's life of any worth is a continual allegory—and very few eyes can see the mystery of his life—a life like the Scriptures, figurative.
>
> JOHN KEATS
> LETTER TO GEORGE AND GEORGINA KEATS, 1819

STORYTELLING IS AS OLD as language itself, but for the theoretician its persistence in human culture raises more questions than it answers. Why *do* we tell stories? And why are human minds endowed with such "seething brains, such shaping fantasies, that apprehend more than cool reason ever comprehends" (*A Midsummer Night's Dream* V.i.5–6)?

This enigmatic gift of the imagination is primarily future-directed. That is, it tells us that man is a being who is innately and fundamentally open to possibility. Imagination's presence in the mind tells us that the human mode of being is not limited to the here-and-now but is always being projected forward, spurred on by the encounter with (imagined) possibility. Human existence is always forward-oriented, and imagination is the way the human mind constantly projects its own self forward toward other possible ways of being. Out of the theoretical infinity of numberless possibilities, imagination conjures up concrete visions of what "might be." Either this "might be" could refer to what might be in the future itself (this is the realistic imagination) or it could refer to the purely fantastic. In this case, the "might be" is projected not so much to a realistic future as to the privileged locale of the imagination itself. But in both instances, imagination gives to "airy nothing / a local habitation and a name" (*A Midsummer Night's Dream* V.i.17) out of the surplus of its imaginative powers.

Narrating history, however, is a peculiar kind of storytelling, and therefore a variant exercise of the imagination. For here imagination is not so much provoked by the possible as disciplined by the past. What is narrated is not the projected imaginings of our "seething brains," but the irrevocable record of the past. And since they are not future-directed, historical narratives testify not so much to that surplus of being which is the object of hope, as to that *deficit* of being which constitutes the sorry record of our past: the failures and the evil; the massacres, plagues, and cruelty; war, strife, and death—that story, in short, that Hegel called a butcher's shop and Cardinal Newman a vision to dizzy and appall:

> [To consider] the tokens so faint and broken of a superintending design, the blind evolution of what turns out to be great powers or truths, the progress of things, as if from unreasoning elements, not towards final causes, the greatness and littleness of man, his far-reaching aims, his short duration, the curtain hung over his futurity, the disappointments of life, the defeat of the good, the success of evil, physical pain, mental anguish, the prevalence and intensity of sin, the pervading idolatries, the corruptions, the dreary hopeless irreligion, that condition of the whole race, so fearfully yet exactly described in the Apostle's words, "having no hope and without God in the world"—all that is a vision to dizzy and appall; and inflicts upon the mind the sense of a profound mystery, which is absolutely beyond human solution. (219–20)

Out of these seemingly diverse perspectives and modes of narration—the one more future-directed and hope-driven and free of the constraints of the actual, and the other past-directed and chastened by the record of human failure—has come the distinction, which appears so obvious and well established to common sense, between fact and fiction, chronicle and myth, legal deposition and novel, truth and fantasy. This distinction has by now been drummed into us with so many reinforcements and social controls—from the way bookstores shelve their wares to the way juries render their verdicts—that nothing would seem to be more obvious than the difference between an historical narrative of past events and a fictional account born of a novelist's imagination.

Recent developments in narratology and the philosophy of history, however, have begun to undermine this common-sense distinction (Atlas, Barthès, Jameson, Kermode, Schama). Historiography is that field, many now feel, where fictional description merges with factual claim. This new trend is not advanced out of an *a priori* conviction that the human mind has no access to the past, that it can know with certainty only the contents of its present consciousness. Such skepticism is primarily a philosophical doctrine, one that claims that the past is forever inaccessible to consciousness in any direct way. And therefore all our knowledge of the past is radically uncertain and reformable.

Recent theories which have attempted to break down the fact/fiction distinction do not build their case on this kind of Humean skepticism. Their thesis that there is something inherently fictive about the writing of history is based on a *literary* criticism of the historian's craft. Thus, the new argument is not so much skeptical as descriptive and phenomenological: based, that is, on a more exact investigation of the constituents of historical narrative itself. For example, Arthur Danto holds that what matters is not so much the secondary distinction between fiction and fact, as the primary category of narrative, which embraces both:

> Narration exemplifies one of the basic ways in which we represent the world, and the language of beginnings and endings, of turning points and climaxes, is complicated with the mode of representation to so great a degree that our image of our own lives must be deeply narrational. (xiii)

Even in philosophy of science, "fictions" (in the sense of imagined hypotheses woven by the human mind out of its imaginative powers) are now seen as valuable heuristic devices without which we would never gain access to the "facts." "Even empiricism," says Fredric Jameson, "is a theory and the exercise of a model" (154), an opinion echoed widely in the world of philosophy:

> The language of natural science is irreducibly metaphorical and inexact, and formalizable only at the cost of distortion of the his-

torical dynamics of scientific development and of the imaginative constructions in terms of which nature is interpretd by science. (Hesse 172)

But it is not enough merely to note that accounts of factual events in the past and works of pure fiction are both examples of narrative. This does not get us very far, for as yet narrative is merely a *formal* category admitting different contents. Simply highlighting the formal commonality of narrative does not inevitably entail an undermining of the fact/fiction distinction. Nonetheless, a closer look at how narratives are constructed shows not merely that narrative is a formal category but also that its structures affect the very presentation of what it narrates, and this primarily through the standard tropes of metaphor, type, allegory, and image (Burke 503–17).

Now, narratology has long recognized the function and place of such tropes as the ligaments and tendons that hold a fictional narrative together and give it cohesion. Traditional historians and philosophers of history have been more cautious, however, in espying the same motifs in historical narrative, but a closer analysis has shown their inevitability in all genres of narration. One of the most influential advocates of this thesis has been Hayden White, himself an important literary critic of the great nineteenth-century historians like Macaulay and de Tocqueville. He makes the important point that in the past

> when an element of figurative language turned up [in historical narratives], . . . it was treated only as a figure of speech, the content of which was either its literal meaning or a literalist paraphrase of what appeared to be its grammatically "correct" formulation. But in the process of literalization, what gets left out is precisely those elements of figuration—tropes and figures of thought, as the rhetoricians call them—without which the narrativization of real events, the transformation of a chronicle into a story, could never be effected. (24)

Thus, with this increasing breakdown of the hard-and-fast distinction between fact and fiction, theoreticians can no longer escape an investigation of how historical narratives are structured by the various literary techniques of internal cohesion. In the rest of this essay, I propose to look at some of these techniques, first generically, and then in their (often hidden) guises in historical narrative. I shall seek to ask how the use of type, pattern, and allegory (broadly defined) operates and functions, and what purpose these techniques serve: both to give internal cohesion to narrative itself and, above all, to provide indications of *meaning*, signs of a hopeful future of invented possibilities for the reader of that narrative.

In cases of historical narrative, this means investigating the implicit presence of typology or allegory embedded in what at first blush seems a merely descriptive narrative. Such narrative strategies become most apparent, to the critic if not to the writer, when we notice how the historian is often forced to describe how much an event, say the Protestant Reformation, is both continuous and discontinuous with what went before. Such judgments require the historian to show how much some events do not just happen but "point to" each other for mutual illumination. Wycliffe, Hus, and Tyndale are thus always discussed as forerunners of a Reformation which, as things turned out, they could only "point to" but not bring to fruition.

Now, before the advent of the fact/fiction distinction, writers of histories, especially in the ancient world, were rather more open—or "naïve," one might say—about their recognition of such patterns. This is particularly true of the biblical authors, particularly but not exclusively the writers of the New Testament, who were confronted with an already nearly closed canon of Scriptures which they too recognized as part of their own inspired "charters" (*graphē*) but which they saw as in some sense overtaken—but also fulfilled—by more recent events of salvation history.[1] The tension between these two polarities was resolved throughout the New Testament by what Paul called "allegory" (Gal. 4:24) and what more discriminating critics today call "typology." But, under the influence of positivism and historicism, such blatant typology was seen to be too flagrantly "interpretive" (that is, distorting) and thus was consciously eschewed. But this rigor proves to obscure another, more subtle naïveté, one that refuses to see how interest in history directly relates to the present, even by the choice of subjects. How, for example, could one even discuss Hus, Wycliffe, or Tyndale without reference to the sixteenth century, without, that is, at least implicitly recognizing a consistent motif that runs throughout a lengthy period of history, influencing even the present in the most direct way?

The presence of such motifs in a work of history testifies to important interpretive realities. Above all, recognition of *pattern* in the writing up of history testifies to an assertion of *meaning* in the events of history. In the words of John Marsh, "typology is a species of historical identification between events which either indicates or applies phenomenal identities between events in order to indicate their identity in meaning" (63).

Recognition of meaning, however, is a projective activity of the human mind. For the historical record, as we have suggested, is in and of itself much more the testimony of the *deficit* of being than it is of its surplus. What the assertion of meaning does is to ground historical narrative in a hope that transcends the warrants of the (mere) past. Typology, therefore, is more than the bald assertion of similarities between two arbitrary points in the past. It is also fundamentally an act of *extrapolation*, that is, an assertion of a meaning to history as such, as furnished not by the record alone but by the projective imagination. As Marsh explains, this is what distinguishes the historian from the mere annalist:

> The annalist writes down events as they occur, without any conscious attempt at interpretation, even if it be no more than the inevitable selection of events to be recorded. . . . This is not history. The historian, when he appears, sees more than a mere series of conjunctions in history. Writing from some temporal perspective, the historian can look back and see continuities and complexes of events, and identities reaching across the boundaries of event complexes, across ages and eras and cultures. So the historian is concerned with "patterns" and "meanings" in history, with connecting one event with another, and with the discovery thereby of the meaning of one event in terms of another. (51–52)[2]

It could perhaps be argued that these acts of meaning recognition are still strictly intrahistorical and empirical, and bespeak nothing about the meaning of the future, let alone of life as such. But this objection holds only if one first posits that the act of meaning recognition is inductive and empirical, spontaneously arising from the facts themselves and imposing its interpretation on the subject from without. This, however, flies in the face of how human beings actually perceive meaning. It is neither a purely arbitrary imposition of subjective projections on neutral data nor a passive recognition of a pregiven pattern. Recognition of meaning arises from the fusion of the subject's relation to the world *which is already narrative in form*. This is a point that the narrative philosopher Donald Polkinghorne has insisted on in his illuminating work, *Narrative Knowing and the Human Sciences*:

> [just as] perception is not originally made up of a confused buzz of isolated sense data but consists of already formed objects, so experience does not originally appear as discrete atoms of experience and then at some later time become organized and patterned. Experience forms and presents itself in awareness as narrative. It is from this original experience that the literary form is derived.... We see that historians do not work with isolated fragments of past actions which they then construct into a story. Rather, for the most part, they work with materials that are already in story form. (68–69)

In other words, it is neither intuitively obvious nor self-evident that meanings percolate upward out of history, and that the task of the historian is but inductively to gather up the scattered evidence for the reality of meaning and pattern in historical events. On the contrary, recognition of meaning is a holistic activity of the human mind, which must encompass a myriad display of evidence from the past and present and see out of that kaleidoscope a pattern that *points to* a purpose. And I argue that such holistic viewing must by definition encompass both past and future in a way that motivates or "gives hope to" the present, which is grounded in the very narrative structure of experience itself. But such combined retrojection and projection moves well beyond the empirical furnishings of mere data (as available, for example, in the chronicles and documentation of history). Because of this fusion of various perspectives in meaning recognition, the perception of pattern is intimately bound with the activity of the imagination, that faculty that is inherently sense-and past-transcendent. For this reason, I believe Frank Kermode is fully justified in his narratology of history-writing when he asserts:

> We . . . inherit, and endorse or qualify, meanings given by others, and the written history on which speculation of this sort must depend may itself be thought of as a kind of imaginative fiction,

or a poem: persuasive, ordered, endowed with at least the simulacra of causality. (49)

The American Civil War provides perhaps the most direct instance of this inevitability. As Matthew Berke says in his review of the historiography of this war, "so tempting are the archetypal themes and patterns in the Civil War that few narratives on the subject—even if they consciously strive to purge themselves of all 'myth,' 'romance,' and 'theology'—can avoid mythic language and constructions altogether" (43).[3]

But in what way is meaning-recognition grounded in the imagination? First of all, to see meanings is a component of recognizing patterns in the world. And pattern recognition depends on the human capacity for juxtaposing diverse realities and seeing in that diversity (often surprising) similarities not at first evident from a cursory glance by the senses. Such juxtapositions, and the concomitant recognition of similarities that arises out of this juxtaposition, take various linguistic forms, from metaphor at the most particular level to narrative at the most general. And thus, in the words of one interpreter, "metaphors and narrative are the preeminent linguistic forms of the passion for the possible—the language of hope" (Vanhoozer 8).

This intersection of various linguistic forms of juxtaposition (metaphor, typology, etc.) with the pattern recognition they produce in the imagination means that the presence of typology in historical narratives is fundamentally a moment in the future-directed activity of the human mind: a supplying to the deficit of history that surplus of being that it is the function of the imagination to provide. In other words, when historiography moves beyond the mere cataloging of events in the manner of the annalist, it thereby and at the same time moves beyond the world of merely observable facts to seeing the meaning behind the human projects that make up the tissue of history.

The reason this move is also future-directed may be seen in the following argument: traditionally, philosophers have treated possibles as "future contingents"—that is, dependent on certain conditions that must obtain in the present, the absence of which creates an impossible. Thus, possibility in this view is what the order of *conditions* (that is, *things*) permits. But this ignores what makes a possibility something that is uniquely possible for a human being. For out of hope and imagination a human being creates not so much an abstract "possibility" as, more accurately, an inspiring "project." A project is a possibility that lies within *my* power, that is, within the order of *human* existence rather than in the order of things.

But because imagination is so teemingly abundant with its productions, weaving scenarios that could never obtain in the conditions of the real order, the temptation arises to dismiss human projects born of the imagination as "figments," that is, as fundamentally unreal because they have not been realized or, more poignantly, because the conditions for their realization will never obtain. Paul Ricoeur, whose analysis I follow here, resists this temptation, driving home the point that "it is by virtue of an unjustifiable reduction that we decide to equate 'world' with the whole of observable facts; I inhabit a world in which there is something 'to be done by me'; the 'to be done by me' belongs to the structure which *is* the 'world'" ("Philosophy" 68).

Now, the world that Ricoeur is referring to here is both the stuff of history and the stuff of historians. For human history in both senses is the story of projects, projects which indeed invariably go awry but which are nonetheless projects born out of inevitable hope and inevitable imagination. And historians who fail to interpret those projects for what they are also—and for that very reason—fail in their task of describing the story of the human.

But to live up to the challenge of that task means that the historian must make a leap of the imagination. It is of course true that this leap must be a disciplined one, unlike the freer flights of fancy the imagination makes in its fictional musings. Partly that discipline entails trying to understand the mental world of the era under investigation, so different from our own. But this effort is not the focus here. I am more interested in this essay in the different mental worlds of other times (Gadamer's "fusion of horizons") that in the relationship of events of one moment—often across wide spans of time and cultures—and events of another.

And this application of the imagination is, I have argued, one of the recognition of patterns. Generally, this pattern will take on certain identifiable teleological patterns, as in Marxist historiography or in the Whig interpretation of history, which posited such events as Magna Carta as the incipient or embryonic moment which eventually led to the constitutional monarchy of Victorian

Great Britain.[4] In our positivistic age, we often flatter ourselves for having outgrown such embarrassing Hegelianism: not for us the subsequently discomfiting notion that history has come to its fulfillment in the Prussian state! But unless history-writing is to revert once more, and entirely, to the annalist school and content itself only with the technical issues of the Cliometricians—busying itself with cataloging the statistics of commerce and populations, charting weather conditions and the like—historians can hardly avoid narrating the patterns of similarity/dissimilarity, continuity/discontinuity, incipient moment/later development.

These recognitions of patterns need not entail a bald assertion of cause-effect, as if one were claiming that the Magna Carta *caused* the Glorious Revolution, etc. In fact, invoking such simplistic cause-effect logic would be to relapse into the world of thing-possibility rather than staying within the world of human project that constitutes the matter of history. Seeing connections in history is a much more complicated affair and involves the application of insight into interrelating patterns and figures. Because such patterns cross boundaries of time, they cannot help but be interpreted in terms of early manifestation versus later full-blown development, or, in biblical terms, earlier promise *vs.* later fulfillment, or foretype/archetype. This was one of the most crucial points made by Erich Auerbach in his influential essay on "Figura":

> Figural interpretation establishes a connection between two events or persons, the first of which signifies not only itself but also the second, while the second encompasses or fulfills the first. The two poles of the figure are separate in time, but both, being real events or figures, are within time, within the stream of historical life. Only the understanding of the two persons or events is a spiritual act, but this spiritual act deals with concrete events whether past, present, or future, and not with concepts or abstractions. (53)

All such positings of linkage between a past event and its later alleged fulfillment are, of course, debatable. Not everyone sees Luther's posting of the Ninety-Five Theses on the Wittenberg church door as the onset of modern self-consciousness or the opening salvo in the battle for individual self-assertion against the forces of obscurantism. Nor is it at all immediately obvious upon a first reading of Magna Carta that King John's barons would have supported the Glorious Revolution, let alone joined the American Civil Liberties Union. But while individual patterns are fit subjects for debate, the *motivation* for finding these patterns arises from the very form of narrative itself into which the telling of the story of our race has been cast. For, as Kevin Vanhoozer explains,

> in giving us an historical consciousness, narrative bestows an identity as well. Indeed . . . personal identity is inherently narrative in nature. To understand who we are is to be able to follow our stories. Narrative also provides the all-important link between the continuity and discontinuity of the self. As historical, the self changes; yet it remains itself. One implication of narrative identity is that we must be "readers" of our own lives. One way of making sense of who we are is to identify with characters in other stories and histories. To the extent that this is so, these narratives "refigure" our lives. (103–104)

And it is this potential of narratives to "refigure" our lives, I argue, that lies behind our ability to recognize the presence of *figurae* in the art of telling. That is why Auerbach sees that one of the essential characteristics of a "figura" in historical narrative (whether that be foretype or later fulfillment) is *contemporary significance*:

> The thing represented must always be something very important and holy for those concerned, something affecting their whole life and thinking, and this something is not only expressed or imitated in the sign or symbol, but is considered to be itself present and contained in it. (56)

With this analysis we are approaching that juncture in the argument where we can finally see why Paul Ricoeur holds that the very art of telling puts us into contact with the entire pattern-structure of the world—*including its future meanings*—and thereby with the most fundamental of religious questions. As he says in his three-volume Summa on these questions, "The most serious question that this book can pose is to know to what extent a philosophical reflection on narrativity and time can help us to think about eternity and death together" (*Time* 87).

What justifies this extraordinary linkage is the intimate connection that bonds the telling of stories to the act of discovering/ inventing religious significance in the universe and in the human life lived out in it.[5] Because of the inventive and future-directed nature of the imagination, it must perforce encounter the boundaries of death and eternity. But doing so means that giving free rein to the imagination is fundamentally a religious act. Imagination in its deepest structures is always religious imagination, for its assertion of meaning is inherently future-directed and teleological, and is therefore, I argue, inevitably grounded in theological assumptions: seeing patterns, recognizing a *Gestalt* in narrative form, is itself an instance of the exercise of the religious imagination.

These statements can be established when we realize how the imagination always weaves its images through the innately mythical structures of its productive powers. As we have seen, imagination always operates within ontological structures that manifest the deficits of being in the past while looking on the future as providing a possible restoration of that deficit out of its possible "surplus." But this is to put abstractly what the imagination conceives of concretely as a myth, a myth that narrates an explanation of that deficit and surplus.

Now history of course is a story of movement within time. But as such it is rooted as a narration in, and borrows the structures of, the prior and more basic mythic movement from Proton to Eschaton. As Ricoeur explains:

> The universality of man, manifested through the myths, gets its concrete character from the *movement* which is introduced into human experience by narration. In recounting the Beginning and the End, myth confers upon this experience an orientation, a character, a tension. Experience is no longer reduced to a present experience; this present was only an instantaneous cross-section in an evolution stretching from an origin to a fulfillment, from a "Genesis" to an "Apocalypse." Thanks to the myth, experience is traversed by the essential history of the perdition and salvation of man. (*Symbolism* 163)

This mythic background in all narrative recognition of pattern (between earlier adumbration and later fulfillment) operates even where the assertions of the myth are explicitly denied; indeed, it is perhaps never more operative than when the myth is denied. For mythical construction of narrative is an inherent aspect of the ontological constitution of man, caught as he is between the deficit and surplus of being: and the effort to deny the role of mythical structure in the formation of narrative does not in any way affect or undermine that inherent constitution.

The ironic upshot of this is that history then becomes *less* historical, that is, less faithful to the event it seeks to describe, when for ideological reasons myths of Beginning and End are not admitted as operative in history. Marxist ideology is in fact the irrefutable proof of the inevitability of mythic consciousness in history, as we see in the very way Marx goes about dismantling mythical consciousness:

> So our campaign slogan must be: reform of consciousness, not through dogma, but through the analysis of that mystical consciousness which has not yet become clear to itself. It will then turn out that the world has merely dreamed of what now it can possess fully if it would but have a clear idea of it. It will turn out that it is not a question of any conceptual rupture between past and future, but rather of the *completion* of the thoughts of the past. (43)

What Marx ends up proving—in direct opposition to his own conscious intention—is that mythic consciousness is rooted in inherent ontological structures in man. Clearly, Marx wants to insist that the denial of the *images* of myth does not thereby entail a denial of the sense that the future represents a surplus in being, one that has the potential for compensating the deficits of current history. But because he has denied any role to the images of myth as a myth, Marx has merely transposed the concrete images of myth into his own historical projects. The upshot of this move is that a mythically imagined Eschaton now becomes an allegedly nonmythical utopia (= "nowhere"!) which Marx claims can be located in a realizable future.

Yet, for all of Marx's alleged purgations of the "mystical" consciousness, the function of his historiography remains the same: to drive home the point to the human person that the present is not what the future will be. This is the point of the implicit utopianism of all forms of progressive historiography. And an analysis of its role, its "demythologization" as it were, only goes to prove the inevitably forward-directed implications of the narration of history, as we see in Ricoeur's analysis of Utopia:

I thus propose to move beyond the thematic contents of utopia to its functional structure. I suggest that we start from the kernel idea of the Nowhere, implied by the word "utopia" itself and by the descriptions of Thomas More: a place which exists in no real place, a ghost city; a river with no water, a prince with no people, and so on. What must be emphasized is the *benefit* of this special extra territoriality. From this "no place" an exterior glance is cast on our reality, which suddenly looks strange, nothing more being taken for granted. The field of the possible is now open beyond that of the actual; it is a field, therefore, for alternative ways of living. (*Lectures* 16)

But these formal similarities should not deceive us into assuming that utopian and mythical projections of the future are interchangeable. For utopian projections hope for a full realization of the Eschaton at some point in the future, however distant; while myth acknowledges the utter transcendence and sheer gratuity of the hoped-for future. By subsuming the Eschaton into a realizable future through a critique of the "ideology" of myth, secularist and Marxist historiographies only serve to abandon man to the Pathos of the real. Utopia, as its name implies, is purely abstract, with no power in and of itself (despite all its pretensions) to realize what it imagines it hopes for.

Utopia remains forever pathetic because it neither "projects" nor hopes for that gracious Presence, the fullness of Being itself, which alone can realize the deficit of our being caught in the web of corroding time. Myth's great advantage is that it can refer to that overarching and transcendent structure of Being within which alone the narrative of history flows. It alone can tell us in eschatological terms of the meaning of that deficit that so characterizes our past, and has marked our history from the beginning.

Utopia, however, when divorced from myth, leaves man stranded in time, with no orientation for anchoring purely intratemporal narratives. In the vocabulary of Gerard Manley Hopkins, the utopian imagination leaves man only with his "motionable mind," ever active, ever searching for a rootedness in that "girth" of history that alone can give it meaning. A hope confined to history alone closes off access to that "quenching ocean" that alone can give our disquieted minds both peace and hope:

> I admire thee, master of the tides,
> Of the Yore-flood, of the year's fall;
> The recurb and the recovery of the gulf's sides,
> The girth of it and the wharf of it and the wall;
> Staunching, quenching ocean of a motionable mind;
> Ground of being, and granite of it: past all
> Grasp God, throned behind
> Death with a sovereignty that heeds but hides, bodes but abides.
>
> (Hopkins, "The Wreck of the Deutschland," Stanza 32)

Religious imagination, however, represents precisely that leap of the projecting mind to the "recurb and recovery" of history's flux and tides. Only religious imagination can take history's patterning, its back-and-forth tidal flow, and see how that pattern of ebb and rise has a girth, a wharf, and a wall. Only through the religious imagination can we hope for that final moment when the deficit of our recorded history will be replenished out of God's surplus, when God will make all things new.

Notes

1. Such "patterning" is by no means confined to the New Testament appropriation of the Old, for it occurs within the canon of the Hebrew Bible as well. One example of such *ex post facto* shaping of the narrative in terms of typology within the Old Testament canon would be Joshua 3:17 ("The priests who carried the ark of the covenant of the Lord stood firm on dry ground in the middle of the Jordan, while all Israel passed by until the whole nation had completed the crossing on dry ground")— a clear allusion to the crossing over the Sea of Reeds (Exod. 14:29).

2. Of course, this distinction between the annalist and the narrative historian can be overdrawn, for even a mere chronicle is still a narrative and as such "employs" a theory of history: "Even the plainest unreflective history—the sheerest, most 'mindless' enumeration of facts, of an annals or a chronicle—implies a whole metaphysics and constitutes through its mere enunciation a whole philosophy of history in its own right" (Jameson 154).

3. Berke goes on to cite a scholar of American literature on this very point: "From its very beginning, the War seemed designed for literary treatment as if history itself had assiduously collaborated with the would-be writer. He had only to plagiarize from the plot of the authorial

Providence who first blocked out the acts and scenes of its cautionary epic, to draw upon the coincidences, portents, climaxes, tragic heroes, and villains of the heavenly scenario" (43).

4. For Marxist historiography, see the excellent three-volume analysis by Kolakowski, and Billingtion; for the Whigs see Butterfield.

5. I have used the fused term "discover/invent" here not to forestall the Feuerbachian challenge which asserts that all theology is the projected inventions of the human mind, but to give credit once more to the genuinely *creative* aspect of human imagination, which though truly inventive is yet cognitively informative: "In short, we must restore to the fine word *invent* its twofold sense of both discovery and creation" (Ricoeur, "Philosophy" 306)

Works Cited

Atlas, James. "Stranger than Fiction." *New York Times Magazine* (23 June 1991): 22–43.
Auerbach, Erich. "Figura." *Scenes from the Drama of European Literature: Six Essays.* Gloucester, MA: Smith, 1973. 12–67.
Barthès, Roland. "Historical Discourse." *Introduction to Structuralism.* Ed. Michael Lane. New York: Basic Books, 1970. 145–55.
Berke, Matthew. "The Myth of the Civil War." *First Things* 16 (October 1991): 42–49.
Billington, James. *Fire in the Minds of Men: Origins of the Revolutionary Faith.* New York: Basic Books, 1980.
Burke, Kenneth. "Four Master Tropes." *A Grammar of Motives.* New York: Prentice-Hall, 1952. 503–17.
Danto, Arthur C. *Narration and Knowledge.* New York: Columbia UP, 1985.
Hesse, Mary. *Revolutions and Reconstructions in the Philosophy of Science.* Brighton, England: Harvester, 1980.
Jameson, Fredric. "Figural Relativism; or, The Poetics of Historiography." *The Ideologies of Theory: Essays, 1971–1986.* Vol. 1. *Situations of History.* Minneapolis: U of Minnesota P, 1988. 153–65.
Kermode, Frank. *Poetry, Narrative, and History.* Oxford: Blackwell, 1990.
Marsh, John. "Christ in the Old Testament." *Essays in Christology for Karl Barth.* Ed. T. H. L. Parker. London: Butterworth, 1956. 39–70.
Marx, Karl. *Early Writings.* Ed. and trans. T. B. Bottomore. New York: McGraw-Hill, 1964.
Newman, John Henry. *Apologia pro vita sua.* 1864. Ed. C. F. Harrold. New York: Longmans, 1947.

Polkinghorne, Donald E. *Narrative Knowing and the Human Sciences.* Albany: State U of New York P, 1988.
Ricoeur, Paul. 1967. *Lectures on Ideology and Utopia.* Ed. George H. Taylor. New York: Columbia UP, 1986.
———. "Philosophy of Will and Action." *The Philosophy of Paul Ricoeur: An Anthology of His Work.* Ed. Charles E. Reagan and David Stewart. Boston: Beacon, 1978.
———. *The Symbolism of Evil.* Trans. Emerson Buchanan. Boston: Beacon, 1967.
———. *Time and Narrative.* Vol. 1. Trans. Kathleen McLaughlin and David Pellauer. Chicago: U of Chicago P, 1984. 3 vols.
Schama, Simon. *Dead Certainties, Unwarranted Speculations.* New York: Knopf, 1991.
Vanhoozer, Kevin J. *Biblical Narrative in the Philosophy of Paul Ricoeur: A Study in Hermeneutics and Theology.* Cambridge: Cambridge UP, 1990.
White, Hayden. "The Question of Narrative in Contemporary Historical Theory." *History and Theory* 23 (1984): 1–33.

II • INTO THE TWENTY-FIRST CENTURY

9 • A View from the Far Side

Andrew Greeley

INTRODUCTION

MY POSITION ON THE INTERPRETATION and criticism of my own work is that anyone who buys the book or at least reads it has the right to his own opinion of what the book is about, provided he does not pull passages out of context and twist their meaning so that the words say the opposite of what they clearly say in their context. It is in the nature of storytelling that many valid interpretations can be drawn from any story. The author is entitled to his own interpretation, however, and, while he can claim no special privilege for that interpretation, it ought at least to be listened to because he knows the characters and the story from the inside. He must recognize, however, that his own interpretation is not the only one possible, or even a privileged interpretation. Similarly, others who engage in hermeneutic on a story also should, to be fair, admit that other interpretations are possible.

At the request of others, I engage in this exercise in self-hermeneutic with some trepidation. It will surely bring down on me the wrath of the people who write for the "liberal" Catholic journals who will argue in effect that self-interpretation is self-serving. But such an argument denies an author the right to explore his own work to find out what it means to him, if to no one else. It is not my intent to judge whether it be "good literature" (as Catholic critics sometimes judge)[1] but only to explore the symbolic themes which seem to hold it together.

Moreover, when I try to do hermeneutic on my own work, I am often surprised at what I find. I do not begin my stories with any clearly thought-out "theme," much less a "moral" to drive home. Yet certain trajectories emerge much, I must say, to my own surprise. It is about these trajectories that I will try to write.

Illumination Not Indoctrination

John Shea has wisely said that a storyteller invites his audience into the world of the story, attempts to enthrall the audience with the story and thus to illuminate them, so that they may go forth from the story with perhaps a new insight or a broadened old insight into how life might be lived. The purpose of a story, therefore, is not to educate or indoctrinate, but to illuminate. Illumination can be reduced to a prose proposition, as long as the one who so reduces it is aware that the flesh and the blood, the muscle and the nerve endings, the hormones and the energies of the story are usually eliminated by the interpretation. There is something, nonetheless, about the contemporary educational system in the Western world which demands that the story be taken apart and analyzed, as if one were writing a high school book report, both by those who earn their living and possibly their academic tenure by such activities and by those who read the book. To reduce poetry to prose, to tear the elements of a story apart and consider them under a microscope, is somehow or the other to master the story and the storyteller and make him subject to oneself.

Such activities, provided they are carried out with sufficient respect for the story and sufficient humility, can be useful, as long as the story itself is left intact. Critics, amateur and professional, often find it difficult to exercise such restraint. The reader's impulse to dominate the storyteller by producing an "opinion" in two or three sentences the moment the last page is finished is childish and contemptuous, but typical of those who once were forced to write high school book reports for class the next day. A story should be permitted to float in our imaginations for some time so that it might take possession of us and its images permeate our personality and permit us to experience it from the inside. It took me a week of such uneasy reflection (precognitive reflection) to grasp the film *The Crying Game*. Then I exclaimed, "Only an Irishman would try something like that and only an Irishman could carry it off!"

A similar period of uneasy "playing" with William Kennedy's *Ironweed* in both its written and its cinematic version was necessary before I could experience the power of its richness. I noted that in the film version, the Meryl Streep character said her final prayer in church not in her bedroom and in front of the statue of St. Joseph, the Catholic patron of a happy death, and that in the book, the author tells us, "she was asking for grace."

I know in my imagination and in my intellect what both stories are about. But if I have to tell you in prose propositions, I am reduced to clichés such as *The Crying Game* was about the power of love. Or *Ironweed* was about redemption. I would much rather say, "Ponder the woman praying to St. Joseph" or "Look at the last scene in the prison in *The Crying Game*." Then I would like to ask, "How do you think the incidents might be illuminating us?" By asking such questions I am not sitting in judgment from on high of the author and his work. Rather, I am inviting the one who has been listening to me to become a co-conspirator with the author and to experience the story from the inside. Then perhaps one can say that a story is about the power of love or the possibility of redemption, and the descriptions are no longer clichés because the aura of the wonder experience gives them life.

It would follow from this approach to a story that a wise reader or viewer or listener should train himself/herself to be sensitive when the moments of peak illumination appear in a story. It is about those moments in my own work as I perceive it that I will try to report in this essay.

It has always seemed to me that one of the best parts of *The Cardinal Sins* is the scene in which Ellen Foley tells Kevin Brennan that she wants to be back inside the Church with all the wondrous images and experiences of Catholicism and she wants these for herself and her children.

> "I'm still waiting for the real sin, the only sin," I said.
> She tilted her head. "I've told everything."
> "You haven't told the one important thing. You were mad at God and mad at the Church and pretended for a long time you could get away from both."
> "I don't want to talk about it," she said.
> "Then no absolution," I said firmly.
> She tugged her hand to free it. I wasn't going to let it go. "Don't you have an ounce of compassion in that ice-cold soul of yours?"

"If you want compassion, Ellen, go to your husband or have him recommend a psychiatrist who will listen sympathetically. If you want absolution, don't play games."

She stopped tugging. We were quiet for a long time.

"That's the only one that does matter, isn't it?" she said. "All right, Kevin, I'll say it, and you'll have to mop up the tears on this hard floor of yours. I blamed the Church and God for things that were inside me and my family. I focused on all the ugly things and forgot about Father Conroy and Sister Caroline and first Communion and May crownings and High Club dances and midnight mass and all those wonderful things that I love so much. I gave them all up because I was angry. I blamed the Church for Tim's death. I loved him so much. I couldn't save him, and I thought the Church should have saved him. Even when I was doing it, I knew I was wrong and that someday I'd be kneeling on the floor before you and pleading to be let back in."

"And now you have done it," I said, feeling a huge burden lift away and go spiraling off into space. "And the damn-fool Church says, 'Ellen Foley Curran Strauss, we really didn't notice you were gone, because we never let you go.'"

I did not plan to write that scene when I began the novel—though I did know where the story was beginning to go. I did not even know that I would write it when I started at my typewriter (before the days of personal computers) that morning. I knew that there would be a reconciliation between Ellen and Kevin and Ellen and the Church. It was only when I actually saw and "heard" the characters talking to each another that the scene exploded in my head. I knew in the writing of it that it would be very important for the book, indeed an encapsulation of the illumination of the whole book and of all my work as a storyteller.

In the scene I am not telling people that the Church will take them back (presumably they know that anyway), much less trying to persuade them that they should return. All I am doing—and I think this is everything—is telling a story about a woman who does return. Moreover, the reaction from readers—hundreds writing or phoning that the scene has attracted them back into the Church—persuaded me that I was correct in judging that the illumination of the scene was crucial to the book.

Yet in the controversy that the book stirred up, the scene was never mentioned. In all the cries of protest against presenting sinful priests, corruption in the Church, the sexual desires of priests, a priest writing about sex, the similarity with Cardinal Cody (there wasn't any!), a priest making money by telling "steamy" stories, etc., etc., etc., this scene was never discussed—by either friendly advocates or hostile critics. I do not think that it has ever appeared in any of the venomous articles in Catholic journals in the last decade and a half. Only some of the scholarly critics have discovered it.

I ask myself how could they have missed it? How could anyone read *The Cardinal Sins* and miss that scene? I conclude that one could miss the scene only if one were rushing to judgment and was not ready to explore the story for illumination. Every reader has the right to do that, of course. But to do so is to violate the storytelling process.

Resurrections and Home-Comings

There are two "myths" that seem to have affected my writing, not exactly consciously but not exactly unconsciously either: the myth of Ulysses and the myth of the Holy Grail—the latter clearly Celtic and the former transmuted into something at least partially Celtic in this century (oddly enough by a man who didn't come home physically, though he never left home spiritually).

I am surprised, when I consider my novels, how many resurrections there are. Lisa Malone revives from a death-like coma in *Happy Are the Clean of Heart*. Catherine Collins's grave has become a shrine in *Virgin and Martyr*, but she returns. Paul Cronin in *Thy Brother's Wife* is reported dead in Korea but comes home when the prisoners of war are finally released, as does Leo Kelly in *Lord of the Dance*. Ciara Kelly disappears from the face of the earth in *Rite of Spring*. Mary Anne Haggerty in *Happy Are Those Who Work for Justice* vanishes on prom night in 1946 and is presumed dead. She reappears forty-six years later. Jerry Keenan says a prayer at the grave of Maggie Ward in San Diego, and yet that worthy reappears in other books to give almost as much advice as Blackie Ryan. Moreover, other protagonists who have gone away return home to wrestle with the demons and the loves they have left behind—Neil Connor in *St. Valentine's Night*, Kieran

O'Kerrigan in *Fall from Grace*, Moira Meehan in *Wages of Sin*, Lisa Malone as a young woman, Jim O'Neill in *Death in April*.

Both those who have been revived and those who return discover that they must struggle painfully to be alive again. Noele Farrell, the brash teenage prophet of *Lord of the Dance* reproves her "cousin" Danny for his discouragement and offers him advice that would be appropriate for all the other returnees: "Daniel Xavier, resurrection isn't supposed to be easy!"

Clearly, there is a kind of Ulysses theme (whether in the Greek or Hibernian versions) in my stories. Men and women go away, sometimes it seems even into the valley of death, and then come back to deal with the problems of winning their Penelope again and routing those who have taken possession of her. In *Fall from Grace*, the smooth, handsome, and ingenious clerical chorus, Father Brendan McNulty (who is half in love, as anyone would be, with the wondrous Kathleen Leary), even announces that he has become Telemachus to Kieran O'Kerrigan's Ulysses.

I did not consciously set out to use the Ulysses myth (though in *Fall from Grace* I was clearly aware that it was operating) any more than I tried to write stories about resurrections—and the struggles involved therein. Intellectually I believe that death and rebirth are the paradigm of human life, experiences that happen often to us. But it was not my intent to teach that lesson. I suppose all that I wanted to do was to write stories that were hopeful, though not quite happy. Resurrection symbolism arose on its own. Indeed, in the one story in which I explicitly involved your man from Dublin, *Happy are the Peace Makers*, the resurrection/return themes are at most latent.

I am happy that upon reviewing these stories I have discovered that I have kept some kind of gender balance. Women as well as men must rise from the dead. Women as well as men must woo their old loves. Penelope returns to recapture Ulysses from the women who have made his life miserable since she went away, most notably Moire Meehan of *Wages of Sin*.

On several occasions I find that I have emphasized the rebirth themes by putting them in an Easter context. The paradigm, I think, is at the end of *Lord of the Dance*.

> "After three hours of shouting we're still in the same room," he said wearily.

And through the argument his desire for her had increased. Fire yearning for water.

Irene was hunched over, her eyes fixed on the carpet.

She looked up and smiled wanly.

"We'll always be in the same room, Danny. From now on. You know that. . . ." She rose from the couch. "I'll make you a cheese omelet. Then we'd better go to St. Prax's for the Easter Vigil. Noele will be furious if we're not there."

"Woman of the house," he yelled after her, "put some ham in my cheese omelet."

He didn't hear her any response exactly, since she was already in the kitchen.

But she did serve him a cheese and ham omelet.

I should have asked for mushrooms, too.

In the brief interlude between the Liturgy of the Word (as they called the Mass of the Catechumens these days) and the Liturgy of the Eucharist (né Mass of the Faithful), the folk group materialized quietly in the sanctuary, the young women mature and self-possessed in dresses and high heels, the young men not too awkward in suits and ties.

They were herded on tiptoe to the Easter candle by a dazzling young woman in an apricot suit. The candle, with 1982 and the alpha and omega engraved on it, stood firm and upright, its flame heralding the renewal of life with the coming of spring.

A phallic symbol, if one was to take the Ace seriously.

Sure, what else was it?

I'm the candle and the water is next to me.

Champagne for breakfast every morning. Will I be bored with it?

Not likely.

The folk group was ready, awaiting—their leader's signal.

He extended the tips of his fingers, searching for his wife's fingers.

They were waiting for him.

"We're going to sing an Easter hymn about young men and young women," Noele informed the congregation. "It's called O Filii et Filiae, which is, like, Latin for teenagers. I'll sing a few of the stanzas in Latin in honor of old priests like the monsignor." She giggled and the congregation laughed. "And then we'll do it in English:

> *O filii et filiae*
> *Rex caelestis rex Gloriae*
> *Morte surrexit hodie*

Et mane prima sabbati
Ad ostium monumenti
Accesserunt discipuli

Et Maria Magdalene et Jacobii
Et Salome venerunt corpus
Ungere Alleluia!

In albis sedens Angelus
Praedixit mulieribus
In Galilaea est Dominus Alleluia!

Discipulis astantibus
In medio stet Christus
Dicens pax vobis omnibus Alleluia!

In hoc festo sanctissimo
Sic laus et jubilatio
Benedicamus Domino Alleluia!

"Now everybody sing it in English," Noele commanded the congregation. Everyone did.

Ye sons and daughters, let us sing!
The King of heaven our glorious King,
From death today rose triumphing, Alleluia!

That Easter Morn at break of day,
The faithful women went their way
To seek the tomb where Jesus lay, Alleluia!

An Angel clothed in white they see
Which sat and spoke unto the three
Your Lord has gone to Galilee, Alleluia!

That night the apostles met in fear
And Christ in their midst did appear
And said, My peace be with you here, Alleluia!

On this most holy day of days
To God your hearts and voices raise
In laud and jubilee and praise, Alleluia!

The Holy Grail and Second Chances

Unlike the rebirth theme, the other major theme that runs through my stories, the quest motif, was self-conscious at the beginning, though later it sank into my preconscious where it continued to have a lasting effect on my stories. I wrote *The Magic Cup* as a deliberate retelling of the Irish version of the Holy Grail quest, in which the hero finds the magic cup and the magic princess (with considerable help from her). The Celtic version of the Grail quest, unlike the version served up to us by the French and the British, is life-affirming, flesh-affirming. It would appear that in its original form it was a narrative to accompany a spring fertility ritual. The girl and the grail and the god were all in some intricate fashion identified with one another. Cormac MacArt finds the Magic Cup and wins the girl (though she might be the one who does the winning) and through the girl (who is not a Christian) discovers what the Christian God is really like.

While we know little about the most ancient rites and stories of the Grail, in Celtic antiquity, as Jean Markale has noted, the grail was probably a sacred vessel in a spring fertility rite which represented life and hence the vulva. But it also may have been, and perhaps more importantly, a symbol of nourishment and hence a cognate of the breast. Even in the life-denying and flesh-denying versions of the legend served up to us by courtiers of the Plantagenet kings, the Holy Grail is profoundly womanly in its implications—a source of life and nourishment.

Markale also argues that the Celts equated their women not with the cold and passive moon but with the warm and life-giving sun. Brigid and Granne were goddesses of light (before the former became a Christian saint), while the male gods lived in the dark, reflecting the light of the sun and requiring its heat to come alive. It is no accident that Brigid in her pagan and Christian manifestations flits through my stories and that my male protagonists to become anything at all must reflect the dazzling light of the women for whom they are questing.

I have heard complaints (from males) that my men protagonists are wimps, men who, while they may be brave in other situations, are incapable of sweeping women they desire off their feet. I would rather think of my men as gentlemen who do the "sweeping off the feet" routine only when they are invited to and then only when the invitation is clear beyond any doubt—and sometimes not even then!

You don't mess with the sun, do you? And you court it very gingerly, don't you?

Are my men afraid of women, even the women they adore? Of course they are and with reason. All men are afraid of women and with reason. Much of the unconscionable oppression and brutalization of women is based on fear (though not justified by it). The difference between my Ulysses and the "sweep them off their feet" heroes is that the former are aware of their fears and the latter repress their fears under the mask of the macho male—a character I dislike in fact even more than I do in fiction.

Neither Homer's hero nor your young man from Dublin's hero were all that macho when it came to pursuing their wives, especially the latter. Both had to be invited.

In most of my novels there is, as a number of the academic critics have observed, a Holy Grail theme. The pilgrim, who is often someone who has returned from the dead or from distant places, is seeking a second chance at an old love which s/he has foolishly lost in the past and through whom perhaps one can fill aching emptiness and find a new direction for life. Clearly, the symbols of resurrection and second chance, of return and search, of old love lost and found anew are closely related to one another. In my reading of my own novels, I find that Ulysses and the Holy Grail create the matrix out of which most of my stories come (not all of them—some of the Blackie mysteries, *God Game*, *Angel Fire*, *Irish Gold*, and *Love Song* have different symbolic orientations). I am quite sure, however, that my imaginative repertory is less shaped by these two myths than drawn to them. I would probably have written stories about a quest that is often a return if I had, *per impossible*, never heard of Homer or your man from Dublin and never read about the Irish version of the Holy Grail story (in a book by the Breton scholar Jean Markale).

Why is the combined myth of quest and return, of return and quest, so much a part of my own preconscious? That is another story and one that I am yet unable (not unwilling) to speculate about till I reach the end of this essay.

Not all my seekers are successful, though most are. Thus, Sean Cronin in *Thy Brother's Wife* does not get Nora (and as a compensation for his loss is sent by God, who is a comedienne, Blackie

Ryan). Nor is Mary Elizabeth Quinlan, heroine of *An Occasion of Sin*, able to hold on to Jumping Johnny McGlynn. There are women searchers, too. Usually my woman who is the Holy Grail who is God is also looking for her own Holy Grail, her own lost love, and her own God. It is debatable whether she is the pursued or the pursuer. Or, to put the matter more positively, the rhythm of death and rebirth, of lost and found, of pursuit and counterpursuit, moves back and forth between the two genders as it often does in life. Danny Farrell, Lorcan Flynn, Neil Connor, and Kieran O'Kerrigan are as much captured by Irene Farrell, Moire Meehan, Megan Keefe, and Kathleen Leary (respectively) as they capture these lost loves. The difference between the two genders as they close in on the Holy Grail is that the women know that they are pursuing as much as pursued and the men do not know it. Moreover, while the women seem hesitant to the men for whom they have become a Holy Grail, in fact it is the men who stumble and bumble and vacillate while the women, when they have made up their mind that this guy is truly their Holy Grail (albeit tarnished and in need of polishing) and can trust themselves to him (more or less), are direct and decisive in their actions. Thus, Kathleen Leary, clad only in her underwear and a robe uncertainly clutched at her waist, rushes from her house and shouts, "Kieran!" when, thinking there is no one home, he is about to drive away. In the subsequent love scene, poor Kieran thinks he is the aggressor.

Thus does the sun pursue the moon.

And both genders learn that Noele is right: resurrection is not easy. Once you've found your lost love and taken that love as well as given yourself over to the love, you must learn to live with the love on a day-to-day basis—a task which, as Eileen Ryan Kane, perhaps more than the others, comes to understand, is neither easy nor dull. A saint in the house can try the patience of a saint, no matter how good he might be in bed—or in the other places he corners her.

In one scene in *Patience* many of these themes are tied together—as always preconsciously and without deliberate planning on my part. Red Kane, having returned from the death of alcoholism, is in bed with his own Molly Bloom. During their love play, she takes charge of the progress of the event because now she has her

Holy Grail back and does not want to lose it again. Then another Lover intrudes and ratifies the event.[2]

> Then he saw the green gem, glowing between her breasts, as she lifted herself off him. The stone captured his eyes and would not release them. It was part of their pleasure, however, not an obsession. Not yet.
> What happened next was utterly distinct from sex, as he told both his shrink, who wouldn't listen, and Blackie, who would.
> He was drowsily slipping along the down side of ecstasy into a contented afterglow. He and Eileen, their bodies greasy with sweat, were more or less automatically disengaging from each other, both of them now seeking a complacent nap as much as they had sought ecstasy a few moments before. Dreamily Red noticed how spectacularly beautiful she was after lovemaking and felt a vague but powerful contentment that he finally knew how to love her in bed and out.
> The light from the emerald grew in power and filled the room.
> The bed, the room, the Doral Plaza, the Chicago skyline, the cosmos turned into fluid chaos. Desperately Red reached for his wife, a last wild gasp for stability and protection.
> So his naked and sweating wife was not exactly a partner, nor a witness, nor even a trigger for the other. Rather she was a hint, an early spring flower promising July warmth: light, heat, fire, overwhelming, invading, possessing love; dazzling truth, beauty, and goodness; confidence, hope, joy, the promise that all would be well; a love so unspeakably powerful that, in the instant it possessed Red, he knew he could never escape from it. Nor would it ever permit him and Eileen to escape from one another. When the joy seemed so intense that he knew he would die, the operator of this transcendental Concorde jet turned on the afterburners and Red thought he had died and was in heaven, a golden city whose ivory walls were his wife's breasts.

Kieran O'Kerrigan wonders whether he should visit Kathleen's home where she is recovering from a brutal beating from her husband.

> I rang the doorbell several times, to no avail. There was no answer. Then I leaned on it.
> Still no answer. I turned to walk back to my car.
> That's when I heard her call my name. I turned around. Red

hair falling to her shoulders, a robe clutched at her waist, she was calling to me. "Kieran, come back!"

It was both an invitation from the present and a cry from the past.

I went to her so quickly, I have no memory of walking down the sidewalk. Inside the door, she threw herself into my arms and wept for joy.

"I've always loved you, Kieran. I always will."

"And I've always loved you, Kathleen. I'll never stop loving you." I held her close, just as I'd longed to do for so many years. "I promised once that I would always take care of you. That promise is operative again."

"I know." She sighed.

She was wearing a plain white bra and panties. I fumbled with the hook and pushed away her bra. I kissed her breasts gently. Then I tugged the panties loose from her hips and let them fall to her ankles.

"Kieran," she murmured, head against my chest. "Oh, Kieran."

She seemed anxious, yet overcome by the same desire, so long deferred, that I felt.

Suddenly she pulled back from me, covered herself with her arms, and turned away. "Oh, Kieran, I'm so afraid. You matter so much to me. I . . ."

I took her hands in mine and pulled her closer.

I was relieved to feel her relax as I kissed her neck, then lips.

She led me to a sofa on the sun porch.

She was more beautiful than in my most erotic dreams of her, round breasts, slim waist, smooth curving hips, trim thighs, and slender legs.

"I've waited a long time, Kathleen."

"So have I. . . ."

My beloved seemed astonishingly inexperienced, but she was eager to learn and to please. She gave herself to me as completely and as trustingly as any woman could give herself to a man for the first time.

I was as gentle as a thoroughly aroused male can be, careful not to hurt her bruises and bumps, cautious with her delicate regions, nurturing in my demands. I caressed her and played with her and fondled her and kissed her until, gradually abandoning all restraint, she opened herself up and capitulated completely.

When we finally rode together on waves of ecstasy, it was better than even my wildest dreams.

Mike Casey and Anne Reilly are about to renew their love after forty years. He knocks at the door of her apartment on the way home from O'Hare late at night. Dressed in a nightgown and a thin robe she lets him in. She gasps but does not protest when he removes the robe and fondles her breasts, and then slips the gown off her shoulders and lets it drop to the floor.

Annie does not resist but seems uncertain. He continues to caress and play with her. He reflects to himself as he arouses her that at last he has her naked after forty years of fantasy. For a moment she hesitates. Gently he pursues his love play.

> Then her body began resonating with his. Her lips returned his kisses and her arms encircled him, moderating the fierceness of his assault and imprisoning him so that he could not change his mind.
>
> Mike lifted Anne off the floor, carried her to a leather couch that seemed to be designed for love-making and, underneath a Vermeer print, consummated the love that had begun forty-one years before in a snowdrift under a street light at the corner of Mayfield and Potomac while American Marines were fighting not in Lebanon but on a forgotten island called Guadalcanal.

The next morning Anne reflects on what has happened from her viewpoint:

> Every cell in her body seemed to tingle in blissful satiety. Men, she thought, never know this kind of contentment with themselves. She felt like a scholar who had won a prize, an actress clutching an Emmy, an artist who had painted a masterpiece. Her womanliness had been put to the tests of intense sexuality and she had performed brilliantly.
>
> You won, darling, she informed herself. He thinks he's won and that's all right because in a way he has won. But you know you have won.
>
> She giggled softly. You really were quite splendid.

Then she luxuriates in fantasies about more love with her conquest, a barbarian slave sent to amuse an empress with new sexual delights each day of her life.

Lorcan Flynn's daughter is engaged to marry the son of a woman who had been his teenage summer love. He meets her again in the lobby of a Chicago hotel to take her to dinner with both families. He searches in vain for any sign that love is still there. The next morning his psychiatrist (Mary Kate Ryan Murphy) reproves him. "Would the poor woman have had to take off her clothes right there in the cab to let you know she was interested in you?"

Lorcan pleads that there were no signs of interest. The doctor replies that she overwhelmed him with signs. Subsequently she stays in his house before the wedding, frolics with him in the swimming pool in the morning, persuades him to walk along the lake front at the end of the day, and then calmly waits in her bedroom for him to come to her, in champagne-colored lingerie with a hair brush in her hand.

> "You look darling in the robe," she said calmly. "If I had been certain you would come, I would have put on something more alluring."
> Unnerved by her beauty, he struggled to find his voice. "It would be hard for any woman to be as alluring as you are at this moment, Moire."
> "I suppose we both knew," she observed thoughtfully, "that this event would be inevitable once we agreed that I would stay in this house."
> "It doesn't have to happen, Moire."
> "Yes, it does. It really does, Lorcan. We've waited too long. Thirty years."
> "Thirty-five."

Later, after she opens the front hook of her bra as a sign that she is ready to make a gift of herself,

> He removed her undergarments and his robe. She opened up her body and gave it to him enthusiastically.
> For the first time in his life, Lorcan Flynn encountered a woman who was a full partner in love, someone who demanded as much as she gave and challenged as much as she yielded.
> Then love ended, as good love should, in laughter.

The next morning she joins him again in the pool, this time with no swim suit beneath her robe. Thus does Penelope hunt down Ulysses.

Another Penelope, Maria in *Ascent into Hell*, hunts her own Ulysses even more aggressively:

He circled her waist with his fingers and drew her close. She put her hands on his head, Sacred love offering her benediction. His fingers moved up to her breasts. Holding one in each hand, he kissed them, first one, then the other, with infinite delicacy. She sighed and her eyes dilated with pleasure.

God in heaven, how he loved her. The only one he'd ever loved.

Then he drew back once more. "Maria . . . I must climb out of hell. . . . I can't . . ."

"No, you don't. You can't escape that way. You should stretch up your hands to God." She recaptured his hands. "And let Him pull you out." She pulled him back to her. "This way."

He wrapped his arms around her.

"Why do you bother with me?" he asked.

Her eyes filled with tears. She leaned her head against his shoulder. "Because I love you, you crazy so and so. I've always loved you and always will, no matter how much you hide from me."

For the first time in four decades, tears spilled out of Hugh Donlon's eyes, tears of agony and pain, of frustration and disappointment, of failure and despair. Maria's arms enveloped him. He buried his head against her chest, his tears washing her breasts, a child in his mother's arms sobbing as though his body would tear itself apart.

And so it was that, close to a monastery named after a garden in which Jesus wept, but not in it, Hugh Donlon forgot about his glacier and experienced peace and happiness.

Later, while he anoints a dying woman in front of Maria's house—for he still has and will always have priestly powers—Hugh experiences a mystical interlude.

"He's here now, Father, and Himself smiling like a young man in the hedges of Galway." The last rays of the sun caught the old woman's weathered faced. For a moment she smiled ecstatically, then slumped forward, unconscious, perhaps dead.

County Galway was long and far away. Yet Grace Monaghan had gone home.

As dusk spread, Hugh felt a burst of light and warmth engulf him, drawing him toward the same Love who had crept out of the hedge in front of Maria's house to take Grace Monaghan home.

It was an implacable and impulsive Love, one that forgave without being asked, never turned away from the beloved, and wanted only that the beloved surrender to Love and be happy.

A Love like Maria.

Hugh tried to flee from the Lover's majestic instancy and unperturbed grace, escape from it, hide from it, turn away from it. There was no exit.

Some observations about these five loves:
- They are the culmination of the quest efforts of the people involved, the moment of high passion in which the Holy Grail is claimed. They are special sexual interludes which renew old loves (which is one of the things for which the evolutionary process selected when it developed human sexuality) but do not eliminate other problems, decisive turning points but not complete solutions. Noele again: "Resurrection isn't supposed to be easy."
- True to the Irish version of the legend, both the man and woman are seeking a Holy Grail. Both come close to the recovering of a lost love, then hesitate because they dread more pain and because they are not sure of their own adequacy as either a man or a woman. Sexual desire, designed as it was by the evolutionary process, to bond and to bind, drives them out of the trenches in which they have been hiding and into each other's arms, often against what they might construe both before and after as their better judgment.
- The men are patient and tender, healing (though they probably do not realize it) the woman's fear that she will not be good enough.
- The women, once they are assured of their sexual worth, are as passionate as the men and more confident and direct than the men. They reason more clearly about their relationships and are more realistic about the possibilities in them. Perhaps like Annie Reilly they also have more creative and more erotic fantasies.
- These interludes of passion are not ordinary sexual interludes between a man and a woman. Rather they are ecstatic turning points in two lives. The argument that they are not typical of human sexual encounters is not relevant. These are very special love-making episodes—though not uncommon experiences, either. They are neither graphic nor pornographic, save to those who for reasons of their own wish them to be.[3]
- The most ecstatic of the sexual affairs described here is between husband and wife—Red and Eileen Kane. For most humans, I believe, the chance to rise from the dead and to make the most of a second chance, to be both Ulysses and a Searcher, arises

between married lovers after their marriage has endured for a couple of decades.

- Kathleen Leary Donahue, Megan Keefe Lane, Irene Farrell, Maria McLain, Anne O'Brien Reilly, Eileen Ryan Kane, and Moire Meehan Hanlon, are all women in their forties and fifties, yet irresistibly appealing to the men who love them, in part because they have kept themselves in good physical condition, but mostly because they are the beloved.[4] As Leo Kelly, half fun and full earnest, tells Jane Devlin Clare in *Summer at the Lake*, a woman does not become really interesting sexually, if she ever does, until she is forty. Whatever may be said about Provost Kelly's reverse ageism, my own research on sex and aging suggests that truly intense passion, involving the totality of two persons, is more likely to exist among passionate and frequent lovers over forty-five.[5]

I am surprised at how many of the lovers in my stories are in the middle years of life or even older. Someone once remarked to me that on the basis of my novels, I take special delight in teenage women and women over forty or even over fifty. I guess I do, but it is the constraint imposed by the two myths that surge up from my preconscious and shape the stories I am trying to tell.

The quest for the Holy Grail is an arduous, dangerous, exhausting search. Only after a certain age can one be compelled by desperate need and insatiable hunger to venture on such a quest; and only after a certain age does one possess (if one ever does) the maturity and the courage to embark on such a pursuit. The quest is too serious and too desperate for those under forty. Thus, the pursuit of the girl who is the grail who is God is not only for the young, but perhaps not at all for the young.[6]

Blackie Ryan, as he often does, explains the rationale for the quest for the Holy Grail in a conversation with his cousin Brendan Ryan (one of the "other" or "quiet" Ryans):

> "You're probably the only person in Grand Beach who read Alfred North Whitehead. If you want, I'll be simple: God is engaged in the business of creating beauty by drawing us forth in hope and love. Sexual attraction is but one dimension of hope, the trickiest of the games that God plays with us. It's Her best technique yet to lure us into generosity and risk-taking which are the raw materials of beauty. Bluntly, your attraction to Ciara Kelly is

a trick God has played on you. 'Love Ciara Kelly, love Me' is what She is saying to you. 'Pursue Ciara Kelly, the will-o'-the-wisp, the Holy Grail, and you pursue Me, the divine will-of-the-wisp. . . ."

In *Love Song* Blackie offers in a Good Friday sermon the appropriate advice for all lovers young or old: run for daylight.

Having thus dramatically denounced his own guilt and responsibility for injustice, why did not Judas hasten to Calvary and accept the proffered forgiveness?

"To be offered a forgiveness we do not deserve—and if we deserve it, then it is not forgiveness but justice—is a terrifying experience as each of us can testify from our own lives. We cannot claim forgiveness, it is pure gift, pure grace, pure mercy, and—ah there's the rub—pure love. If we have betrayed the intimate other, only absurdly foolish love can possibly forgive us.

"The young persons in Erich Segal's novel *Love Story* are wrong to say that love means you don't have to say you're sorry. You do, but that merely opens the communication links, clears away the landslide rubble so that the love, which is a given, can function again. Once the plea for pardon has been made, it becomes irrelevant. The trouble with being the object of a love that is too absurdly foolish to resist is that it is terrifying to be that lovable. It is an assault on our consoling self-rejection and our soothing self-hatred. If Judas was the focus of such a love, if he were really that lovable, then he would have to live again, love again, try again, laugh again, despite his own conviction of his ugliness and worthlessness. That was no mean challenge. Judas, we learned in school, was the victim of pride. Doubtless, but pride meant a self-rejection and a self-contempt which told him that he could never have earned again the love which he betrayed.

"Judas, you see, represents that part of our person which wants only the love that it can earn and thus control. Peter represents that part of our personality that realizes that love is unlearnable and therefore surrenders helplessly to a love which is beyond merit, beyond control, beyond manipulation, beyond negotiation, beyond anything but grateful acceptance and—here's the catch: with Jesus there is always a catch—enthusiastic response. Judas thought he was not good enough to respond, so he went out and hanged himself with a rope. Peter knew that he was not good enough to respond but that it didn't matter. If you're loved with an absurdly foolish love that is irresistible, 'good enough' doesn't compute. Only acceptance and response do, an acceptance which is response and a response which is self-acceptance. We need not hang ourselves with a rope, we need not despair because love, unlearnable, is nonetheless given. Love is gift, love is graceful, love is grace. And grace, needless to say, is love.

"On Good Friday the Peter in us wrestles with the Judas in us. What shall we do about the love in our lives, especially the human love that may most powerfully and passionately reflect God's love? Shall we agonize over the obligation to win it, earn it, prove ourselves worthy of it, do penance because of our failure to be worthy of it, or shall we, like Walter 'Sweetness' Payton when presented with the pigskin by one of the painfully numerous Chicago Bear quarterbacks take our love and, in company of our beloved, run for daylight?

"In the Name of the Father and of the Son and Holy Spirit."

There's no point in my trying to improve on the good Bishop's words. Sexual love, as St. Paul knew,[7] is a sacrament, a hint of God's love. The wonder and the surprise of the Grail and Ulysses myths, the illumination to be found in them (as Leopold Bloom discovered) is that the quest and the homecomings need never end as long as there is life.

I did not set out to write novels with the "run for daylight" illumination. I am surprised as I do this analysis how much of my fiction fits into the matrix of Holy Grail and Coming Home: one goes forth on a search and returns home to finish the search. The theme of G. K. Chesterton's *Colored Lands* and of Eliot's "The end of all our searching" is to return home and know it for the first time. At any rate that's what I find in my stories when I reconsider them.

Conclusion

There are other themes I find in reconsidering my novels which are either a surprise or would have been a surprise if some of the scholarly critics had not called them to my attention: Sacred Time in the Church's Liturgical Year; Sacred Place in the parishes and neighborhood and in the City and the Lake (and even, in the next Blackie, the River). Sacred persons in angels and saints—and, of course, priests.

If you believe the writers in Catholic journals, both on the left and on the right, I write about priests who violate their vows. In fact, only one of my priests leaves the priesthood (Hugh Donlon) and three others (Patrick Donahue, Sean Cronin, and John McGlynn) break their celibacy vows,[8] for which both of them do appropriate penance.[9] Such critics pay no attention to all the good, virtuous, hardworking, and wise priests who inhabit my stories—Kevin Brennan, Dick McNamara, Laurence O'Toole McAuliffe, John Raven, Mugs Branigan, Brendan McNulty, Jamie Keenan, Sean Cronin in his later days, and especially John Blackwood Ryan.[10]

Such matters may perhaps be left aside for another day.

By way of a final word, the issue of the effectiveness of a story cannot be judged either by a book reviewer or by the author—academic critics may well do better.[11] The worth of a story depends on how much wonder and surprise it creates in its audience and how much illumination it offers them while they are inside the story (whether actually reading it or reflecting on it afterward). If I am to judge by my mail, many people do go forth from my stories with some such illumination. The illumination comes hardly at all from what I plan to write. Rather it comes from the elements of the story as they emerge in the process of writing it and thus from my preconscious, my agent intellect, my poetic imagination (call it what you will). In this essay I have tried to depict some of the illuminations that I have discovered in reconsidering my stories after fifteen years.

Notes

1. With discouraging lack of imagination such reviewers announce that I am not a Graham Greene. They never suggest why that comparison is appropriate or why I must be a Graham Greene. My talents are less that Greene's (so are the talents of most other writers), and my vision of Catholicism profoundly different. As Chuck O'Malley remarks in *A Winter's Tale*, Greene was a convert who never lived in a parish like St. Ursula and hence did not really understand Catholicism. It escapes me why I am not to be permitted by such reviewers to tell my own stories.

2. My research on mystical experiences shows that sexual love and childbirth are the two most frequent "triggers" of mystical experiences.

3. I assume that I need not persuade anyone that none of the scenes

cited in this essay are either "steamy" or "dull" as the Catholic right and left have called them. Much less are they "nineteen fifties soft-core porn," as Mary Gordon has claimed. Whether they represent skilled writing or not is not for me to say—though most of the readers I have surveyed find them to be "tasteful," "sensitive," and "delicate." Ingrid Shafer in her research on my fiction has found that such passages are often ranked higher than "erotic" passages from Saul Bellow or John Updike *as long as the author of the passage is not identified.* Catholic reviewers, especially resigned priests, delight in saying either that the sexual passages betray knowledge that a celibate should not and could not have or that they are the sign of sexual "innocence." Heads they win, tails I lose. In fact, the notion that one must have sexual experience to comprehend what sex means in human life is absurd.

4. Some women write letters of protest to me in which they claim that the women in my novels are all beautiful. It is not fair, they say. Some of my heroines, they argue, should not be beautiful—a curious notion of affirmative action. The envy that some women feel for their attractive "sister" even in stories is hardly edifying. In any case, with the exception of Kathleen Leary Donahue (whose beauty captures even the fantasy of Brendan McNulty), the women described in this section are beautiful because their men love them (and because they have, as all humans should, taken care of themselves).

5. Some "feminist" critics say that my women are a man's picture of women. What the hell else would it be? I think their point is that no man, especially no celibate priest, should write about women. I note for the record that while my women characters have their moments of fear and doubt, there is not a weak person in the whole lot. They are able to take care of themselves and their children and have done so often under very trying circumstances. They do not need men to protect them or get them out of trouble. They have goals and careers of their own. While vulnerable and often quite fragile, they are also tough-minded and independent. I surely do not apologize that, with the exception of Maria, they are all Irish. I suppose that the real objection of "feminist" complainers to these women is that they like men and men find them attractive. For that I do not apologize either—especially given the fact that after a certain age in life, attractiveness is under a person's control and is not the result of genetic luck. I also reject the charge that all my women characters are "bosomy." Some (like Moire Meehan, Annie Reilly, and the spectacularly lovely Kathleen Leary) have generous figures. Others are more deftly carved (Maria, Maggie Ward, Noele Farrell, Marbeth Quinlan), their allure created by indirection. Still others like Megan Keefe Lane are explicitly described as diminutive with small breasts. Yet others, like Diana Lyons and Mary Elizabeth "Candibeth"

Cain, are tall and sturdy women athletes—in her case a "power forward" on the basketball team of St. Ignatius College Prep. I find it hard to understand why people engage in such sweeping generalizations, but, having paid for the books, it is their right to do so, even if they are demonstrably wrong. As to the other charge that I have a breast fixation, I can reply only that so does every other heterosexual male member of our species. The evolutionary process selected both for the phenomenon of large breasts in human females (as opposed to other higher primates) and for the male delight and indeed obsession with them.

6. Twenty-two percent of American married men and women (25% of the men and 19% of the women) say that their spouse is often like God to them. Among those who see in the spouse a metaphor for God, the judgment that the spouse is physically attractive does not diminish with age. For the others it declines sharply with age. If your spouse is the Grail, it does not matter how old she or he is, the spouse is still attractive. In fact, at first encounter, Lorcan Flynn thinks that Moire Meehan Hanlon is simply an ordinary woman of her generation, not striking at all. Then at dinner, he finds himself haunted by her mysterious appeal. Later, when he encounters her in her lingerie and eventually naked, he is mesmerized by her beauty. It might be argued that she was more attractive than his first impression suggested, but less attractive than his lovesick fantasies imagined. But debates about her objective attractiveness are beside the point (as the one from whose imagination she emerged, I think she is the kind of woman who would turn the head of any man over forty, but my testimony is unimportant in the matter). To the eyes of her lover, the man for whom she is the Holy Grail, she is gorgeous. Her beauty truly is in the eyes of the beholder.

7. And as my sociological work has confirmed—if it needed to be confirmed.

8. A "feminist" critic (writing in *Commonweal*) complained that my priests treat women brutally, a charge which is not true save of Pat Donahue in his younger days. Quite the contrary, my priests (most notably Blackie and Lar McAuliffe) are tender and sensitive with women. I should, the critic insisted, present models of priestly behavior toward women which will educate Catholic laymen on how to treat women. Clearly, she wishes a return to the days when it was believed that "Catholic novels" should edify and indoctrinate rather than illuminate. There are a lot of bishops who would agree with her.

9. A reviewer in the *National Catholic Reporter* informed his readers that I was not a Sigrid Undset because Sean Cronin and Nora (the "brother's wife") were not banished to monasteries for their sins. Not only do these guys want to dictate your sensibility, they want to outline the plot for you—and deny characters a "second chance."

10. Two other critics, also writing in *Commonweal*, compare Blackie to Chesterton's Father Brown, to the former's disadvantage as one might have anticipated. Blackie, they said, uses "power"—ecclesiastical and civil—which Father Brown never did. So I guess I am not a G. K. Chesterton as well as not a Sigrid Undset or a Graham Greene. These two critics, I am sure, would not object to revolutionary power by "base communities" in South America who believe in "Liberation Theology." Power is bad only when it is practiced by a character in stories written by someone you do not like. Incidentally, they fail to mention that Blackie uses his "clout" only to protect his parishioners from the powers of evil.

11. The two *Commonweal* reviewers contend that I believe the worth of a story is determined by the sales figures for the book. To my reply that I believed no such thing, they replied that they knew what I believed even if I could not admit it to myself. Right!

Works Cited

Greeley, Andrew. *Angel Fire*. New York: Warner, 1988.
———. *Ascent into Hell*. New York: Warner, 1983.
———. *The Cardinal Sins*. New York: Warner, 1981.
———. *Death in April*. New York: McGraw-Hill, 1980,
———. *Fall from Grace*. New York: Putnam, 1993.
———. *God Game*. New York: Warner/Tor Books, 1986.
———. *Happy Are the Clean of Heart*. New York: Warner, 1986.
———. *Happy Are the Peace Makers*. NY: Jove Books, 1993.
———. *Happy Are Those Who Work for Justice*. New York: Mysterious P, 1987.
———. *Irish Gold*. New York: Forge, 1994.
———. *Lord of the Dance*. New York: Warner, 1984.
———. *Love Song*. New York: Warner, 1989.
———. *The Magic Cup*. New York: McGraw-Hill, 1980.
———. *An Occasion of Sin*. New York: Putnam, 1991.
———. *Patience of a Saint*. New York: Warner, 1987.
———. *Rite of Spring*. New York: Warner, 1987.
———. *St. Valentine's Night*. New York: Warner, 1989.
———. *Summer at the Lake*.
———. *Thy Brother's Wife*. New York: Warner, 1982.
———. *Virgin and Martyr*. New York: Warner, 1985.
———. *Wages of Sin*. New York: Putnam, 1992.

10 • The Tyranny of the Secular Imagination

Gavin D'Costa

THE STUDY OF RELIGIONS has become a major part of the academic curriculum in many European countries, the United States, and Canada. Christian students and staff involved in such enterprises find themselves faced with difficult questions: How do I study Buddhism, Hinduism, and Islam? Do I allow my Christian presuppositions to interfere with issues of methodology and evaluation? What place does the Christian theological imagination play in this activity? In our academic institutions (and most of my comments are based on the British scene) such students will tend to receive the answer that they need to study these religions in their own right and with a methodology that is both scientific and humanistic. Thankfully, the days are long past (the answer will continue) when a Christian imperialism dominated the "study" of other religions, whereby they were deemed demonic, in error, or perhaps breathtaking, but not of God—all this in advance of a real study and understanding of the Other. Imaginative empathy in this new mode is the key to understanding the Other. Answers may differ in church institutions, although many are structurally (culturally and academically) aligned to their secular academic counterparts. I suspect matters are not so different in the United States (see Westerhoof and Hauerwas, eds.).

If this brazen sketch has any truth in it, and I think it has, then it will be worth outlining the thesis I wish to advance here. My argument is that the secular imagination exercises a tyranny over the theological imagination. This tyranny is employed and embedded in the secular culture of most Western nations, including the academy. The tyranny is most insidious, for it exists unseen, claiming to be the way things are, claiming the authority of tradition and learning, claiming an unchallenged norm. This has meant that the dominant methodology in the study of religions is inimical to most of the religions studied and certainly not in keeping with a Christian theological imagination. I will need to define "secular imagination" and "Christian theological imagination" as the argument proceeds. Both are highly specific sociopolitical moments, presuming and developing projects that shape culture, practice, and virtue. My argument will be against this tyranny, and I will suggest instead the possibility of a Christian imagination that facilitates critical engagement with the Other without distorting it *a priori*. Hence, there will be two parts to this essay. The first will be a critique of the secular imagination in Religious Studies. The second will be a proposal for a theological imagination methodologically appropriate to "Religious Studies," or what would better be be called (if my arguments are accepted) "Theology of Religions."

Iago and the New Imperialism

Let me turn to a definition of the secular imagination that will allow me to engage with my first topic. To define the secular imagination one might adopt Iago as the symbolic enactment of the concept. I take this image from a discussion about modernity and the imaginative power of empathy, drawn to my attention by Talal Asad's *Genealogies of Religion* (11–12). In a discussion of modernization in the Middle East, Daniel Lerner defined the West's success in terms of the "mobile personality," able to ceaselessly invent, adapt, change, and empathize. Imaginative empathy was central to this personality, and this was defined as "the capacity to see oneself in the other fellow's situation" (50). Stephen Greenblatt criticizes Lerner's analysis with the succinct point: "what Professor Lerner calls 'empathy,' Shakespeare calls 'Iago'" (225). I want to quote at greater length, because Greenblatt's point highlights the specific cultural-political nature of this secular imaginative empathy, not so different, I shall argue, from the imaginative empathy employed in Religious Studies. Greenblatt notes that improvisation, the ability to grasp the unforeseen and turn it to one's own advantage, is the key to Iago as empathy:

The spur-of-the-moment quality of improvisation is not as critical here as the opportunistic grasp of that which seems fixed and established. Indeed, as Castiglione and others in the Renaissance well understood, the impromptu character of an improvisation is itself often a calculated mask, the product of careful preparation.... What is essential is the Europeans' ability again and again to insinuate themselves into the preexisting political, religious, even psychic structures of the natives and to turn those structures to their advantage.... Lerner is right to insist that this ability is a characteristically (though not exclusively) Western mode, present to varying degrees in the classical and medieval world and greatly strengthened from the Renaissance onward; he misleads only in insisting further that it is an act of imaginative generosity, a sympathetic appreciation of the situation of the other fellow. For when he speaks confidently of the "spread of empathy around the world," we must understand that he is speaking of the exercise of Western power, power that is creative, but that is scarcely ever wholly disinterested or benign. (227-28)

The point here is that empathy is not just an innocent imaginative skill that allows us to get into the "other woman's situation.". We need to be aware that this skill is generated and employed in a specific history which has a colonial and capitalist context, hence, the "spread of empathy around the world" and the point that empathy is "scarcely ever wholly disinterested or benign." One might transpose this point to say that all forms of knowledge (and imaginations) are related to the exercise of power of one sort or another. And such power is always at the service of some end or other, spoken or implicit. What I want to argue is that a Christian study of other religions is methodologically better justified than the secular methodology of Religious Studies. I want to go so far as to suggest that the history of such a methodology has a counterpart in the emergence of a consumer-capitalist ethos, such that religions are reproduced in open markets as objects for the Western gaze, to be consumed, appropriated, or rejected—as objects of individual choice. Hence, despite the arguments of those who are antitheology in Religious Studies, they succeed in replacing one alleged distortion with another. Iago spells a new imperialism!

Before focusing more specifically on imaginative empathy in Religious Studies, a few comments about the context and presuppositions of the emergence of this discipline require attention. In such a short space I can only be impressionistic. (For a closer documentation of this reading, see my "End.") First, Religious Studies emerged in British Universities in the 1960s. This was a time of rapid secularization, the history of Christian mission was closely aligned by many with the history of Western imperialism and both were condemned, and immigration patterns and international communications meant that most Western city dwellers knew about other religions. Hence, there is a sociological explanation for the rise of this discipline. Second, such a context must also be read in tandem with the secularization of theology and theological method. This explains the lack of resistance to this secular tyranny. The process of secularization had begun in the Enlightenment and had accelerated during the nineteenth century with the rise of liberal Protestantism. Secular history and methodologies became the criteria by which theologies were judged. Theology in most British universities boasted a strength in Biblical Criticism—a textual discipline which was entirely secular and "scientific" in its philological origins. Furthermore, with the general secularization of the universities, Theology struggled for respectability by systematically denying any theological bias in its forms of investigation. One form of sectarianism replaced another.

Hence, the increasing secularity of theology, both institutionally and methodologically, had produced a situation where many felt that actually what in practice existed was the study of religion (not theology), and that the religion so selected for historical reasons was Christianity. Furthermore, in the context of England's multireligious nature, worldwide communications, and the growth of Indology and Orientalism, many argued that religions other than Christianity (and "Judaism" which tended to be "Old Testament" studies) should be taught. If the study of religion was an academic specialty, it seemed right and obvious that to limit the menu to Christianity was parochial to say the least. The final and related factor worth mentioning, and perhaps the most significant in the English context, was the introduction of an allegedly scientific, objective, and academic method appropriate to the study of religion: phenomenology. It is no accident that the supporter of such a method in Britain was also the founder of the first British Department of Religious Studies at Lancaster in 1967.

Ninian Smart tellingly wrote about this new discipline (in contrast to the old Theology) that the "theological establishment is, therefore, a problem in that it is a kind of conceptual albatross round the neck of religious studies" (*Religion* 8). Smart at least realized that Theology and Religious Studies could not coexist, contrary to the innocence of some theologians who often think they can. Smart's *The Phenomenon of Religion* (1973) is central for understanding this program.

Faith as a starting point was both unscientific and unscholarly according to the canons then acceptable to the secular academy and the cultured despisers of theology. Hence, the phenomenological method started with *epoché* or bracketing, so as to allow imaginative empathy. *Epoché* meant the suspension of one's own beliefs, attitudes, values, etc., in order to avoid contaminating one's description with personal prejudice or one's own personal religious commitments. It was allegedly only in this fashion that the enquirer could really get at the object of enquiry and understand it correctly through the exercise of empathic imagination: standing in the "other fellow's situation." *Epoché* and empathy were central to the phenomenological enterprise. The resemblance to Descartes' and Locke's stripping-down process to get to the foundations of knowledge is again not incidental; neither is the positivism so reminiscent of Hume. In one sense the new scientific methodology of Religious Studies was clearly a child of the Enlightenment. While acknowledging much debate about Smart's model, I wish to make this point: while the methodology and subject of Religious Studies in its institutional setting was increasingly successful (there are now a number of Religious Studies Departments, while prior to 1967 there were not), intellectually the presuppositions of this approach are deeply problematic. And its problematic nature lies in its Enlightenment marriage to objectivity and scientific neutrality. Recall Iago's providing objective evidence to Othello!

There are important objections against *epoché* and imaginative empathy as a method and subsequently all that follows from it. As was mentioned above, the success of the phenomenological method was in part due to the social episteme which looked favorably upon such an enterprise. This consensus is crumbling, and the episteme is shifting. The natural sciences and social sciences have tended to move away from the positivistic assumptions that they both shared at the turn of the century—and that were imitated in Religious Studies. Both the former disciplines have tended to eschew objectivity and neutrality and increasingly acknowledge that the role of the investigator and her sociopolitical location is crucial to the production of knowledge. Thomas Kuhn's notion of scientific paradigms is widely, though not uncritically, accepted in the natural sciences. There would be few scientists who would deny that the scientific imagination, the language of investigation, the methods and controls of experimentation, and the very questions asked in scientific exploration are shaped by the paradigm inhabited by the research scientist. And there is no one who is not operating within a paradigm, even if that paradigm is on the verge of collapse. This insight need not lead to relativism, for of course the very fact of paradigm shifts proves the possibility of error and change. *Epoché* and imaginative empathy as outlined above is not only epistemologically impossible—for how could one suspend all one's beliefs?—but actually undesirable, for it both masks a new set of beliefs taken on by the investigator (the character of Iago) and obscures the forceful eviction of contenders for intellectually respectable methods of study (Theology). Kuhn's point can be seen to have its counterpart in the social sciences in regard to the work of Alasdair MacIntyre. In *After Virtue* MacIntyre had argued against Enlightenment liberalism, for its presumption to neutrality is the very source of its contradictory authoritarianism. Then, in *Whose Justice? Which Rationality?* he argued persuasively against the possibility of neutrality or a universal rationality, and showed the tradition-specific nature of all moral and philosophical enquiry.

To take just one more example: in anthropology, Bernard McGrane has argued in *Beyond Anthropology. Society, and the Other* that anthropologists and ethnologists should eschew their desire for objectivity and neutrality, for it simply masks forms of ethnocentricism that can be discerned properly only when the location of the studying subject is taken into consideration. Imaginative empathy is highly problematic when coupled with *epoché*. His survey of ethnographic work from the sixteenth century on is provocative and clearly shows that the construal of objects of study always take place within a definite and specific horizon—and in this sense is historically tradition-specific and cannot assume a universal neutral platform for enquiry. The notion of *epoché* and neutral objectivity aligned with the skill of imaginative empathy has been radically questioned in just those citadels which the method of Religious Studies sought to emulate.

But what precisely has imaginative empathy concealed? It has concealed the presuppositions in Religious Studies which, while appearing neutral and objective, simply sacralize the secularity of the investigating subject. This predetermines the question of religious truth as it has already been resolved in favor of the secular, privileging the free zone of uncluttered transactions, without the bias and prejudice that characterized theological forms of investigation. Hence, the Christians studying Buddhism are told to leave their Christianity behind, for this is unscholarly and inappropriate to the exercise of imaginative empathy and *epoché*, alone capable of rendering a proper understanding of Buddhism. This logic reflected the free market in allowing religions to be produced and exhibited so that the consumer was left to choose, pick and mix, or leave the assembled products. It also reinforced a highly textual production of religion, so that, for example, people were introduced to Hinduism through a study of its "scriptures," of books which sometimes came into book form only to serve Western encyclopedic translations, such as Max Müller's *The Sacred Books of the East*.[1] It allowed the Western gaze to survey its objects of production, insinuating itself into the preexisting religious "structures of the native and to turn these structures to [its own] advantage." By producing these religions on the open market, Western power, or modernity to be more precise, continues to control and order the native universe. The moors must be tamed!

To summarize: Religious Studies was born into English universities partly because of the anachronism of theology's being located within secular academia; partly due to the search for scientific and objective ways of carrying out research on religions to avoid theological sectarianism (but nevertheless creating another form); and to gain the approval of the secular academy (which has, in many other disciplines, moved on). The secular imagination, Iago, has entered the academy and dictated the study of religions. It has been the burden of this first section to question the assumptions of the secular imagination as a privileged form of undistorted access to the Other. In fact, precisely the opposite has often been the case. It is now time to turn to the definition of the "Christian theological imagination" to see whether it can regain its lost position. With Iago, one might close this section:

> But he that filches from me my good name
> Robs me of that which not enriches him
> And makes me poor indeed.
> (*Othello* III.iii.159)

The Theological Imagination and the Other

If, as I have been arguing, every imagination is a context-tradition specific form of critical inquiry, then so is the Christian theological imagination. (In a certain sense, the title of this book is misleading in essentializing religion). But even within this term of reference (the Christian theological imagination), there are many forms of dogmatics, so it is necessary to say that what I am proposing is a Roman Catholic form of theological imagination to be employed in the encounter with the Other. This means that in shaping the imagination, certain and necessary constraints proper to the Roman Catholic theologian will be required as part of the proper freedom of inquiry rather than, as viewed by Religious Studies, a constraint to free enquiry (see Congregation for the Doctrine of the Faith). To study other religions in the comparative mode of Religious Studies already concedes the hidden starting point outside the various religions being investigated and thereby locates the inquiring subject as secular, with the presumed virtue of fairness and neutrality.

What I will be proposing is a theologically informed engagement with the Other, which attempts to navigate between modernity's homogenizing tendency to reduce the Other to the Same and the counter movement to transform the Other into demonic difference—as was attributed (often correctly) to the old theological engagement with the Other. This is also the presumption of some currents of nihilistic postmodernity, where the demonic is exchanged for sheer incommensurability, totally Other. This secular demonization finally authorizes force as the answer to conflict—as is so persuasively argued by John Milbank in *Theology and Social Theory*. Hence, I will argue that *epoché* must be replaced by Roman Catholicism (the concrete church in particular acts of engagement). And imaginative empathy, the seeing "oneself in the other fellow's situation," must be replaced by a theological critical engagement (which is thereby sociopolitical) with the situation of the Other in the specific location of engagement. Before turning to an example of the practice I want to advance, I need to clarify a little more carefully the sense of this theological imagination in a place that readers may find surprising (for its anti-Roman Catholic polemic): Karl Barth's *Church Dogmatics* (1.1, s. 1–2).[2]

Barth begins the *Dogmatics* by locating dogmatics properly as a theological science (as opposed to other quasi-sciences that dominate the academy and secular culture), with its own methods and presuppositions peculiar to its ecclesial and Christological character. "Theology follows the talk of the Church to the extent that in its question as to the correctness of its utterance it does not measure it by an alien standard but by its own source and object" (4). Theology is thoroughly intratextual, sensing, exploring, and confessing the truth in terms of its own biblical and ecclesial authority. "The question of truth, with which theology is concerned throughout, is the question as to the agreement of the Church's distinctive talk about God with the being of the Church. The criterion of past, further and therefore present Christian utterance is thus the being of the Church, namely, Jesus Christ, God in His gracious revealing and reconciling address to man" (4). All inquiry by the Christian theologian therefore falls within this context, refusing alien criteria for investigating the question of truth, requiring intratextual authorization for its reading of the world. George Lindbeck, a neo-Barthian, puts the same point by saying: "Intratextual theology redescribes reality within the scriptural framework rather than translating scripture into extrascriptural categories. It is the text, so to speak, which absorbs the world, rather than the world the text" (118). A theological reading of the Other is called for when this sense of Christian imagining is envisaged.

Two points are clear from this. First, a neutral methodology for evaluating Christianity, or any religion for that matter, is out of the question. Iago cannot return to the stage. In contemporary literature two influential writers, Keith Ward and John Hick, both suggest certain criteria by which all religions are evaluated (including Christianity), such as internal coherence, freedom from contradiction, conformity to other forms of knowledge (mainly science and history).[3] Barth responds to a contemporary, Heinrich Scholz, who accommodates theology to the concept of science then current (although analogous to the criteria advanced above by Ward and Hick) in demanding that all theology correspond to "(1) formal consistency, (2) inherent consistency, (3) openness to control through a community of verifiers, (4) antecedent credibility, (5) impartiality or positively stated, according to the principle of sufficient reason, and (6) formalisability" (8).[4] Barth's response to Scholz can be appropriately applied to Ward and Hick, when he writes:

> [T]heology can only say point-blank that this concept is unacceptable to it. Even the minimum postulate of freedom from contradiction is acceptable to theology only when it is given a particular interpretation which the scientific theorist can hardly tolerate, namely, that theology does not affirm the principle that the 'contradictions' which it makes cannot be resolved. But the statements in which it maintains their resolution will be statements concerning the free activity of God and not therefore statements which 'dismiss contradictions from the world' (9).[5]

Second, the process by which theologians learn to speak, pray, and act is a process whereby "Christian speech must be tested by its conformity to Christ. This conformity is never clear and unambiguous" (13). This is a most important point for the theological imagination engaged with the Other. In one sense, truth is always conformity to Christ and therefore ecclesial (8), but a constant and painstaking process which is never clear and unambiguous, involving a "laborious movement from one partial human insight to another with the intention though with no guarantee of advance" (14). Hence, in engaging with the Other, although in a way that Barth may not have envisaged, Christian speech and practice may discover its own truthfulness—not in simply trying to see in the Other a reflection of Christ already known, comprehended, and captured, but Christ who is still unknown, while being known, still veiled, while unveiling, still far, while being close. Before going on to indicate what this might look like in practice, two brief asides are in order.

I will forbear defending Roman Catholicism from what are

Barth's incorrect readings of its ecclesiology and its understanding of revelation (40–41). Barth finds idolatry both in its alleged closure to the freedom of Christ—in restricting and conditioning revelation to "certain concrete forms of human understanding" authorized by the Church (40)—and in its marriage with the secular through the *analogia entis* (41).[6] Secondly, my reading and use of Barth is defensible in the light of his own later essay in the *Dogmatics* (IV, 3, i, s. 69), "The Light of Life," whereby his thought follows a direction not inimical to the one being advanced here.

To return to the main argument: it will best be advanced by showing an example of the new form of "Religious Studies" I am urging, which employs a theological imagination and is therefore best called "Theology of Religions," for that is precisely the only conceivable relation to the Other: a theologically imaginative critical engagement. I want to offer a close outline of one of the most important books to be published recently in the field of both "Religious Studies" and "Theology of Religions" which seems to exemplify the practice I support. It will not be surprising that its author, a Sanskritist and specialist of Hinduism, is also a Roman Catholic priest and Jesuit, deeply influenced by George Lindbeck and the neo-Barthian heritage.

Francis X. Clooney's book is called *Theology after Vedanta: An Experiment in Comparative Theology*. The title is to my mind a little misleading in using the term "Comparative," which still employs a metaphor of comparing two things that are external to the comparer, which is not the case in Clooney, although he is sometimes a little ambiguous on this point (170–71). I also think Clooney slightly misleading in calling his project comparative "Theology," for Advaita Vedanta is here assumed under an inappropriate category of "theology," where "God" does not have the same role or reference as in Christianity. But he uses this term to avoid "comparative religions" which assumes that the project is being carried out neutrally, not from any faith tradition. These are rather minor qualifications.

Clooney's argument is simple. Immerse yourself in the commentarial tradition that constitutes Advaita Vedanta. Then, as a Christian wishing to think comparatively (or, as I would say, think using the theological imagination), read Aquinas's *Summa Theologiae*. This (re)reading will constitute "theology after Vedanta," for the Christian comparativist will now be reading Aquinas in a new context in which the Vedanta texts constitute the horizons of questioning and reflection on Aquinas. Subsequent rereadings of Advaita are similarly transformed. The process goes on indefinitely, and questions of comparative truth claims are not necessarily infinitely deferred but must certainly await long and patient readings and rereadings. Hence, there is no easy assimilation of the Other, either negatively or positively, but a long and patient critical engagement, while keeping the question of truth constantly at hand. Notice, too, that the role of the theological imagination is central, for the exploration advances in terms of the new space created between the texts that call for interpretation and insight. There is no consistent rational method, but rather a process of going to and fro, rather like the conversation between people.

Hence, in Clooney's terms, "comparative religion" is properly rendered as "comparative theology" so that there is constant mutual interrogation. If one is a Christian (who also reads Vedanta), then one is committed to inscribing the world within the biblical and Christian viewpoint. Likewise for the Advaitin. Here Barth and more directly Lindbeck supply the theological framework for Clooney's intra-and intertextualism. But this is no triumphalistic inscribing, for Clooney is all too aware that closure is exegetically improbable when working with such complex and sophisticated traditions. His project of readings and rereadings shape his theology of religions, and in this Clooney successfully breaks free from the often over-abstract discussions in this field. While Clooney is wary of the threefold typology of exclusivism, pluralism, and inclusivism, he locates his project within inclusivism, but breathes concrete life into "its distinctive tension between an adherence to the universal claim of one's own religion and an acknowledgment of the working of the truth of the Christian religion outside its boundaries" (194–95; see also his "Reading").

Clooney's merit is to marry the theological with the Indological. His earlier book on Purva Mimamsa (1990) set the groundwork for seeing Advaita as performance, ritual, and textualism against the dominant Western rationalization in its mode of production of Advaita. This latter is found in the overly philosophical image of Advaita generated by scholars such as Paul Deussen and Eliot Deutsch. The latter, for example, took Sankara's hierarchy of truths at face value and tended therefore to denigrate words, rites, and texts in Advaita and concentrated exclusively on its philosophical non-dualism. Advaita was thereby transformed into a kind of profound rational insight independent of its texts, not untypical of the German Romantic appropriation of Hinduism as charted by Halbfass and Schwab.

Clooney convincingly argues that Advaita's own commentarial tradition powerfully challenges this view. Rather, it suggests itself as thoroughly textual: that is, while reality is extratextual, the avenue for discovering this reality is exclusively textual. Advaita demands and trains its reader, so that only a carefully educated reader of Advaita has access to its truth, and this truth is communicable only through the act of reading. In fact, the "Text resists summation based on major themes, conclusions, or the important intentions of its authors; it resists a (merely) linear reading that moves either toward an expressible conclusion, or from a generally stated theory to its (mere) exemplification." But this is positively viewed, for it educates its readers "in certain ways of thinking and organizing what is learned from reading, so as to implicate them in ongoing acts of commentary from which the readers cannot simply disassociate themselves" (38). To defend this reading he shows how the "great sayings" (*mahavakya*) which seem precisely to be "expressible conclusions" such as "I am Brahman" and "You are that" are not such conclusions. Rather, they are ways of grading and qualifying textual readings, not a way of getting rid of them. This is also convincingly argued for Sankara's distinction between nirguna and saguna Brahman. While Clooney's argument makes Advaita look very much like Lindbeckian textualism, his case is vigorously argued from within Advaita. He is also well aware that had he instead dealt with the Tamil Alvars, from the south-Indian Srivaisnava tradition, the tensions would revolve not around textuality but around the dynamics of hearing and seeing. This is an important point, for in acknowledging the specificity of his project, Clooney is rightly cautious about generalizing greatly from this particular engagement. The engagement might take very various forms dictating different strategies and uses of the theological imagination, ranging from social and political issues, texts from "dead" religions, as is exemplified by David Tracy, to forms of lifestyle and ritual, and so on.

The minor misgivings that I have only highlight the value of the book as a project working in the right direction, breaking new ground in the contemporary debate (but also following old territory in his close affinity, not without significant differences, with Swami Abhishiktananda's *Hindu-Christian Meeting Point*, and Raimundo's Pannikar's first edition of *The Unknown Christ of Hinduism*). I think Clooney plays down his contribution by giving the comparative reading of Aquinas only twenty-four pages (156–68, 175–87), in contrast to three very full chapters on Advaita. This diminishes the impact of the potential fruitfulness of his method. He shows, all too briefly, that the question of theological language is one issue raised when reading Aquinas after Advaita (more specifically Amalananda's commentaries). Clooney intelligently explores similarities and differences between Aquinas and Amalananda on this point. He then takes the Passion of Christ (*ST* III.46.3) to show that apparent incomparability is not a necessary hindrance to the process of cross-readings. He also, in the light of the commentarial tradition, reflects on the role of Scripture in the *Summa* and the significance of the commentaries, taking Cardinal Cajetan as an example. But without more detailed exploration these excursions fail to be as promising as they should be.

The reason for spending so much time on Clooney's book is that it exemplifies the methodology that I have been arguing for. It eschews traditional Religious Studies for a genuine theological intra-and intertextual engagement using the theological imagination. Here the Other is not encountered as Same or rendered totally Other, but critically engaged with in regard to the questions of both truth and transformation. Here we see the abandonment of the barren secular imagination in favor of a more fruitful strategy: "fruitful" not in the sense of always rendering positive results (whatever those might be), but in the sense of allowing a real and unpredictable engagement with the Other, while still retaining Christian theological integrity.

If my arguments for the reinstating of a Christian theological imagination are found to be in the least convincing, then this is just the beginning of a study that must be continued. I have left untouched many institutional questions regarding the structural enforcement of the secular imagination in our Western academies, the shifts of power and realignments that would be required for the successful pursuit of a theology of religions. Furthermore, such questions also raise the issue regarding the appropriate theological training that is required in contrast to the secularization of theology in much of the academy. To develop a genuine Catholic theological imagination requires schooling in the virtues, such that the imagination be led by hope, charity, and patience, and the encounter with the Other must be directed by such phronesis.

Notes

1. See the literature regarding the distortion of the study of religion in the grid of Western modernity: Said, Asad, Smith.)
2. Subsequent page references in the text refer to this volume.
3. See Ward, Hick, and criticisms of each in D'Costa, *Hick's* and "Whose," respectively.
4. This is the editor's summation of Barth's characterization of Scholz's requirements stated in "Wie ist eine evangelische Theologie als Wissenschaft möglich?" Z.d.Z 1931: 8–53.
5. The final citation is from Scholz 44.
6. See Urs von Balthasar and Küng's defense in the light of Barth's criticisms and the rereading of Barth employed by both. Elsewhere (D'Costa, "Whose") I have offered an interpretation of the Catholic axiom that revelation is closed with the death of the apostles.

Works Cited

Abhinishiktanada, Swami. *Hindu-Christian Meeting Point: Within the Cave of the Heart*. Rev. ed. Delhi: SPCK, 1976.
Asad, Talal. *Genealogies of Religion: Discipline and Reasons of Power in Christianity and Islam*. Baltimore and London: Johns Hopkins UP, 1993.
Barth, Karl. *Church Dogmatics*. .1. Edinburgh: Clark, 1975
———. *Church Dogmatics*. IV.3.1. Ed. G. W. Bromiley, Edinburgh: Clark, 1961.
Clooney, Francis X., s.j. "Reading the World in Christ. From Comparison to Inclusivism." D'Costa 1990, 63–80.
———. *Theology after Vedanta: An Experiment in Comparative Theology*. New York: State U of New York P, 1993.
———. *Thinking Ritually: Rediscovering the Purva Mimansa of Jaimini*. Vienna: Institut für Indologie der Universität Wien, 1990.
Congregation for the Doctrine of the Faith. *Instruction on the Ecclesial Vocation of the Theologian*. London: Catholic Truth Society, 1990.

D'Costa, Gavin, ed. *Christian Uniqueness Reconsidered. The Myth of a Pluralistic Theology of Religions.* New York: Orbis, 1990.

———. "The End of Theology and Religious Studies." *Theology.* 1995.

———. *John Hick's Theology of Religions.* New York: UP of America, 1987.

———. "Revelation and Revelations: Discerning God in Other Religions. Beyond a Static Valuation." *Modern Theology,* 10.2 (1994): 165–83.

———. "Whose Objectivity? Which Neutrality? The Doomed Quest for a Neutral Vantage Point from Which to Judge Religions." *Religious Studies,* 29 (1993): 79–95.

Greenblatt, S. *Renaissance Self-Fashioning.* Chicago: U of Chicago P, 1980.

Halbfass, Wilhelm. *India and Europe: An Essay in Understanding.* New York: State U of New York P, 1988.

Hick, John. *An Interpretation of Religion.* London: Macmillan, 1989.

Küng, Hans. *Justification: The Doctrine of Karl Barth and a Roman Catholic Reflection.* London: Burns & Oates & Nelson, 1964.

Kuhn, Thomas. *The Structure of Scientific Revolutions.* 2nd ed. Chicago: U of Chicago P, 1970.

Lerner, D. *The Passing of Traditional Society: Modernizing the Middle East,* New York: Free Press, 1958.

Lindbeck, George. *The Nature of Doctrine: Religion and Theology in a Postliberal Age.* London: SPCK, 1984.

McGrane, Bernard. *Beyond Anthropology. Society, and the Other.* New York: Columbia UP, 1989.

MacIntyre, Alasdair. *After Virtue.* 2nd ed. London: Duckworth, 1985.

———. *Whose Justice? Which Rationality?.* London: Duckworth, 1990.

Milbank, John. *Theology and Social Theory: Beyond Secular Reason.* Oxford: Blackwell, 1990.

Müller, Max. *Sacred Books of the East.* 49 Volumes. Oxford: Clarendon, 1879–94.

Pannikar, Raimundo. *The Unknown Christ of Hinduism.* London: Darton, Longmann & Todd, 1964.

Said, Edward. *Orientalism: Western Conceptions of the Orient.* London: Routledge, 1978.

Schwab, Raymond. *The Oriental Renaissance: Discovery of India and the East, 1680–1880.* New York: Columbia UP, 1984.

Smart, Ninian. *The Phenomenon of Religion.* London: MacMillan, 1973.

———. "Religious Studies in the United Kingdom." *Religion,* 18 (1988): 1–11.

Smith, Wilfred Cantwell. *The Meaning and End of Religion.* New York: Macmillan, 1962.

Tracy, David. *Dialogue with the Other: The Inter-Religious Dialogue.* Louvain: Peeters, 1990.
Urs von Balthasar, Hans. *The Theology of Karl Barth.* New York: Rinehart, 1971.
Ward, Keith. *A Vision to Pursue: Beyond the Crisis in Christianity.* London: SCM, 1991.
Westerhoof, John H., and Stanley Hauerwas, eds. *Schooling Christians: "Holy Experiments" in American Education.* Grand Rapids, MI: Eerdmans, 1992.

11 • Religious Polyphony in the Novels of Nuruddin Farah

Norman R. Cary

MIKHAIL BAKHTIN'S NOTIONS of dialogism *vs.* the monological, of carnivalesque heteroglossia *vs.* conservative monoglossia, link internal and external discourse with historical/social power, and can be "translated" into postcolonial and feminist readings of Anglophone texts throughout the world (Pechey; Sullivan). Particularly helpful are Bakhtin's opposition to monophonic ideological authoritarianism and his countervailing endorsement of the polyphonic, and the subversive nature of the carnivalesque in literature. His paradigm is provided by the novels of Dostoevsky, in which there is a "plurality of independent and unmerged voices and consciousnesses." Bakhtin asserts that Dostoevsky's characters articulate not the views of the author; rather they embody in their personalities fully contradictory "idea feelings" regarding class behavior, politics, morality, and religion (*Problems* 6, 10). Farah, by contrast, has usually been viewed as a monological writer who incorporates in his fiction his strong views against political and gender oppression in Somalia, though Petersen recognizes the polyphonic in Farah when she notes "the characters' (and perhaps the author's) inability or unwillingness to commit themselves to a final point of view" (93). If most of the critics are correct in identifying Farah's monophonic authority, one would expect his attitude toward Eurocentric Christianity and the dominant Somali Islam to be negative as well; instead, Farah is as suspicious as Bakhtin of any authoritative truth about religion, composing instead a polyphony of religious "voices" ranging from the cynically hypocritical to the sincerely mystical. These "voices" include minor characters who have no notion of their contradictory beliefs, and major characters who resemble Bakhtin's notion of the Dostoevskian hero and are more or less aware of an inner heteroglossia of competing beliefs (*Problems* 28–29).

Bakhtin claims that Dostoevsky in his fiction embodied the contradictions of his time and place (*Problems* 27). The same can be said about Farah, for Somali religious life in the twentieth century includes not only Islam but elements of African Traditional Religion (Lewis, *Religion* 96–103), as well as the influence of the Christianity which missionaries and European conquerors brought with them. The function of religion in Somalia is also contradictory. Islam often supports the forces of sexual and political oppression, so that Ewen is partially correct when he says that "it is no longer effective as a spiritual or moral force" (204). It is often hybridized with African Traditional Religion, so Somalis often attempt to solve their problems through magic—a practice that, in Farah's novels, usually proves powerless. But Farah does not monologically enforce a pessimistic view of religion, for there are characters who interpret Islam as a liberating force; that they typically fail is not due to any defect in their religion but because they are beset by an inner dialogue between opposing beliefs which marks them to be as "unfinalizable" as Dostoevsky's characters, an inner conflict which hinders their ability to devise effective strategies against the Siyaad Barre dictatorship. Christianity is also the occasion for inner psychic juxtaposition: on the one hand, it is associated with colonialism and postcolonial oppression; on the other hand, Joycean rebelliousness provides a model for one major character.

Islam is often felt by Farah's characters to be complicit in sexual and political repression; in some, the two are linked. It is used cynically by men who have no religion, and by devout people who believe that female subordination is sanctioned by Allah. The two men Ebla marries in *From a Crooked Rib* observe the forms of Islamic matrimony, though they have no respect for it. Awill, the young bureaucrat Ebla accompanies to the city, acts out of an inner dialogue between Islam, customary male behavior, and his European education. He swears by "the Great Allah" that he will call in the sheikh to solemnize their marriage; then beats her until he can deflower her like a traditional Somali groom who forces himself on his bride, exulting in her pain as a sign of his virility. He also beats her, a traditional gesture of male domination (Lewis, *Marriage* 29; Petersen 100). Because of this inner dialogue Awill sees no inconsistency between this conduct and his participation in the religious ceremony the next day. He is also unable to see the inconsistency between his unorthodox method of obtaining a wife outside the clan system, and his abuse of her. Tiffo, the rich man who takes up with Ebla after Awill flies off to Italy, has no more respect for Islamic marriage than Awill has. Tiffo too calls in a sheikh, but despite this formality, Ebla seems little to him but a woman of convenience to take the place of his estranged wife. His inconsistency, however, is not the result of an inner dialogue but is rooted in the traditional Somali double standard: "wives are expected to remain faithful to their husbands and misconduct by women is regarded as more serious than a man's illegitimate relations" (Lewis, *Marriage* 35).

More reprehensible but equally complex is the religiosity of Keynaan, the twins' father in *Sweet and Sour Milk*. Keynaan was a career policeman until he was dismissed for his womanizing; now, anxious to be rehabilitated, he cooperates with the regime's effort to make his son Soyaan a martyr to the revolution. Keynaan is also cruel to the present women in his life, beating Qumman, his wife, and getting his mistress, Beydan, pregnant. He justifies his misogyny in religious terms, reproving the surviving twin Loyaan for discussing ideas with women: "Women are for sleeping with, for giving birth to and bringing up children; they are not good for any other thing.... They are not to be trusted with secrets. They can serve the purposes Allah created them for originally, and no more" (84). The other element of his psychic dialogue is African Traditional Religion which moves him to blame his wife for bewitching his mistress and causing her to die in childbirth. But he thinks in Islamic terms when, after Soyaan's death, he orders Loyaan to read from the family Koran:

> Read on. Bless us. Bless your mother who has sinned. Bless your brother who died an innocent death. Bless us all. Bless us so that Allah may deliver us from our sins and the sins we harbour inside of ourselves. Bless your mother, the woman who consulted and paid for evil and the death of others. Bless the newly-arrived, welcome him. (236)

Other characters, more pious than Keynaan, also support male domination, and sometimes political domination as well. The inner dialogue which characterizes Ebla's grandfather is between Islamic piety and Somali custom. He is a devout man who has loved his granddaughter; but when she avoids an arranged marriage by disappearing, he curses her. Resentment at his granddaughter for breaking tribal convention overshadows his piety. Another sexual traditionalist is Idil, Medina's mother-in-law in *Sardines*, whose ideas about sex are ostensibly Islamic but in fact are tribal (King 6). Idil advocates infibulation (female circumcision) for her granddaughter despite its painful disfiguring. She also feels it her duty to provide a replacement for Medina after she leaves her husband. Like Ebla's grandfather, she has no inkling that her feelings are contradictory, maintaining that all her values are sanctioned by the Koran: "What I always say is this . . . we can tell the world what pleases the ears of the world. But facts are facts, and God is God. It is all in the book. Allah says it very clearly in His book, the Holy Koran. Clear and distinct as the Sacred Word" (79).

Idil's conduct does not seem to have any political effect, but this is not so with Qumman in *Sweet and Sour Milk*, who is suspicious of Western medicine but accepts African Traditional medicine along with her Islamic faith. She calls in a native healer to Soyaan's bedside, and after he dies, she refuses permission for an autopsy, assuming that her son's death is due to witchcraft. Her traditional beliefs unwittingly assist the government coverup of the poisoning. Africanized belief in *From a Crooked Rib* does not harm Ebla, but neither does it help her. After Awill's departure she is unhappy, and Asha, the landlady, takes her to a *savant*; the interpretation of a woman's frustration over a jilted love as spirit-induced is conventional (Lewis, *Religion* 29). The fortune teller appeals to both Islam and Traditional Religion: "Take her to a medicine-man, a priest, and then he should read the Holy Book over her" (148). Asha arranges for a sheikh to come to the girl's room, where he writes words in Arabic which Ebla assumes are from the Koran, washes the ink off the slate with water, and has her drink the water as a cure. This treatment of Scripture as a talisman, an example of the Somali practice of seeking spiritual remedies for sickness (Lewis, "Islam"" 140).

Sometimes religion is seen to be supportive of liberation. When

Ebla is unsure whether she should join a caravan out of her village, she "put her faith and her fate along with it into the hands of God," praying, "I am certain that God will understand my situation. And of course, He won't let me down" (19). In town at her cousin's, she asks God to decide whether she should stay or leave; but when God does not respond, she reassures herself in a long prayer that Allah wants her to make up her own mind. Her prayer could be construed as a rationalization of her desire to escape, or as evidence that she is a strong-willed woman. Certainly, she seems to have few religious qualms later about marrying Tiffo. She wonders to Asha whether her marriage to Awill is legal according to Islamic law, then quickly drops Tiffo when Awill returns.

Ebla's "unfinishedness," to use Bakhtin's term, is emphasized when she reappears in *Sardines* sophisticated and wealthy. She remembers that she has broken with the traditional restrictions on women but still argues to her Westernized daughter Sagal, who is pregnant, that a woman should not avoid childbearing. God decides one's fate, she says; Allah blessed childbearing when Mary conceived without knowing a man; then she repeats the legend of woman being made of Adam's crooked rib. Despite the status Ebla has acquired, the language of belief is still powerful for her. As if to complement the power of religion, Sagal's acquiescence to her mother's advice is motivated in part by the timely reappearance of a mendicant who had been told by his "favourite saint" in a dream to appreciate his female children. This is more than just a hint of "a greater human possibility" (Adam 40); devotion to saints is a central feature in Somali piety (Laitin and Samatar 45), though in the context of Somali misogyny, such a religious validation of the worth of female children is surprising.

Commendable attitudes toward politics and gender roles do not, however, guarantee success, especially when they lead to violence. A number of religious figures in the novels collaborate with the government—Loyaan thinks of such people as clowns and *arrivistes*:

> they were those who were willing to search for and find in their concordances references which legitimized the tyranny with which the country was being ruled. Turn into a soviet-inspired Marxist-Leninist state a country with a hundred per cent Muslim popula-

tion. In one hand, the Blue Book of the General and Lenin's writings in improvised translations; in the other, the Holy Koran. In one instant: "We have blind faith in Allah's doctrine" in the same: "We are Marxist-Leninist and Mohammedan." (*Milk* 133)

Loyaan's cynicism should be seen in the context of recent history. After he seized power in 1969 and instituted what he called socialism, General Siyaad Barre tried to associate himself with earlier heroes of Somali history, including Sayyid Muxammad Cabdillle Xasan, a religious leader who led a revolt against the British in the first quarter of this century. But when Siyaad Barre "proclaimed himself the divinely guided saviour of his people, some Somalis were heard to mutter, under their breaths, that Somali socialism was a religion" (Lewis, *History* 225). To counter such an accusation of infidelity to Islam, Siyaad Barre tried to enlist the support of religious leaders, and when this was not effective, he executed ten sheiks for opposing his regime(Laitin and Samatar 109–10; Samatar 95). Loyaan's inner dialogue is between distrust of religion and respect for Islam; despite his skepticism, he seems to admire the sheikhs' integrity—he even told the General that their sentencing was unconstitutional and against the Koran. Neither religious opposition nor Loyaan's remonstrations have had any observable political effect.

Old Deeriye in *Close Sesame* is even more contradictory than Ebla's grandfather. Like the grandfather, Deeriye is a follower of Sayyid Muxammad. Like his hero, Deeriye is not bound by clan-divisiveness and, like his hero, he opposes tyranny; his favorite poem, composed by the Sayyid, vividly describes the bloody death of the madcap British soldier Colonel Richard Corfield in 1913(Samatar 176). Unlike the Sayyid, whose religion was austere and puritanical, and also unlike Ebla's grandfather, Deeriye has a positive attitude toward the women in his life. He respected and loved his wife, he has not stood in the way of his daughter when she pursued an advanced education in medicine, and he is even fond of his Jewish daughter-in-law.

As admirable as Deeriye is, his religious feelings are finally directed to suicidal violence. His prayers and love of the Koran, and his nonlegalistic approach to religion, are characteristic of the Sufi approach (Lewis, "Sufism" 149–51). He also has somber discussions with his son Mursal about the appropriateness of retaliative violence against a tyrant, for he has a deep concern for all who are oppressed. Deeriye is such a virtuous character that the reader is also prepared to accept his visions of his dead wife, Naadifa, as authentic, even though they might be labeled pagan by fundamentalist Muslims (Lewis, *Religion* 63, 95). After Mursal vanishes, Deeriye begins to think of his son, who he suspects has been involved in a plot to assassinate the General, as a martyr for the cause of God. In addition, he feels that Naadifa is accusing him of fruitless political gestures and quietistic devotion and urging him to revenge Mursal's death. But, when he confronts the dictator, he pulls out his Sufi rosary instead of a gun, and is killed by the General's bodyguards.

How do we interpret a character whose inner dialogue includes a deep faith and a broad tolerance but also a propensity for violence? The clue may be in his veneration of the Sayyid, a man who similarly was both a religious mystic, a Sufi who was sometimes guided by visions, and a bloodthirsty warrior. Samatar concludes that the Sayyid "wanted wholeheartedly to satisfy both the pious tranquillity of his faith and the stormy duties of his career as a warrior chieftain, and the dogged pursuit of these contradictory objectives led him, on occasion, into 'erratic behavior'" (194).

Religion in *Maps* is again quixotically associated with self-defeating violence. Askar, the protagonist, is a younger, less devout version of Deeriye whose inner dialogue is even more confusing, for it includes not only the attraction to revenge-murder but conflicting religious vocabulary (both Islamic and Christian) and sexual confusion (Kelly 20–26). In the depiction of Askar, Farah has gone beyond confusion to a polyphony of madness. Askar is a personality who can be associated with the macabre side of the "carnivalesque," the overturning of normal restraints of normality to celebrate the irrational and erotic (Bakhtin, *Rabelais*). Many of Askar's memories and dreams are about Misra, who brought him up after his parents' death. As a child he was so attached to her that he disliked her lover Aw-Adan the priest, who beat him and thought him satanic. Askar remembers his youthful religion in sexual terms; he recalls sleeping with the Holy Word between his legs for comfort. Now he cannot forget religion even under the aegis of his secularized uncle in Mogadiscio. After Askar apparently learns that Misra has been mutilated and killed, he remembers that during a rite when meat was "read" as a clue to the future, she prophesied disaster and perhaps her own death—surely this is a ritual with its roots in African belief. He recollects the divination after deciding that even Salaado, his uncle's wife, has become religious and wants to sacrifice a goat. It is not clear how accurate Askar's perceptions are at this point, for his rambling about blood and guilt may be symptomatic of an unbalanced psychic state. By the end of the novel Askar is beginning to resemble Deeriye in his self-questioning and his hinted involvement in the revenge-death of Misra, who has been suspected of aiding murderous Ethiopians.

Christianity in *A Naked Needle* is also faulted, because of its association with Italian imperialism and its cooperation with European and Somali dictatorships. The young bureaucrat Koschin is reminiscent of the young Awill in his internalization of conflicting impulses, though he is more lost and less vicious. He is knowledgeable about avant-garde Western literature (he has written a thesis on James Joyce) but is estranged from his own culture, although he momentarily seeks its power when he desires the magical wisdom in an amulet left him by his dead mother—though he cannot even get the amulet open. Is the alternative Eurocentric Christianity? Koschin contrasts his inability to access traditional wisdom to the serene Christian faith of Nancy, his European mistress. Still, he imagines himself telling her he is repulsed at both her white color and her religion, which is associated with the violence of Fascism. Christianity has not been averse to Somali dictatorship either; Koschin expresses his disapproval of the special tax-free status the General's government gives to the Church's enterprises, probably a vestige of ecclesiastical privilege under Italian rule.

Koschin thinks of himself as a skeptic, and in fact uses the language of Christian and Muslim eschatology to reinforce a kind of metaphysical nihilism. When a widow approaches him and Nancy as they tour Mogadiscio, Koschin speculates ironically that the woman "[m]ust have lost her man into the earth. From which he will resurrect only with the accompaniment of the Bugle of the Angels, *Insha'allah!*" (22). When his friend Meyran welcomes him to her apartment, Koschin misquotes to himself the first stanza of *The Divine Comedy*:

> Midday this day I'm bound upon
> I woke to destruction in a dark day
> Where the right path is wholly gone!
>
> (48)

Here he may be providing a hint that the novel is a parody of the pilgrim's quest: he is also lost in a spiritual and cultural wood, and finds what fulfillment he can in a woman, but neither Meyran nor Nancy is a Beatrice, and there is certainly no beatific vision. Much later, he mentally rambles for an entire paragraph about last things:

> . . . heaven is neither up nor is it down nor is it before the Judgement. Heaven is neither lukewarm, of tepid temper. . . . What am I saying? . . . But the roll-call and the Judgement are all antecedents to the blowing of the bugle which is preceded by the epicentrum. Those who laugh a little here in this Vanishing World cry a lot later in the Next Everlasting World, it is said. . . . Time in the Next World is a long expansion of nothingness and everythingness with no dimensions, no days, no nights, not even a change of climate. (117)

This passage brings to mind the retreat sermon in Joyce's *Portrait of the Artist as a Young Man* which precedes Stephen Daedalus's renunciation of Christianity; here Koschin is alluding to his own dismal experience with bureaucracy as well as voicing his despair.

Koschin is unable to escape the God he wants to deny, however. He imagines his friend Barre as a Buddhist monk "pulling him towards the arena where he may recognize the complete inability of man to turn his back totally on God" (30). What he thinks is a cynical attack on religion may be rather an admission that he cannot forget the religious question:

> I'm a Muslim, surely, although I don't practice it. The early morning and the afternoon prayers, my God! But why have all the important religions, all the faiths that continue to flourish, why have they all originated in the Middle East and its environs? I ask. That I have yet to find out. Perhaps it is the knack of Asiatic craftsmanship? I don't know. (102)

For all his fulminating against religion and his alienation from his own culture, Koschin too will become an impotent rebel; the last we hear of him he has been tortured into mental incompetence.

Farah's latest novel, *Gifts*, once more presents the dialogical relationship among religions—Islam, Christianity, as well as indigenous Somali religion—and secularism. Islam is associated with the subordination of women by Duniya's young brother Mataan:

> "*Xabs* is interpreted by Islamic scholars as the right of obedience," explained Mataan, "although the word shares its root with another misunderstood to mean detention. The point is that women aren't permitted to leave their husbands' homes without their husbands' prior notification, and any woman who violates this right maybe described as rebellious. . . . A homeless woman is one who has no husband or a male relation to provide her with shelter." (173)

Obviously Mataan is conversant with Islamic scholarship, and his remarks have a somewhat pedantic tone; but there is no evidence at all that he is a practicing Muslim. Duniya's dialogue, between Islam and secularism, is more inward: she reflects often on the subordinate status of women in Somali society, and is quite touchy about being manipulated by men. She is reticent about wearing her hair uncovered, but pleased at the freedom it gives her. She overcomes her initial reserve with Bosaaso and experiences idyllic sex with him, but she seeks the approval of her elder brother for their relationship. Her speech, her daytime fantasies, and even her dreams include Islamic superstitions and legends, though she and her friends also allude to Islamic "mythology," a term which suggests a certain psychological distance from Islamic faith. The dialogue is also inter-religious. There are allusions to Christianity by Duniya's friends, who are aware of what is happening in Europe and North America. Duniya's first husband Taariq, for example, caustically refers to the self-serving motives of Bible-Belt Christians of North America when they give aid to starving Africans. Pre-Islamic Somali religion seems as plausible as Islam to Dr. Mire when he delivers his disquisition comparing indigenous and monotheistic creation myths. Taariq goes further, comparing an imposed Islam to modern neocolonial aid to Africa:

> "If I could afford to be cynical I would say that the African, knowing no better, accepts whatever he is given because it is an insult to refuse what you're offered. If his cousin or a member of the extended family doesn't give, God will or somebody else will.

God, as we know Him, has been 'given' to us, together with all the mythological paraphernalia, genealogical truisms that classify us as inferior beings, not to forget the Middle Eastern philosophical maxim that God (in a monotheistic sense) is progress. Yes, the truth is our Gods and those of our fathers, we have been told, do not give you anything; and since they have a beginning, they have an end too." (196)

Retrospectively surveying Farah's seven novels, we see that his presentation of religion is richly polyphonic, though it is often more political and less psychological than the religious heteroglossia in Bakhtin's Dostoevsky. Farah does not charge Christianity directly with Eurocentrism or imperialism, as many African writers do, though Christianity is linked to indigenous authoritarianism as well as imperialism and neocolonialism. With respect to Somalia's dominant religion, Turfan is correct that "Farah's own attitude towards Islam is by no means hostile. Rather, it is the distortion of Islam by its practitioners and by those who seek to use it to their own advantage that provokes his criticism" (177). On the other hand, despite the fact that Islam is part of the thought-world of Farah's characters, they do not find it to be an effective source of social and political liberation, though it sometimes provides inspiration to those who seek sexual and political freedom. When these characters fail, it is likely to be not because of a lack of religious faith but because the polyphony of impulses they experience hampers effective action against sexual and political oppression. And when they succeed, religion does not seem to be decisive to their achievements.

Works Cited

Adam, Ian. "Nuruddin Farah and James Joyce: Some Issues of Intertextuality." *World Literature Written in English* 24 (1984): 34–43.

Bakhtin, Mikhail. *Problems of Dostoevsky's Poetics*. Trans. Caryl Emerson. Minneapolis: U of Minnesota P, 1984.

———. *Rabelais and His World*. Trans. Helene Iswolsky. Bloomington: Indiana UP, 1984.

Ewen. D. R. "Nuruddin Farah." *The Writing of East and Central Africa*. Ed. G. D. Killam. London: Heinemann, 1984. 192–210.

Farah, Nuruddin. *Close Sesame*. London: Allison, 1983.

———. *From a Crooked Rib*. London: Heinemann, 1970.
———. *Gifts*. London: Serif, 1993.
———. *Maps*. 1986. New York: Pantheon, 1987.
———. *A Naked Needle*. London: Heinemann, 1976.
———. *Sardines*. London: Allison, 1981.
———. *Sweet and Sour Milk*. 1979. London: Heinemann, 1980.
Kelly, Hilarie. "Somali Tragedy of Political and Sexual Confusion: A Critical Analysis of Nuruddin Farah's 'Maps.'" *Ufahamu* 16.2 (1988): 21-37.
King, J. S. "The Practice of Female Circumcision and Infibulation Among the Somal." *Journal of the Anthropological Society* [Bombay] 11 (1890): 2-6.
Laitin, David D., and Said S. Samatar. *Somalia: Nation in Search of a State*. Boulder, CO: Westview, 1987.
Lewis, I. M. "Islam." *Somalia in Word and Image*. Ed. Katheryne S. Loughran et al. Bloomington: Indiana UP, 1986. 139-42.
———. *Marriage and the Family in Northern Somaliland*. East African Studies No. 15. Kampala: East African Institute of Social Research, 1962.
———. *A Modern History of Somalia*. Rev. ed. Boulder, CO: Westview, 1988.
———. *Religion in Context: Cults and Charisma*. Cambridge: Cambridge UP, 1986.
———. "Sufism in Somaliland: A Study in Tribal Islam." *Bulletin of the School of Oriental and African Languages* 18 (1956): 149-61.
Pechey, Graham "On the Borders of Bakhtin: Dialogisation, Decolonisation." In *Bakhtin and Cultural theory*. Ed.Ken Hirschkop and David Shepherd. Manchester: Manchester UP, 1989. 39-67.
Petersen, Kirsten Holst. "The Personal and the Political: The Case of Nuruddin Farah." *Ariel* 12.3 (1981): 93-101.
Samatar, Said S. *Oral Poetry and Somali Nationalism: The Case of Sayyid Muhammad Abdille Hasan*. Cambridge: Cambridge UP, 1982.
Sullivan, Zohrah. "The Postcolonial African Novel and the Dialogic Imagination." *Approaches to Teaching Achebe's 'Things Fall Apart.'* Ed. Bernth Lindfors. New York: MLA, 1991. 101-106.
Turfan, Barbara. "Opposing Dictatorship: A Comment on Nuruddin Farah's *Variations on the Theme of an African Dictatorship*." *Journal of Commonwealth Literature* 24.1 (1989): 173—84.

12 • The Social and Political Vision of Sri Aurobindo

K. D. Verma

As A PROPHET of Indian nationalism, Sri Aurobindo occupies an important place in the history of Indian political thought.[1] When we recall the early Aurobindo, we think of a fiery, aggressive, and uncompromising revolutionary who had cast his lot with the larger destiny of India and her people. His active involvement in the struggle against the British Empire in general was an expression of his staunch conviction that imperialism and colonialism, whether mercantile or political, are manifestations of repressive egoism or hubris on the part of a nation or a group who simply happened to possess an expedient superiority of means over its relatively less favored subjects. The Caesars and Napoleons of history have been guilty of exercising this hubris, of perpetuating slavery, tyranny, and injustice in the world, of devising and enforcing negative and immoral political, economic, and social systems, and, hence, of denying man his basic freedom and individuality. Man, as Aurobindo believed right from the very beginning of his involvement, is entitled to freedom, equality, and basic human dignity. He fully shared the ideas of Rousseau, Voltaire, and other thinkers of the European Enlightenment, and the bases of the French Revolution, although later on, especially as one finds in *The Human Cycle* and *The Ideal of Human Unity*, his ideas of liberty, equality, and fraternity assumed a much more metaphysical and philosophical dimension. The early Aurobindo believed quite religiously that nationalism is an immediate and irrevocable necessity, an inevitable phenomenon, much like the powerful thrust of a destined natural cycle of change.[2] He further believed that revolutions in the history of mankind are healthy and fruitful expressions of the creative energy in men, and that they occur and would continue occurring unchecked and uncontrolled at predicated successive intervals of history. The psychology of the history of human progress was later fully developed and synthesized by Aurobindo in his evolutionary philosophy of human growth. Readers of Blake may remember the conflict between Orc and Urizen: the revolutionary energy, symbolized in the figure of Orc, manifests itself in the cycle of human destiny as a formidable agent of change against tyranny, oppression, the law, and decay. Himself a fiery Orc of Indian nationalism, Aurobindo was resolutely determined to help the peoples of India not only in getting rid of the foreign yoke but also in achieving a happy and honorable condition of existence.

Evil, according to Aurobindo, appears at various periods during the course of the evolutionary growth of man, nature, and society, but it has no permanent existence of its own. The pattern of evolutionary progress, as envisaged by Aurobindo, is no doubt cyclical, but it does not admit Spenglerian regression and pessimism.[3] The young Aurobindo, as Zaehner notes in *Evolution in Religion*, was "a left-wing politician," and had evinced "sympathetic interest in Marxian socialism," perhaps fully sharing the Marxian prophecy of a possible materialization of a new social order "in which the free development of each is the condition for the development of all" (4). Whatever the nature of the obvious similarity between Aurobindo and Marx,[4] we know that Aurobindo's emphasis is on the divinization of man and of this earth and on the ultimate liberation of man. In Aurobindo, the two dreams, one of individual freedom, the other of collective salvation, are integral parts of the one unified dream; and national independence or nationalism is a preparatory condition to the realization of the larger dream.

For the Indian intelligentsia, especially for men like Aurobindo, Gandhi, Nehru, and others who were educated in England and steeped in Western intellectual thought, it was not difficult to comprehend the meaning and significance of nationalism. One can argue that modern nationalism is a typical European phenomenon and that it emerged in India mainly as a reaction against British colonialism and racism.[5] In England, of course, nationalism had been imbued with powerful religious feelings: as a result of this amalgam of religion and nationalism, the English have always regarded themselves as God's chosen race, and the monarchy as a divine institution. It is this overpowering sense of nationalism which later outgrew into colonialism and imperialism. France and England, as Murray remarks in *Studies in the English Social and Political Thinkers of the Nineteenth Century*, fought the Hundred Years' War "for a prize of incalculable worth, the leadership of the colonial world" (2: 210). Ironically, Blake thought this inchoate and expedient mixture of politics and religion an infectious perversion, and clairvoyantly prophesied the fall of the Empire. But Disraeli, Mill, and Carlyle were happy colonialists:[6] underlying their pious convictions was perhaps the paternalistic assumption that God's chosen people had the moral obligation to spread light—to educate and reform the savages and natives, to devise means of introducing European education and civilization and to ensure progress and advancement. If this sanctimonious principle had effectively dictated the governance of India, much of the history of the British Raj in India would have been written entirely differently. But the fact remains that British colonialism—and European colonialism for that matter—was an expression of the powerful urge to gain political and economic supremacy; and it had the blessings of "feudalized Christianity."[7]

As the colonial umbrella grew phenomenally bigger and more unmanageable, the English politicians at home became overly concerned with the problems of unity, homogeneity, and consolidation of the imperial power. People like Lord Morley thought that "the empire was united, if it were united, by community of interest, whereas Seeley conceived it as bound together by community of race and religion" (Murray 2: 211). The phrase "community of interest" is no doubt dubious, but it is pregnant with rich irony: it certainly did not imply uniform interest of people or national units within the Empire. Earlier, of course, Edmund Burke had formulated the clear possibility of forming one commonwealth more expediently and readily by the states of Europe rather than by the racially heterogeneous nations; and for Burke nationalism was the key element in the unification of the European states. Burke, like Coleridge, had accepted the metaphysics of Divine Providence, but he was vehemently opposed to the use of divine authority by England for the gratification of "the lowest of their passions."[8] That is why Burke who was in favor of preserving the integrity of the Indian civilization and maintaining peace in India had proposed a political trusteeship for India. But the questions that intrigued Indian intellectuals like Aurobindo pertained to fundamental humanistic values and moral principles underlying the essential structure of British colonialism. Why is the principle of absolute sovereignty of a people, even if it were the most genuine and authentic expression of their will, not universally and unreservedly acknowledged? If the English as a nation have the absolute right to assert their sovereignty, why should Great Britain deny the same right to Canada, Ireland, or India? Why is the Christian ideal, according to which the denial of human rights is supposed to be an offense to God, generally considered to be compatible with the political reality of colonialism? Does colonial politics, especially when its authority and sanction are explicitly derived from religion, have any moral basis?

It is abundantly clear from Aurobindo's early writings that he was very distrustful of British justice, for the British, in their injudicious and oppressive governance of India, were essentially led by their boastful pride—"the pride of race, the pride of empire and the pride of colour" (BCL 1: 904). The unpropitious school of toryism and conservatism had made its political views on India too sharply pronounced to incite any feelings of hope and trust, but Aurobindo was equally suspicious of the British liberals.[9] Such parabolic and insensitive vocabulary of colonial consciousness as indubitably defines the incongruous relationship between Prospero and Caliban, the master and the slave, and the ill-conceived obsession of Kurtz ("exterminate all the brutes")[10] is only reminiscent of the unchaste collective guilt and of the self-destructive political reality that writers like Conrad and Forster were to dramatize in their works. Aurobindo was convinced that the colonial rule, in its lustful intent and approach, was engaged in robbing the subjects of their national and cultural identity and that it had, in the due course of history, firmly established a bureaucratic and despotic system based on fear, repression, and tyranny. Because of the rapid debilitation of Indian consciousness prompted by racial bigotry and because of the pervasive colonial hubris, Aurobindo remained vehemently opposed to the idea of India's becoming a satellite province or otherwise a confederate state of the Empire.

Metaphysics and religious thought had played a significant role in shaping the political ideas of Dante, Milton, and Coleridge. Likewise, in the case of Aurobindo—a poet, a radical, a philosopher—it goes without saying that his political vision of India's nationhood and sovereignty derives its essential outline from his spiritual vision of man's freedom and enlightenment. In fact, both Aurobindo and Gandhi were inspired by Indian spiritual thought,[11] although it is a well-known fact of history that Aurobindo did not share the Mahatma's position on several issues.[12] Aurobindo was an out-and-out revolutionary—he was dubbed an "extremist"—who did not believe in the policy of mendicancy, appeasement, and compromise. His vociferous criticism of the moderate position centered on their psychological vulnerability to the repressive and intimidating measures of the despotic regime and to the self-defeating programs of the Raj. It was practically the same sort of political process that had made people like Sir Syed Ahmed Khan support the colonial regime.[13] "To recover possession of the State," reiterates Aurobindo categorically and emphatically, "is therefore the first business of the awakened Indian consciousness" and not "to revive the old dissipation of energies, to put social reform first, education first or moral regeneration first and leave freedom to result from these" (BCL 1: 882). Later, it turned out that the disastrous historical tragedy, the partition of Bengal, not only enabled the radicals to consolidate their own strength, but also forced the moderates to see the truth of Aurobindo's vision. The moderates, it seemed, had followed Burke's exhortation to the Irish of preferring the path of pacific resistance to that of an open rebellion. Aurobindo's spiritual vision had enabled him to invest divinity upon his country, his land, and his nation, to see in each man the sleeping divinity that needs to be awakened, and to believe firmly that the solemn and unequivocal affirmation of the will of people can wipe out the stains of slavery. It is this unique vision of divine nationhood or of India as Mother that gave him the inspiration and strength to wage an incessant struggle for the sacred cause of freedom. Aurobindo believed that once India regained its nationhood, the task of strengthening national consciousness and of achieving progress would be much more relevant to the larger goals, for those who had been enslaved and subjugated too long would not otherwise know the meaning of true liberty.

During the period of his active political involvement, Aurobindo advocated the idealistic position—a position which admitted no compromise with the colonial rule on fundamental principles and which called for an equally firm and unequivocal commitment to a comprehensive program of revolutionary action. For Aurobindo, nationalism was a *dharma*, and the revolution was a *yudha*. "*Dharma*," as Aurobindo explains, "is the Indian conception in which rights and duties lose the artificial antagonism created by a view of the world which makes selfishness the roots of action . . ." (BCL 1: 760). This *dharma*, the selfless act, *nishkam karma* of the *Gita*, is "the basis of democracy which Asia must recognize . . ." (BCL 1: 760). Since the struggle was not merely political but ethical and spiritual, he could, therefore, morally justify the use of violence as a means of achieving the larger ends. In the beginning, however, most of his ideas on freedom, nationalism, and revolution were inspired by manifold experiments in the West, especially the long, intrepid struggle of the peoples of Europe to attain basic human dignity. Rousseau and other European thinkers, we may remember, did characterize slavery as immoral. The entire history of the French Revolution and the European Romantic movement, especially in its unswerving commitment to the cause of liberty, had a moral basis. Some of the English Romantic poets, especially Wordsworth, viewed the French Revolution as a fulfillment of the biblical prophecy contained in the Revelation. In the history of European political thought and particularly at the time of the American and the French revolutions clear-cut distinctions had been drawn between morality which is politically functional and expedient, and morality which has its reference to larger and more fundamental humanistic values. Undoubtedly, Aurobindo considered the latter the only justifiable basis of a revolution which was inspired by a comprehensive vision of liberty.

Liberty for Aurobindo did not mean simply the abolition of foreign rule and the achievement of self-government based upon the blind imitation of the West. Nor did it mean the attainment of empty and selfish materialistic progress hitherto sought by great nations. Nationalism meant the true awakening of the "Indian proletariat" to a collective vision of such cultural greatness as would enable India to contribute to the progress of human civilization:

> . . . we advocate the struggle for Swaraj [self-rule], first, because Liberty is in itself a necessity of national life and therefore worth

striving for for its own sake; secondly, because Liberty is the first indispensable condition of national development intellectual, moral, industrial, political . . . ; thirdly, because in the next great stage of human progress it is not a material but a spiritual, moral and psychical advance that has to be made and for this a free Asia and in Asia a free India must take the lead, and Liberty is therefore worth striving for the world's sake. India must have Swaraj in order to live; she must have Swaraj in order to live for the world . . . as a free people for the spiritual and intellectual benefit of the human race. (BCL 1: 465)

While egoistical nationalism is morally destructive, true nationalism, as is evident from this lucid exposition of the larger responsibilities of freedom, is neither callously selfish nor inherently antagonistic; on the contrary, such nationalism as marks the intellectual and cultural growth of a nation or a group of people is directly and positively related to the welfare of the entire community of mankind. Swaraj is an inner discipline, both at the individual level and at the national level, and it cannot be realized without cleansing one's perceptions. "The true source of human liberty, human equality, human brotherhood," maintains Aurobindo, "is in the freedom of man's inner spirit" (BCL 1: 757). Liberty, equality, and fraternity are teleological and epistemological concepts, and their place in a social structure is dependent on man's ability to perceive the truth of each of these concepts. In the structure of political reality envisaged by Aurobindo, the recognition of the constitutional or legal rights of liberty and equality is not enough, for the ideal of liberty is not fully achieved without equality and fraternity, and, more important, without fraternity. Teleologically, of course, the term *swaraj* simultaneously refers to nation and to liberty.

Aurobindo considered "political Vedantism" to be the basis of the struggle and the strategy: not only did this "political Vedantism," the wisdom of the Vedas, and especially of the *Gita*, spiritualize the struggle, but it also gave him a much more profound and authentic political vision of liberty. The kind of swaraj that Aurobindo envisioned was not merely a political liberty; and the kind of struggle that Aurobindo championed was again not merely a political struggle, but a total and endless struggle for true freedom. Generally speaking, most revolutionary struggles are viewed as reactionary insurgences or temporary volcanic eruptions. But for Aurobindo the revolution meant more than a series of sporadic boycotts, fiery protests, and violent demonstrations; it included a large-scale program of political, economic, educational, social, and spiritual reconstruction. As a *dharma yudha*, it must be continuously fought simultaneously on several planes.

Aurobindo's early political radicalism was motivated by his uncompromising commitment to the ideals of liberty, equality, and fraternity and by his optimistic faith in the ability of man to become perfect. Indeed, his early political writings are an important contribution to Indian literature and thought; but, what is significant, as he progressed in his self-realization, the direct political anxiety and commitment were transformed into a much more universal and comprehensive concern for true human freedom and a new world order. The later Aurobindo, that is, the Aurobindo of the period following his dramatic exit from the active political scene,[14] has given us not only one of the most subtle analyses of man and society but also a unique vision of human progress and perfection.

One no doubt gathers from *The Human Cycle* and *The Ideal of Human Unity* that Aurobindo is a close student of history, but his philosophic vision is not centered in history, that is, in the past. Aurobindo is essentially an evolutionist, and the evolutionary theory (which, in spite of some of its obvious similarities with scientific and materialistic theories of evolution, is not Darwinian) implies that man, forms of society, and other structures must continue evolving. Since man is capable of realizing his true divinity, the form and level of perfection arrived at by man at one particular stage is not absolute. In fact, in *The Human Cycle*, Aurobindo, using Lamprecht's phraseology, conceives five psychical stages in the evolutionary development of the human race: symbolic, typal, conventional, individualistic, and subjective.[15] The movement from the symbolic to the subjective marks a process of divinization of man. However, Aurobindo does not believe that there is a straightforward path which the process of development follows. Nor does he think that man should be overly dependent upon either the past or the future, although for the purpose of immediate development the past and the future must coalesce in the present, such that the point of history absorbed in the present becomes only another point in history. As Aurobindo states:

It is true that the world's movement is not in a straight line; there are cycles, there are spirals; but still it circles, not around the same point always, but around an ever advancing centre, and therefore it returns exactly upon its old path and never goes really backward. As for standing still, it is an impossibility, a delusion, a fiction. (BCL 16: 317)

Since man is capable of becoming perfect, the highest point that he is capable of achieving is the highest point of his divinization only at one particular stage. Similarly, society is not merely a stagnant and abstract political structure; its progress depends upon the degree and nature of perfection achieved by its individual members. In a true sense, an ideal society is a community of mankind, a brotherhood that apprehends the individuality of man. But since none of the political structures so far invented by man allows any one of the two possibilities to be realized in the most ideal sense, political solution alone is no satisfactory solution of the problem of human existence, individual or collective.

While the movement from the symbolic level to the typal and conventional levels may ordinarily be regarded as symptomatic of man's fall from unity, in Aurobindo it characterizes an essential phase of continuous human advancement without the slightest implication of any pessimistic regression. At these levels, the law is established and enforced strictly according to the dictates of rational and empirical reason. Also, at these levels, the age of scientific advancement has made some of its major claims: our priorities here are confined strictly to the external world of material existence. What is valued more is the shastra (that is, established rules and the logical order), and not Atman, the spirit. The Urizenic government of the shastra (coded morality) is primarily created to safeguard man in his fallen condition of disorder and disunity. No political structure based upon this constrictive reason, however ideal—and be this democracy, communism, or socialism—will apprehend the true individuality of man. Under these various political and social systems, whatever liberty and equality are granted are given according to the law, the code, and are not consistent with man's fundamental right to be absolutely free and with his evolutionary nature. For example, in a democracy, political liberty or political equality is what is conferred upon an individual at the pleasure of the philistine majority.

Therefore, even a democracy, and still worse of the mediocre kind, is limited in scope and nature; and at best it gives only political freedom. In any political structure, including democracy, absolute freedom breeds egoism; and whether it is individual egoism or national egoism, it will destroy the ideal conception of liberty. As Aurobindo states:

> Freedom, equality, brotherhood are three godheads of the soul; they cannot be really achieved through the external machinery of society or by man so long as he lives only in the individual and the communal ego. When the ego claims liberty, it arrives at competitive individualism. When it asserts equality, it arrives first at strife, then at an attempt to ignore the variations of Nature, and, as the sole way of doing that successfully, it constructs an artificial and machine-made society. A society that pursues liberty as its ideal is unable to achieve equality; a society that aims at equality will be obliged to sacrifice liberty. For the ego to speak of fraternity is for it to speak of something contrary to its nature. . . . (BCL 15: 546)

Indeed, Aurobindo's concern with the nature and scope of liberty is teleological. And he advocates absolute freedom:

> . . . man cannot build greatly whether in art or life, unless he can conceive an idea and form of perfection and, conceiving, believe in his power to achieve it out of however rebellious and unductile a stuff of nature. Deprive him of his faith in his power for perfection and you slay or maim his greatest creative or self-creative faculty. (BCL 15: 609–10)

If man's salvation, as Aurobindo maintains, lies in "a religious or spiritual idealization of a possible future humanity" (BCL 15:609), man must continue to evolve, by means of the synthetic discipline of yoga, to the apex of what Blake would call human form divine. Aurobindo, like Blake, is not advocating licentious freedom with which man nourishes his titanic ambitions (*asura pravriti*) into egoism or hubris, be it Apollonian or Dionysian. But while most political systems are inherently fearful of such egoism, their repressive and sanctimonious laws, paradoxically enough, become a fertile soil for the nefarious perversion of ego as well as for the loss of individuality. After all, political slavery is only one kind of slavery, but the most frightful form of slavery is mental slavery—which is what the passivity of the spirit really means. It hardly needs to be stressed that any amount or degree of political freedom given to an individual whose mind has been conditioned by the language of laws and rights is not only useless but also harmful. That is why Nietzsche, while advocating intellectual anarchism, proposes the annihilation of the stubborn structure of the obsolete system. If absolute freedom implies anarchism, political or intellectual, this kind of freedom, in a sense, is a negation of that divinity which entitles man to seek his freedom and which when realized is in itself true liberty. In the anarchist thought on the whole, we are talking about only partial or one kind of liberty, not about total and comprehensive freedom. The conception of superman, according to Aurobindo, suggests the fully integrated and realized whole, an heroic consciousness. Therefore, neither the Apollonian man nor the Dionysian man is a whole man; and for the same reason, neither the ethical being nor the aesthetic being is a whole being. Such wholeness and realization as Aurobindo proposes are not anarchical in character, for his conception is based neither on the rejection of history nor on a self-centered alienation from the body of the universe. Rebellion against the yoke of law and its manifest tyranny and general "putrid waste" is a significant step forward toward a program of social reform; but a total rejection of history and of law as generally emphasized by a variety of anarchist thought suggests not only an unnatural discontinuity and disruption in the process of evolution but also a refusal on the part of the systems to recognize man's achievement.

Here we may emphasize a significant difference between a political revolutionary and a karm yogi. In Aurobindo's *Savitri*, King Ashwapathy is a karm yogi, but Savitri is both a karm yogi and a radical. Savitri's heroic consciousness enables her to wage a successful war against the god of death and of a deterministic order of lower nature and to restore to the earth the paradisal vision of life and happiness. The heroic man, according to Aurobindo, is charged by his own consciousness to create a paradisal condition on earth: such heroic souls as Plato's men of gold are agents of the Brahman engaged in the redemptive act of regenerating this virile universe. The individual belongs to mankind on the whole, and his true *dharma* is *manav dharma*: the principle and the process which bring him together with his fellow man are summed up by the word *lokasangrah*—which means "the holding together of the race in its cyclic evolution"" (BCL 15: 59). Man creates his new higher self by participating in the good of others. He enjoys absolute freedom and equality, but with one imperative—that is, brotherhood. The vision of one consciousness, and of reintegration and wholeness, places Aurobindo in an enviable company of such great figures as Plato, Dante, and Shelley. But, what is most significant, he shows the practical way of making this earth a paradise.

In Aurobindo's vision of human freedom and unity, as a nation's freedom and progress basically depend upon the nature of individual consciousness, so does the progressive movement toward one-world community depend upon the quality of the "aggregates" of people. Aurobindo maintains that people should be able to organize themselves into nations or "aggregates" in accordance with the principles of free association and unity. As free and equal people are brought together by a communal consciousness, so free and equal nations are brought together, not as a conglomeration of "imperial aggregates" that are motivated merely by political and commercial designs of expansion, but as "an ideal aggregate of humanity" that aspires to a vision of spiritualized community. True nationalism will lead, not to antagonism, domination, and confrontation, but to understanding, collaboration, and cosmopolitanism—and hence, to creating a better and happier community of mankind. Since Aurobindo's vision of universal humanity is based upon the spiritualization of man, all forms of national and imperial egoism, including such racial egoisms as Europeanism, Asiaticism, and Americanism, must be overcome. Man will cooperate with fellow man, not because he is a *homo economicus* or because he is a political or social animal, but because he has the inner urge to establish a spiritual brotherhood. It is abundantly clear that Aurobindo does not accept the Hobbesian thesis of a basic distrust in man's capacity to become free and of an avowed supremacy of the state. Nor does he regard Utilitarianism, Marxism, and Socialism as sufficiently powerful structures for resolving the problem of human suffering. Most social and political theories of contractual obligation and entitlement are fundamentally inconsistent with the larger vision of human freedom, since all conceptions of contracts and rights are essentially founded on inveterate prejudices, especially fear, distrust, and hatred, that in turn provide a pretentious basis of human subjugation and exploitation, economic, political, and social, and, hence, of an invidious social anarchy.

Evidently, Aurobindo's conception of human freedom is very bold and radical. Aurobindo tells us that man is the author of social and historical destiny, and that all forms of social, political, and religious structures are hindrances to his freedom and creativity. The idealist position, beginning with Plato, recognizes the divinity of state: in *The Republic*, the soul's liberation from the cycle of existence is ultimately dependent upon social good. Kant, of course, considers individual freedom more important than an unequivocal commitment to the state, although Hegel's belief in the divinity of a nation, which incidentally constitutes the basis of social ethics, is directly the opposite of the Kantian position. But among the English thinkers it is, indeed, Coleridge who emphasizes the divinity of state, categorically affirming organicism—not the Spencerian organicism but Romantic organicism—according to which man, nature, and society evolve together discovering "the transcendental and divine force of life."[16] In his conception of the evolution of a new society, Aurobindo, as might be construed, takes a daring leap beyond social morality, rational ethicism, nationalism, and statism. In a message delivered on August 15, 1947, Aurobindo says that "Nationalism will then have fulfilled itself; an international spirit and outlook must grow up . . . " (BCL 26: 403). While Burke will still insist upon the need of nationalism as the basis of a European common community or a confederation of nations, Aurobindo envisions the formation of an international brotherhood, a new community of man, where voluntary fusion of cultures takes place, where nationalism and its militancy will have outlived its usefulness, and where narrow national boundaries will eventually become redundant. It is somewhat paradoxical that nationalism or the state as a moral entity carries only a limited value in Aurobindo's vision of the progress of human society: the divinity that was once attributed to the state is now vested in mankind as a whole, the divine humanity. We must note this significant difference between the early Aurobindo of the Pondicherry period—the serene, the contemplative, and the philosophical mind. In his vision of human freedom, Aurobindo may be called a spiritual anarchist, but he is not a nihilist.

He is a reconstructionist and a progressive thinker who believes that all precipitous impediments to human progress, whatever their generic form, must be overcome, and that modern socioeconomic and scientific progress and spiritual growth are not incompatible with each other. Undoubtedly, behind this vision of affirmation is the hope and belief in the unhindered progress of man to the highest possible point in the human divine image: obviously, on a projected scale of continuous evolution, state, religion, and other institutional structures, because of their regressive conservatism and cryptic inertia, do not remain compatible with man's progress. That is why Aurobindo stresses the need for newer forms of social and political structures that will eliminate the problem of historical obsolescence and redundancy and help in the fusion of tradition and modernity.

Since evil belongs to history and the order of nature—and, hence, to the world of Maya—it appears at periodic stages in the evolutionary process of life.[17] In a sense, evil, as Aurobindo would have us believe, is a fortuitous agent of beneficial change, and, hence, of good, since without evil the redemptive appearance of good will not take place. But moral evil and physical evil are real, not illusory; and Aurobindo deals with the problem of evil with full force in his philosophy of evolution. At the individual level, however, it is egoism that breeds evil. In *The Life Divine*, Aurobindo's view is clearly monistic: evil and falsehood, according to Aurobindo, result from ignorance (*avidya Maya*), but there is no absolute evil as there is no absolute ignorance. Evil and falsehood, as Aurobindo observes, "are a by-product of the world movement: the sombre flowers of falsehood and evil have their root in the black soil of the Inconscient" (BCL 18: 598). The world or life as a whole is not evil; nor is man inherently evil. This conception of evil, which essentially comes from Aurobindo's view of human nature, has unmistakably shaped his vision of liberty, equality, and brotherhood and of man's salvation—and, hence, of a progressive journey from political freedom to spiritual liberation. One of the most significant elements in Aurobindo's social and political vision is that there is no room for repressive measures and laws based on a system of rewards and punishments. Nor is there any room for negative and punitive religious morality governed by the fear of evil and the self-dissipating bigotry of damnation. Religion that rejects life in preference to the over-zealous pursuit of other-worldliness and esoteric goals and rituals, that creates an unwarranted division between life and spirit, and that promotes pain, suffering, fear, and retribution is an exercise in spreading ignorance and as such does not hold any hope for man. In *The Human Cycle*, Aurobindo addresses "the historic insufficiency of religion as a guide and control of human society" (BCL 15: 165): while sharply distinguishing between institutional religion and the spiritual religion of humanity, Aurobindo maintains that neither religion nor industrialization should be permitted to thwart human progress and world unity. Hence, it is clear that the way to resolving the problem of evil is not rational and orthodox religion but spirituality. As Aurobindo explains "the idea and spirit of the intellectual religion of humanity,"

> Man must be sacred to man regardless of all distinctions of race, creed, colour, nationality, status, political and social advancement. The body of man is to be respected, made immune from violence and outrage, fortified by science against disease and preventable death. The life of man is to be held sacred, preserved, strengthened, ennobled, uplifted. The heart of man is to be held sacred also. . . . the mind of man is to be released from all bonds. . . . (BCL 15: 542–43)

Such a cohesive and profound vision of unity and progress of the human race is not utopian: on the contrary, it directly focuses on the intricate muddle of human existence in a comprehensive context and on the ultimate goal of life. Aurobindo's political vision is compatible with his spiritual vision of man's total freedom:[18] political freedom provides a fertile soil needed to pursue the path of spiritual awakening and to discover that intelligent principle which binds men together as a unity and which enables them to evolve into one divine humanity. But politics, education, and religion are merely tools of facilitating man's evolutionary progress and his search for Reality and Truth, and are not ends in themselves. An ideal political structure that guarantees such individual freedom as enables man to pursue his search for truth voluntarily, unreservedly, and fearlessly is an expression of the most genuine self-assertion and the will of awakened minds, but not of the philistines and the bourgeoisie. In this sense, Aurobindo is a fearless and astute champion of individual freedom and human dignity: in the struggle between collectivity and the individual, the state, as Aurobindo asserts with Kant, has absolutely no right to force an individual to surrender his freedom, whatever the pretext. The individual has the unquestionable right to strive to achieve the highest form of wisdom, since it is only by awakening divinity in oneself that one would know how to apprehend divinity in another. The recognition of this underlying principle of unity implies that an individual and clusters of people can hope to coexist in the world today in a fraternal trust of love and hope without being trampled, devoured, and vitiated. This vision of human freedom and progress and of realizing an ideal condition of human existence on this earth is not a devaluation of the political vision[19] but a fulfillment of the larger and more comprehensive vision of human freedom.

Notes

1. See Karan Singh, V. P. Varma, and Sisirkumar Mitra. R. C. Majumdar notes: "Today Arabinda is known more as a Rishi or a spiritual leader than anything else. But we can look upon him as a great political seer and leader who played the most important role in the last phase of India's struggle for independence. . . . He was indeed the prophet of Nationalism. For the two chief characteristics of nationalism which brought about a radical change in our politics were initiated by Arabinda. These were a clarion call to look upon complete independence of India as our goal and to substitute for the policy of mendicancy followed by the then Congress a policy of self-help and passive resistance to achieve the goal" (qtd. by Mitra, 115–16).

2. See, for example, the views expressed in the *Bande Mataram* of February 6, 1908: "Nationalism is itself no creation of individuals and can have no respect for persons. It is a force which God has created, and from Him it has received only one command, to advance and advance and ever advance until He bids it stop, because its appointed mission is done. It advances, inexorably, blindly, unknowing how it advances, in obedience to a power which it cannot gainsay, and every thing which stands in its way, man or institution, will be swept away, or ground into powder beneath its weight. Ancient sanctity, supreme authority, bygone popularity, nothing will serve as a plea" (*Bande Mataram: Early Political Writings*, vol. 1, Sri Aurobindo Birth Centenary Library Edition of the Collected Works: 669). A more expanded and comprehensive analysis of this conception appears in *The Human Cycle*. All textual refer-

ences, unless otherwise indicated, are to the Sri Aurobindo Birth Centenary Library edition of the collected works, to be referred to as BCL.

3. See Maitra, "Comparison". Maitra argues that Aurobindo's philosophy of evolution is not cyclical in the same sense as Spengler's is, although Aurobindo himself calls the pattern cyclical. For an exposition of the "cyclical" pattern in Aurobindo, see Gandhi.

4. I believe Zaehner's point is that Marxism was one of several possibilities—Vedanta, Christianity, and others—which during the process of transvaluation and synthesis should have converged into a common structure of reality. For a detailed comparison between Aurobindo and Marx, see Chattopadhyaya. For a criticism of Zaehner, see Sethna.

5. In *Nationalism*, Carlton J. H. Hayes notes that "modern nationalism, as we know it today, has its original seat in England" (39), that nationalism which was supposed to be a spiritual force degenerated into an intolerant and belligerent force (chap. 7), that nationalism became "the seed and product of the New Imperialism" (chap. 8), and that nationalism was a cause of World War I (chap. 9).

6. Colonization, according to Coleridge, is "not only a manifest experiment, but an imperative duty in Great Britain. God seems to hold out His finger to us over the sea. But it must be a national colonization" (qtd. by Murray 1: 177). In Carlyle's writings, notes Murray, there is a strong note of a happy imperialist (1: 350–51); and Disraeli, according to Murray, "was always an imperialist, anxious to consolidate the empire by evoking the sympathies of the colonies for the Mother Country" (1: 231).

7. The issue of the origin and growth of colonialism is, indeed, controversial. Marx, for example, considers colonialism originating from economic imperialism or capitalism. Moin Shakir observes that Marx had "firmly established a correlation between colonialism and capitalism" (260). British imperialism in India, according to Marx, proved "regenerative" (Chattopadhyaya 96).

8. Burke had spearheaded the impeachment proceedings against Warren Hastings; and "had called on the country [England] to fit itself for world-wide dominion by abandoning old parochial limitations, or rather by expanding them to the utmost limits of Empire" (Cobban 48). Concerning the allegations against Hastings, "George III wrote of 'shocking enormities in India that disgrace human nature'" (Marshall xviii).

9. Note Aurobindo's poignant criticism of Lord Morley, "The Radical philosopher, the biographer of Voltaire and Rousseau," . . . "for the life of John Morley is a mass of contradictions, the profession of liberalism running hand in hand with the practice of bastard Imperialism which

did the work of Satan while it mouthed liberal Scripture to justify its sins" (BCL 1: 863).

10. I agree with Meenakshi Mukherjee's main thesis that Africa in Conrad's *Heart of Darkness* and India in Forster's *A Passage to India* "are in each case metaphors for a larger human experience," but I do not agree with her observation when she says that these works are "basically not about racial and political issues at all" (219). If India and Africa are comprehensive metaphors, then political reality must be an integral part of the total structure of reality that these metaphors represent.

11. Note Nehru's observation: "It is significant to note that great political mass movements in India have had a spiritual background behind them. In Sri Aurobindo's case this was obvious. . . . Mahatma Gandhi's appeal to the people of India . . . was essentially spiritual" (7). Surendra Verma maintains that Gandhi "makes religion his soul objective." "What he really wants to achieve is self-realization and his ventures in political field are directed towards this very goal" (9).

12. For these two divergent positions, the extremists and the moderates, see McLane 152–78 and Masselos 93–118. Aurobindo did accept the idea of passive resistance, but the type of passive resistance he advocated meant a categorical moral war against slavery and exploitation. In this connection, see "The Doctrine of Passive Resistance" and "The Morality of Boycott" (BCL 1: 85–128). See also "Revolutions and Leadership" (BCL 1: 668–70); and the play "The Slaying of Congress" (BCL 1: 671–96). Even after his retirement from active political struggle, his position on the subject remained unchanged. For example, in his letter of December 1, 1922, to Barindera Kumar Ghose, he reiterates: "As you know, I do not believe that the Mahatma's principle can be the true foundation or his programme the true means of bringing out the genuine freedom and greatness of India, her Swarajya and Samrajya. On the other hand others would think that I was sticking to the school of Tilakite nationalism. That also is not the fact, as I hold that school to be out of date" (BCL 26: 438–39).

13. "In November 1886, before the Congress met," remarks Anil Seal, "Syed Ahmed Khan publically declared India unready for representative or popular government, and condemned Congress as 'seditious'" (320). Indeed, it was the interest of Muslims—the fear of Muslims being reduced to the status of a perpetual minority—which led Sir Syed Ahmed Khan to support the colonial regime.

14. Aurobindo's withdrawal from the active political scene has been a subject of some speculation and concern. But Aurobindo, as this essay explicitly shows, did not divorce himself from the social and political problems of India. Although the writings in the *Arya* from 1915–18, which later on appeared as *The Psychology of Social Development* and *The*

Ideal of Human Unity (BCL 15), sufficiently show the nature and scope of Aurobindo's commitment. We may especially refer to the following excerpt from his letter of the Pondicherry period: "Pondicherry is my place of retreat, my cave of tapasya, not of the ascetic kind, but of a brand of my own invention. I must finish that, I must be internally armed and equipped for my work before I leave it. . . . I do not at all look down on politics or political action or consider I have got above them. I have always laid a dominant stress and I now lay an entire stress on the spiritual life. . . . all human activity is for me a thing to be included in a complete spiritual life, and the importance of politics at the present time is very great. But my line and intention of political activity would differ considerably from anything now current in the field. I entered into political action and continued it from 1903 to 1910 with one aim and one alone, to get into the mind of the people a settled will for freedom and the necessity of a struggle to achieve it in place of the futile ambling Congress methods till then in vogue. . . . I hold that India having a spirit of her own and a governing temperament proper to her own civilization should in politics as in everything else strike out her own original path and not stumble in the wake of Europe" (Letter to Joseph Batista in response to his invitation to accept the editorship of an English daily newspaper, BCL 26: 430–31). There is enormous evidence, as Brown notes, concerning Aurobindo's active interest in India's political development: synthesis of East and West into an international brotherhood; his open expression of support for the Allies during World War II; his fear of German aggression in Asia; his enthusiastic support of the Cripps's Mission Proposal; and the formation of linguistic provinces under the new constitution (123).

15. Kishore Gandhi maintains that after the first few chapters of *The Human Cycle* Aurobindo did not follow Karl Lamprecht's rigid categorization which was based on a "materialistic-economic conception of history and society" (86) and that he subsequently used his own broad divisions, namely, infrarational, rational, and suprarational. The infrarational stage includes Lamprecht's three stages, symbolic, typal, and conventional; the rational stage is common to both; and the "suprarational stage is an extension of the subjective age of the earlier sequence" (87).

16. Spencer, observes Barker, learned from Coleridge that life is "a transcendental principle, in virtue of which nature as a whole, and society as a part of nature, evolve from within outwards towards a final 'individuation' . . . but it was Coleridge, and Schelling through Coleridge, who gave precise form to the hypothesis [of evolution]. In all nature, he came to argue, and therefore in human society, there is transcendental and divine force of life. Hence it follows that nature and society are living organisms: it follows that in virtue of immanent life

they develop; and this development may be regarded as a process of individuation or differentiation, which is combined with co-ordination of the differentiated elements" (71).

17. Aurobindo, as Reddy maintains, "steers clear of two extreme views of evil. The first extreme view, sponsored by India, looked upon evil as unreal and as product of ignorance. . . . The other extreme view . . . is one which has generally found favour in the West and which treats evil as a permanent feature of the world" (324-35). For a lucid discussion of the problem of evil in Aurobindo see Maitra (*Meeting* 111-50). For Aurobindo's own view of evil, see *The Life Divine*, chap. 14 (BCL 18). It should be noted that while denying absolutism of evil, Aurobindo readily admits absolutism of good.

18. David L. Johnson, for example, raises the issue of the failure of synthesis between political goals and spiritual goals. "And given the complete isolation from politics, as well as the duration of isolation," remarks Johnson, "I would maintain that Aurobindo was convinced of a basic incompatibility between spiritual goals and political goals" (119). See June O'Connor's comment on Johnson's criticism (123ff.): "But in the later (spiritual) period, to integrate the two was no longer necessary, for Aurobindo no longer viewed political involvement as a value to be nourished. His vision of the supramental provoked to devalue the political forum as an 'impure form' unworthy of one's energy. To say that Aurobindo dramatically exemplifies an 'ideal blending of social-political activism and spiritual discipline' at most refers to chronological sequence, not to matured philosophical conviction nor intended contribution" (137). I am inclined to believe that both Johnson and O'Connor have contradicted themselves, and have not shown adequate and clear understanding of Aurobindo's spiritual vision of human progress and unity. Furthermore, it is difficult to see the relevance of social and political activism to the nature and scope of a poet's or a philosopher's vision, for a poet or a philosopher does not have to prove the validity of his vision by his activism.

19. "Is it possible," wonders O'Connor, "that Aurobindo's impact might delay or even impede the progress of social reform in India" (318)?

Works Cited

Barker, Ernest. *Political Thought in England, 1848 to 1914*. 2nd ed. London: Oxford UP, 1963.

Brown, D. Mackenzie. *The White Umbrella*. Berkeley: U of California P, 1964.

Chattopadhyaya, D. P. *History, Society, and Polity: Integral Sociology of Sri Aurobindo.* New Delhi: Macmillan, 1976.

Cobban, Aldred. *Edmund Burke: The Revolt Against the Eighteenth Century.* 1929. London: Allen & Unwin, 1962.

Gandhi, Kishore. *Social Philosophy of Sri Aurobindo and the New Age.* Pondicherry: Sri Aurobindo Society, 1965.

Ghose, Aurobindo (Sri Aurobindo). *Sri Aurobindo Birth Centenary Edition of the Collected Works.* 30 vols. Pondicherry: Sri Aurobindo Trust, 1970–72.

Hayes, Carlton J. H. *Nationalism: A Religion.* New York: Macmillan, 1960.

Johnson, David L. *The Religious Roots of Indian Nationalism.* Calcutta: Mukhopadhayay, 1974.

McLane, John R. *Indian Nationalism and the Early Congress.* Princeton: Princeton UP, 1977.

Maitra, S. K. *The Meeting of the East and the West in Sri Aurobindo's Philosophy.* 1956. Pondicherry: Sri Auribindo Ashram, 1968.

———. "Sri Aurobindo and Spengler: Comparison Between the Integral and the Pluralistic Philosophy of History." *The Integral Philosophy of Sri Aurobindo: A Commemorative Symposium.* Ed. Haridas Chaudhuri and Frederic Spiegelberg. London: Allen & Unwin, 1960. 60–80.

Marshall, P. J. *The Impeachment of Warren Hastings.* London: Oxford UP, 1965.

Masselos, Jim. *Indian Nationalism: An History.* New Delhi: Sterling, 1985.

Mitra, Sisirkumar. *Sri Aurobindo.* New Delhi: Indian Book, 1972.

Mukherjee, Meenakshi. "Caliban's Growth: Impact of Colonialism on Commonwealth Fiction." *Colonial Consciousness in Commonwealth Literature.* Ed. G. S. Amur and S. K. Desai. Bombay: Somaiya, 1984. 216–27.

Murray, Robert H. *Studies in the English Social and Political Thinkers of the Nineteenth Century.* 1929. 2 vols. Cambridge: Heefer, 1972.

Nehru, Jawaharlal. Foreword. *Prophet of Indian Nationalism: A Study of the Political Thought of Sri Aurobindo Ghose, 1893–1910.* By Karan Singh. London: Allen & Unwin, 1963. 7–8.

O'Connor, June. *The Quest for Political and Spiritual Liberation: A Study in the Thought of Sri Aurobindo Ghose.* Rutherford, NJ: Fairleigh Dickinson UP, 1977.

Reddy, V. Madhusudan. *Sri Aurobindo's Philosophy of Evolution.* Hyderabad: Institute of Human Study, 1966.

Seal, Anil. *The Emergence of Indian Nationalism: Competition and Collaboration in the Later Nineteenth Century.* Cambridge: Cambridge UP, 1968.

Sethna, K. D. *The Spirituality of the Future: A Search apropos of R. C.*

Zaehner's Study in Sri Aurobindo and Teilhard de Chardin. Rutherford, NJ: Fairleigh Dickinson UP, 1981.

Shakir, Moin. "Karl Marx on Colonialism." *Colonial Consciousness in Commonwealth Literature.* Ed. G. S. Amur and S. K. Desai. Bombay: Somaiya, 1984. 259–72.

Singh, Karan. *Prophet of Indian Nationalism: A Study of the Political Thought of Sri Aurobindo Ghosh, 1893–1910.* London: Allen & Unwin, 1963.

Varma, V. P. *The Political Philosophy of Sri Aurobindo.* Bombay: Asia, 1960.

Verma, Surendra. *Metaphysical Foundation of Mahatma Gandhi's Thought.* New Delhi: Orient Longmans, 1970.

Zaehner, R. C. *Evolution in Religion: A Study in Sri Aurobindo and Pierre Teilhard de Chardin.* Oxford: Clarendon P, 1971.

13 • Feminist Providence: Esther, Vashti, and the Duty of Disobedience in Nineteenth-Century Hermeneutics

Joyce Zonana

> A history of biblical interpretation by women would not only give us much insight into the ways women have read and used the Bible throughout the centuries but would also make us conscious of a rich feminist history now almost completely lost to us.
> ——Elizabeth Schussler Fiorenza

AT A KEY MOMENT IN *The Princess*, Tennyson's ambivalent 1847 meditation on the woman question, Prince Hilarion receives a lesson in nineteenth-century feminist biblical hermeneutics. Cross-dressed as a woman so that he might infiltrate Princess Ida's separatist college, the disguised Prince urges Ida to honor the marriage agreement established by their fathers. "'As to precontracts,'" Ida replies,

> "we move, my friend,
> At no man's beck, but know ourself and thee,
> O Vashti, noble Vashti! Summon'd out
> She kept her state, and left the drunken king
> To brawl at Shushan underneath the palms."
>
> (3.210–214)

The "noble" Vashti invoked by Ida is the first wife of Ahaseurus, king of Persia, banished by an unalterable law because she "refused to come at the king's command" (Esth. 1:12). Like Vashti, Ida takes her stand against the arbitrary commands of despotic but ignoble men.

In Charlotte Brontë's *Jane Eyre*, also published in 1847, Ahaseurus and Vashti similarly serve to represent extremes of patriarchal despotism and female independence: just at the moment when Rochester decides to marry Jane while remaining married to his first wife, he describes himself as passing a law, "unalterable as that of the Medes and Persians" (169), that he is justified in his decision to put aside the "intemperate and unchaste" (334) Bertha. Later, in the midst of a playful discussion about money and power, Jane calls Rochester "Ahaseurus," and he responds as had the biblical king to his second queen, Esther, by offering to give her half his estate.

Although today these allusions to Ahaseurus, Vashti, and the plot of the Book of Esther are lost on most readers, Tennyson and Brontë writing in the mid-nineteenth century could rely not only on their audience's knowledge of the biblical narrative but also on their familiarity with an array of competing contemporary interpretations, both homiletic and imaginative. Described by prominent London preacher Henry Melvill as "among the most interesting narratives contained in the Old Testament" (51), Esther drew nineteenth-century audiences through its Oriental locale (and Orientalist thematics),[1] its matter-of-fact illustration of "non-miraculous providence" (Taylor 209), its structure as a *Bildungsroman*, and, most important, its exploration of both public and private gender politics.[2] Writers both male and female, conservative and radical, turned to Esther for validation and elaboration of their views on women's place. While men composed sermons and commentaries, women—debarred from most pulpits and from the writing of biblical commentary—produced poems, plays, fictions, and "sacred heroine" narratives that embodied their visions of the lessons of Esther and laid the groundwork for the development of twentieth-century feminist biblical hermeneutics.

In her recent *Feminist Revision and the Bible*, Alicia Ostriker argues that

> feminist hermeneutics finds at the textual fault-lines [of biblical narratives] the obsessively told and re-told moment of transition

from a world in which women were humanly and socially powerful because divinity was in part female, to a world in which that divinity and power were repressed. (49)

Yet the Book of Esther tells a story in which women's power is not so much repressed as asserted.[3] The king who banishes one queen finds himself submitting to the will of another; liberal feminist readers in the nineteenth century might find in Esther an empowering story of women's emergence from oppression: a story of divine providence that could amply justify—and represent—the contemporary struggle for women's social advancement and emancipation. In addition, as Grace Aguilar put it in 1851, "to the women of every faith, race, and land, . . . [Esther's] history is alike instructive and inexpressively consoling" (367). For some nineteenth-century women and men, the Book of Esther served as a cornerstone for meditations not only on women's rights but also on the rights of all "marginalized persons in their struggles for freedom, justice, and well-being" (Fiorenza 5). Nineteenth-century readers who discovered and explored the link between the Hebrew Esther and the Persian Vashti set the stage for that still more radical contemporary feminist critique that "reads biblical texts not just in terms of the sex/gender system but with reference to the Western patriarchal system with its interlocking structures of racism, classism, colonialism, and sexism" (Fiorenza 43).

In this essay, I explore a variety of nineteenth-century readings of Esther, focusing on both commentaries by men and literary treatments by women. I conclude with some remarks on Charlotte Brontë's *Jane Eyre* and *Villette*, demonstrating how these novels emerge from the larger context of debate on the meanings of Esther. While *Jane Eyre* relies on an opposition between Esther and Vashti to justify the liberal feminist triumph of its heroine, *Villette*, I argue, presents a more radical identification of the two biblical queens as the grounds for the success of its heroine, Lucy. Both novels, however, are alike in their reliance on the Book of Esther, and the nineteenth-century commentary on it, as sources for Brontë's conception of a "feminist providence" that rewards the young, solitary Protestant woman who stands up for herself in a despotic, patriarchal environment.

The Book of Esther is distinguished among the books of the

Hebrew Bible as being the only one not to mention God or any specific Hebrew practices or customs. It recounts a crisis faced by the entire Jewish people during their exile in Persia (perhaps during the seventh century B.C.E.), and serves as the historical justification for the annual celebration of Purim.[4] The book opens with a chapter describing the power and wealth of the Persian ruler, Ahaseurus. During a lavish feast in the third year of his reign, the king orders his queen, Vashti (who had been holding a separate feast for women), to "display her beauty to the peoples and the officials" (1:11). Vashti peremptorily refuses the king's command, and the king, "greatly incensed" (1:12), asks his counselors for advice. At the suggestion of Memucan, Ahaseurus banishes Vashti, and establishes an an unalterable law that "every man should wield authority in his home" (1:22). Otherwise, Memucan reasons, "the queen's behavior will make all wives despise their husbands" (1:17).

The second chapter opens "some time afterward" (2:1); no longer angry, the king is thinking of his banished queen. His advisers suggest that he select, from all the virgins in the kingdom, a new consort. After a leisurely sampling of the variety Persia has to offer, Ahaseurus chooses Esther, an orphaned Hebrew girl who has been raised by her cousin Mordecai, and who, at Mordecai's insistence, conceals her identity as a Jew. Some time after that, Mordecai refuses to bow before Haman, the king's highest official. Enraged, Haman asks that the king punish not only Mordecai, but all the Hebrews, a people "whose laws are different from those of any other people and who do not obey the king's laws" (3:8). Haman easily persuades Ahaseurus to pass another unalterable law—that all the Hebrews (men, women, and children) in Persia be killed on a specific day. This is tantamount to an order for complete extinction of the Hebrews, for at this time all the Hebrews are living in Persia.[5]

When he learns of the order, Mordecai sends word to Esther, asking that she appeal to the king on behalf of their people. Esther, who has not been "summoned to visit" him for thirty days (5:11), responds that she will be killed if she approaches the king without having been invited. Mordecai reminds Esther that she will die one way or another:

> "Do not imagine that you, of all the Jews, will escape with your life by being in the king's palace. On the contrary, if you keep

silent in this crisis, relief and deliverance will come to the Jews from another quarter, while you and your father's house will perish. And who knows, perhaps you have attained to royal position for just such a crisis." (4:12-14)

The queen makes her decision: she asks that Mordecai instruct all the Jews in the capital city of Shushan to fast for three days and nights; she takes on the same fast herself with her maidens, and she decides to "go to the king, though it is contrary to the law" (4:16). "If I am to perish, I shall perish!" she declares.

Esther does not perish; nor do the Jewish people, thanks to her intervention. When, on the third day, she approaches the king, he extends his golden scepter as a sign of his favor and asks what her petition might be, offering up to half the kingdom should she desire it. Esther asks that Haman be invited that day to a banquet; at the banquet she asks that he be invited again on the next day. Only then does she reveal his treachery and plead for the preservation of her people. The king is persuaded; he orders that Haman be impaled, and because he cannot reverse his law ordering the killing of the Hebrews, he orders instead that they be permitted to fight back on the day appointed for their slaughter. Esther then requests a second day of fighting in Shushan, and the king grants her request. Afterward, Mordecai is given the position of high counselor; he issues a decree ordering the annual observance of Purim—days of "feasting and merrymaking" to commemorate the transformation of a month of "grief and mourning to one of festive joy" (9:22). Esther writes a second letter, "confirming with full authority" that of Mordecai (9:29), and her ordinance is "recorded in a scroll" (9:32).

This, in bare outline, is the story of Esther, clearly a narrative rich in interpretive possibilities. Before the Reformation, most Christian readings of Esther were allegorical. For example, Ahaseurus might be viewed as Christ, the repudiated Vashti as the Jewish synagogue, Esther as the Church, Haman as the devil, and Mordecai as the apostles. Or Ahaseurus might be God, Mordecai Christ, Esther the Church, Vashti the "world, proud and luxurious, and therefore excluded heaven," and Haman the devil. John Donne, in a moving sermon, suggests that Esther is the type of the penitent Christian soul, pleading her case before the Lord, who will always accept her.

With the development of more literal and pragmatic approaches to biblical interpretation, the Book of Esther became prized for its historical documentation of the workings of Providence: it was regarded as a factual account of a momentous event in the history of the Hebrew people, an event making possible the eventual birth of Christ from a descendant of David. Further, as Matthew Henry wrote in 1706, "though the name of God be not in it, the finger of God is, directing many minute events for the bringing about of his people's deliverance" (2: 1168).

Esther's significance for Henry, whose five-volume *Commentary on the Holy Bible* was a standard well into the next century, is primarily in its demonstration of what a later writer would call "non-miraculous providence," the working-out of the Hebrews' deliverance with "no interference with the operation of the laws of nature" (Taylor 209). As Henry bluntly puts it,

> we cannot now expect such miracles to be wrought for us, as were for Israel when they were brought out of Egypt, but we may expect that in such ways as God here took to defeat Haman's plot, he will still protect his people. (2: 1168)

Henry contrasts the events of the Book of Esther with those in Exodus; underlining the parallel between Queen Esther and Moses, he implies that while there may be no latter-day Moses, there may well be contemporary Esthers.

Although Henry focuses on the factual basis of Esther, and how the narrative of providential deliverance can be "edifying and encouraging to the faith and hope of God's people in the most difficult and dangerous times," he also finds moral significance in some of the particulars of the action. Thus, while it is necessary that Vashti be banished in order to make way for Esther, and though her disobedience demonstrates the "foresight and vast reaches of Providence" (2: 1168), she is also at fault for disobeying her husband. Her "bad example" would indeed have a "bad influence" on wives throughout the kingdom, making them "haughty and imperious" (2: 1171), and Henry insists that Vashti must be "humbled for her height" even as Esther is "advanced for her humility" (2: 1171).

In contrasting Esther's obedience with Vashti's disobedience, Henry perpetuates the bifurcated reading initiated by the allegorists. He does not note that while Esther may apparently (and only after some deliberation) obey Mordecai, her foster-father, she disobeys Ahaseurus, her husband. Not surprisingly, Henry reads the text as supporting rather than critiquing patriarchal norms, and he fails to see that the triumphant Esther manifests courage, intelligence, and foresight as well as humility—or that the banished Vashti might have had good reason for her decision not to comply with the king's command.

The categories established in Henry's brief commentary on Esther served as the standard for the many more detailed and extended commentaries on Esther that proliferated throughout the nineteenth century in England and America.[6] For example, in his 1804 *Discourses on the Whole Book of Esther*, a set of sermons on Esther, George Lawson praises Esther for her "humility" and "filial obedience" (55); and he criticizes Vashti for her disobedience, noting that—as the king's counselors had feared—she is "too often imitated by women who have promised obedience to their husbands" (20).

Like Henry, Lawson sees in the Book of Esther "one of the most wonderful interpositions of God" (2), and he finds in it a multitude of lessons for contemporary Christian life—young women, particularly, even in difficult circumstances, would do well to model themselves on the humble and obedience Esther. Yet Lawson, while echoing and developing many of Henry's observations, also reveals his awareness and approval of early liberal feminist arguments. He criticizes the "domestic tyranny" (34) of the Persians who hold women "in the chains of ignorance and slavery" (30), and calls Vashti's offense "pardonable," her fate "unmerited" (52). Lawson does not condone Vashti's choice: women are bound to obey, he believes, but husbands must "always be reasonable in their commands" (20). He wonders what Ahaseurus might have felt had he been a "subject" (41) rather than a king and he praises the lot of European women, who must be thankful for the "laws of Christ" that free them from the "slavery imposed upon women in the East" (54). Thus Lawson has it both ways, arguing against an extreme of patriarchal tyranny that he locates in the (ancient and pagan) East while insisting on the obedience of wives in the contemporary Christian West—("because you have promised it" [31]).

While struggling to come to terms with Vashti, Lawson glosses over Esther's marital disobedience. Yet he urges that her story be told "for the encouragement of women": "Women are too ready to say, what can we do to serve the public interest? . . . But Esther is not the only woman that has gained just praises by her public spirit" (225). Clearly, Lawson is sensitive to, and to some extent approving of, the feminist potential of Esther, though he is also careful to insist upon the duty of both marital and filial obedience for women.

Thomas McCrie, in 1838, continues Lawson's efforts with a series of eighteen lectures on Esther, "a golden leaf in the book of providence" (308). In harsher language than Lawson's, McCrie condemns Vashti as "proud," "haughty and unyielding" (38), yet he also accuses Ahaseurus of "foolish" (34) and "imprudent" (35) behavior. Noting that Vashti loses her crown but not her life, McCrie concludes that the ancient Persian treatment of women was less inhumane than the current "Eastern" custom of viewing them as "slaves" (37). Like Lawson, McCrie upholds the norm of female obedience while criticizing cultures that take that norm to too great an extreme. On the other side of the Atlantic, in 1859, William Scott insists that "the unalterable decree of the king of Persia is also the unchangeable law of Heaven. . . . [M]an should be the head and woman the heart of society" (107–108). Scott unambiguously condemns Vashti while he praises Esther as "a model girl . . . kind, respectful, obedient to her foster-father" (134–35).

The views of Lawson, McCrie, and Scott set the patriarchal standard for providential interpretations of Esther and Vashti, reading the one as a triumphant model of "Christian" obedience, and the other as a properly punished example of pagan pride. Yet as early as 1804, counter-readings emerged, beginning with the views of Joseph Priestley, who regarded Ahaseurus's decree against Vashti "foolish" and who speculated that her "spirit" might well have caused him to "admire her still more" (2: 127). In *Hadassah, the Jewish Orphan*, an 1834 text written for the American Sunday-School Union, Vashti is unabashedly applauded for her choice: "Better was it for her . . . to go into disgrace and obscurity with an unspotted character and a good conscience, than to keep her place on the throne with guilt and self-reproach" (16). Here disobedience is justified because of conformity to the "higher" law of feminine modesty: by refusing the king, Vashti upholds the Persian rule that enjoins the separation of men and women. Similar praise for Vashti recurs throughout the century: in 1859, Alexander Davidson reasons that Vashti "only acted in accordance with all standing law," calling Ahaseurus's decision to banish her a "sin" (29); Bernard O'Reilly in 1871 finds in Vashti "the self-respect of a true woman, and the lawful pride of a queen" (192). While praising the "piety and courageous self-devotion of Esther," O'Reilly reminds readers not to forget the "modesty and magnanimity of the beautiful though unfortunate Vashti" (192).

By the end of the century, William H. Gill in Philadelphia calls the king's command to Vashti a "cruel outrage" (19) and applauds the queen's preference of "the risk of death to dishonour" (20). Similarly, William H. Taylor in 1891 finds Vashti's action "worthy of all praise" (121). Taylor is perhaps the only nineteenth-century male writer to establish a clear parallel between Vashti's refusal of the king and Mordecai's defiance of Haman: he identifies both acts as manifestations of "conscience" (163, 122), a "fidelity to principle" (161) necessary in both domestic and political relations. Yet while Taylor wishes to avoid the errors of commentators who "think it needful to degrade Vashti in order to exalt Esther" (121), having exalted Vashti he proceeds to undermine Esther, calling her un-Christian in her "vindictive and revengeful" request for a second day of killing (254).[7]

As the century progresses, then, male commentators are increasingly willing to champion Vashti, though, for the most part, they uphold patriarchal norms by praising her for her "feminine" modesty. Thus, when they liken her to Esther, it is in terms of "obedience" (to a higher law) rather than disobedience (of their common husband). It remains difficult for these writers to see in *both* Esther *and* Vashti a praiseworthy (and providential) form of *dis*obedience. Yet beginning as early as 1820, women write plays, poems, novels, and popular books about "sacred heroines" that offer more daring interpretations. Through dialogue, plot transformations, and elaboration of the setting in the Persian harem, women focus on the parallels between Vashti's and Esther's disobedience; reading both women as "wives," they work to show the difficulty of their choices, and to give insight into both their characters. In celebrating Esther, the (typically) middle-class white women who write about her use her as a model for tales of social mobility and individualistic triumph; but in the recuperation of

Vashti, some of these writers approach the more radical feminist hermeneutics that challenges not only sexism but racism and classism as well, establishing genuine links between women in different social situations.

One of the first of these women's revisions of Esther appeared in Boston in 1820, "By a lover of the fine arts," Maria Gowen Brooks. Brooks's narrative poem portrays Esther as a "weak and artless woman" (24) caught in a situation that requires her "disobedience" (25) of her husband. Aware of all that the "dishonoured" Vashti suffered for her "slight offense" (25), Esther remembers that her "throne and bed" (25) were once Vashti's, that indeed Vashti was loved as she is loved by Ahaseurus. Afraid more of the king's "displeasure" (iv) than of death, Esther nevertheless prays for assistance, and, with her "bosom throbbing" (27), succeeds in conquering the king by the "soft controul" (27) of her beauty. Brooks's Esther—replete with an "ivory form," "hair of wavy gold," and "azure eyes" (26)—is hardly defiant or willingly disobedient, but she is nevertheless noteworthy for her awareness of her affinity with Vashti and for her self-conscious sexuality. This is a woman who is a wife, not simply a dutiful daughter.

Elizabeth Polack's 1835 play *Esther, the Royal Jewess*, performed for two nights at London's Pavilion Theatre, presents a far more fiery Esther—a woman who disobeys not only her husband, the Persian king, but also her foster-father, the Jew. Polack transforms Esther from a reluctant into a willing heroine, a woman who from the first actively challenges Mordecai as she seeks a role in history. Long before the crisis facing the Jews, Polack's Esther dreams that she is queen of Persia, "who has saved her people" (14). Countering Mordecai's objections to her entrance into the king's harem, she insists, "I'll hazard all; misery—danger—yea, even death—to make my people free!" (15). Esther triumphs over Mordecai, as she deliberately works to become the savior of her people—the Moses figure commentators so often compare her with. Vashti in this play is also a defiant woman, though—unsustained by the Hebrew God—she is brutally sacrificed to the will of a despotic tyrant: in her final scene, she screams and "laughs hysterically": "—Gods! he has struck me!—my brain is on fire!—madness!—death!—banishment!" (13).

Esther as publicly powerful woman consciously choosing to

intervene in history is similarly invoked by abolitionist Angelina Grimke in her 1836 "Appeal to the Christian Women of the South"—a text which opens with an epigraph from Esther. "Is there no Esther among you?" asks Grimke. "If there were but *one* Esther at the South, she *might* save her country from ruin; but let the Christian women there arise . . . and that salvation is certain" (25). Like Brooks and Polack, Grimke emphasizes, not Esther's obedience, but her disobedience to Ahaseurus.

Two years after Grimke's "Appeal," Eliza Cushing published in *Godey's Lady's Book* a long dramatic version of Esther that goes even further in challenging patriarchal assumptions. At first Cushing's text seems merely to portray a conventionally reluctant Esther, a demurely resistant Vashti. Both queens are thoroughly feminine heroines who offer Ahaseurus "the balm of a woman's love" (16: 244). The king, remorseful after his banishment of Vashti, asks forgiveness for his "sin," and doubts whether another woman can "fix" his "wand'ring heart" (16: 244). Desolate until he discovers Esther, Ahaseurus turns to her as one who "sweetens every joy, / And makes that life, so valueless before, / A precious boon" (17: 75). Thus, when Esther comes unasked before him—afraid more of losing his love than of losing her life—Ahaseurus recalls the error of his earlier treatment of Vashti. He names Esther his "dearer self" and vows to "protect" her nation and "reverence" her God (17: 262).

In demonstrating the vanity of the "earth-born pride" (16: 242) that leads Ahaseurus to assert power over both Vashti and the Jews, Cushing establishes clear parallels between Vashti's defiance and Esther's. Vashti asserts that she "has a spirit, that will not be chain'd"; she is "Persia's queen" who "stoops not to such disgrace!" (16: 243). Similarly, Esther, while at first afraid that she will suffer the fate of "beauteous Vashti" (17: 4), decides to "rise assured," "unaw'd" and "fearless" before the king, for,

> Great as he is, our God is greater far,—
> He is a king—our God is king of kings,
> And the sole arbiter of life and death.
>
> (17: 81)

Cushing thus suggests that Esther and Vashti are united in their opposition to despotism and in their reliance on a power "greater" than the king's. And while Cushing's Esther at first characterizes herself as a "clinging vine," a "timid maid" (17: 4), she is by the drama's conclusion celebrated as a "rod of power, in God's directing hand" (17: 263) equivalent to "Moses' rod, instinct with power divine" (17: 4). In chronicling the transformation of her heroine from a timid girl like Brooks's Esther to a powerful queen like Polack's, Cushing offers an especially instructive model for women who might wish to escape from patriarchal control.

Far more conservatively, Eliza Steele, in her 1842 *Heroines of Sacred History*, concludes her account of Esther with a pious celebration of the Hebrew woman's self-sacrifice and filial obedience, citing Esther as a "beautiful example of the duty we owe our guardians and aged relatives" (146). Yet Steele's insistence on duty breaks down in her portrayal of Vashti, whose refusal of the king is chronicled in elaborate, almost loving detail. When her banquet is interrupted by the king's messenger, Steele's "tall and commanding" Vashti, "panting with all the anger of outraged dignity and womanly delicacy" asserts, "'I will not come!'" Her companions take up her cause; one of them, named "Roxa" after Montesquieu's rebellious Roxanna, asks, "shall we be abject slaves to our husbands?" and she urges the others, "Let us imitate the strength of mind of our royal mistress" (93–94). All the women present "resolve[]" to "demand . . . more freedom" (94), thus fulfilling Memucan's worst fears. And though Steele neither returns to the fate of Vashti nor offers any explicit commentary on the harem-rebellion she portrays, she provides one tantalizing, subversive summary of the action: "the refusal of a Persian queen to obey her husband, prevented the massacre of thousands of innocent persons" (98). Vashti's refusal is providential; her rebellion necessary to the preservation of the Jewish people.

Still more explicit celebrations of Vashti emerge in women's writing in the closing decades of the nineteenth century, particularly in the United States. In 1871, Frances Ellen Watkins Harper devotes a poem to Vashti as an example of "earnest womanhood." Here "Persia's Queen" sadly though steadfastly refuses to accept the king's command; she is "A woman who could bend to grief / But would not bend to shame." Harper's celebration of Vashti's dignified resistance to domination acquires special resonance when it is remembered that Harper is an African-American woman, who, in a poem entitled "Learning to Read" describes reading the

Bible as giving a woman a sense of being "as independent / As the queen upon her throne." It is tempting to speculate that Harper, perhaps familiar with Grimke's "Appeal," would choose as her model Vashti, the "other" woman first introduced, but then abandoned, in the biblical narrative. In contemporary African-American womanist theology, Vashti continues to play a prominent role as a representation, like Hagar, of the woman forgotten within the dominant white culture.

For Harriet Beecher Stowe, in her 1873 *Woman in Sacred History*, Vashti's refusal to come at the king's command is the "first stand for women's rights" (197); and she calls attention to the strength of character it embodies:

> If we consider the abject condition of all *men* in that day before the king, we shall stand amazed that there was a woman . . . that dared to disobey the command even of a drunken monarch (197).

Similarly, in the *Woman's Bible*, Vashti is hailed as "the first woman who dared" (2: 87). Elizabeth Cady Stanton laments, "I have always regretted that the historian allowed Vashti to drop out of sight so suddenly" (2: 90), for the narration of her story is "the first exhibition of the individual sovereignty of woman on record" (2: 87); until her, there had been no example of "a self-respecting womanhood which might stand for a higher type of social life than was customary among men" (2: 87). For these self-consciously feminist women writing at the end of the century, Vashti even more than Esther becomes the laudable model—a woman who acted for women without even the sanction of the Hebrew God.

The relationship between Vashti's rebellion and Esther's triumph are central to understanding Charlotte Brontë's *Jane Eyre* and *Villette*. Each novel is, like the Book of Esther, a "romance of providence" (Gill 8), a *Bildungsroman* detailing the rise to power and position of "an orphan and an exile" (McCrie 312); in each, a tyrannically Orientalist—or darkly Catholic—background provides the context for the heroine's assertion of alternative Protestant values. Focusing in each novel on the transformation of despotic men, Brontë uses the underpattern of Esther to explore the consequences of overt defiance of patriarchal power and to provide religious sanction for the class mobility and romantic fulfillment of her struggling young women. Each of her heroines writes the story of her life like Esther who "with full authority" writes to confirm the annual celebration of Purim (9:29)—and who was believed by some commentators to have been the author of her Book. And in each novel, Brontë's heroine, as Esther, encounters a Vashti whose rebellion makes possible her own ultimate success.

In *Jane Eyre*, Vashti is rewritten as Bertha, the woman who is banished for her refusal to conform to Rochester's expectations of feminine behavior: when Rochester decides to marry Jane while remaining married to Bertha, he describes himself as passing a law, "unalterable as that of the Medes and Persians" (169), that his aims and motives are right. Responding to Rochester's assertion, Jane quietly protests: "The human and fallible should not arrogate a power with which the divine and perfect alone can be safely entrusted" (169). Her words echo the language of Thomas McCrie's comment on the irrevocability of ancient Persian law, and suggest that his *Lectures on the Book of Esther* may have been close at hand when she was composing *Jane Eyre*:

> A most preposterous provision! . . . proceeding on the presumptuous assumption of infallibility, and arrogating the right which belongs exclusively to the Supreme Being. . . . No human authority . . . is free from error. (240–41)

Later, Jane pointedly calls Rochester "Ahaseurus" (290); the man who seeks to transfer Bertha's estate to the woman he sees as more deserving cannot do so until he pays—in proper Old Testament fashion, with his eyes and his hand—for his initial transgression against female (and divine) sovereignty.

In *Villette*, the allusions to the Book of Esther are even more elaborate—an entire chapter is called "Vashti"—although the narrative line is less clearly a transposal of the Esther story.[8] Still, Brontë seems to be working with the same essential elements of the biblical text, and deliberating on the issues that concerned nineteenth-century readers of Esther: the justifications and consequences of female self-assertion and disobedience, and the role of providence in supporting and vindicating the oppressed female subject—who is portrayed both as an individual and as a member of a group.

At the theater for a performance of a celebrated actress named Vashti, Lucy finds in her "the strong magnetism of genius" (340). Characterized as a fallen angel—"insurgent, banished" (340), this "sinister and sovereign" (341) Vashti is "Wicked, perhaps, . . . but also she is strong" (340), triumphing over conventional images of womanhood and morality. The actress deeply affects Lucy, drawing her "heart out of its wonted orbit" (340); Lucy is dismayed to find that her beloved companion, Dr. Bretton, condemns Vashti with a "callous" and "branding judgment" (342). While conflicted about Vashti, Lucy discovers in her something worthy of imitation, some strong call to "what was wild and intense, dangerous, sudden, and flaming" (341); significantly, in the analogy typically used for Esther, Lucy sees Vashti as the "rod of Moses . . . whelming the heavy host with the down-rush of overthrown sea-ramparts" (340). Brontë here has her heroine—an adept in biblical exegesis—transpose Vashti and Esther, an interpretive act that has powerful implications for her own self-image.

Thus, not much later in the narrative, having witnessed and been inspired by Vashti, Lucy assumes the role of Esther, resolutely entering the despotic M. Paul's classroom after he has threatened death by hanging to anyone who ventures in (410). The scene is written as comedy, but the allusion is to the Persian queen who risks her life when she enters Ahaseurus's chamber. The episode marks the beginning of Lucy's improved relationship with M. Paul, the man who eventually becomes her beloved "king" (587) and who, although a Catholic, "freely" leaves her to her "pure faith" of Protestantism (594)—in a gesture that recalls Ahaseurus's acceptance of Esther as a Hebrew.

Identified as she is with Esther, Lucy Snowe also models herself on Vashti—establishing a clear identity between the banished and the reigning queens. At the theater, Lucy notes ʻashti's ferocity in the face of death: "panting still defiance," the actress "fought every inch of ground, sold dear every drop of blood, resisted to the latest the rape of every faculty, *would* see, *would* hear, *would* breathe, *would* live, up to, within, well nigh *beyond* the moment when death says to all sense and all being—'Thus far and no farther'" (342). Similarly, when Lucy confronts the "secret junta" opposed to her relationship with M. Paul, she notes:

> The sight of them thus assembled did me good. I cannot say that I felt weak before them, or abashed, or dismayed. They outnum-

bered me, and I was worsted and under their feet; but, as yet, I was not dead. (558)

A little later, telling M. Paul of her fear that the "junta" has led him to be engaged to another, she notes: "To my very self I seemed imperious and unreasonable"; she calls this her "moment of utmost mutiny" (591). Yet her king, at this juncture, gives her his love: "Be my dearest, first on earth," he says, and Lucy discovers, for the first time in her life, an experience of "home" (591). Instead of being banished for her defiance, this "imperious and unreasonable" queen enters into her "estate."

Brontë goes a long way, then, toward uniting Esther and Vashti. Whereas in *Jane Eyre* she allows the middle-class heroine's success to be contingent on (and justified by) the providential displacement of the "other" woman, in *Villette* she suggests that the "other" woman can (and must) be integrated into the "self." Lucy is both Esther and Vashti, and her story suggests that Brontë has come to a more radical feminist reading of Esther. For Brontë now offers a king who does not banish a woman in mutiny: while Lucy's first love, Graham, reacts to Vashti as Ahaseurus does, her ultimate beloved, Paul, does not. Brontë's new plot in fact suggests that it is Lucy, as queen, who seeks a more suitable king, replacing the first man she loves with one who will not require conventional femininity of her.

Brontë's manipulations of the Esther plot in *Jane Eyre* and *Villette* are perhaps the most subtle and provocative in the nineteenth century. These transformations acquire their greatest meaning when seen in the light of the nineteenth-century debate on disobedience, duty, and the workings of Providence in the Book of Esther. Brontë's Esthers are advanced not for their humility but for their 'height,' and her rebellious Vashtis do not gracefully depart despite their kings' best efforts to banish them. It is in these plots that we see a truly feminist providence at work, bringing rewards to women who are proud, diosbedient, and not afraid to take risks to improve their circumstances—and those of their sisters. Read against the background of Esther and its nineteenth-century interpretations, the powerful religious resonance of Brontë's novels increases: if Jane and Lucy are indeed like Esther, then these novels demonstrate that the Judeo-Christian God sanctions the feminist aspirations of women. Such a use of Esther could not have been possible without the proliferation of conservative Protestant readings praising Esther for her humility and regarding the text as a "romance of providence"; yet by turning interpretive categories upside down, Brontë and her sisters remain truer to the spirit of the original Hebrew text. For Esther in fact celebrates a radical reversal of power in ancient Persia, and it forms the basis for a unique Jewish festival in which cross-dressing, public drunkenness, and the blurring of all traditional boundaries are the norm. At Purim, Jews are enjoined to drink so much that they cannot tell the difference between Mordecai and Haman. Jewish tradition here betrays its patriarchal bent; for surely, as Brontë shows so well, being unable to tell the difference between Esther and Vashti might be an even more appropriate way to celebrate this festival of glorious triumph over patriarchal and religious or ethic oppression.

Notes

1. For a discussion of the general appeal in the nineteenth century of things Oriental—as well as of the specifics of Orientalism, a "Western style for dominating, restructuring, and having authority over the Orient" (71), see Said. For a detailed examination of the tradition of feminist Orientalism, a discourse that "displaces the source of patriarchal oppression onto an 'Oriental' . . . society" (593)—and which emerges throughout nineteenth-century discussions of Esther, see Zonana.

2. In his recent study, Michael Fox calls Esther the only book in the Bible "with a conscious and sustained interest in sexual politics" (209). For a twentieth-century reading that forcefully argues that the Book of Esther is feminist in the sense of demonstrating "the fragility of male sovereignty" (83), see Fewell. For an alternative contemporary feminist perspective, claiming that Esther is "in full compliance with patriarchy" (216), see Laffey. For other current readings of Esther that explore the text's gender politics, see Fuchs, Rosenheim, and White.

3. While many commentators have suggested that Esther's name is a version of Ishtar, the ancient Sumerian goddess, few have considered that the biblical book bearing her name might tell a story of that goddess who was a consort to human kings. In her recent authoritative study, Tikva Frymer-Kensky demonstrates that Innanna/Ishtar was a "liminal deity" (58) who combined "the passions of sex and violence" (67), and at whose festivals "men dress as women and women as men" (29). The parallels to Esther, who is both alluring and willing to order a second

day of slaughter, and to the celebration of Purim, are striking. Might it be that the Book of Esther, long regarded as anomalous within the context of the Hebrew Scriptures, tells a story, not of the successful repression of a goddess, but of her powerful return?

4. Although I here offer a summary of the Book of Esther, readers are encouraged to examine the text for themselves. Any summary, as my study of nineteenth-century accounts has made me acutely aware, involves choices that represent interpretations. My own "reading" of Esther inevitably reflects my interpretation of the narrative—an interpretation grounded in nineteenth-century readings but also reflecting my own feminist and structuralist biases.

5. It should be evident that Haman's response to Mordecai is exactly parallel to Ahaseurus's response to Vashti: in each case the disobedience of an individual results in punishment of the entire group to which the individual belongs—wives in the case of Vashti, Hebrews in the case of Mordecai. The parallel incidents serve to characterize the excesses (and weaknesses) of what the Western writer of Esther saw as "Persian" despotism; in addition, they serve to set up the necessary emergence of Esther as the only appropriate "savior." As both a wife and a Hebrew, Esther can set things right for both women and Jews; and although the text (and most interpretation by men) foregrounds her intervention on behalf of the Hebrews, readers with feminist leanings need make no great leaps to interpret her behavior as redressing the wrongs of women as well.

6. The precise number of commentaries exclusively on Esther is difficult to establish. The National Union Catalogue lists seven published in the United States and England between 1750 and 1900. However, Robert Paton's 1908 study lists a great many more. And the catalog of the New York Public Library, where I conducted much of the research for this essay, lists still others neither mentioned by Paton nor included in the NUC. In preparing this essay, I consulted seven books of sermons or lectures on Esther published in the nineteenth century.

7. Taylor's perspective on Esther and Vashti finds a disturbing and bizarre fulfillment in the 1897 play *Vashti, A Tragedy* published pseudonymously by "Zeto" in London. In this play, Vashti is portrayed as a Christ-like figure who continues to love Ahaseurus after her banishment and who is killed by a power-hungry Esther who cannot believe that her "rival" would bear love for her. Instead of reading the ancient Hebrews as the progenitors of Christians, and Esther as their savior, the play is violently anti-Semitic, portraying Esther and Mordecai as rapacious and greedy "Jews" who kill a new (female) Christ—Vashti. The play succeeds in recuperating Vashti but only by creating another "other."

8. Gilbert and Gubar discuss the "Vashti" chapter in their analysis of *Villette*, as do Brownstein, Stokes, and Larson, *Prophecy*. All these critics agree, however, in seeing the "cool" Lucy as separate from the "fiery" Vashti.

Works Cited

Aguilar, Grace. *The Women of Israel, or, Characters and Sketches from the Holy Scriptures and Jewish History Illustrative of the Past History, Present Duties, and Future Destiny of the Hebrew Females, as Based on the Word of God.* 1851. New York and London: Dutton and Routledge, 1888.

American Sunday School Union. *Hadassah, the Jewish Orphan.* Philadelphia: American Sunday-School Union, 1834.

Berg, Sandra Beth. *The Book of Esther.* Society for Biblical Literature Dissertation Series 44. Missoula, MT: Scholars P, 1979.

Brontë, Charlotte. *Jane Eyre.* 1847. New York: Penguin, 1985.

———. *Villette.* 1853. New York: Penguin, 1979.

[Brooks, Maria Gowen.] *Judith, Esther, and Other Poems.* Boston: Cummings & Hillard, 1820.

Brownstein, Rachel M. "Representing the Self: Arnold and Brontë on Rachel." *Browning Institute Studies* 13 (1985): 1–24.

Cushing, Mrs. Eliza Lansford. "Esther, a Dramatic Sketch in Five Acts." *Godey's Lady's Book.* 16: 241–44; 17:2–8; 73–81; 216–221; 260–64. (1838). Reprinted in *Esther, With Judith, a Poem.* Boston, 1840.

Davidson, Alexander D. *Lectures, Expository and Practical, on the Book of Esther.* Edinburgh: Clark, 1859.

DeJong, Mary. "God's Women: Victorian American Readings of Old Testament Heroines." *Old Testament Women in Western Literature.* Ed. Raymond-Jean Frontain and Jan Wojcik. Conway, AR: UCA P, 1991. 238–60.

Fewell, Danna Nolan. "Feminist Reading of the Hebrew Bible: Affirmation, Resistance, Transformation." *JSOT* 38 (October 1987): 77–87.

Fiorenza, Elisabeth Schussler. *But She Said: Feminist Practices of Biblical Interpretation.* Boston: Beacon, 1992.

Fox, Michael V. *Character and Ideology in the Book of Esther.* Columbia: U of South Carolina P, 1991.

Frymer-Kensky, Tikva. *In the Wake of the Goddesses: Women, Culture, and the Biblical Transformation of Pagan Myth.* New York: Free Press, 1992.

Fuchs, Esther. "Status and Role of Female Heroines in the Biblical Narratives." *Mankind Quarterly* 23.2 (Winter 1982): 149–60.

———. "Who is Hiding the Truth? Deceptive Women and Biblical Androcentrism." *Feminist Perspectives in Biblical Scholarship*, ed. Adela Yarboro Collins. Chico, CA: Scholars P, 1985. 137–44.

Gifford, Carolyn De Swarte, "American Women and the Bible: The Nature of Woman as a Hermeneutical Issue." *Feminist Perspectives on Biblical Scholarship*. Chico, CA: Scholars P, 1984. 11–33.

Gilbert, Sandra, and Susan Gubar. *The Madwoman in the Attic: The Woman Writer and the Nineteenth-Century Literary Imagination*. New Haven, Yale UP, 1979.

Gill, William Hugh. *Esther: A Drama of Jewish History: Being the Story of the Book of Esther Elucidated by Interpolation for Popular Use*. Philadelphia: Jacobs, 1899.

Grimke, A. E. "Appeal to the Christian Women of the South." *Anti-Slavery Examiner* 1.2 (September 1836).

———. *Letters to Catherine E. Beecher in reply to An Essay on Slavery and Abolitionism Addressed to A. E. Grimke*. Boston: Knapp, 1838.

Harper, Frances Ellen Watkins. "Vashti." *The Norton Anthology of Literature by Women: The Tradition in English*. Ed. Sandra M. Gilbert and Susan Gubar. New York: Norton, 1985. 830–32.

Henry, Matthew. *A Commentary on the Holy Bible*. 5 vols. 1706. New York: Funk & Wagnalls, 1890.

The Holy Bible. King James Version. New York: American Bible Society.

Japp, Phyllis M. "Esther or Isaiah?: The Abolitionist-Feminist Rhetoric of Angelina Grimke." *Quarterly Journal of Speech* 71.3 (August 1985): 335–48.

Kelsey, David H. "Protestant Attitudes Regarding Methods of Biblical Interpretation." *Scripture in the Jewish and Christian Traditions: Authority, Interpretation, Relevance*. Ed. Frederick E. Greenspahn. Nashville: Abingdon, 1982. 133–61.

Laffey, Alice L. *An Introduction to the Old Testament: A Feminist Perspective*. Philadelphia: Fortress, 1988.

Larson, Janet L. "The Battle of Biblical Books in Esther's Narrative." *Nineteenth Century Fiction* 38.2 (1983): 131–60.

———. "'Who Is Speaking?': Charlotte Brontë's Voices of Prophecy." *Victorian Sages and Cultural Discourse: Renegotiating Gender and Power*. Ed. Thais E. Morgan. New Brunswick: Rutgers UP, 1990. 66–86.

Lawson, George. *Discourses on the Whole Book of Esther. To Which Are Added Sermons, on Parental Duties, on Military Courage, and on the Improvement to be Made of the Alarm of War*. 2nd ed. Edinburgh: Oliphant & Balfour, 1809.

McCrie, Thomas. *Lectures on the Book of Esther.* 1838. New York: Robert Carter. Rpt. Lynchburg, VA: James Family, 1979.

Melvill, Henry. "The Sleepless Night." *Sermons.* Ed. C. P. M'Ilvaine. 2 vols. New York: Stanford and Swords, 1850. 2: 51–60.

Moore, Carey A., trans. *The Anchor Bible: Esther.* Garden City: Doubleday, 1971.

O'Reilly, Bernard. *Heroic Women of the Bible and the Church.* New York: Ford, 1877.

Ostriker, Alicia Suskin. *Feminist Revision and the Bible.* Cambridge, MA: Blackwell, 1993.

Paton, L. G. *A Critical and Exegetical Commentary on the Book of Esther.* New York: Scribner's, 1908.

Peterson, Linda H. "Gender and Autobiographical Form: The Case of the Spiritual Autobiography." In *Studies in Autobiography.* Ed. James Olney. New York: Oxford UP, 1988. 211–22.

Polack, Elizabeth. *Esther, the Royal Jewess: Or, The Death of Haman: An Historical Drama in Three Acts.* London: Duncombe, 1835.

Priestley, Joseph. *Notes on All the Books of Scripture. For the Use of the Pulpit and Private Families.* 4 vols. Northumberland: Kennedy, 1804.

Rosenheim, Judith. "Fate and Freedom in the Scroll of Esther." *Prooftexts* 12.2 (May 1992): 125–49.

Scott, William Anderson. *Esther, the Hebrew-Persian Queen.* San Francisco: Bancroft, 1859.

Said, Edward. *Orientalism.* New York: Vintage, 1979.

Stanton, Elizabeth Cady, and the Revising Committee. *The Woman's Bible.* 1895, 1898. 2 vols. Seattle: Coalition Task Force on Women and Religion, 1974.

Steele, Eliza. *Heroines of Sacred History.* 2nd ed. New York: Taylor, 1842.

Stokes, John. "Rachel's 'Terrible Beauty'": An Actress Among the Novelists." *ELH* 51.4 (Winter 1984): 771–93.

Stowe, Harriet Beecher. *Women in Sacred History: A Series of Sketches Drawn from Scriptural, Historical, and Legendary Sources.* New York: Ford, 1873.

Taylor, William M. *Ruth the Gleaner and Esther the Queen.* New York: Harper, 1891.

Tennyson, Alfred Lord. *The Princess. The Poetical Works of Tennyson.* Cambridge Edition. Ed. G. Robert Stange. Boston: Houghton Mifflin, 1974. 115–62.

Trapp, John. *A Commentary or Exposition Upon the Books of Ezra, Nehemiah, Job, and Psalms.* London: Newberry, 1657.

Weems, Renita J. *Just a Sister Away: A Womanist Vision of Women's Relationships in the Bible.* San Diego: Luria Media, 1988.

White, Sidnie Ann. "Esther: A Feminine Model for Jewish Diaspora." *Gender and Difference in Ancient Israel*. Ed. Peggy L. Day. Minneapolis: Fortress, 1989. 161–77.

Zeto. *Vashti, A Tragedy, and Other Poems*. London: Kegan Paul, 1897.

Zonana, Joyce. "The Sultan and the Slave: Feminist Orientalism and the Structure of *Jane Eyre*." *Signs* 18.3 (1993): 592–617.

14 • The Buddhist Imagination in Chinese Fiction

Sheng-Tai Chang

IN THE COURSE OF ALMOST TWO THOUSAND YEARS, Buddhism has exerted a profound, pervasive influence on Chinese culture.[1] Though of Indian origin, it has been so thoroughly integrated into Chinese culture that it is often spoken of as one of the three fundamental paradigms of traditional China, the other two being Confucianism and Taoism. This essay will give a brief account of the presence of the Buddhist imagination in Chinese fiction, based on a reading of selected traditional and modern texts, and then speculate on their contributions to Chinese literary sensibility.[2]

Buddhism has a vast canon and has evolved a great many sects and schools in its long history. Common to all Buddhist traditions is the basic doctrine known as the "Four Noble Truths": "1) that all life is inevitably sorrowful; 2) that sorrow is due to craving; 3) that it can only be stopped by the stopping of craving; and 4) that this can be done by a course of carefully disciplined and moral conduct, culminating in the life of concentration and meditation led by the Buddhist monk" (De Bary 266–67). Buddhism holds that "[a]ll things are composite, and as a corollary of this, all things are transient, for the composition of all aggregates [is] liable to change with time. Moreover, being essentially transient, they have no eternal Self or soul, no abiding individuality" (De Bary 267). Buddhism conceives of existence as composed of twelve links (*Dvadasanga pratityasamutpada* in Sanskrit), which begin with ignorance and actions in the past, continue with birth, sensations, desires, sexual union, aging, and death. And this cycle of birth and death will be repeated ad infinitum according to the law of karma until one achieves enlightenment and enters nirvana. In Theravada ("Hinayana," or the "Lesser Vehicle") Buddhism, one emphasizes moral self-discipline to achieve enlightenment and deliverance. In Mahayana (or the "Greater Vehicle") Buddhism, one emphasizes delivering all sentient beings from the sea of suffering; the ideal is the Bodhisattva, an enlightened being who delays his or her entrance into nirvana in order to help others to become enlightened. Chinese Buddhism is basically of the Mahayana tradition.

The history of Chinese Buddhism is largely the history of how Buddhism adapted itself to Chinese culture and in turn influenced and transformed it. It is a long and complicated story of interactions among the "Three Teachings," namely, Confucianism, Taoism, and Buddhism. When Buddhism was introduced into China, Buddhists borrowed Taoist terminology to explain thier concepts. Buddhism also made accommodations to Confucian ethics.[3] Generally speaking, Buddhism appealed to the Chinese mind with its promise of afterlife, its sophisticated metaphysics and logic, and its philosophy of universal compassion. Taoism and Buddhism shared much in their criticisms of secular life and in their common interest in intuiting truth beyond language. Since each functioned as a tradition antithetical to dominant Confucianism, in the syncretic Chinese mind they often became closely allied or even interchangeable. Chan (i.e., Zen) Buddhism, a unique invention of Chinese Buddhism, may be seen as a result of the confluence of Buddhism and Taoism. On the other hand, Mahayana Buddhism's commitment to save the world paralleled the secular orientation of Confucianism. The Buddhist art of mind training also contributed to the development of Neo-Confucianism, especially its "mind philosophy" (xinxue).

In traditional Chinese thought, Confucianism and Taoism were regarded as complementary, "appealing to two sides of the Chinese character" (De Bary 48). Mahayana Buddhism seemed to reproduce the Confucianism-Taoism polarity within its simultaneous denial of secular life through the philosophy of emptiness and its accommodation to or even affirmation of secular life through the Bodhisattva ideal. How does Buddhism reconcile this apparent contradiction? In *Madhyamika Sastra* (*The Middle Doctrine*), Nagarjuna argues: "all causally produced phenomena, I say, are unreal [empty, *kong*], / Are but a passing name [provisional designation, *jia*] and indicate the mean [transcending duality, *zhong*]" (qtd. in Soothill and Hodous 76–77). The Tiantai school of Buddhism developed this into the "Perfectly Harmonious Threefold Truth," which means: "that 1) all things or dharmas [i.e., phenomena] are empty because they are produced through causation and therefore have no self-nature; but that 2) they do have temporary existence; and that 3) being both Empty and Temporary is the nature of dharmas and is the mean" (De Bary 310). In other words, a Buddhist must balance the absolute truth (that all phenomena are empty, i.e., devoid of self-nature) with the relative truth (that the phenomenal world is real to the extent that it has temporary existence). In a similar formulation, the phenomenal world is equated with emptiness (*se kong bu er*). In practice this allows Buddhists to see through the seeming permanence of life while involving themselves in this life and committing themselves to benefiting others. As Nagarjuna tries to prove in *The Middle Doctrine*, "emptiness" itself can be negated, that is, made "empty." Thus, in order to transcend duality, the theory of Madhyamika attempts to steer a middle course between extremes. This mode of thought strikes a chord of sympathy in the Chinese mind, which treasures the Confucian ideal of the golden mean (*zhongyong*) and the Taoist penchant to seek truth in paradox.

Buddhism has brought into Chinese literature a series of new themes and reinforced others that were already in existence. The following Buddhist themes are common in Chinese fiction: the suffering of life; the inconstancy or transience of all phenomena; life as a dream; karma, which causes reincarnation and dispenses retribution; spiritual awakening and conversion to Buddhism; and compassion for all and the self-sacrificing desire to benefit others. Broadly speaking, two major issues emerge from these themes: first, how to perceive the truth of emptiness hidden behind deceptive appearances, which is often formulated as the question of true *vs.* false; and, second, how to act upon the knowledge of emptiness and practice Buddhism as a religion of infinite compassion, which is often posed as the dialectic of simultaneously detaching oneself from the world and engaging it.

The epistemological issue of seeking truth by debunking the deceptive appearances of life involves a range of themes, motifs, and devices. In the *Diamond Sutra*, Buddha concludes his teaching in these celebrated lines: "All activities [or phenomena] / Should be looked upon merely as being like a dream, / A phantasm [or illusion], a bubble, a shadow, / A drop of dew, or a flash of lightning" (qtd. in Hamilton 116).[4] These similes emphasize the insubstantial, unreal, fragile, and fleeting nature of experiences and phenomena, and form a paradigm for dramatizing the key Buddhist notion of emptiness. Of the figures in the quoted lines, the two that appear most commonly in fiction are illusion and dream.

In a tale by Li Fuyan (early ninth century) entitled "The Spendthrift and the Alchemist" ("Du Zichun"), a series of illusory scenes are invoked by magic to underscore the point that unreality has the quality of reality, and consequently that ego-clinging, based on the assumption of solid reality, is groundless. The protagonist, Du Zichun, a reformed spendthrift, submits himself to a test given by a priest, his benefactor. The priest tells him not to utter any sound, "[n]ot even if you see deities, devils, vampires, wild beasts, the horrors of Hell, or your relatives bound and in agony—it will all be an illusion" (139). Sure enough, Du is subjected to the threats of a rainstorm, beasts of prey, and soldiers, and he even has to witness the torture of his wife before his eyes. All these, including his wife's plea for one word from him so that she could be spared, he ignores, bearing in mind the priest's teaching that they are all illusory. Then he is killed and subsequently reincarnated as a woman, who grows up mute and in time marries and has a son. The woman's husband tries to make her talk but fails. In exasperation, he seizes the child by the feet and dashes his head against a stone. "The little boy's skull was smashed, and blood spurted out several feet. Love for the child made Du forget the pledge and give an exclamation of horror" (142). At that instant, Du comes out of the illusions and realizes that he has failed the test of emotional detachment. Although the story is framed in a Taoist setting, the theme, that one must view emotional experiences as essentially unreal and be detached in order to reach an egoless state, is clearly Buddhist, and such details in plot as reincarnation and Hell also derive unmistakably from the Buddhist tradition. In fact, Shi Yongxiang has traced this story to an early Buddhist parable contained in Volume 7 of Xuan Zang's (596–664) *Da Tang xiyu ji* (*Records of the Western Region of the Great Tang*) (see Shi 193–94).

In "The Spendthrift and the Alchemist," the illusory scenes are brief and disconnected (they achieve unity only in that they are varied assaults on the protagonist's ego); the story appears to be an artistically crude religious parable. The more popular and sophisticated dream tales present a coherent, realistic story as a dream. In "The World Inside a Pillow" ("Zhenzhong ji") by Shen Jiji (750?–800?), for instance, a struggling scholar napping on a pillow given him by a Taoist priest has a dream in which he leads a full life of wealth, enjoys marital bliss, a distinguished career, and supreme honors, and finally dies at the age of eighty. At that point he wakes up to find that his sleep has been so brief that even the millet the host has been cooking is not yet ready. But he learns a lesson from the dream and realizes the vanity of his worldly ambitions. "The World Inside a Pillow" offers a formula for many dream tales: a religious teacher (Buddhist or Taoist) causes an unenlightened man, usually a disgruntled Confucian scholar, to realize his fondest ambitions in a dream, and as the man wakes up from the dream, he is made to see that his ambitions—and, by extension, his life—is also like a dream.

"Governor of the Southern Tributary State" ("Nanke taishou zhuan") by Li Gongzuo (770–850), another gem of a dream tale, is praised for "its charming blend of reality and fantasy," which makes it, in Lu Xun's opinion, "infinitely superior to" "The World Inside a Pillow" (105). In this story, the hero, Chunyu Fen, gets drunk under a large ash tree outside his house and falls asleep after he has been helped inside. In his dream he is invited to the "Great Kingdom of Ashendon," where he marries the princess, raises a large family, becomes the governor of its southern tributary state, and enjoys enormous influence and popularity. His fortune declines after the death of the princess and when the king forces him into retirement for fear of his rising power. He is finally sent back to the world of men with the king's promise to take him back in three years. At that point he wakes up from his dream. The story continues with the revelations that Ashendon is an anthill under the ash tree and that events in the dream world correspond to those in this world. Chunyu dies three years later, fulfilling the ant king's promise. Unlike "The World Inside a Pillow," in which the dream world is bracketed off from the real world in terms of plot, "Governor of the Southern Tributary State" deliberately blurs the distinction between the two worlds to make the point that life is not merely *like* a dream, that it *is* a dream.⁵

In Cao Xueqin's (1715?–64?) *Honglou meng* (*The Dream of the Red Chamber* or *The Story of the Stone*),⁶ the greatest of traditional Chinese novels, the dream theme is exploited in a most consummate way. *The Dream of the Red Chamber* is a monumental work of realism with an allegorical framework. In its voluminous pages, the novel describes the vicissitudes of the aristocratic Jia family against the broad backdrop of eighteenth-century Chinese society. In the foreground and at center stage is the tragic love story of Baoyu, the hero, and his cousin Daiyu. Surrounded by other young girls his age, who are either his relatives or maids serving them, Baoyu lives an idyllic life in a secluded part of the Jia estates called Prospect Garden. He is a sensitive adolescent who has the "feminist" idea, rather surprising for his time and for a boy of his social status, that girls are made of water and therefore pure and men are made of mud and therefore dirty. Although a privileged member of the family, he treats even the servant girls as equals and has fine sentiments for all of them. In the eyes of his father, who is an official and Confucian scholar, Baoyu is wayward and rebellious because he "wastes" his time playing around with the girls instead of devoting himself to the study of Confucian classics in preparation for an official career. Baoyu's true love, Daiyu, is a hypersensitive, frail, and self-pitying beauty. Eventually the family chooses another cousin, the more worldly Baochai, to be Baoyu's wife. Baoyu goes mad, Daiyu dies, and Baochai is heartbroken. When Baoyu recovers from the derangement, his personality is totally changed: he becomes inexplicably cold. He goes on to take the civil service examination to accommodate his family's wishes and shortly afterward leaves home to become a Buddhist monk. Baoyu's personal tragedy unfolds against the declining fortunes of the family. By the end of the novel, the two Jia mansions have been raided twice by imperial guards suspecting corruption and political entanglement.

Without an account of its mythic and allegorical dimension, however, the novel would be much impoverished in meaning and structure. In the opening chapter, the reader is told the origin of the story. In fact, Baoyu is the incarnation of a magic stone which was left unused when the goddess Nuwa was repairing the sky.⁷ This divine stone later takes a fancy to a plant growing by the

Magic River and waters it everyday with sweet dews. The plant, known as the Crimson Pearl Flower in Heaven, is incarnated as Lin Daiyu to repay for the kindness of the Stone, now Baoyu, with tears. In the view of the otherworldly Buddhist monk and the Taoist priest who take the Stone on a little trip to the human world, Baoyu has to undergo the full range of human experiences, especially bittersweet love, to awaken to the illusory nature of life. Thus, Baoyu's story, told against the background of the fortunes of the aristocratic Jia family, with meticulous attention to realistic details, is structurally framed as a "dream."

Dreams indeed provide a device by which characters travel between this world and the other in *The Dream of the Red Chamber*. The most important of such dreams is Baoyu's dream adventure in the "Land of Illusion." In that dream he meets the fairy Disenchantment, who makes her home in the Land of Illusion and whose business "is with the romantic passions, love-debts, girlish heartbreaks and male philanderings" of the human world (130). There Baoyu is shown the Celestial Registers in which "are recorded," in cryptic verses, "the past, present, and future of girls from all over the world" (131). The fates of the twelve leading female characters in the novel are thus foreshadowed. There Baoyu is also introduced to the art of lovemaking; the purpose is, paradoxically, "to shock the silliness out of him" (137), according to his ancestors in Heaven, or to "disenchant" him about the "illusions of life," as the fairy Disenchantment is trying to do. Thus, Baoyu's dream of the Land of Illusion provides a mythic or allegorical explanation of the fates of Baoyu and other characters. In the context of the novel, it may be regarded as a revelation of Reality, compared with which the realistic story, with its confusing, shifting, and ambiguous details, has the quality of a dream.

That a dream may reveal Reality while quotidian reality may conceal Truth represents a major theme of *The Dream of the Red Chamber*. At the entrance to the Land of Illusion there is a couplet which reads: "Truth becomes fiction when the fiction's [made *or* treated as] true; Real becomes not-real where the unreal's real" (55). This couplet can be read on several levels. First, it most immediately applies to the Land of Illusion. When the fictive (as suggested by the name of the realm) is experienced as emotionally real, the essential Buddhist truth of emptiness (also as suggested by the name of the realm) contained in the fiction, along with the fictive, appears to be fantastic or unreal from a conventional point of view (indeed, on the realistic level of the story, it is dream-talk pure and simple). Second, as the idyllic Prospect Garden is, in a sense, an earthly projection of the Land of Illusion (see Yu, *Haiwai* 33), so what Baoyu and his companions take for real in their daily lives is misleading and obfuscating from a Buddhist perspective. Third, the interpenetration and interdependence of the true/real and the false/fictive also apply to the microlevels of plot. The play on the words *zhen* (real) and *jia* (false) by way of homonyms results in the pair of Jia Baoyu and his double, Zhen Baoyu, and in another important pair, Zhen Shiyin (Real Happenings Concealed) and his counterpart Jia Yucun (False Talk [*or* Fiction] Presented). By further extension, the play on the idea of the real and the false is found wherever the apparent is contradicted and subverted by the actual, the true, and the essential. The complicated interweaving of the real and the unreal, the apparent and the actual at all levels of the work makes a naïve differentiation of the real from the unreal impossible. As a central fictional device in the novel, the interweaving of the real and the unreal carefully balances the work between an allegorical structure and a realist style of writing.

Paralleling the sophisticated use of the dream theme is the process by which Baoyu (the Stone) awakens to the dream that is life and becomes a Buddhist monk. It may seem curious that the divine Stone must go through all the complications of mundane life before it can return to Heaven enlightened, but the detour is necessary for several reasons. From the perspective of art, it is human life, with all its passions, emotions, allurements, and disappointments, which makes absorbing reading. The reading process, i.e., the empathetic process of experiencing the fictional universe, is more important than knowing the endpoint of that process. On the religious level, spiritual growth occurs, not in spite of the "snares of life," but because of them. In other words, transcendence is possible only through descent into the thick of human experience. In Buddhist terms, this process is formulated as the Buddhist-Taoist priest Vanitas's spiritual *Bildungsroman*: Vanitas, "starting off in the Void (which is Truth), came to the contemplation of Form (which is Illusion); and from Form engendered Passion, entered again into Form; and from Form awoke to the Void (which is Truth)" (51). Then Vanitas changes his name to "Brother Amor, or the Passionate Monk," and the title of the book from *The Story of the Stone* to *The Tale of Brother Amor* (51). What Vanitas goes through here in the first chapter is a rehearsal of what Baoyu is to go through; in that sense, Baoyu is Brother Amor. Now we can see that in the *Dream* the allegorical structure is not a mere framework imposed on a realist story; it permeates the entire story and gives it deep metaphysical resonances.

Compared with *The Dream of the Red Chamber*, *The Journey to the West* (*Xiyou ji*) by Wu Cheng'en (ca. 1500–82) is more clearly a Buddhist allegory of enlightenment, using the journey as its main figure.[8] The novel, popularized in the West by Arthur Waley's abridged version entitled *Monkey*, is based on the Chinese monk Xuan Zang's (596–664) historic pilgrimage to India to study Buddhism and to bring home Buddhist scriptures.[9] In the novel, Tripitaka, protected by his three disciples, Monkey, Pigsy, and Sandy, undertakes the arduous journey through difficult terrains and encounters many obstacles and calamities along the way. On the religious level, the action of the novel is motivated by the law of karma. All the members of the pilgrim party, Tripitaka, Monkey, Pigsy, and Sandy, as well as the horse, are making a spiritual journey to achieve "redemption through atoning merit" (Yu, *Companion* 416). It turns out that they are all celestial beings who were amiss in their conduct before they are reincarnated on earth. The story of Monkey is especially interesting. Born from a stone egg, Monkey in time learns magic, acquires immortality, and challenges the authority of the Jade Emperor in Heaven—in fact, he singlehandedly makes a havoc of Heaven—and is finally subdued by the Buddha Tathagata and imprisoned under a mountain. His chance for expiation and freedom comes when he agrees to be Tripitaka's disciple and escort him on his pilgrimage. The others have their own karmic destinies to work out, too. This explains why Monkey cannot use his miraculous skill to take Tripitaka to the destination.[10] In response to such a query from Pigsy, he answers:

> But it is required of Master to go through all these strange territories before he finds deliverance from the sea of sorrows; hence even one step turns out to be difficult. You and I are only his protective companions, guarding his body and life, but we cannot exempt

him from these woes, nor can we obtain the scriptures all by ourselves. (1: 436)

If the goal of the pilgrims is to reach Western Heaven to obtain Buddhist scriptures, one wonders why they must get sidetracked in situations that do not pose obstacles to their journey. In other words, as one demon in the novel asks, why must they mind "others' business" (3: 349)? Structurally, this could mean a meandering plot. To be sure, the pilgrims have to go through trials and ordeals of all kinds (eighty-one calamities in total) to dispel their store of karmic demerits before they can reach enlightenment. But were they only objecting to "paying a karmic debt," they would not be truly enlightened. What motivates them in such cases is also compassion, which makes them unable to bear watching sentient beings suffer. Whereas the law of retribution may "convey an air of ethical determinism" (Bantly 518), the exercise of compassion liberates the pilgrims from such determinism and gives them the freedom to do good. In the larger picture of the novel, since other characters are each working out their karmic fates, the compassionate acts rendered by the pilgrims, uncalled-for either by their own atonement or by a "progressive" structure of the journey, help to bring to fruition the karmic destinies of these characters.

Overcoming obstacles and vanquishing enemies are what the pilgrims must do to reach their destination; acting compassionately is what they should do as Buddhists. What can they do if the two apparently get in each other's way? In fact, many demons and monsters in the novel exploit the compassion of the pilgrims to attain their evil goals by transforming themselves magically into the forms of helpless women or tottering old folk. Tripitaka, obsessed with not violating the principle of compassion and unable to see through the appearances, falls for their tricks. It is Monkey who is able to see the demons for what they are, no matter how they disguise themselves, and mercilessly wipes them out so they cannot harm Tripitaka or innocent people. Monkey obviously comprehends both compassion and the emptiness of Form and is able to act both ethically and wisely, whereas Tripitaka sticks to the principle of compassion blindly and falls victim to his own delusion. Tripitaka's problem is that of the average person who tries to do good in a world of appearances where evils are rife.

The relation between Buddhism and modern Chinese fiction is an ill-explored subject. But toward the end of the nineteenth century and the beginning of the twentieth, amid the general decline of Chinese Buddhism as an institution, there was a resurgence of interest in Buddhism among progressive intellectuals. Kang Youwei (1858–1927), Tan Sitong (1865–98), Liang Qichao (1873–1929), Zhang Taiyan (1869 [1867]–1936), and others delved into Buddhist classics and found parallels between Buddhism and modern Western thought; the political and social reforms they advocated were thus inspired by their understanding of both Buddhism and Western thought (see Tan 5–6). Buddhism exerted a considerable influence on modern Chinese writers in various ways. In the turmoil of Chinese society in the early twentieth century, amid the sufferings many modern writers experienced as they were caught between idealism and the sordid reality of a society in transition, the Buddhist teachings about the sufferings of life, about the need and ways to effect release from the oppression of reality, about compassion for the suffering masses, and about the selfless sacrifice for the good of others were quite appealing (see Tan 7–10). In the following pages, I will discuss Buddhist influence on selected works by three major modern writers, Lu Xun (1881–1936), Xu Dishan (1896–1945), and Qian Zhongshu (1910–).

Lu Xun's short story "Diary of a Madman" ("Kuangren riji") (1918) is the first vernacular story written in modern China; it marks the beginning of modern Chinese fiction. "Diary of a Madman" consists of thirteen brief diary entries prefaced by an editorial note. The diary proper portrays a man from a family of landed gentry who apparently suffers from paranoia. In the hostile, gloating, sinister looks he thinks he receives, he sees the cannibalistic intentions of those around him—men, women, children, neighbors and family members alike. He then recalls the man-eating practices in the past and consults history to find out what's what. There beneath the words "Confucian Virtue and Morality," "scrawled all over each page," he discovers two words between the lines: "Eat humans" (4). Chinese history turns out in the Madman's reading to be one of cannibalism. This discovery only deepens his sense of spiritual isolation, however. He realizes that within this all-encompassing cannibalist tradition, he himself is not innocent, that he may very well have eaten of his sister inadvertently. The despair this agonizing knowledge engenders leads him, in the last entry of the journal, to an attempt to break out of the claustrophobic "iron house" of history and to a plea to "Save the children" (12).

On the symbolic level, the Madman is a radical rebel to traditional Chinese society, and his voice is that of a visionary. That the Madman is a conduit for Lu Xun to proclaim his own antitraditional stand and to voice his condemnation of Confucianism as a feudalist ideology is confirmed by the author himself. Lu Xun wrote in a letter to a friend: "'Diary of a Madman' is truly my humble work. . . . One day I was browsing *Zi zhi tongjian* [*A Mirror of History to Aid Government*], and it dawned upon me that the Chinese are still a cannibalistic people. Hence my story. This is a significant discovery which few are aware of yet" (*Shuxin* 1: 18). "Diary of a Madman" and Lu Xun's revelation of its genesis highlight two major themes that will recur in his later fiction: namely, indictment of the feudal tradition and the pathos of the revolutionary or progressive intellectual who must endure the apathy, noncomprehension, and even persecution of the very masses whom he or she tries to enlighten and liberate.

Though "Diary of a Madman" has been well researched in terms both of the foreign influences it has received (see, e.g., Chen, "Kuangren") and in the tradition of mad characters in literature (see, e.g., Guan), its possible connection to Buddhism has not been recognized. As I mentioned earlier, an important theme of the "Diary" is that an enlightened one is besieged by benighted people and, consequently, right (sanity) and wrong (insanity) are inverted. Thematically, it recalls a parable from *Za biyu jing* (*Miscellaneous Parables*), which may be summarized as follows. In a certain country, poisonous rains often fell to pollute rivers, lakes, moats, and wells, causing drinkers of the polluted water to be drunk and crazy for a week. Knowing this, the wise king covered his well to shelter it from rain. When his ministers went crazy after drinking the polluted water, they appeared in court naked, their heads bespattered with mud, and accused the normal-acting king of being insane. The king, fearful of a rebellion, offered to take medicine for his "illness." He retired to cover his face with mud and then came out as naked as his ministers. The next week, all the ministers went back to normal and were surprised to see the king sitting on his throne naked, his face muddy. To their query, the king answered: "My mind has remained constant as it has always been. You call me crazy because you are crazy."[11] In a variation on this story, a folk tale from the *Songshu* changes the poisonous rain to an insanity-inducing spring and has the subjects force the king to receive painful treatment for his "insanity" until the king gives up by drinking from the same spring to conform to the majority. The Madman faces essentially the same problem as the king in the Buddhist parable faces: how to convince others that those who consider him crazy are themselves insane? In the end, the Madman in Lu Xun's story is "cured" and leaves home to become a candidate for official positions, as the editor indicates in the prefatory note. In terms of plot, especially the outcome, "Diary" seems to bear closer resemblance to the story from the *Songshu*; but in terms of the spiritual isolation the protagonist experiences and the glimmer of hope that insanity may be cured, the author, of whom the Madman is a voice, would probably identify himself with the wise king, who has to compromise but will not surrender.

That Lu Xun's story may have been influenced by the Buddhist parable from *Miscellaneous Parables* is very plausible. During the 1910s, Lu Xun systematically studied Buddhism and collected stone rubbings of Buddhist images.[12] According to Xu Fancheng, a disciple of his, this period of dedicated work and self-discipline gave Lu Xun the necessary training in spiritual serenity and resilience which proved useful in coping with the tremendous pressures in his life (see Tan 10). Lu Xun's knowledge of and insight into Buddhism can be found throughout his writings. In a preface to a new edition of *Baiyu jing* (*One Hundred Parables*), retitled *Chihuaman*, which is perhaps the best-known of *avadana* literature (Buddhist parables), Lu Xun praises the rich tradition of Indian fables as found in Chinese translation of Buddhist scriptures, and mentions that there are five or six books of *avadana* literature extant. Although *Miscellaneous Parables* is not named, Lu Xun must have been familiar with this work and the parable quoted above. In a more general way, Lu Xun must also have been familiar with the fundamental Buddhist question of appearance and reality. The quoted parable shows how unreality caused by insanity and reality represented by sanity can be inverted in a community dominated by the wrongheaded majority. Although the "Diary" had a very different agenda from the said Buddhist parable, the spiritual affinity between the Madman—and the author himself—and the king in the parable is apparent.

Xu Dishan is a major modern writer whose work shows clear influence of Buddhism.[13] Suggestive of "popular Buddhist tales and medieval Christian legends" (Hsia, *History* 85), his early work dramatizes the suffering of life by treating marital and family problems and extols the spirit of endurance, acceptance, and transcendence. "The Merchant's Wife" ("Shangren fu") (1921) is a good example. Hsi Kuan helps her husband, Lin Yin-chiao, emigrate to Singapore after he has gambled away his business in China. Ten years later, Lin has become rich and remarried there. Hsi Kuan, in keeping with Lin's promise, goes to Singapore to look for him, only to find him remarried and herself soon sold by him to an Indian Muslim merchant as the latter's sixth wife. Hsi Kuan suffers under the tyrannical new husband in a loveless marriage and is abused by his other wives except for one. After her husband's death, she flees home with her half-Indian son and, with the help of a friend, goes to college and finally becomes a schoolteacher. Later she goes to Singapore in search of Lin. Failing to find him, she returns with her son to India. Hsi Kuan has suffered extraordinarily in life, yet she is not embittered. She says:

> in all human affairs, there is basically no distinction between the painful and the pleasurable. When you try too hard, it is painful; when you have hope, it is pleasurable. In other words, everything in the present is filled with suffering. The past, recollections of it, and hope are pleasant. (50)

She then advises the narrator, who expresses sympathy for her suffering, to "take things easy" (50). Hsi Kuan's simultaneous acceptance of suffering and affirmation of hope and, in doing both, transcending suffering are truly remarkable.

> When the ship nears Singapore, Hsi Kuan tells the narrator: My happiness is the same as it was nine years ago when I first [saw the dancing leaves of the coconut trees on the coast and the seagulls flying back and forth to welcome strangers]. In the blink of an eye these years have passed—like an arrow—yet I can't find any difference between what I saw then and what I see now. So the

expression "Time is like an arrow" doesn't refer to the speed at which an arrow flies, but to the arrow itself. For no matter how fast time flies, things show no change—as something attached to an arrow, although it may fly with the arrow, doesn't go through any changes at all. (49)

Traditionally, the Chinese are fond of contrasting the apparently unchanging scene with the passage of years and the changed circumstances of an individual's life and then uttering a sigh over the impermanence of life. But because Hsi Kuan is able to free herself from the entrapping force of her immediate experiences, she sees an unaltering reality beyond them, which delights her.

Acceptance of adversities in life and attempts to transcend the ego need not imply passivity or withdrawal from life. While she calmly accepts her fate, Yu Kuan also sees herself as a "female Crusoe." Through diligence and perseverance she has made something of herself. What is most remarkable about this woman is that, despite the injustices she has suffered, she still has a large heart. She helps others in need and forgives Lin. Religious faith and perspective enable her to cope with adversities and sufferings in life with courage and dignity. Obviously, in describing Hsi Kuan as both resigned to her fate and persevering, trying to take control of her life, Xu Dishan attempts to balance the two basic thrusts in Mahayana Buddhism—detachment from life and engagement of it—and apply them to modern life. One critic notices these "contradictions" and believes that Xu's Buddhist visions compromise his humanism (Qiu 6). It may be argued that Xu attempted to integrate humanism in a modern version of Buddhism and to complement humanism with religious transcendence. Whether the task is successful or not, the effort is significant.

Besides being the author of *Fortress Besieged* (*Wei cheng*), "regarded by many to be the crowning achievement of modern Chinese literature" (Huters [13]), Qian Zhongshu is known worldwide as an erudite scholar. The Belgian sinologist Pierre Rickmans said of Qian in an interview in *Le Monde* in 1983: "His knowledge of Chinese literature, Western tradition, and universal literature is prodigious. Qian Zhongshu is unequaled in China and even in the world today" (15). Two preoccupations figure prominently in Qian's writings, both literary and scholarly: first, his critical examination of tradition, convention, received opinions, and common sense; second, his abiding interest in observing the clashes and interactions between Chinese and Western culture. In his short story "Shangdi de meng" ("God's Dream") (1946), both these tendencies may be observed.

In "God's Dream," at an unspecified future time, the accelerated process of evolution finally leads to the extinction of the human race because humans have no time to mate. Then God emerges as the supreme creation of evolution. God wants to create for himself a companion smart enough to appreciate his greatness but not enough to emulate it, a servant who knows how to flatter him right to the point. God keeps fantasizing and falls sleep. In his dream, he creates man and woman. However, God and humans become increasingly estranged because of mutual suspicion and distrust. To reassert his authority, God decides to make the life of humans hard by creating beasts of prey, mosquitoes, and germs. In time humans fall sick and die. While this proves that God is powerful, it also defeats his original purpose in creating obedient companions for himself. Finally, God wakes up from his dream, stretching and yawning at the endless time and loneliness ahead.

"God's Dream" is clearly a satire of the accelerated pace of evolution or "progress," with its underlying notion of linear history, imported from the West and sanctified in modern Chinese discourse. Linear history is essentially a Judeo-Christian conception of history, which begins with Genesis and ends with doomsday, and human history so conceived becomes an interlude in divine eternity, something like God's dream. In Qian's story, God's creation and decreation of humans may be regarded as a *reductio ad absurdum* of human history. That they exist only in a dream invalidates not only Genesis but the entire linear human history issuing therefrom. As I discussed above, the dream is a major device in the Buddhist tradition for belying the phenomenal world and proving the groundlessness of ambitions based on what it considers to be an erroneous understanding of life. "God's Dream" resembles "The World Inside a Pillow" and "Governor of the Southern Tributary State" in that in all these stories the protagonists have their fantasies of self-aggrandizement fulfilled at one point in their dreams, and the height of glory they reach in their dreams contrasts ironically with the reality they wake up to face. The difference is that while the protagonists in the two classical tales awake to the dreamy character of life as they wake up from their dreams, God in Qian's story is not shown to have had this epiphany.

In "God's Dream" the God that comes out of evolution is presumed to be existent, whereas the biblical God is alluded to as if he had existed only in a rumor. Yet the later God unknowingly parodies the biblical God and his genesis. At the end of the story, God wakes up from his dream—a not very successful rehearsal of genesis—and is undecided about whether to go ahead with his project of creating man. In other words, the post-"Creation" moment turns out to be a pre-Creation moment. This structure of repetition and circularity reminds one of Buddhist cosmic cycles. In Buddhist cosmology, the universe, encompassing an unlimited number of worlds, is in an unending process of emerging, being, decaying, and destruction. The time between the creation and re-creation of a world is called a kalpa. From a Buddhist perspective, the biblical conception of history, which stretches between Genesis and doomsday, makes only one kalpa. Without the later God's knowledge, his existence has already been anticipated by the biblical God and his genesis preceded by the biblical Genesis. Even his own genesis, if it is to take place at all, is already a repetition of his dream. Qian of course is not preaching Buddhist cosmology as a religious dogma. What interests him most is to counter "oneness"—one God, one genesis, one linear history, with all the absoluteness each of these suggests—with duplicity and multiplicity.

Not only is the later God's genesis unreal, his own being is also in question. Let us see how God emerges from evolution:

> The set rule of evolution is that the thing that comes later is superior. Out of time and space evolved inorganic matter; inorganic matter progressed to animals and plants; from fixed plants came quiet and clinging woman; from active animals came crude, adventurous man; and man and woman creatively produced children; and dolls evolved from children. The supreme God, therefore, should be the last product of evolution. (Huters 99)

The absurdity of the narrator's summary of evolution makes God's emergence a plain joke. When God creates man in his dream, the narrator says that "[b]y now, all records of making man out of dust that we find in the sacred books of all religions had finally proved to be a valid prophecy" (5). Ostensibly, the validity of the biblical genesis is confirmed; yet by calling it a "prophecy" and by relegating its fulfillment to a dream, the text finally denies its validity. If both Gods and both instances of genesis are unreal, how can history grounded in either of them be valid? Thus, despite the suggestion of Buddhist cosmic cycles, the story does not substitute cyclical history for linear history *ultimately*. Qian counters not only Genesis but the whole of Judeo-Christian cosmology with a Buddhist perspective, showing everything to be illusory and empty. The way Qian goes about his argument in the story recalls the way Nagarjuna reasons in *The Middle Doctrine* (see above). Ontologically and epistemologically, the story shows that there is no transcendental signified to anchor the discourse of linear history, upon which the notion of accelerated social evolution or "progress" is grounded.

"God's Dream" is ideologically significant in several ways. In twentieth-century China, modernization is often equated with Westernization.[14] The discourse of "progress" based on the conception of linear history has enormous prestige and influence and supports a range of ideologies imported from the West, such as Darwinism and Marxism. By drawing upon Buddhism and other Eastern cultural resources, Qian playfully challenges the discourse of "progress." From a global perspective, Qian's critique of modernity parallels the postmodernist critique of the metanarrative of the Enlightenment in the West. In fact, the themes of "God's Dream," the techniques used in it, and the author's sensibility revealed in the work are typically "postmodern."[15] The possibility of a Buddhist-Taoist postmodernism effectively challenges the Western view of twentieth-century world literature and calls for a rethinking of postmodernism, which is generally considered a Western phenomenon.[16]

From the rather sketchy discussion above of a small selection of texts, one can already see the extent and depth of influence that Buddhism has exerted on the Chinese literary imagination as manifested in Chinese fiction, both traditional and modern. Hu Shi (1891-1962), a modern scholar and one of the initiators of China's literary revolution in the early twwentieth century, argues that for the indigenous Chinese mind dominated by realism, the introduction of Indian imaginative literature via Buddhism had an enormous liberating power (*History* 195). For proof one could point to the multilayered Heaven and Hell with their hosts of gods and demons, or to karmic retribution that extends over lives and brings together individuals in a vast network of possible relations. These new supernatural or mythic elements no doubt extended the imaginative range of the Chinese mind, but the most abiding contributions made by Buddhism had to do with epistemological and ontological issues. Indigenous Chinese thought was generally more concerned with ethics, social philosophy, and the individual's role in society as defined by both; it seldom ventured into sustained metaphysical speculations (Zhuang Zhou was a possible exception). Buddhism supplied sophisticated answers to many epistemological and ontological questions basic to human existence. For instance, the Chinese, like other peoples, did have empirical observations of the impermanence of life,[17] but Buddhism systematized them into a doctrine of emptiness. After Buddhism came to China, the figure that "Life is a dream" became one of the basic visions of life in Chinese culture and attained the status of a cliché.

As may be seen from the above discussion, a broadly defined tradition of dream tales has enriched Chinese fiction tremendously. The four texts surveyed may be used to sketch the evolution of the genre. In "The Spendthrift and the Alchemist," a rewriting of a Buddhist parable, the theme of dream or illusion is delivered highhandedly; religious intent overwhelms artistic merit. In "The World Inside a Pillow" and "Governor of the Southern Tributary State," the plot becomes more plausible, and the dream theme is executed fairly persuasively. *The Dream of the Red Chamber* brings this genre to an unsurpassable height and taps its metaphysical and artistic potentials to the full. More than just a vastly expanded dream tale, *Dream* is also a masterpiece of realism. The Mahayana argument that there is no gap between phenomena and emptiness (*se kong bu er*) allows the author to explore the complicated relations between dream and life, fantasy and reality, fiction and truth. Ultimately, *Dream* can be read as an epitome of social life, a myth about human existence, and an allegory of fiction all at the same time.

The Journey to the West uses the Buddhist doctrine in a fairly systematic way, despite its syncretic nature in the Chinese cultural context. In fact, Bantly has argued for its canonization as Buddhist literature (52–53). The use of karmic action and the principle of compassion allow the author to spin a vast story about Tripitaka's pilgrimage. The repetitions and digressions in plot may make the work seem structurally weak if one compares it with a typical *Bildungsroman* in the West; but from the perspective of karmic retribution and compassionate action, these "negative" features become fully motivated.[18]

In modern Chinese fiction, Buddhism proves to be a tradition more vital than many have recognized. Lu Xun's "Diary of a Madman" seems to be indebted to Buddhist parables both in plot and in the theme of the spiritual isolation of the awakened loner. More important than to establish direct influence, the reader would appreciate the affinity between the Madman (and Lu Xun) and the king (the bodhisattva) who must save the very masses who misunderstand and even persecute them. In "The Merchant's Wife," Xu Dishan attempts to offer Buddhism as a viable way of life in modern times—the stormy age of the May Fourth Movement—which is not very receptive to the idea of individual endurance and transcendence of suffering. While continuing the tradition of dream tales, Qian Zhongshu's "God's Dream" shows a significant way Buddhism may be used to serve the Chinese fictional imagination in modern times. Qian's use of the dream theme and Buddhist cosmology, along with his use of Zhuang Zhou's Taoism, to deconstruct the notion of linear history, grounded in the Bible and dominant in modern Chinese discourse, may be characterized as "postmodern." That quite a few contemporary avant-garde fiction writers in China seem to exhibit a Buddhist-Taoist sensibility suggests that Qian's precedent is being followed.

In conclusion, one can say confidently that by supplying the Chinese writer with ideas, examples, and techniques the Buddhist imagination has contributed substantially to the achievements of Chinese fiction, both traditional and modern.

Notes

1. Founded by Siddhartha Guatama (ca. 563–483 B.C.E.), Buddhism was introduced to China from Central Asia probably in the early

first century C.E. Although there are speculations that the Chinese may have heard about Buddhism as early as the second century B.C.E., the first official reference to it occurred in 65 C.E. (see Shi 11–16 [esp. 12] and De Bary xxi).

For the impact Buddhism has made on Chinese culture, see Zurcher, and K. Chen. One indication of the pervasive influence of Buddhism on Chinese culture is in language. According to Liang Qichao, a modern Chinese scholar, the large-scale translation of Buddhist works into Chinese over a period of one thousand years added 35,000 words and phrases to the Chinese language (27). These include many words and expressions still in common use, e.g., *shijie* ("world"). Also see Zhu Ruiwen, ed.

2. By "the Buddhist imagination" I mean the characteristic ways Buddhism views life and the world. This term is flexible enough to include anything from Buddhist philosophy, theology, to the individual "sensibility" shaped by Buddhism in various ways. Because the topic is vast, this essay is of necessity sketchy and highly selective in the choice of texts and themes for discussion. Within the limited space available, I have attempted to strike a balance between survey and textual analysis. For a general account of Buddhism and Chinese literature, see Jan Yun-hua. For a survey of Buddhist influence on Chinese fiction in themes and artistic expression, see Sun Changwu 259–89.

3. For instance, the Buddhist monastic practice of celibacy was attacked by Confucians for violating the principle of *xiao*, or filial piety, which gave first importance to men's obligation to continue the family line. Buddhists later reinterpreted taking the religious order as a great act of *xiao*, because the merits created by the individual could benefit the family and the parents in ways no other filial sons could.

4. The translation is by Shao Chang Lee. Alternative wording is from Lu Kuan-Yu's translation in *Vajracchedika-Prajna-Paramita Sutra*, 23.

5. The idea that waking life and dream are not distinguishable was most dramatically expressed by Zhuang Zhou (360?–280? B.C.E.), a Taoist master, when he said that he did not know whether he was Zhuang Zhou who had dreamt he was a butterfly or a butterfly dreaming he was Zhuang Zhou (see Zhuang 45). Zhuang Zhou's skepticism and relativism were often found compatible with the Buddhist sensibility.

6. *Honglou meng* has two major textual traditions. By general scholarly consent, the first 80 chapters are attributed to Cao Xueqin and the remainder of the 120 chapters to Gao E (ca. 1740–1815). The first 80 chapters circulated in manuscript form as early as the mid-eighteenth century, while the complete 120-chapter version was first published in 1791 by Cheng Weiyuan and Gao E, who claimed that their complete book was an edition of the original manuscript. Despite differences and minor inconsistencies between the first 80 and the later 40 chapters, most

scholars agree that the Gao text follows the inner logic of the Cao text fairly closely and the work as a whole maintains its thematic and artistic integrity. For a description of the textual history of the work, see Hsia, *Novel*.

7. In Chinese mythology, the Goddess Nuwa, described as a being with a human face and the body of a serpent, is known for creating humans out of "yellow earth" and repairing the sky when it was damaged by Gong. The latter, angry at losing the battle for the heavenly throne with Zhuan Xu, another god, ran his head against Mount Buzhou, which was a pillar supporting the sky, and broke it, causing the sky to tilt. Nuwa set up a smelter and repaired the sky with colorful stones. For further details of the myth, see Yuan 16–41.

8. *The Journey to the West* is read by most modern scholars as a political satire, a comical novel, or an instance of the rich syncretic mixture of the "Three Religions," i.e., Confucianism, Taoism, and Buddhism. See, e.g., Sherman Han. Recently Francisca Cho Bantly argues cogently that "the most compelling reading of the *Journey* is an explicitly Buddhist one" (512).

9. Wu's novel may be regarded as the culmination of a long tradition of tales about Xuan Zang's pilgrimage to India. It follows the tendency in this tradition to shift the emphasis from Tripitaka, Xuan Zang's fictional counterpart, to Monkey, his disciple. Waley's abridged translation gives further prominence to Monkey. Hence, the justification of his title, *Monkey*.

10. For doubts over the necessity of the journey, see Plaks 243. Similar questions were raised by other scholars (see Plaks, note 178).

11. Both the parable from *Miscellaneous Parables* and the folk tale from the *Songshu*, quoted below, can be found in Shi 92–93.

12. For an account of Lu Xun's affinity with Buddhism, see Cai Huiming.

13. Xu Dishan studied comparative religion at Columbia and Oxford. Although he was converted to Christianity, his creative spirit and art are mainly Buddhist (see Tan 9).

14. The most striking example of this equation is Hu Shi's call in the late 1920s and early 1930s for "wholesale Westernization," which he later replaced with "wholesale modernization" (see Hu Shi, "Chongfen shijiehua yu quanpan xihua."

15. For a detailed argument, see Chang.

16. For example, Fredric Jameson specifically relates it to "post-industrial or consumer society, the society of the media . . . or multinational capitalism" in the West (112–13). Douwe Fokkema argues: "The Postmodernist code can be linked to a particular way and view of life, common in the Western world, including parts of Latin America" (55).

Linda Hutcheon also holds that postmodernism is "primarily European and American (North and South)" (4).

17. In the Bible, there are numerous references to the transience of life (see, e.g., Gen. 3:19, Job 7:6–7 and 10:20–22; Pss. 39:4, 89:47, 90:10; Rev. 12:.12) and even the phenomenal world at large (see, e.g., 2 Cor. 4:18). In early Chinese thought, the best example of the changeability of the world is found in the *Book of Changes* (*Yi jing*).

18. Many Western scholars believe that karmic causality in popular Chinese fiction provides "facile moral explanation" (Jaroslav Prusek) or creates an "air of childish unreality" that "only makes for melodramatic or pietistic contrivance in a novel" (C. T. Hsia) (see Bantly 517). Bantly disagrees with this harsh judgment, citing the *Journey* as evidence (see 517–18).

Works Cited

Bantly, Francisca Cho. "Buddhist Allegory in the *Journey to the West*." *The Journal of Asian Studies* 48.3 (1989): 512–24.

Cai, Huiming. "Lu Xun xiansheng de fojiao yinyuan" ("Lu Xun's Buddhist Connection"). *Fayin* 1 (1987) 38–39.

Cao, Xueqin, and Gao, E. *The Story of the Stone* (also known as *The Dream of the Red Chamber*). Trans. David Hawkes (vols. 1–3) and John Minford (vols. 4–5). London: Penguin, 1973–1982.

Chang, Sheng-Tai. "Reading Qian Zhongshu's 'God's Dream' as a Postmodern Text." *Chinese Literature: Essays, Articles, Reviews* (1994): 1–17.

Chen, Kenneth K. S. *The Chinese Transformation of Buddhism*. Princeton: Princeton UP, 1973.

Chen, Yuankai. "Kuangren riji de wailai yingxiang" ("The Foreign Influences on 'Diary of the Madman'"). *Ershi shiji Zhongguo wenxue yu shijie* (*Twentieth-Century Chinese Literature and the World*). Xi'an: Shaanxi renmin chubanshe, 1987. 226–42.

De Bary, William Theodore, Wing-tsit Chan, and Burton Watson, comps. *Sources of Chinese Tradition*. Vol. 1. New York and London: Columbia UP, 1960. 2 vols.

Fokkema, Douwe. *Literary History, Modernism, and Postmodernism*. Amsterdam and Philadelphia: Benjamin, 1984.

Guan, Xixiong. "Cong lilai zuojia bixia de kuangren dao Lu Xun bixia de kuangren" ("From Madmen in General Literature to Madmen in Lu Xun's Work"). *Lu Xun yanjiu dongtai* 12 (1989) 33–38.

Hamilton, Clarence H. *Buddhism: A Religion of Infinite Compassion: Selections from Buddhist Literature*. Indianapolis: Bobbs-Merrill, 1952.

Han, Sherman. "An Anatomy of the Political Satire in *Hsi yu-chi*." *Tamkang Review* 13 (1983): 227-38.

The Holy Bible. The authorized edition.

Hsia, C. T. *A History of Modern Chinese Fiction*. New Haven: Yale UP, 1961.

———. *The Classic Chinese Novel*. New York: Columbia UP, 1968.

Hu, Shi. *Baihua wenxue shi* (*A History of Vernacular Literature*). Vol. 1. Shanghai: Xinyue shudian, 1929.

———. "Chongfen shijiehua yu quanpan xihua" ("Full Cosmopolitanization and Wholesale Westernization"). *Hu Shi Wencun* (*Collected Works of Hu Shi*). Vol. 4. Taipei: Yuandong tushu gongsi, 1975. 541-44.

Hutcheon, Linda. *A Poetics of Postmodernism: History, Theory, Fiction*. London: Routledge, 1988.

Huters, Theodore. *Qian Zhongshu*. New York: Twayne, 1982.

Jameson, Fredric. "Postmodernism and Consumer Society." *The Anti-Aesthetic: Essays on Postmodern Culture*. Port Townsend, WA: Bay, 1983.

Jan, Yunhua. "Buddhist Literature." *The Indiana Companion to Traditional Chinese Literature*. Ed. and comp. William Nienhauser, Jr. Bloomington: Indiana UP, 1986. 1-12.

Li, Fuyan. "The Spendthrift and the Alchemist" ("Du Zichun"). *Tang Dynasty Stories*. Trans. Yang Xianyi and Gladys Yang. Beijing: Chinese Literature P, 1986. 136-43.

Li, Gongzuo. "Governor of the Southern Tributary State" ("Nanke taishou zhuan"). *Tang Dynasty Stories*. 56-69.

Liang, Qichao. *Foxue yanjiu shiba pian* (*Eighteen Essays in Buddhist Studies*). Taipei: Zhonghua shuju, 1966.

Lu, Xun (Hsun). *A Brief History of Chinese Fiction*. Trans. Yang Hsien-yi (Xianyi) and Gladys Yang. Beijing: Foreign Languages P, 1959.

———. "*Chihuaman* tiji" ("Preface to *Chihuaman*"). *Lu Xun quanji* (*Complete Works of Lu Xun*). Vol. 7. Beijing: Renmin chubanshe, 1973. 458-59.

———. "Diary of a Madman" ("Kuangren riji"). *The Complete Stories of Lu Xun* (*Calls to Arms* and *Wandering*). Trans. Yang Xianyi and Gladys Yang. Bloomington: Indiana UP; Beijing: Foreign Languages P, 1972. 1-12.

———. *Lu Xun shuxin ji* (*The Letters of Lu Xun*). 2 vols Beijing, Renmin wenxue chubanshe, 1976.

Plaks, Andrew. *The Four Masterworks of the Ming Novel*. Princeton: Princeton UP, 1987.

Qian, Zhongshu. "Shangdi de meng" ("God's Dream"). *Ren, shou, gui*

(*Humans, Beasts, Ghosts*). Fuzhou: Fujian renmin chubanshe, 1983. 1–17.

Qiu, Wenzhi. Preface. *Xu Dishan daibiaozuo* (*Representative Works of Xu Dishan*). Ed. Qiu Wenzhi. Zhengzhou: Huanghe wenyi chubanshe, 1987. 1–15.

Rickmans, Pierre. "Rencontre avec Pierre Rickmans, alias Simon Leys: Fou de chinois" ("Meeting with Pierre Rickmans, Also Known as Simon Leys: Crazy About Chinese"). Interview with Alain Peyraube and Nicole Zand. *Le Monde* 10 June 1983: 15, 18.

Shen, Jiji. "The World Inside a Pillow" ("Zhenzhong ji"). Trans. William Nienhauser. *Traditional Chinese Stories: Themes and Variations*. Ed. Y. W. Ma and Joseph S. M. Lau. Boston: Cheng & Tsui, 1986. 435–38.

Shi, Yongxiang. *Fojiao wenxue dui Zhongguo xiaoshuo de yingxiangjj* (*The Influence of Buddhist Literature on Chinese Fiction*). Kaohsiung: Foguang chubanshe, 1990.

Soothill, William Edward, and Lewis Hodous, comps. *A Dictionary of Chinese Buddhist Terms*. Rev. Shih Sheng-kang, Li Wu-jong, Tseng Lai-ting. 1962. Kaohsiung: Foguang chubanshe, 1988.

Sun, Changwu. *Fojiao yu Zhongguo wenxue* (*Buddhism and Chinese Literature*). Shanghai: Shanghai renmin chubanshe, 1988.

Tan Guilin. "Foxue yu Zhongguo xiandai zuojia" ("Buddhist Learning and Modern Chinese Writers"). *Wenxue pinglun* 4 (1993): 5–18.

The Vajracchedika-Prajna-Paramita Sutra and *The Prajna-Paramita-Hrdaya Sutra* (*The Diamond Sutra* and *The Heart Sutra*). Trans. from Chinese by Lu Kuan-yu. Chinese and English bilingual ed. Hong Kong: H. K. Buddhist Book Distributor, 1985.

Wu, Cheng'en. *The Journey to the West* (*Xiyou ji*). Trans. Anthony C. Yu. 4 vols. Chicago: U of Chicago P, 1977–83.

———. *Monkey*. Abridged and trans. Arthur Waley. New York: Grove, 1958.

Xu (Hsu), Dishan (Ti-shan). "The Merchant's Wife" ("Shangren fu"). Trans. William Nienhausser, Jr. *Modern Chinese Stories and Novellas, 1919–1949*. Eds. Joseph S. M. Lau, C. T. Hsia, and Leo Ou-fan Lee. New York: Columbia UP, 1981. 41–50.

Yu, Anthony C. "Hsi-yu chi" ("The Journey to the West"). *The Indiana Companion to Traditional Chinese Literature*. 413–18.

Yu, Yingshi. "*Honglou meng* de liangge shijie" ("The Two Worlds in *The Dream of the Red Chamber*"). *Haiwai Hongxue ji* (*Essays on Redology From Overseas*). Ed. Hu Wenbin and Zhou Lei. Shanghai: Shanghai guji chubanshe, 1982. 31–55.

Yuan, Ke. *Gu shenhua xuanshi* (*An Anthology of Ancient Myths, With Annotations*). Beijing: Renmin wenxue chubanshe, 1982.

Zhu, Ruiwen. *Chengyu yu fojiao (Idioms and Buddhism)*. Beijing: Beijing jingji xueyuan chubanshe, 1989.

Zhuang, Zhou (Chuang Tzu). *Chuang Tzu: Basic Writings*. Trans. Burton Watson. New York: Columbia UP, 1964.

Zurcher, E[ric]. *The Buddhist Conquest of China: The Spread and Adaptation of Buddhism in Early Medieval China*. 2 vols. Leiden: Brill, 1972.

15 • "Behind the Curtain": Derrida and the Religious Imagination

Terence R. Wright

DECONSTRUCTION IS OFTEN THOUGHT to display a dry, cerebral, destructive approach to literature and a negative, critical, atheistic attitude to religion, leaving no room for any recognition of the role of the imagination. Terry Eagleton describes it as a return to formalism, only worse:

> because whereas for New Criticism the poem did in some indirect way discourse about extra-poetic reality, literature for the deconstructionists testifies to the impossibility of language's ever doing more than talk about its own failure, like some bar-room bore. Literature is the ruin of all reference, the cemetery of communication. (146)

Derrida has recently denied that deconstruction is nihilistic in this way: truth is not denied or "destroyed in my writings, but only reinscribed in more powerful, larger, more stratified contexts" (*Limited* 146). The infamous phrase "there is nothing outside the text," he insists, does not mean that "all referents are suspended, denied, or enclosed in a book" but that "every referent, all reality has the structure of a differential trace, and that one cannot refer to this 'real' except in an interpretive experience" (*Limited* 148). There is no getting beyond the veil or web of textuality, no drawing of the curtain to reveal an unmediated inner truth.

Much of the point of Derrida's early work, it cannot be denied, was to indicate the difficulty of representation and communication, "to introduce into the manger of speech acts, a few wolves" such as the *pharmakon*, the supplement, the hymen, and the gift, all of which point to the radical ambiguity of language, the complexity of this textuality in which all our understanding is enmeshed (*Limited* 75). The gift of language may be poisoned, to use one of his favorite German/English puns. But if writing, in the eyes of so many Western thinkers represented in *Of Grammatology*, is contaminated, its fall into polysemy can also be seen as fortunate, allowing as it does for the generation of unforeseen, accidental meanings. Much of Derrida's later writing celebrates rather than bewails the creative potential of this textual web, which is not so much a trap as a playground, a source of endless pleasure in which apocalypse, understood etymologically as the unveiling of secret inner meaning, is perpetually deferred. This, as I hope to show, is the whole point of literature, in which the text in its material uniqueness is regarded as sacred.

Derrida can sometimes be apocalyptic in the eschatological sense; in his recent autobiographical "Circumfession," he calls himself "the last of the eschatologists" (75). The opening section of *Of Grammatology*, for instance, announces "The End of the Book and the Beginning of Writing," bringing with it "the death of speech" and the closure of the "age of the sign." This, he claims, had been "essentially theological," its signifier replete with the full presence of a transcendental signified (8, 14). The opening sentence of the final chapter of *Writing and Difference*, "Ellipsis," is equally dramatic, declaring "the closure of the book" and "the disappearance of an exceeded God or of an erased man" (294). The essay on "Différance" in *Margins of Philosophy* goes out of its way to deny any supposed similarities between his understanding of the limits of language and that of negative theology. Différance, he insists, does not exist in any category of being; it is simply a name for the process of differing and deferral by which meaning is generated. The aspects of its functioning which he attempts to describe

> are not theological, not even in the order of the most negative of negative theologies, which are always concerned with disengaging a superessentiality beyond the finite categories of essence and existence, only in order to acknowledge his superior, inconceivable, and ineffable mode of being. (6)

"This unnamable," he repeats, "is not an ineffable Being which no name could approach: God, for example"; it involves no "prophetic annunciation"; there is "nothing kerygmatic about this 'word'" (26–27).

Throughout Derrida's early work, theology is aligned with logocentrism. The name of God, Derrida argues in *Of Grammatology*, is "the name of indifference" (71), involving a denial of the endless deferral of language. He also acknowledges, however, that to speak of "God's death" would be as metaphysical as to announce his presence (68). In "Violence and Metaphysics," Derrida notes that Levinas's theology involves talk *with* rather than *on* God, but even this is too metaphysical for Derrida, who suggests that God is rather "an effect of the trace . . . the movement of erasure of the trace in presence" (*Writing* 108). Derrida has recently denied that this involves any negative metaphysical claim: "To say that something is an effect of the trace—God for example—doesn't mean that it's an illusion" (Hampson 218). It is merely to describe how the word is produced.

The point, as John Caputo has seen, is that deconstruction is a critical practice that is "ontically neutral," that has "no ontological commitments"; it can be utilized by negative theologians or by atheists (24). Many of the early popularizers of deconstruction, literary critics such as Christopher Norris and Jonathan Culler, happened to be hostile to religion, Culler in particular seeing one of the "historic tasks" of criticism as "combating superstition . . . and fighting religious dogmatism" (78). Theologians such as Mark Taylor and Don Cupitt also developed Derridean ideas in radically atheistic ways, though Taylor tried to balance on the slash in "a/theology," caught between belief and unbelief (10). More recently, Kevin Hart has utilized deconstructive methods to illustrate the inadequacy of our concepts of God without denying His reality (28) while Graham Ward has argued that theology can benefit from a greater attention to the materiality of its discourse. But most important, as Ward points out, it is Derrida himself over the last decade or so who has turned with renewed interest to the religious imagination as it manifests itself in a range of texts including, of course, the Bible. It is on these more recent works that I wish to concentrate now, moving toward a reassessment of the supposedly negative, antireligious nature of deconstruction. What will emerge as the real target of deconstruction is not the religious imagination itself, which Derrida finds fascinating, but the belief that its product, religious discourse, can be the last word, the final solution, transparent upon a fixed and absolute truth. He has been seen as rabbinic in his understanding of the endlessness of interpretation, his refusal to go beyond the veil of discourse, the letter of Scripture, the materiality of the signifier, to pronounce upon the inner truth of the spirit or ultimate reality (Handelman 167–76).

It is Hegel's confidence that he can talk about Absolute Truth (*Savoir Absolu*), which comes in for such mockery in *Glas*, published in French in 1974 but not translated into English until 1986. Derrida highlights Hegel's attack on the Jews for their lack of imagination or appreciation of beauty, his castigation of their stony hearts for failing to respond to Moses's appeal to their imagination. The Jews, according to Hegel, could attain only to "the negative sublime," incapable of "expressing the infinite into phenomenal representation": "A stranger to the symbol, to the concrete and felt union between the infinite and the finite, the Jew has access only to an abstract and empty rhetoric. . . . His iconoclasm itself signifies the coldness of his heart." The Tabernacle exemplifies

> a signifier without a signified . . . the structure encloses its void within itself, shelters only its own proper interiorized desert, opens onto nothing, confines nothing, contains as its treasure only nothingness: a hole, an empty spacing, a death. . . . Nothing behind [*derrière*] the curtains.

A gentile such as Pompey, violating the tabernacle, finds nothing there at the "secret center" (*Glas* 44a, 47a–50a).

How personally Derrida feels this attack upon the Jews becomes apparent in a passage later in *Glas* which confesses to the way the word *Derrière*, capitalized, at the beginning of a sentence, conjured up the image of his father's name in golden letters on a tomb:

> *A fortiori* when I read *Derrière le rideau* [Behind the Curtain].
>
> *Derrière*, behind, isn't it always already [*déjà derrière*] a curtain, a veil, a weaving. (68b)

Another very personal memory recounts a child in Algeria in a mosque transformed into a synagogue watching the Torah being "brought forth from behind the curtains" and "promenaded" before the faithful (240b). These cryptic fragments defy authoritative interpretation but signal a recognition on Derrida's part that his refusal to go beyond the veil, to draw back the curtain of textuality to discuss an unmediated inner "truth," derives from a religious sensibility nurtured within Jewish traditions of reverence. To quote Levinas, as Derrida does in *Writing and Difference*, "To love the Torah more than God" is "protection against the madness of a direct contact with the Sacred" (qtd. in *Writing* 102).

The difference between Christian confidence in revelation and Jewish reticence before a veiled mystery, captured in a phrase quoted in a footnote to *Memoirs of the Blind*, "*Vetus testamentum velatum, novum testamentum revelatum*" (18), emerges in the contrast Derrida makes in *Glas* between the Christian Hegel and the "Jewish" Kant. For Hegel "God's being is absolutely present, manifest, there (*da*)" and the Christian religion,

> the only one that expressly named itself revealed religion. It calls itself the revealed (*ausdrücklich die geoffenbarte heisst*). No other religion is absolutely true—not for being false—but for not being of the truth, for not having made of the truth (of the unveiling) of the manifestation, of the open (and openable) its own proper essence.

For Kant, therefore, to talk of "God's being-hidden" and to build religion on "non-manifestation" is "to comprehend nothing about revelation." That is why Hegel claims that "Kant is Jewish: he believes in a jealous, envious God, who hides and guards his *Da*." Hegel's God is a solar deity who lights up all, a generous father who does not hide himself, in contrast with Judaism's "nocturnal God," a God who is "jealous, dissembling his *Da*, moral and castrating, giving himself to be seen, as the galaxy structure, only by scintillating, glimmering, twinkling on the background of night—lighted by a sun that is not seen" (*Glas* 233a–34a). Derrida characteristically hides behind his texts, refusing to comment overtly in his own name. But it is clear throughout *Glas* that his sympathies lie much more with Jewish reticence before the veil than with the claims of reason or of revelation to disclose inner truth to the clear light of day.

Derrida turns to the Book of Revelation itself to explore the biblical understanding of apocalypse as unveiling in his 1981 essay "Of an Apocalyptic Tone Recently Adopted in Philosophy." The Greek word *apocalypsis* (literally, "uncovering") translates the Hebrew *gala*, which "recurs more than a hundred times in the Hebrew Bible," often of physical things such as the body, for instance, when the drunken Noah is uncovered in his tent, but also assuming a "terrifying and holy gravity" when it is the glory of YHWH which is revealed to men's astonished ears or eyes (Ap 64–65). Just as Kant had complained of an "overlordly" tone recently adopted by contemporary philosophers who were turning poets and mystics, so Derrida notices an eschatological tone in the writings of his contemporaries:

> I tell you this in truth; this is not only the end of this here but also the first of that there, the end of history, . . . the death of God, the end of religions, the end of Christianity and morals (that [*ça*], that was the most serious naïveté), the end of the subject, the end of man, the end of the West . . . *Apocalypse Now* . . . the fire, the blood, the fundamental earthquake, . . . the nuclear thunder and the great whoring, and also the end of literature, the end of painting, the end of the university, the end of phallocentrism and phallogocentrism, and I don't know what else. . . . ("Of an Apocalyptic Tone" 80)

Derrida is partly mocking his earlier self, of course, but he also feels ambivalent about Kant's fears that to turn to the poetic or the supernatural is to bring about the death of philosophy, which requires a rational standpoint and a neutral tone. Kant pours scorn upon the "mystagogues" who try to seduce others into a mysterious secret:

> The mystagogues claim to possess as it were in private the privilege of a mysterious secret (*Geheimnis* is the word that recurs most often). The revelation or unveiling of the secret is reserved to them: they jealously protect it. Jealousy here is a major trait. They never transmit the secret to others in the current language, only by initiation or inspiration. (69)

The leap from philosophical "concepts to the unthinkable or the irrepresentable" brings with it, according to Kant, a "crypted" style, "a poetico-metaphorical abundance," "a crypto-poetics, a poetic perversion of philosophy" (72–80). As in his much-quoted essay on "White Mythology," Derrida pokes fun at the philosopher's suspicion of figurative language. Here he quotes Kant railing against the abuse of metaphors or "figurative expressions (*bildliche Ausdrücken*)," particularly in religious contexts. Two examples cited by Kant talk of approaching "so near the divine wisdom that one can perceive the *rustle* of its garment" and of not raising "the veil of Isis" but making it "so thin (*so dünne*) that one can have a presentiment of the goddess under it" (75). Kant has no time for rustles and presentiments; he wants to see and talk clearly and rationally. And Derrida has some sympathy, although as in "White Mythology" he does not take sides "between metaphor and concept, literary mystagogy and true philosophy" but shows their interdependence, their reliance upon the opposite or other to fashion their own identity (76). Kant will bow before no "veiled goddess" but that of "the moral law," rejecting "an *aesthetic* manner of representing (*eine ästhetische Vorstellungsart*) in the name of "a logical method" which "is alone properly philosophical" (79). Derrida sees the limitations of Kant's "rational" understanding of language but does not want to abandon Enlightenment principles altogether:

> We cannot and we must not . . . forgo the *Aufklärung*. In other words, we cannot and we must not forgo what compels recognition as the enigmatic desire for vigilance, for the lucid vigil [*veille*], for clarification, for critique and truth, but for a truth that at the same time keeps within itself enough apocalyptic desire, this time as desire for clarity and revelation, to demystify, or, if you prefer, to deconstruct the apocalyptic discourse itself and with it everything that speculates on vision, the imminence of the end, theophany, the parousia, the Last Judgement, and so on. (82)

Derrida too refuses to kneel uncritically before the veil but analyzes as clearly as possible how it is woven.

The apocalyptic text he turns to in this essay is the Book of Revelation, noticing its "interlacing of voices and *envois*," the way in which John's "disclosure (*apokalupsis*)" is not the direct "word of Elohim" but the testimony of Jesus relayed through his messenger or angel; "so many sendings." Comments Derrida, "so many voices, and this puts so many people on the telephone line" (86). Apocalypse, in other words, involves no direct revelation or disclosure but an "interminable" series of literary stratagems; it is "an apocryptic, apocryphal, masked, coded genre" which can "give some detours in order to mislead another vigilance, that of censorship" (89). The Book of Revelation ends by inviting Jesus to "Come," blurring the distinction between what is inside and what is outside the text. Some would argue that the "Come" performs its apocalypse, calls the Lord into being. But Derrida characteristically ends on an anticlimax, telling his listeners, in an ironic echo of Christ Himself, that "there is no more time to tell the truth on the apocalypse . . . it's finished, I tell you this, that's what happens, that's what comes" (94–95). The implication is that all endings are arbitrary, acts of interpretation (or imagination) whose validity is only temporary, to be augmented by future texts.

Derrida turns to the Book of Genesis in his other sustained piece of biblical analysis, "Des Tours de Babel" (1985), which explores the necessary detours of language, "the inadequation of one tongue to another" and "the need for figuration, for myth, for tropes." The myth of the Tower of Babel signals once again "the impossibility of finishing, of totalizing, of saturating, of completing something," in this case a building and also a language (3). The sons of Shem want to make a name for themselves and build a tower reaching to the heavens, but God disseminates their meaning, confounds their single language, and deconstructs their tower, proclaiming his own name Babel, signifying both the name of the father and confusion, making translation both "necessary and impossible" (4–7). For God's name is a proper name and therefore "forever untranslatable," disrupting the "linguistic imperialism" of the Semites, their attempts to impose a "rational transparency," an "impossible univocity" upon language (8–10). Derrida draws upon Walter Benjamin's discussion of the impossibility of translation to emphasize the uniqueness of the literary event as of the proper name. Poetic and sacred texts do not have "a communicable content"; they are not about "communication" or "enunciation" (14–15); they are "less a revelation . . . than an annunciation," an unrepeatable event. In a sacred text "meaning and literality are no longer discernible as they form the body of a unique, irreplaceable, and untransferable event": "What comes to pass in a sacred text is the occurrence of a *pas de sens*," something which does not make transparent, literal sense but performs its meaning as in a dance (32–33). Hence the reverence Derrida accords to the body and letter of the text, his resistance to any attempt to "spirit" it away.

The myth of Babel recurs in *The Ear of the Other* (1982), where Derrida dwells again on God's "disshemination" of the language of the sons of Shem, making his name untranslatable by being ambiguous. Babel thus "gives a good idea of what deconstruction is: an unfinished edifice whose half-completed structures are visible, letting one guess at the scaffolding behind them" (102). Again Derrida cites Benjamin to the effect that a "sacred text is untranslatable . . . precisely because the meaning and the letter cannot be dissociated" (103). For Benjamin all literature "gets sacralized" in this way, becomes sacred by being untranslatable (148).

Even Derrida's early work, *Writing and Difference*, *Margins of Philosophy*, and *Dissemination*, emphasized the sacred nature of literature, the untranslatable excess of meaning which cannot be reduced to a closed system, a restricted economy "in which there is nothing that cannot be made to make sense" (*Margins* 20), opposing to this a notion of a general economy which allows for "the absolute sacrifice of meaning: a sacrifice without return and without reserves" (*Writing* 257). He quotes Bataille attacking the Hegelian philosophical system for making nothing of laughter, poetry, ecstasy, and the sacred: "The poetic or the ecstatic is that *in every discourse* which can open itself up to the absolute loss of its sense," renouncing all "*theme* and meaning" (*Writing* 261). For Bataille, writing becomes worthy of that name by exceeding the *logos* of meaning, by refusing to "tolerate the distinction of form and content" (*Writing* 267), erupting from the circle of absolute meaning and philosophical system.

Derrida's more recent work on literature has continued this emphasis on the physicality, the sacredness, and the untranslatability of literature. His 1986 essay "Shibboleth" stresses the physical conditions which made the Ephraimites unable to pronounce that word and likens poetry to circumcision, a similarly sacred but untranslatable cut in the body of a language (323–24). His 1988 meditation "Che cos'è la poesia" likens literature to a hedgehog, a creature with "an absolutely unique form" in which meaning is not separated from "the body of the letter" (*Derrida* 229). A 1992 interview with Derek Attridge in *Acts of Literature* acknowledges the difficulty of identifying "the literary object" rather than "a *critical* experience of literature"; literature is a product of an intentional relation to a text, an experience rather than an essence, a suspension of thetic or transcendent reference, a particular attention to the singularity of the linguistic event. But, as he admits, there are certain texts that lend themselves better than others to such a reading (*Acts* 41–45).

Literature, Derrida insists in *Given Time* (1991), is a gift, an act of grace which exceeds the circle of exchange:

> It must not circulate, it must not be exchanged, it must not in any case be exhausted, as a gift, by the process of exchange, by the movement of circulation of the circle in the form of return to the point of departure. If the figure of the circle is essential to economics, the gift must remain *aneconomic*. (6)

A gift is original, "an intervention that interrupts the continuous chain, the program, or the economy" (73); it is an event, even a revelation, Mauss himself, the first theorizer of the gift, being likened by Lévi-Strauss to Moses as establishing, albeit in fragmented and incomplete form, the founding revelation of sociology (74). Derrida, circling around a story of Baudelaire's about the counterfeit gift of a false coin to a beggar, develops the links between credit, faith, literature, and belief (97). Literature is seen as an institution that passes itself off as natural (and is received as the real thing) while remaining necessarily "superficial, without substance" or secret inner truth (153, 170).

It is not that deconstruction diminishes the importance of literature, or denies its force. Rather, it insists, in Hartman's words in the "Preface" to *Deconstruction and Criticism*, that "the force of literature" lies in the "priority of language to meaning," the excess of figurative language over any "assigned meaning," "the strength of the signifier vis-à-vis a signified" (vii). Hartman wants to "save the text" in this sense of preserving its physical phenomena rather than spiritualizing or stabilizing them into "stabilized reference" (*Saving* xxi). This is why Derrida devotes a whole book to the analysis of the word "spirit," that Hegelian word which was also the subject of *Of Grammatology*, which complained about the way in which "writing, the letter, the sensible inscription" had always been considered by Western philosophers as inferior "body and matter external to the spirit, to breath, to speech, and to the logos" (35).

Of Spirit, first published in French in 1987, looks at the checkered history of Heidegger's use (or avoidance) of the word *Geist* and its compounds. He tries to avoid it in *Sein und Zeit*, draping it when it does appear in quotation marks to signal its use in a "deconstructed sense" outside the system of Hegelian ontology (23). These quotation marks are likened by Derrida to "two pairs of pegs" which hold in suspension a sort of drape, a veil or a curtain. "Not closed, just slightly open." In the *Rectorship Address* of 1933, however, the curtain is raised and *Geist* appears in its full glory upon the stage as Heidegger not only sanctifies Nazism but also reintroduces a full-blooded metaphysics (31–32). By the time of the lecture on Georg Trakl of 1953, even the word *geistig* is withdrawn as inevitably contaminated by the Platonic opposition to the material (95–96). Derrida is rather skeptical about Heidegger's attempt to de-Christianize Trakl, ending the book with an imaginary debate between Heidegger and some Christian theologians in which Heidegger claims not to be opposed to Christian discourse, whether of salvation, resurrection, or the spirit, but simply trying to understand the way in which that discourse functions (111). This could be taken as the model for deconstruction itself, which does not necessarily undermine religious language but simply unearths the oppositions upon which it is constructed.

There is certainly a more eirenic quality about Derrida's more recent writing about theology, in particular negative theology, than there was in "Différance" or *Of Grammatology*. In "How to Avoid Speaking: Denials" of 1987, for example, Derrida accepts that his negative rhetoric appears similar to that of negative theology, insisting that key terms such as Différance are "neither sensible nor intelligible, neither positive nor negative, neither inside nor outside," but exceed these conventional oppositions (4). But he sees his own work as falling short of "that ontological wager of hyperessentiality" characteristic of negative theologians such as Dionysius and Meister Eckhart (9), whose work he proceeds to analyze. Dionysus describes sacred symbols, "the signs and figures of sacred discourse," as "'shields' against the many," an "allegorical veil" which protects the inner mystery of God and which can only be trusted on God's authority: "Without the divine promise," they "would be merely conventional rhetoric, poetry, fine arts, perhaps literature." As it is, they can be trusted to take a believer beyond the veil to the inner truth of God (23). Eckhart makes a similar claim to penetrate the veil of language: "a certain signification of unveiling, of laying bare, of truth as what is beyond the covering garment, appears to orient the entire axiomatics of this apophasis" (45). In Eckhart the symbols and figures of religious discourse lead to the unfigurable "Simplicity," and one learns finally to be silent. Derrida writes sympathetically about Heidegger and Marion, who avoid metaphysical theology by using terms such as Being and God only under erasure, crossed through to indicate their inadequacy. What Derrida finally objects to in negative theology as such is the condemnation of writing as finally falling silent before inner truth. He ends this essay by positing that

> there would be no prayer, no possibility of prayer, without what we glimpse as a menace or as a contamination: writing, the code, repetition, analogy or the—at least apparent—multiplicity of addresses, initiation. If there were a purely pure experience of prayer, would one need religion and affirmative or negative theologies? Would one need a supplement of prayer? But if there were no supplement, if quotation did not bend prayer, if prayer did not bend, if it did not submit to writing, would a theology be possible? Would a theology be possible? (62)

This is a point that Derrida develops further in his contribution to the volume on *Derrida and Negative Theology* published in 1992, "Post-Scriptum: Aporias, Ways, and Voices." For negative theology is itself a genre, a discourse with identifiable conventions and traditions within which individual mystics write. Despite the figure of the desert, a paradoxical figure for the aporia or pathless path, "what we call negative theology grows and cultivates itself as a memory, an institution, a history, a discipline. It is a culture, with its archives and its tradition." It is a discourse on language which denounces "images, figures, idols, rhetoric" at the same time as employing its own ("Post-Scriptum" 297–99). It is a "sweet rage against language," a "wounded writing that bears the stigmata of its own proper inadequation" (303–304). Derrida goes so far as to say, "I trust no text that is not in some way contaminated with negative theology," by which he presumably means a recognition of its own limits (309–10). He certainly celebrates the work of Augustine, who writes of "doing the truth" (*veritatem facere*) rather than "revealing, unveiling" or "informing in the order of cognitive reason" (286), and clearly admires the "poetic flashes" of Angelus Silesius (289). He ends this essay by celebrating negative theology as a powerful and economic form of poetry: "Inexhaustible literature, literature for the desert, for the exile, always saying too much and too little" (321–22).

Derrida's deep interest in religion and the religious imagination is confirmed by *Memoirs of the Blind*, his introduction to an exhibition of paintings at the Louvre in 1991, an exhibition which he chose to focus on the connection between physical blindness and spiritual vision. As it happened, in the process of preparing the material he suffered from a virus which paralyzed his own face, transfixing his left eye, and experienced "a feeling of conversion or resurrection" on recovery (32). The book begins with reference to belief: "Do you believe this [*vous croyez*]?" which the translator glosses as "ranging from its everyday meaning, 'Do you think so?' to the more literal 'Do you believe?' to the more incredulous 'Do you really believe this?'"(1). It ends too with reference to weeping eyes, in Marvell and others, the notion that tears "unveil the eyes" (127), allowing the beholder to see what had previously remained hidden. The last two lines read,

> —Tears that see . . . Do you believe?
> —I don't know, one has to believe. . . .

The tone here slides between the colloquial, the flippant, and the serious. At one level, however, it can be taken as a recognition of the need for faith.

Literalness earlier in the text is taken as a Jewish quality, the New Testament condemning the Old, Christians condemning Jews for being limited in their vision, for seeing

> with an eye that was too natural, too carnal, too external, which is to say, too *literal*. Blindness of the letter and by the letter. Here is a symbol: the blindfolded synagogue. The pharisees, these men of letters, are, when you come right down to it, blind. They see nothing because they look outside, only at the outside. They must

be converted to interiority, their eyes turned towards the inside; and a fascination must first be denounced, the body and exteriority of the letter reproached. (18)

Derrida goes on to quote Jesus calling the pharisees "blind guides" and "blind fools"(Matt. 23:15–17ff., 26) and recalling Isaiah's prophecy about those who will "look" but not "see" (Mark 8:22, John 9:6). After recounting a dream about blind old men, "ancestors, or rather, fathers, perhaps even grandfathers" (20), Derrida turns to three blind old men of the Old Testament, Eli, Isaac, and Tobit, all of whom fall, "for the blind are beings of the fall" (21), but all of whom have a legacy to pass on to their children. Derrida's most sustained analysis is reserved for Tobit, blinded by the droppings of sparrows and healed after eight years by his son, whose hand is guided by the angel Raphael. Raphael tells Tobit that what he has seen "was a vision" (*"je me rendais visible"*) and that he should now "acknowledge God [*rendez grâce à Dieu*]" and "Write down all these things that have happened to you" (29; Tob. 12:17–19). Derrida's comment here is important:

> Whether it be in writing or in drawing, in the *Book of Tobit* or in the representations related to it, the thanksgiving grace [*grâce*] of the *trait* suggests that at the origin of the *graphein* there is debt or gift rather than representational fidelity. More precisely, the fidelity of faith matters more than the representation, whose movement this fidelity commands and thus precedes. And faith, in the moment proper to it, is blind. It sacrifices sight, even if it does so with an eye to seeing at last. The performative that comes on the scene here is a "restoring of sight" rather than the visible object, rather than a constative description of what is or what one notices in front of oneself. Truth belongs to this moment of repayment that tries in vain to render itself adequate to its cause or to the thing. (30)

Faith, in other words, is a gift that no amount of hard work can repay.

Part of the purpose of *Memoirs of the Blind* is to speculate on the origin of drawing, "the invisible condition of the possibility of drawing" (41), in the same way as Derrida has earlier explored the origins of writing. As with writing, there is an abyss "between the thing drawn and the drawing *trait*" or stroke (45), between perception and representation. Derrida finds himself again employing theological terms:

> Is it by chance that in order to speak of the *trait* we are falling back upon the language of negative theology or of those discourses concerned with naming the withdrawal [*retrait*] of the invisible or hidden god? The withdrawal of the One whom one must not look in the face or represent, or adore, that is, idolize under the *traits* or guise of the icon? the One whom it is even dangerous to name by one or other of his proper names? (54)

He proceeds to explore the sacrificial element in visionary blindness, the violence that "is always at the origin of the mythic narrative or of the revelation that opens one's eyes and makes one go from the sensible light or the *lumen naturale* to the intelligible or supernatural light" (92). This sometimes takes the form of mistake, as in Isaac's providentially mistaking Jacob for Esau, of punishment, as in Paul's striking Elymas with blindness, or of conversion, as in Paul's own three-day bedazzlement.

Derrida dwells at length on Jan Provost's painting of *Sacred Allegory*, with its huge divine eye, which is an "allegory of drawing as apocalypse . . . a revelation or a laying bare, an unveiling that renders visible, the truth of light: light that shows itself, as and by itself." This revelation is cataclysmic, unveiling itself in a moment of catastrophe. Sacred allegory is not passive:

> It makes something happen or come, makes something come to the eyes, makes something well up in them, by producing an event. It is performative, something vision alone would be incapable of if it gave rise only to representational reporting. . . . By blinding oneself to vision, by veiling one's own sight—through imploring, for example—one *does* something with one's eyes, *makes* something of them. (121–22)

Which brings Derrida to weeping eyes, tears that unveil, and the need for faith, with which the book ends.

Memoirs of the Blind, like many of Derrida's recent works, has a number of veiled autobiographical elements, for instance, the confession that he turned to writing, "another *trait*, the graphics of invisible words," partly because his older brother was a more talented draftsman. The same passage refers to the way their grandfather, Moses, "though not a rabbi, incarnated for us the religious consciousness" (37). He also brings in their father, like Tobit, liking to bury the dead of their community (24), and their mother on her lingering deathbed, "eyes veiled by cataracts" (39). This autobiographical impulse comes into the open in "Circumfession," published in French in 1991 as a prolonged footnote responding to Geoffrey Bennington's systematic exposition of Derrida's thought in *Jacques Derrida*. The contract between them was that Derrida was to surprise Bennington, to produce something that would not fit into his system. Apparently it succeeded (in surprising Bennington), but anyone who has followed the course of Derrida's interest in religion as I have tried to chart it up to now will not be that shocked to find that it mimics Augustine's *Confessions*, letting flow his own "profession of faith or confession" (4), dwelling on his relationship with his mother just as Augustine dwelt on Monica (there are pictures of both mothers and sons to underline the parallel). There is much too on circumcision, drawing on material prepared from 1976 for a projected book on the subject to be called "The Book of Elijah" (Derrida's secret name, not on his birth certificate). There is a reproduction of Rembrandt's painting *Circumcision*, with a caption from *Memoirs of the Blind* on the way Paul sees circumcision as "pointless after the revelation or the 'unveiling' of Christ" (29). Bennington's biographical notes at the back of the book, "Curriculum Vitae," explain more about Derrida's sense of "double rejection" at being expelled as a Jew from his Lycée in 1942 but secretly absenting himself from the Jewish school in which he was then enrolled. Bennington also comments on the links Derrida sees in his current seminar between the exhibition of the circumcised body and the Eucharist's gift of the body (326–27), a subject dwelt on in *Glas*. He mentions too the period Derrida spent in "intense reading of Simone Weil (in a pathos of vague Christian mysticism)" (328).

Derrida's own circuitous confession begins by quoting Augustine's meditation on why he confesses to God in writing when He knows everything anyway: it is a matter of *making* truth before a witness, presenting oneself to God, and asking for pardon, an activity that is a matter both of religion and of literature (47–49). In his own case, he admits, that "great pardon ... has not yet happened":

this is why I am addressing myself here to God, the only one I take as a witness, without yet knowing what these sublime words mean, . . . and not only do I pray, as I have never stopped doing all my life, and pray to him, but I take him here . . . as my witness, . . . and why I talk to him in Christian Latin French when they expelled from the Lycée de Ben Aknoun in 1942 a little black and very Arab Jew who understood nothing about it. (56–58).

Derrida reveals that he and his family, like other Algerian Jews disguised their religious difference: "one scarcely ever said 'circumcision' but 'baptism', nor Bar Mitzvah but 'communion'" (72). Much of his early religion, he recalls, came from his mother, whom he can remember praying (117) and who continues, like Monica with Augustine, to monitor his religious progress, a development "about which nobody understands anything." Derrida complains about her "not wanting to talk to me about it" but asking others "if I still believed in God":

> she must have known that the constancy of God in my life is called by other names, so that I quite rightly pass for an atheist, the omnipresence to me of what I call God in my absolved, absolutely private language being neither that of an eyewitness nor that of a voice doing anything other than talking to me without saying anything . . . that feminine figure of a Yahweh who remains so strange and so familiar to me, but the secret I am excluded from. . . . (154–55)

The implication here is that he is reluctantly excluded from this secret rather than deliberately excluding himself.

Derrida presents himself at this point in "Circumfession" as a rather sorry figure, part Jewish, part the product of French Catholic culture (170), "sad, deprived, destitute, disappointed, impatient, jealous, desperate, negative and neurotic" (268), unable to express "anything other than an interest as passionate as it is disillusioned for these things, language, literature, philosophy" (270). Bennington too, in his section on "The Jew," posits a Derrida as depicted by a Hegelian who "would make himself the slave of an infinite that he admits he cannot understand. Whence the wandering in the desert . . . of deconstruction which will never announce the truth" (296–97). Derrida accepts that he remains to some extent the "Jew expelled from the Ben Aknoun school," escaping into literature:

> he runs he flies so young and light futile subtle agile delivering to the world the very discourse of this impregnable inedible simulacrum, the theory of the parasite virus, of the inside/outside, of the impeccable *pharmakos*, terrorizing the others through the instability he carries everywhere. . . . (307–308)

He makes no attempt to hide some of the psychological motives behind his thought.

In "Circumfession," it is tempting to say, the real Derrida can be glimpsed through the partially drawn curtain. But, of course, it is not as simple as that (it never is, as deconstruction tries always to demonstrate). Nor do I see this text as a dramatic reversal of what went before. Right from the beginning there was a deeply religious vein in Derrida's thought. His critique of Greek metaphysics, with which Christianity was early infected, makes him still deeply suspicious of the language of presence, of meaning becoming fully incarnate in the word. For Derrida all representation will always be incomplete, always in need of interpretation, always textual, enmeshed in codes whose construction can be painstakingly analyzed. This veil of language can never be wholly removed; nor should we want it to be. It is the veil itself which is the religious imagination which Derrida both analyzes and celebrates.

Works Cited

Berry, Philippa, and Andrew Wernick. *Shadow of Spirit: Postmodernism and Religion.* London: Routledge, 1992.

Caputo, John D. "Mysticism and Transgression: Derrida and Meister Eckhart." *Derrida and Deconstruction.* Ed. Hugh J. Silverman. London: Routledge, 1989. 00–00.

Culler, Jonathan. *Framing the Sign: Criticism and Its Institutions.* Oxford: Blackwell, 1988.

Cupitt, Don. *The Long-Legged Fly: A Theology of Language and Desire.* London: SCM, 1987.

Derrida, Jacques. *Acts of Literature.* Ed. Derek Attridge. London: Routledge, 1992.

―――. "Circumfession." *Jacques Derrida*. Ed. Geoffrey Bennington and Jacques Derrida. Chicago: U of Chicago P, 1993. 3–315.

―――. *A Derrida Reader: Between the Blinds*. Ed. Peggy Kamuf. Hemel Hempstead: Harvester, 1991.

―――. "Des Tours de Babel." *Semeia* 54 (1991): 3–34.

―――. *Dissemination*. Trans. Barbara Johnson. Chicago: U of Chicago P, 1981.

―――. *The Ear of the Other: Otobiography, Transference, Translation*. Trans. Peggy Kamuf. Ed. Christie V. McDonall. New York: Schocken, 1985.

―――. *Given Time*. Trans. Peggy Kamuf. Chicago: U of Chicago P, 1992.

―――. *Glas*. Trans. J. P. Leavey, Jr., and Richard Rand. Lincoln: U of Nebraska P, 1986.

―――. "How to Avoid Speaking: Denials." *Languages of the Unsayable: The Play of Negativity in Literature and Literary Theory*. Ed. Sanford Budick and Wolfgang Iser. New York: Columbia UP, 1989. 3–70.

―――. *Limited Inc*. Ed. Gerald Graff. Evanston, IL: Northwestern UP, 1988.

―――. *Margins of Philosophy*. Trans. Alan Bass. Brighton: Harvester, 1982.

―――. *Memoirs of the Blind: The Self-Portrait and Other Ruins*. Trans. Pascale-Anne Brault and Michael Naas. Chicago: U of Chicago P, 1993.

―――. "Of an Apocalyptic Tone Recently Adopted in Philosophy." *Semeia* 3 (1982): 63–97.

―――. *Of Grammatology*. Trans. Gayatri Spivak. Baltimore and London: Johns Hopkins UP, 1976.

―――. *Of Spirit: Heidegger and the Question*. Trans. Geoffrey Bennington and Rachel Bowlby. Chicago: U of Chicago P, 1987.

―――. *The Post Card: From Socrates to Freud and Beyond*. Trans. Alan Bass. Chicago: U of Chicago P, 1987.

―――. "Post-Scriptum: Aporias, Ways, and Voices." *Derrida and Negative Theology*. Ed. Harold Coward and Toby Foshay. Albany: SUNY P, 1992. 283–325.

―――. "Shibboleth. *Midrash and Literature*. Ed. Geoffrey H. Hartman and Sanford Budick. New Haven: Yale UP, 1986. 306–47.

―――. *Writing and Difference*. Trans. Alan Bass. Chicago: U of Chicago P, 1978.

Eagleton, Terry. *Literary Theory: An Introduction*. Oxford: Blackwell, 1983.

Gasché, Rodolphe. *The Tain of the Mirror: Derrida and the Philosophy of Reflection*. Cambridge: Harvard UP, 1986.

Hampson, Daphne. "After Christianity: The Transformation of Theology." *Literature and Theology* 8 (1994): 210–18.

Handelman, Susan A. *The Slayers of Moses: The Emergence of Rabbinic Interpretation in Modern Literary Theory.* Albany, NY: SUNY P, 1982.

Hart, Kevin. *The Trespass of the Sign: Deconstruction, Theology, and Philosophy.* Cambridge: Cambridge UP, 1989.

Hartman, Geoffrey. Preface. *Deconstruction and Criticism.* Ed. Harold Bloom et al. New York: Continuum, 1979.

———. *Saving the Text: Literature/Deconstruction/Philosophy.* Baltimore and London: Johns Hopkins UP, 1981.

Leavey, John. *GLASsary.* Lincoln and London: U of Nebraska P, 1986.

Norris, Christopher. *Derrida.* London: Fontana, 1987.

Taylor, Mark C. *Erring: A Postmodern A/theology.* Chicago: U of Chicago P, 1984.

Ward, Graham. "Why is Derrida Important for Theology?" *Theology* 95 (1992): 263–70.

CONTRIBUTORS

NORMAN R. CARY ("Religious Polyphony in the Novels of Nuruddin Farah") is Associate Professor in the Department of English at Wright State University. He has published widely on world literature.

SHENG-TAI CHANG ("The Buddhist Imagination in Chinese Fiction") is Assistant Professor in the Division of Humanities of South Puget Sound Community College. He has published in *Studies in Modern Chinese Literature, Canadian Review of Comparative Literature,* and elsewhere.

PAUL G. CROWLEY, S.J. ("Dialectical Structure of Ignatian Imagination") is Associate Professor of Religious Studies at Santa Clara University. His articles have appeared in *The Heythrop Journal* and *Theological Studies.*

GAVIN D'COSTA ("The Tyranny of the Secular Imagination") lectures in the Department of Theology and Religious Studies at the University of Bristol. Among his publications is *Theology and Religious Pluralism* (Blackwell).

WILLIAM FRANKE ("Blind Prophecy: Milton's Figurative Mode in *Paradise Lost*") is Assistant Professor of Comparative Literature and Italian at Vanderbilt University. His articles on Hermeneutics and Christian Prophetic Poetry have appeared in *Comparatio, Italian Quarterly,* and *Rivista de studi italiani,* for which he regularly reviews scholarship on Dante.

ANDREW GREELEY ("A View from the Far Side") is Professor of Social Science and directs the National Opinion Research Center at The University of Chicago. He publishes both novels and sociological studies.

JOHN C. HAWLEY ("Introduction") is Associate Professor of English at Santa Clara University. He has edited *Reform and Counterreform: Dialectics of the Word in Western Christianity Since Luther*, and served on the Modern Language Association's Executive Committee on Religious Approaches to Literature.

JANE KRISTOF ("Rouault and the Catholic Revival in France") is Associate Professor of Art History at Portland State University. She has published in *The Sixteenth Century Journal*, and elsewhere.

CHRISTIAAN THEODOOR LIEVESTRO ("Erasmus, Education, and Folly") is Associate Professor Emeritus of Comparative Literature at Santa Clara University. His publications include articles and translations in The Library of Christian Classics: Spiritual and Anabaptist Writers, the *Journal of the History of Ideas*, and the *Mennonite Quarterly Review*.

FRANCO MORMANDO, S.J. ("An Early Renaissance Guide for the Perplexed: Bernardino of Siena's *De inspirationibus*") is Assistant Professor of Italian at Boston College.

EDWARD T. OAKES, S.J. ("A Life of Allegory: Type and Pattern in Historical Narratives") is Associate Professor of Religious Studies at Regis University in Denver, Colorado. He has recently published a major study of the Swiss Roman Catholic theologian Hans Urs von Balthasar, *Pattern of Redemption*, and edited a collection of classic texts in German philosophy of religion and theology, *German Essays on Religion*.

JO ELLEN PARKER ("A Lesson in Reading: George Eliot and the Typological Imagination") is President of the Great Lakes Colleges Association. She writes on George Eliot and on composition, most recently in the *ADE Bulletin*.

BRENDA DEEN SCHILDGEN ("The Gospel of Mark as Myth") lectures in the Comparative Literature Department at the University of California at Davis. Her essays have appeared in *Dante Studies*, *Poetics Today*, *The Medieval World of Nature*, and *Countercurrents*.

KAMAL D. VERMA ("The Social and Political Vision of Sri Aurobindo"), Associate Professor of English at the University of Pittsburgh, Johnstown, has guest-edited the Sri Aurobindo number of the *Journal of South Asian Literature* and the Mulk Raj Anand number of the *South Asian Review*.

TERENCE R. WRIGHT ("'Behind the Curtain': Derrida and the Religious Imagination") is Lecturer in English at the University of Newcastle. His books include *John Henry Newman* (1983), *The Religion of Humanity* (1986), and *Theology and Literature* (1988).

JOYCE ZONANA ("Feminist Providence: Esther, Vashti, and the Duty of Disobedience in Nineteenth-Century Hermeneutics") is Associate Professor in English at the University of New Orleans. She has published in *Signs*, the *Journal of Narrative Technique*, *Victorian Poetry*, and *Tulsa Studies in Women's Literature*.

www.ingramcontent.com/pod-product-compliance
Lightning Source LLC
Chambersburg PA
CBHW051419290426
44109CB00016B/1354